The Yoga of Kirtan

Conversations on the Sacred Art of Chanting

Steven Rosen

The Yoga of Kirtan

Conversations on the Sacred Art of Chanting

FOLK
BOOKS

First printing 2008
Cover and interior design by Barbara Berasi

CD Compilation:
Mastered by Nathan Bliss
at Barnaby Bright Studios, Brooklyn NY
www.BarnabyBright.com

Printed in the United States of America
ISBN softbound: 978-0-615-20510-6

Persons interested in the subject matter of this book
are invited to correspond with the publisher:

FOLK Books
PO Box 108,
Nyack, New York, 10960
U.S.A.
info@yogaofkirtan.com
www.yogaofkirtan.com

To the "Kirtan Tree" in Tompkins Square Park, New York City

On November 18, 2001, a plaque was placed in Tompkins Square Park in honor of the first kirtan in the Western world. The inscription on the plaque describes the context. Here it is in full:

One of Tompkins Square Park's most prominent features is its collection of venerable American elm (ulmus americana) trees. One elm in particular, located next to the semicircular arrangement of benches in the park's center, is important to adherents of the Hare Krishna religion. After coming to the United States in September, 1965, A. C. Bhaktivedanta Swami Prabhupada (1896–1977), the Indian spiritual leader, founded the International Society for Krishna Consciousness in New York. He worked from a storefront on near-by Second Avenue that he used as the Society's American headquarters. Prabhupada and his disciples gathered in Tompkins Square Park in the fall of 1966 to introduce the East Village to the group's distinctive 16-word mantra:

Hare Krishna, Hare Krishna, Krishna Krishna, Hare Hare
Hare Rama, Hare Rama, Rama Rama, Hare Hare

On October 9, 1966, Prabhupada and his followers sat beneath this tree and held the first outdoor chanting session outside of India. Participants chanted for two hours as they danced and played cymbals, tambourines, and other percussive instruments; the event is recognized as the founding of the Hare Krishna religion in the United States. Prabhupada's diverse group that day included Beat poet Allen Ginsberg (1926–1997). Krishna adherents continue to return to the tree to acknowledge its significance.

—OCTOBER 2001,
CITY OF NEW YORK, PARKS AND RECREATION
RUDOLPH GIULIANI, MAYOR
HENRY J. STERN, COMMISSIONER

{ TABLE OF CONTENTS }

"God respects me when I work, but He loves me when I sing."

—RABINDRANATH TAGORE

Yoga is popular, and there are numerous reasons for this. Some of those reasons directly relate to what yoga is all about, and others — well, not so much. Although the word itself literally refers to "linking with God," the common perception, especially outside India, leans more toward taking care of the body. Western *yogis* want to keep their body in shape. Unfortunately, it's often to attract the *yogi* or *yogini* on the mat next to them — which really isn't what yoga is all about.

But there's also an upside to keeping the body in shape. In fact, a healthy body is a step toward a healthy mind, and a healthy mind is an absolute necessity when trying to meditate — when trying to link with God. Thus, in pursuance of this healthful state, modern-day practitioners tend toward elevating and positive lifestyles — a remnant, perhaps, of yoga's metaphysical dimensions — embracing vegetarianism, animal rights, environmental awareness, and other, related concerns.

Part of that tendency for enhanced living is a love for enriching music—the desire to imbibe nourishing, inspirational sounds as part of the meditative experience. New Age, World Music, classical, and the sounds of the ocean, sure. But modern-day *yogis* have now discovered the music of their forebears as well. In a word, they're now opening their ears to kirtan, a call-and-response form of yogic chanting that vibrates in the Western world like never before.

Go into any yoga studio, health food store, or New Age center and you'll likely find the exotic sounds of kirtan wafting through the atmosphere. Whether it's Krishna Das crooning in his own inimitable style, Jai Uttal delivering his particular brand of East-West fusion, Vaiyasaki evoking the emotional moods of Medieval Bengal, or Sean Johnson serving up the spicy grooves of a New Orleans melody—kirtan is leaving its mark.

Its new Western form is intriguing, making prodigious use of well-established Indian motifs along with the sounds and sensibilities of diverse ethnic cultures; it combines the music of the ancient world with the tones of modernity.

In this book, we are introduced to *kirtaniyas* (i.e., lead kirtan singers) who hail from Jewish and Christian backgrounds, and others who have Sikh and Hindu roots. We meet a wandering musician from the islands who saw in kirtan his native Carnival made divine, and an Israeli who became a Latin pop star by way of devotional chanting. We talk to West Coast seekers who have made kirtan the central focus of their lives, and to urbane New York intellectuals who have done the same; we even walk through life with a New Zealander who revolutionized Eastern Europe by chanting for Gorbachev. Young and old, rich and poor, male and female, black and white. The diversity of those touched by kirtan is astounding.

The interviewees in this book come from various traditions: Some are disciples of A. C. Bhaktivedanta Swami Prabhupada, representing ISKCON and the Gaudiya Vaishnava Sampradaya—put simply, they are Hare Krishnas. Others represent the lineage of Vallabha, and still others come in the traditions of Ramanuja and Russill Paul. The book gives a platform for devotees of Neem Karoli Baba to share their stories and realizations, and it offers a similar venue for disciples of Swami Rama, Osho Rajneesh, and Swami

Muktananda. We even look at "kabbalistic kirtan" and Sikh kirtan as well. Some of these interviews represent traditional viewpoints and time-honored devotional communities; others are more free-flowing and innovative, with a view toward recent developments in kirtan lore. Again, the variety is considerable.

And why not? Call-and-response devotional singing is anything but staid; it is alive, dynamic, and always growing, and its universality has been documented many times in the past. It is, after all, the soul crying out for God, which transcends racial and sectarian limitations or the confines of a particular tradition.

Robert Gass, author of *Chanting: Discovering Spirit in Sound*, believes that ritual chanting is among the most universal of human impulses, as well as one of the first: "We have no recordings of the earliest humans," he writes, "but when we encounter indigenous tribes who've had little contact with modern civilization, they all have sacred chants that their oral history traces back to their earliest origins. And if you look into creation myths from different cultures, in almost every case the world is said to come into being through sound, through chant. It's in Hinduism, Christianity, Judaism, and Native American religions. That's evidence, in a way. The other evidence you can look at is young children: Almost all young children make up repetitive songs—they lose themselves in the rapture of singing."

In Judaism, the *hazzan*, or cantor, is a type of *kirtaniya*, directing all liturgical prayer and chanting in synagogues around the world. If no cantor is available, a less qualified "*kirtaniya*" is called in—known as the *ba'al tefilah*. This person then chants the prayers, and the congregation repeats his every utterance, as in a traditional kirtan. The basic practice comes from a principle found in the Bible (*Psalms* 150.4-5), "Glory ye in His holy name. Praise Him with the timbrel and dance: praise Him with stringed instruments and organs. Praise Him upon the loud cymbals." If that's not kirtan, what is? Indeed, one of Judaism's greatest mystics, the Baal Shem Tov, might be considered the ultimate *kirtaniya*—his very name means "Master of the Good Name," and he encouraged his followers: "Chant, chant, chant!"

Jesus, coming from the same tradition, taught his disciples how to pray: "Our father who art in heaven, hallowed be Thy name." This was the basis of early Christianity. In his *Epistle* to the Romans (10.13), St. Paul writes, "For whosoever shall call upon the name of the Lord will be saved." Baptist choirs and church singers take this mandate to heart, often with marked enthusiasm, embodying the essence of Indian kirtan parties.

Calling on the name became a formal part of the Roman Catholic Church during the days of Pope Gregory I (circa 540–604 C.E.). Even so, the Gregorian chant is only one of many, with the Christian tradition claiming hundreds of thousands of "mantras" — which are often recited in responsorial fashion, like kirtan. Along similar lines, Christian mystics have given the world the Jesus Prayer — "Lord Jesus, son of God, have mercy on me" — a continuous mantra-like incantation whose practice resembles *japa*, repetitive rosary chanting, in the mood of Indian *sadhus*.

The Muslim Qari are those who professionally recite the Koran. In tone and passion they easily bring to mind kirtan singers. Though demonstrative singing is not generally permitted in mainstream Islam, chanting to Allah is, and it is viewed as a particularly effective form of prayer. In fact, the Qari are *kirtaniyas* whose chanting is called *tajwid* — which is Arabic for "vocal music." The ninety-nine names of Allah, called "the Beautiful Names," are chanted on beads, inscribed on mosques, and glorified in countless ways.

In particular, the Sufis, Islamic mystics, seek to evoke God's presence by uttering His names. This is called "Qawwali," a form of sacred Islamic vocal music originating in Pakistan and India — it is an art form or ecstatic ritual based on classical Sufi texts. One of its primary functions is to guide its listeners — those who delve deeply into its poetry and meaning — to a state of ecstatic trance (*wajd*), much like expert *kirtaniyas* of old.

In Japan, followers of the Shinto religion engage in ritualistic chants, known as *norito*, which is their version of kirtan. Buddhist hymns are referred to as *shomyo*. This is a form of kirtan as well. In India, kirtan is a way of life. Sikhs, for example, view kirtan as central to their religious practice, as any google search on kirtan quickly reveals. Naturally, all forms of Hinduism make use of kirtan, too, and this is true whether we're talking about South Indian Ramanujites or Gaudiya Vaishnavas in Bengal; Marathi devotees who glorify God as Vitthala, or Devadasis who sing to their beloved Jagannath. Call-and-response chanting is the very basis of religion, and it was developed into a meticulously well-defined system of knowledge in India, as this book will soon show.

But before our magical journey into the world of kirtan, let's be clear about its connection to yoga. According to most of India's renowned sages, if yoga is about linking with God, kirtan is the best way to facilitate that link. Here's why. When you sing to someone, you develop intimacy with that person. In fact, *such singing presupposes intimacy* — you generally sing to those who are near and dear. And the singing brings you closer, too. In this way, kirtan sparks something buried deep within the heart, rekindling memories of an all but lost relationship with the Divine. And it accelerates that relationship, putting you in proximity to God, which, of course, is what yoga is all about.

In the *Bhagavad-gita*, one of the world's foremost yoga texts, Lord Krishna briefly describes, among other practices, Raja-yoga — that is, yoga as we know it today, with breathing exercises, sitting postures, and so on. But Arjuna, the adept to whom Krishna is speaking, finds yogic technique too difficult, and by the end of the *Gita*'s Sixth Chapter, Krishna accedes to Arjuna's point, saying that of all *yogis*, "he who abides in Me [Krishna] with great faith, worshiping Me in transcendental loving service, is most intimately united with Me in yoga and is the highest of all." Elsewhere in the *Gita* (9.14), Krishna says that such great souls are always chanting His glories.

Thus, kirtan is the essence of yoga, for by chanting the names of the Divine, one can develop intimacy with Him, which is the ultimate goal of yoga. Again, chanting can employ Krishna's original name or any of His hundreds of millions of names, in any language, from any tradition. It should be clear that, in this book, when we say "Krishna," we simply mean God, and God appears in variegated ways, to numerous peoples. In fact, Krishna has unlimited forms: He mercifully appears in both genders—as Sita-Rama, Radha-Krishna, Lakshmi-Narayana, and so on—and incarnates in various species of life, as Varaha, Matsya, Kurma, Hayagriva, ad infinitum. All these forms are discussed in Vedic texts and in other sacred literature. Ultimately, He incarnates in His holy name, and He comes to us through kirtan.

Finally, kirtan shouldn't be intimidating. While there is a great art or science to chanting the Lord's names, it can be appreciated on a simple level as well. It doesn't have to be a religious experience. Just by hearing the sound and letting it in, you can take part in the kirtan process. Thoughts about God and the universe can come later, if at all. In the beginning, if you just relish the melody, you begin the process. Anyone can do that. And the results are uplifting, healing, and enlivening. A child can benefit from it, as can an accomplished sage. The kirtan leader feels closer to the Divine while chanting, but so does the audience—and anyone else who hears it.

As Arjuna noted, yoga and meditation aren't easy for most people. And that's where kirtan comes in. Anyone can chant, and the nature of chant is such that it immediately engages the senses, the mind, the heart. Its participatory method pulls you right in, and before you know it, you're absorbed, concentrating on the divine name like an accomplished *yogi*. And that's the point: By allowing the chant to enter your ears and your heart, you *are*, in a sense, a *yogi*, without making a conscious endeavor. And while that might only be the beginning, you have, indeed, taken part in the yoga of kirtan.

Special note to readers: The recurring word "Das" appended to the names of most of our *kirtaniyas* is not about family connection or ancestral relations. It is rather a title given to all who live their lives in service to the Divine. It literally means, "servant," as in, for example, "Krishna Das," which means "servant of Krishna."

{ INTRODUCTION }

"It is difficult to find Me in the spiritual kingdom,
Or for yogis to find Me in their heart of hearts;
But where My devotees are chanting,
There, O Narada, stand I!",

— Lord Krishna, *Padma Purana*

For countless ages, seekers have journeyed to the Ganges, or to similar holy places, to absorb themselves in sacred mantras, hymns that have been passed down for generations. These same seekers would often perform kirtan, celebrating special mantras with song and dance. Much to our good fortune, these mantras have finally come West, and kirtan now contributes to the rhythms of modernity. As a result, an exotic musical movement is emerging worldwide, turning age-old sacred chants into a new cultural phenomenon.

I remember the first time I heard kirtan. The year was 1972, and though only seventeen years old, I had been around the corner. In fact, I had been around many corners. The late 1960s was a no-holds-barred time of experimentation and change, offering young whippersnappers like me a whirlwind education in music, sex, politics, and drugs. Ours was a generation that reconsidered values and beliefs like few before us. Harsh realities made themselves known: the Cuban missile crisis, the bullets with names Kennedy and King on them, the Vietnam War. But there were good

1

things, too. And a lot of it: the Civil Rights movement was progressing rapidly, and women's libbers were getting ever closer to liberation. There was Dylan and Davis. Cream and Coltrane. Sly wanted to take us higher, and Jimi actually got us there. Mushrooms were anything but portabello and the Maharishi was on the cover of *Time* with the tag-line, "Meditation: The Answer to All Your Problems?"

The question loomed large, especially as the Beatles went off to India in search of an answer. I, too, had dabbled in Eastern mysticism, though mainly by way of pop culture. To be more precise, I was reading the popular imports of the day: Suzuki and Watts, Isherwood and Mascaro, Castaneda and Gibran. And I was pondering the big questions: "Who am I? Why am I here? Is there a God?"

But even so, nothing could have prepared me for that group of otherworldly Hare Krishnas—complete with exotic dress, hand-cymbals and double-headed Indian drums—making their presence known near my favorite New York concert hall. I was there to hear loud, raucous rock music, but instead I would hear the sweet call of Krishna's flute.

Like rock-n-roll icons from another time and place, these shaven-headed and *sari*-clad strangers swept through the area, affecting everything around them. Including me. I was mesmerized by their visual image, and more so by the melodic chants. At first they seemed to blend with the horn-honking cars and general cacophony of New York City streets. But then a sharp contrast emerged— an enticing oasis in the desert of my urban landscape. These were clearly American and European youths, peers perhaps, but their bright saffron robes and multi-colored *saris* spoke to me of something foreign. I read into their mysterious visage: monasticism and psychedelics, serious meditation and joyful romp. Whatever the case, these people were clearly on another platform of existence, coming from a totally different place, representative of an alternate state of consciousness.

How was I to know that these were Gaudiya Vaishnavas, that— despite their Western bodies—they were the modern-day spiritual inheritors of Sri Chaitanya's Vedanta? At the time, I had no awareness that "Hinduism" was a misnomer—an umbrella term for the many, diverse religions of India—or that Vaishnavas constituted the Hindu majority. Nor could I know that, 500 years ago, Sri Chaitanya—revered by his followers as a combined manifestation of Radha and Krishna—revolutionized the subcontinent with his method of ecstatic chant, using spiritual vocalization as yoga and developing it into a sophisticated science of ecstasy. How could I know that these were his emissaries, making a public display that would soon change my life?

Their sounds were energizing and, for me, somehow strangely familiar. Though I couldn't understand the words, which, I knew, were either gibberish or some distant, sacred language, their songs spoke to me with an unmistakable message: "Arise sleeping soul! Move beyond the mundane and become situated in transcendence! Don't delay! The time is now!"

I was captivated as I watched these surreal, spirited souls position themselves among the hippies and concert-goers on that particular New York evening. They seemed to be in full color while the rest of us were in black and white—a cliché, I know, but true nonetheless. Just then, a large group of about a dozen assumed center-stage, to ensure their presence would be felt. And indeed it was.

The lead Krishna vocalist deftly vibrated his startling if pleasing melodies, and his battery of robed brothers and sisters responded dynamically, electrically, with each line stimulating a current of bouncy spirituality. Call and response, call and response, over and over in euphoric manner. They went through their hypnotic refrain again and again, methodically speeding up the tempo with each verse. The lead singer clearly knew what he was doing, his confidence brimming as he looked smilingly at his enthusiastic comrades. They, in turn, accommodated him, singing progressively faster, their bodies moving to the thunder-like rhythms of their drums. As they teased each mantra from their leader's lips, the chanting grew louder and more forceful, until the entire area was overtaken by their performance.

After a few moments, I fell into it—not that I joined in. Something stopped me. Perhaps it was conditioning, or maybe it was the fear that, allowing myself their ecstasy, I would never find my way back. Whatever it was, and despite the fact that my body showed no hint of it, my mind gradually obscured the alien nature of the spectacle before me; I somehow ousted the idea that it was unusual. Gradually, without warning, it became simpatico, comfortable. I found myself fundamentally enthralled, until I became one with the chant, at least emotionally. The now frenetic singing and dancing seemed like an old friend, a distinct part of me. I felt deep kinship with these harmonious strangers.

As it went on, their intensity and volume reached dramatic proportions—faces completely flushed, ear-to-ear smiles, eyes rolling. Losing focus, some of them swayed with senseless abandon, while others jumped high, exhibiting blissful glee. Their intoxication seemed to surpass that of the concert-goers around them, and it was obviously more wholesome, triggered, as it was, by natural means and not by drugs. I looked at each of them, their absorption complete, their enthusiasm contagious. Going far beyond what I thought would be the climax of their earth-shattering exhibition, the now much appreciated—and somewhat envied—street chanters reached a breathtaking crescendo. And then, suddenly, the chanting stopped, and everyone within ear's reach was visibly stunned. This was my introduction to kirtan.

What Exactly is Kirtan?

Kirtan in the East—on its home turf—is another matter altogether. The alien component simply doesn't exist, since, in India, especially, it is not uncommon to see a kirtan party rousing through the streets—or in temples and homes—fiery singers using their voices and talents in praise of the Divine.

Kirtana (pronounced keer-ton-uh) is a Sanskrit word that means "praise" or "glory." The more common Hindi pronunciation is "keerton," dropping the final "a." Simply understood, it is a form of song that centers on glorifying God, commonly performed in a "call and response" style of singing. There is Nam-kirtan, which are songs composed of God's sacred names, and Lila-kirtan, or songs that celebrate the esoteric activities of the Divine. There is Sankirtan, when the songs of praise are performed in a group setting, and Nagara-Sankirtan, when the group is taken into the streets. And there are numerous variations on these terms and themes. But kirtan, in any form, is ecstatic.

A closely related idiom is *bhajan* (bah-jon), prayerful song, which involves an internal, more meditative technique, usually in a sitting position. This is in contrast to kirtan, normally performed while standing, at least, if not dancing. *Bhajan* literally means "worship" and is often conceived as a more solitary practice, though it is also generally performed in a group, like kirtan. In addition, *bhajan* is generally softer, whereas kirtan can become quite strident. Various sects and regions in India will attribute different labels to different forms of prayerful song, sometimes defining *bhajan* as a subcategory of kirtan and vice versa.

Those particularly adept at such singing are called *kirtaniyas* (keer-ton-nee-uhs) or *kirtan-wallahs* (keer-ton-wahl-uhs), and it is wonderful to watch them perform. Usually, traditional, exotic instruments accompany their song and dance. In your average kirtan, you can expect to find a *khol* — also called a *mridanga* — which is a double-headed folk drum originating in northeast India. It has a body made of clay or fiberglass, with a small head on the right side (some four inches in diameter), and a larger one on the left (approximately ten inches). A pair of brass hand cymbals, known as *kartals*, is also a staple in any kirtan performance — the two cymbals, commonly two to five inches in diameter, are tied together by a piece of string or cloth and employed rhythmically, according to the beat of the chant.

Devotional singers often use *harmoniums*, too — especially in *bhajan*. Originally from France, the *harmonium* is a free-reed wind instrument with a keyboard somewhat akin to a piano or an organ. When it first made its way to India, *kirtaniyas* eschewed its use for devotional music; it was considered only suitable for low-caste street musicians. But in due course it found a home in the yoga of chant. The *ektar* — a single-stringed relative of the Western guitar — is also used in kirtan, though not as frequently as the other instruments just described. For those who know its tradition, this instrument

d the paradigmatic female devotee, Mirabai, who,
century India, played the *ektar* while singing her now
e-songs to Krishna. Bowed chordophones, such as the
the *esraj*—violin-like in nature—are sometimes used as
well, as are flutes and *tablas*, and a background drone might be provided by a *tamboura*, too. But these are for more elaborate kirtans—
the *khol, kartals,* and *harmonium* are the standard instruments, along
with hand clapping. Contemporary *kirtaniyas*, it should be noted,
tend to engage more modern instrumentation, too, because ideally
any form of musical accompaniment can serve kirtan's purposes.

In short, kirtan is an uncomplicated and effective way of communing with God. The *Padma Purana* tells us, "Because the holy
name and the 'holy named' are nondifferent, the name is fully complete, pure, and eternally liberated. Indeed, it is Krishna Himself."
Philosophically, this idea can be summarized as follows: matter and
spirit are opposites. Thus, since in the material world, all things are
relative, and part of that relativity manifests in a thing and its name
being different, in the spiritual realm, the opposite must be true: a
thing and its name are one. This is the nature of the Absolute.

The implications here are tremendous. If God and His name are
the same, by chanting one can get close to Him in every sense of
the word. The chanter gets close to Him in terms of proximity,
since the name is on his or her lips—and the name, remember, *is*
God. The chanter gets purified by close association and becomes
"godly," cleansed, divinely inspired—thus becoming closer to God
in nature. And the chanter gets close to God by achieving the goal
of yoga, or linking with Him, through the intimacy of calling His
name with love and devotion.

This is the ultimate effect of kirtan, even if, in the beginning stages, one usually remains blissfully unaware of it. Kirtan does not
ask us to achieve the highest level. Instead, it dutifully takes us
there, sometimes in spite of ourselves. And at any stage, it is joyfully performed, leading to higher and higher modes of spirituality.
It gradually takes us beyond the physical, mental, and intellectual
strata of existence and situates us in transcendence. Thus, whether
we approach chanting as mere entertainment; as part of a yogic reg-

imen; as a night out; or as a method for getting close to God—we benefit from the practice and move upward toward the Supreme.

Kirtan Origins

According to the sages of India, kirtan transcends history: It is "imported from the spiritual realm." That is, in the highest heaven, one will find God—Krishna, Vishnu, El, Allah, or whatever one chooses to call Him (or Her)—glorified with blissful song and dance. Then, as kirtan makes its way to the material world, we find it in humanity's earliest cultures and civilizations, as mentioned in the Prologue.

For example, the Vedas and the Upanishads, which are among the world's oldest religious texts, describe the power of sound in minute detail, elaborating on how certain mantras, when properly recited, reveal Ultimate Reality. Kirtan, then, claims both divine origin and a history traceable to the world's earliest scriptures.

Vaishnavism, which constitutes the majority tradition in what we today know of as Hinduism, developed kirtan into a methodical practice, some would say a science, leading to the goal of yoga. With the help of Vaishnava scriptures, such as the *Bhagavata Purana* and the *Bhagavad Gita*, adherents came to understand chanting as a highly technical—if also blissful—discipline through which they could expect definite results on the spiritual path.

Indeed, the scriptures state that for each world age, a specific method of God realization is particularly appropriate: In Satya-yuga, millions of years ago, one attained the Absolute through deep meditation; in Treta-yuga, through opulent sacrifices; in Dvapara-yuga, through Deity (iconic) worship; and in Kali, the current age, through chanting the holy name of the Lord.

Even the celestial beings mentioned in the Vedic literature want to take part in this celebration of sacred sound. Vishnu Himself, for example, sounds His conch as a call to spiritual awakening, and, in His original form as Krishna, bewitches all living beings with His silky smooth flute playing. Shiva, god of destruction, plays his threatening drum during the dance of cosmic dissolution. The Goddess Sarasvati, too, is always depicted with *vina* in hand; she is the divine patron of resonance and bestows blessings on all students of God-centered music. Lord Brahma, the husband of Sarasvati, creates musical scales with the mantras of the *Sama-Veda*, and uses the specific mantra "OM" to create the universe. Interestingly, this teaching — that material existence is generated through sound — resonates with the Bible: In the beginning was the Word (*John* 1:1). Vedic texts state it directly: "By divine utterance the universe came into being." (*Brihadaranyaka Upanishad* 1.2.4) These same texts tell us that just as sound had once instigated the original flow of cosmic creation, so, too, does it play a significant role in humankind's ultimate goal: "Liberation through sound." This is a catchphrase in the Vedantic tradition. (*Vedanta-sutra* 4.4.22) Hence: kirtan.

This is the core practice of Vaishnavas, originating from hoary times and the revelation of the Vedas. Then, in as early as the sixth century CE, when *bhakti* ("devotion") emerged as a vital force, powerful *yogis* and alluring singer-poets with mystic powers transformed the countryside, conveying truths not only in Sanskrit, drawing on the original Vedas, but in vernacular languages, making full use of new compositions and contemporary song. Most productive were the Shaivite Nayanars and the Vaishnava Alvars, whose devotional poetry might be seen as first steps in the development of modern kirtan. A *bhakti* movement was in full flower, emphasizing the heart, the essence, rather than rituals and rigid observances.

Bhakti literature and devotional song spread rapidly, accommodating the growing wave of seekers and spiritual adepts that inundated the land. As a result, four major lineages arose in South India, allowing primeval knowledge to flow north and, eventually, around the world. This was done through commentary and explication, practice and revelation. The four lineages owe a debt of gratitude to the following seers: Ramanuja (1017–1137), the initial systematizer for the Sri Sampradaya; Nimbarka (ca. 1130–1200), of the Kumara Sampradaya; Madhva (1238–1317), who appeared in the Brahma Sampradaya; and Vishnu Swami (dates unknown), who reinvigorated the Rudra Sampradaya, which was then reformulated by Vallabhacharya (1479–1545) as Pushti Marg. Many branches, sub-branches and diverse traditions sprouted from these essential four. The most significant in terms of kirtan would be that of Sri Chaitanya Mahaprabhu (1486–1533), who in many ways was the cap on the Vaishnava tradition (See Appendix I). His Gaudiya Sampradaya, an offshoot of the Brahma-Madhva line, inspired all of India with ecstatic song and dance, illuminating the science of kirtan as never before.

Sophisticated love poetry, systematic theology, and new revelations came from many quarters. Chief among these, perhaps, was the *Gita-Govinda*, Jayadeva's twelfth-century Sanskrit work on the love of Radha and Krishna. Mentioning the names of the great *kirtaniyas* who developed Jayadeva's theme might appear like a meaningless litany to the layman, but to those who know the tradition, reciting these names is on a par with the most profound kirtan: Sur Das, Tulasi Das, Tukaram, Namdev, Mirabai, Vidyapati, Chandidas, Swami Haridas, Narottam, Bhaktivinode Thakur. And there were countless others who wrote devotional songs on the same subject, elaborating on divine love as found in the spiritual world. The practice of kirtan is forever indebted to them.

The Maha-Mantra

The Hare Krishna *maha-mantra* — Hare Krishna, Hare Krishna, Krishna Krishna, Hare Hare/ Hare Rama, Hare Rama, Rama Rama, Hare Hare — is known as the greatest (*maha*) of all mantras, because it is said to contain the potency of all other spiritual sound vibrations, at least when properly chanted. It is thus the most popular form of kirtan.

The mantra is also considered "the greatest chant" because it is totally selfless: Unlike other prayers, in which the chanter asks for something personal, whether it be health, the protection of loved ones, or daily bread, in this mantra one merely asks to be used as God's instrument, to serve Him in love and devotion, without any expectation of return. The sages of India give us the following translation: "O Lord! O energy of the Lord! Please engage me in Your divine service!"

Since it is a mantra composed solely of the names of God, how do India's sages arrive at this translation? To begin with, the initial word of the mantra forcefully calls out to Radha, the embodiment of devotional energy: "O Radhe! Please engage me in divine service!" One may wonder: If the first word is "Hare," how is the mantra connected to "Radha"? In fact, "Hare" and "Radha" are one—both names refer to the same Supreme Goddess. But, also, "Hare" is in the vocative, and so the mantra is not merely a passive recitation of Her name. Rather, it beseeches Her, calling out to Mother Hara (Radha) for Her undivided attention. And since She is the embodiment of devotional energy, calling out to Her is, in essence, a prayer passionately asking to be engulfed in that energy—and that with great urgency. The basis of the mantra's urgency is revealed in the esoteric Gaudiya tradition: Divine service cannot be attained or practiced without recourse to the Goddess, Radha. Thus, the mantra is basically an intense request to be engaged in spiritual service (*seva*).

Yet there is another dimension to this mantra's greatness: According to the ancient, mystical teachings of Gaudiya Vaishnavism, Radha, the feminine Divine, is supreme, in some ways eclipsing even Krishna, the male Godhead, and this is realized through the chanting of the mantra. Overall, the tradition views God as both male *and* female—which is more inclusive than the usual patriarchal and matriarchal conceptions of divinity. Radha and Krishna are one, but have become two in order to relish spiritual exchange. And yet the lovely Radha surpasses even Him, for He is totally controlled by Her love. The message is clear: *Bhakti*, devotional love, conquers God by His own divine arrangement. This is a spiritual phenomenon that reveals itself more and more as one becomes adept in the chanting. On a basic level, it can easily be appreciated as follows: Radha and Krishna, the dual-gendered divinity, are a beautiful vision of the divine, showing perfect egalitarianism, even if, ultimately, Sri Radha is Supreme.

The Book You Hold in Your Hands

Kirtan is alive and well. It is embraced by Occidental people as much as by those of the East; by women as well as men, by black and white, young and old. We have chosen to present our theme primarily through dialogue, an interview-style format that allows individuals to speak in terms of authoritative sources but also of their own realizations. This is important, since kirtan is as much a personal experience as it is a traditional practice. The bold text is comprised of my questions and comments, followed by the responses of my distinguished interviewees.

The conversations are intimate and a bit like kirtans themselves, with a back-and-forth dynamic that makes them easy to read and accessible. Thus, the chapters focus not only on kirtan as such but on the lives of those being interviewed. This is intentional, because kirtan is first and foremost *performed by people*. Accordingly, our goal is to offer readers a peek into the world of kirtan by warmly acquainting them with the personalities who perform kirtan—whether recording artists who have a career in music; *sadhus* who practice kirtan as a way to unite with God; or people like you or me, sojourners in the world of matter, trying to make sense of all that we see around us.

The book also includes two appendices: The first, "Chaitanya Mahaprabhu: the Father of Modern Kirtan," will introduce readers to a sixteenth-century ecstatic—someone whose name might be familiar but who often remains something of a mystery to the general public. His relative obscurity is easily understood: While Sri Chaitanya is often briefly mentioned in popular yoga literature in the West, few details of his life and teachings make their way into such books. Rather, his story has largely been confined to academic volumes and inaccessible tomes meant for experts, when not entirely limited to Sanskrit and Bengali sources. Here, then, *The Yoga of Kirtan* seeks to fill this lacuna by sharing some much-needed information about this consequential personality. In the second appendix, "What Does OM *Really* Mean?," readers will learn the history and context of OM, not only as popularly understood in the yoga world but according to original Vedic sources.

For those who want to hear the joyous sounds of kirtan first-hand, we have included a CD of some, but not all, of the artists represented here. Space simply did not allow the full spectrum of voices that could have ideally graced this disk. Nonetheless, readers (and listeners) will get the essence of kirtan through these representative pieces. The track listing is as follows:

1. Ragani, "Hare Krishna Govinda." (7:16) From the album "Ancient Spirit" (Kirtan Café, Vol. II)

2. Dave Stringer, "Devakinandana Gopala (minor)." (8:27) From the album "Mala."

3. David Newman, "Sita-Ram." (4:43) From the album "Lotus Feet: A Kirtan Revolution."

4. Sean Johnson and the Wild Lotus Band, "Bhajarangi Hanuman." (6:07) From the album "Calling the Spirits."

5. Krishna Das, "Jaya Bhagavan." (4:47) A previously unreleased live recording.

6. Dravida Das, "Namaste Sri Radhe." (3:23) From the Temple Bhajan Band.

7. Havi Das, "Nam-Sankirtan." (4:43) From the album "Bhakti: Devotional Chants from India."

8. Keshav Das, "Govinda Jaya Jaya." (4:34) From the album "Barefoot in the Heart."

9. Jai Uttal, "Radha Rani." (9:18) From the album "Kirtan! The Art and Practice of Ecstatic Chant."

10. Karnamrita Dasi, "The Glories of Sri Radha." (4:07) From the album *"Dasi: Prayers by Women."*

11. Vaiyasaki Das, "Radhe Radhe Shyam Milade." (12:18) From the album "Transcendence." Though this track is some twenty-five years old, it is among my favorite kirtan recordings, so I've included it here.

The CD is just a sample of what kirtan sounds like, but there is no substitute for joining in a kirtan oneself, for immersing oneself in a live kirtan with others — to see the faces of those who allow themselves to become absorbed, to feel one's body move, one's heart dance. Just thinking about it takes me back to 1972, to my first actual experience of live kirtan on those New York City streets. Hopefully, reading this book will inspire you to go out and find a live kirtan performance. It will be life-altering.

KRISHNA DAS

Krishna Das is the unassuming icon of kirtan in the West. Yoga Journal *famously dubbed him, "The Pavarotti of Kirtan," and it is indeed impossible to spend any time in a yoga studio — whether in America or in Europe — without hearing him call out to the divine, either by his personal presence in the form of a live concert, or through his many CDs, which inevitably resound through such studios as a matter of course.*

In the winter of 1968, a young Jewish seeker named Jeffrey Kagel — soon to become Krishna Das — met Richard Alpert (Ram Dass), who had just returned from his first trip to India. After living and traveling with Ram Dass in the States — all the while hearing from him stories about his extraordinary teacher, Neem Karoli Baba — Krishna Das journeyed to India, eventually finding and spending time with Baba himself.

While living in India for almost three years, Krishna Das was introduced to the art of sacred chanting, and it stayed with him for the rest of his life. Neem Karoli Baba, or Maharaji, as he is affectionately called, helped his new disciple penetrate the depths of kirtan — chanting the names of God. When the young kirtan-wallah emerged in the States, some time later, he would find the chanting to be his only true repose, even as life offered its usual struggles and difficulties.

In 1990, KD, as Krishna Das came to be known, founded Karuna/

Triloka Records with Mitchell Markus, a label now famous for its world music recordings, including releases from East-West fusionist Jai Uttal, Native American vocal phenomenon Walela, the legendary Hugh Masekela, Indian classicalist Ali Akbar Khan, and others.

Krishna Das' debut album, "One Track Heart" (1996), quickly popularized his inimitable baritone chanting style, making use of kirtans culled from the ancient tradition of Bhakti-yoga. Several albums followed, his most popular being "Pilgrim Heart"(1998), which has sold over 50,000 copies. Touring constantly, he has now sung with Sting and given instruction to Madonna. He has worked with producer extraordinaire Rick Rubin and continues to revolutionize kirtan in the 21ˢᵗ century. This is the phenomenon known as Krishna Das.

✳ ✳ ✳

Let's begin with some background. I suspect readers will want to know who you were before you became Krishna Das. Of course, there's the Wikipedia, where one becomes privy to simple facts like your former name and your birth date: May 31, 1947. But let's hear what really happened . . .

Well, the setting: I was born in New York City, in Manhattan, and I grew up on Long Island in New Hyde Park, Mineola. I went to Herricks High School, and then I went on to Stony Brook, on and off for a few years, transferred to New Paltz College, upstate New York, and then I quit school sometime during the first semester there—that's when I met Ram Dass.

Now I'd like you to elaborate on that. How did you meet him?

I lived on a farm in upstate New York, in Rosendale, which is near New Paltz; I lived there with some wild people, and they knew Richard Alpert, aka Ram Dass, from the old days. He had just come back from India and had lectured in New York City. One of my friends, from that farm community, had been to the lecture and came back telling us that Ram Dass was now living in New Hampshire and that they were going up there to visit him. I thought it would be cool to meet him and just got in a car and drove up. So that's when I met him for the first time. It was late winter, in 1968.

And then you lived and traveled with him, as the story goes. Do you have some anecdotes, like about places you went together?

Well, during that period I wasn't living and traveling with him, although I followed him around a lot. We spent the winter together with a few other people up in the mountains in New Mexico, at the Lama Foundation—we were meditating, chanting, just living and breathing. It was really nice.

Was that your first exposure to chanting?

More or less, I think. I mean, the ISKCON people were around, and I heard their chanting quite a bit. And Swami Satchidananda was probably around by then—so I heard that kind of chanting and stuff like that.

Was there any attraction to the chanting?

No, not really; not at that time. There was a mild attraction. When Ram Dass came back he used to sing this nice melody, actually, a couple of nice melodies, for "Sri Rama, Jaya Rama," and I liked that. But, no, I had no special attraction for chanting yet. It was interesting, though. When I went to see Swami Satchidananda at Ananda Ashram once . . .

In Monroe, right?

In Monroe, yeah. He was sitting outside in the afternoon and there was a very austere-looking swami sitting next to him. After Swami Satchidananda gave his lecture, instead of the usual "Hari Om," and that's it, you know, this other swami broke out in song: "Sri Rama, Jaya Rama, Jaya Jaya Rama." And I was shocked, because my eyes were closed and I was expecting the other thing—but this was great. It was like electricity; it was unbelievable.

Who was the swami?

I didn't know who he was at the time, but I never forgot him, because of the intensity of that experience. So, now, this is, say, 1968, or thereabouts. Four years later, I'm in India in the temple living with Maharaji and a car full of swamis pulls up. They all race in, going right into Maharaji's room. And as soon as they got in the room and closed the door: "Sri Rama, Jaya Rama . . ." It was the same guy! That's when I found out it was Swami Chitananda, who was the head of the Divine Life Society. Maharaji had known him for many years and always asked him to sing for him. Great, great kirtan. And so Swami Chitananda had been singing "Sri Rama" to Maharaji before I even knew about Maharaji, and yet when he sang it that day with Swami Satchidananda, I felt it.

Through the connection . . .

Through the connection, yeah.

Fantastic. So then, after that Swami Chitananda experience you became enamored with this Eastern stuff and went to India. Can you talk about your first meeting with Neem Karoli Baba? Or did something happen before you met him?

No, we went there to see him, specifically to see him, because Ram Dass told all these amazing stories. Well, you know, we did meet Muktananda in London, on the way to India. We enjoyed our exchange with him, and he said to us that since we were going to land in Bombay, we might want to check out his ashram for a week and relax, which we did. It was a really nice introduction to India for us. It's interesting, though: He was on his way to America for the first time, and we were on our way to India. But he was very nice to us, and so we went to his ashram for a week and then after that we went up north.

This is the early 1970s?

This is in September 1970, or actually August. I remember because when I arrived in Delhi, it was a couple of days after Jimi Hendrix died, which was in September. The death was mentioned in *Time* magazine there in Delhi.

Anyway, so then we went up north and we found Maharaji in

Kainchi. At first, we didn't know where he would be, and we only knew the address of this devotee who had helped us get there.

You see, Ram Dass had not given us details of where to go. This is because Maharaji had told him not to talk about their experiences together; Maharaji didn't want a bunch of Westerners to come. Of course, all Ram Dass *did* was talk about him — he couldn't stop talking about him. But he never told you who he was, what his name was, and where you could find him. It was all quite secretive.

But I was at a point where I had to go. I mean, I was being pulled too strongly, aggressively, spiritually — so Ram Dass said, "Okay. Look, I'll give you this devotee's address; you write to him; he and I are very close. He'll ask Maharaji what we should do."

I see. So you almost didn't meet him. I mean, if it were not rearranged by providence . . .

Exactly. So I wrote to this devotee named KK, Krishna Kumar Shah, and he wrote back saying that Maharaji wasn't in the hills at the time, because KK lived up in the mountains, but when he returned he would take my letter to him and then write back to me. So I got a letter back a few weeks later, I guess, saying that after some time Maharaji had returned to the hills and that he had finally had an opportunity to go the temple at Kainchi, where Maharaji was staying. And he ends his letter by saying, "As you know, Maharaji doesn't encourage people to come to him, but his doors are always open, and if you are traveling in India, you can come and have his darshan."

Ah, a point of entry.

[laughter] Right. All I saw was a green light — "All right, here we go." But let me give you some background on KK.

First of all, you've got to understand that KK grew up in Maharaji's lap, from the time he was eight years old. Maharaji was like his grandfather and a member of the family. Of course, Maharaji was a member of all these families — that's the way, the emotion, that he had with all the people around him; he was like the grandfather of all these families. And KK, especially, had developed a relationship with Maharaji like that of a spoiled boy, you know, who just did what he wanted, feeling totally free in front of Maharaji, to do as he pleased. He didn't necessarily obey him, as one would one's guru. In fact, if Maharaji said sit down, KK would stand up; if he said eat, KK would fast.

Lovingly rebellious.

Right, that's the way he was. Of course, the love was astoundingly intense. Anyway, with this much background, I'll go on with the story. So KK came into the room with Maharaji, and he put my letter down in front of him. Now, there were two other letters, from Danny and Jim. And he places them down right next to Maharaji. Then he began peeling an apple to feed to Maharaji. So this is going on, and there were others in the room—Maharaji was talking to them. At one point, Maharaji happened to look down and he sees these letters. He says, "What's that?" And KK said, "Oh, these are letters from students of Ram Dass and they want to come to see you."

"No! Tell them not to come." So KK began to pout, and he looked down and dejected—he even stopped feeding Maharaji the apple. And he was just sitting there with an upset look on his face. Maharaji noticed and then pushed KK's head in a loving manner, saying, "Kailash"—that was his nickname—"what's the matter?" KK wouldn't even look at him; he would just turn his eyes away, even though Maharaji was holding his head up. So after a few of these interactions, Maharaji said, "Alright, tell them what you want."

See, KK wanted to do the right thing for Ram Dass, who was his friend. He felt that he was serving Ram Dass by getting us darshan. That's how we got in. I never got a whiff of all that back then. He told me the story many years later.

That's a sweet story.

But it's also indicative of the kind of person Maharaji was. He had such love for his devotees. But also, he accomplished a lot of things by apparently doing nothing, just by submitting to the desires of those around him. He appeared to do nothing, but he accomplished everything from another place entirely. Everything was taken care of perfectly, and God's will was done in all cases perfectly, because of the depth of his realization and surrender. So, it always appeared that he was uninvolved and unconcerned, so to speak. Even if he was concerned, he would say, "Well, just pray to Hanumanji and then anything is possible." And, you know, we knew that that was really true, *really* true. This is what he taught us, and what we experienced, firsthand.

Well, for me this brings up an interesting question: What lineage does Neem Karoli Baba come from? Usually, Hanumanji is seen as devotee, not as Bhagavan, not as God, so . . .

His past is shrouded in mystery, but he certainly hails from the lineage of Rama and Hanuman. That's definitely his line. Some people say he was a Vaishnava *sadhu*, but nobody really knows.

His lineage is unclear.

I don't think anybody really knows. Maharaji never talked about it—he never talked about his past or stuff like that, although there are a lot of stories. He never talked about having one particular guru. He didn't have any pictures of his guru anywhere. All he had were pictures or *murtis* of Hanuman, and Rama, and Shiva, too.

But he had an intense spiritual power that attracted you . . .

He had God's love . . . he *has* God's love. That's what attracts.

How much time did you spend with him?

Well, for the first nine months or so there was a lot of coming and going. He would send us away, we would come back, and he'd say come back in two days. Then we'd leave and come back. After that, he'd say come back in three days; we'd come back; he'd say come back in a week. And we'd just be sitting around in this North Indian town with nothing to do.

What town is it?

Nainital and Kainchi. The temple is about an hour from there, between Nainital and Almora, in northern India.

Kainchi means "scissors," and this valley is like a pair of scissors; the river runs north right by the temple.

So you'd wait around for him to call you back, like when he said to come back in a few days . . .

Right. And it was kind of like that for a while — not spending a lot of time with him. Going back and forth. So from that fall until the spring there was mostly coming and going — we weren't allowed to spend a lot of time there. Come the spring, we all moved up into this devotees' hotel, in Nainital, and every day we'd come to the temple and spend all day there, only going back at night.

Then he would disappear in the late fall. He would go down to the plains and maybe go off on some pilgrimage — nobody would know where he was. You see, that's what he did; he'd start out someplace and then he would disappear, and nobody knew where he went, or when he'd show up. And then when he did show up somewhere, word would get out and people would come from wherever they were — and then he would go off again.

He was a wanderer, and that's that. Totally free. He had no place of his own, and not even the temples were in his name — nothing was in his name. There was a temple trust, but the properties themselves belonged to the government. He owned nothing — he traveled with a blanket and his simple *dhoti*, and that was it. And when he wandered off, he never took anything with him. He might take one devotee to one town and then send him back and take another devotee to the next town. Or he would disappear and get on a train, nobody really knowing where his next destination would be.

He would show up and people seemed to know him, no matter where he went. He knew everybody, everywhere. I mean, he would just walk into houses unannounced, uninvited, and sit down and say, "Hello, from now on I'll stay here." And then those people would become devotees, because he knew who was who and where they were and what they needed to happen in their lives. He would show up anywhere at any time if you needed him, even if you didn't know you needed him. Or if he didn't show up himself, you would get a phone call in the middle of the night from somebody saying, "Please hold. Baba wants to talk." And then he'd get on the phone and say, "Please, don't worry," and hang up. He would constantly travel like that, ministering to people's needs.

It was only when the body got a little older and he slowed down that he spent significant periods of time in places like Kainchi, or in the winter he would stay at a devotee's house in Allahabad; then in the fall, spring and summer he would stay up in the mountains, where there's some quiet, not traveling too much. That's when we got to spend time with him.

Now, that's when you hooked into the chanting. But I read that you were a *pujari*, a priest, at his Durga temple, too. That's pretty far out.

Right. Of course. This all happened Maharaji-style, in his own inimitable way. The *murti* of Durga Devi, the Goddess, had come, and the time for consecration was imminent. But he wanted the temple to be opened right away, before the consecration ceremony, because it was Durga Puja, a big, big festival in the fall, and people were coming. So he wanted them to have darshan at the temple. Accordingly, they brought in a priest and they opened the temple, and then after a couple of days they found that the priest was stealing the donations. They sent him home and got another one, and the same thing happened; and this happened again and again. So, finally, the temple trust came to him and said, "Baba, we can't find a priest that won't steal!"

Maharaji answers, "My priest won't steal!" And they say, "Your priest? Who is your priest?"

"Krishna Das!" No training, no nothing. But now I'm his priest.

He had already given you this name, Krishna Das?

Yeah. So they said, "Okay," and they came to me, asking me to do the job. "Maharaji wants you to be the *pujari*." So I did it; I sat there all day, giving out *prasadam* [food offered to the deity], accepting the donations.

You knew how to do formal *puja*, to worship the deity, like a Brahmin?

No, but I used to close the deity doors and hang out a lot. [laughter]

I see. Very informal . . .

Very informal, and then the deity had a caretaker. That was the main thing. Priests would come by and do the *puja*, when it was going on at other temples. My job was just to sit there and take care of her, to take care of the Goddess, when nobody else was around. Actually, she was taking care of me.

So you'd give out *prasadam*. . .

Give out *prasadam*, yes, when people came for darshan. But the funny thing was, since I was sitting there anyway, I started to think, "Well, maybe I should learn some mantras." And that's when I began to start doing Devi-puja, learning the formulas . . .

Okay, so this is good. This is how you started studying mantras.

That's how I started. It all happened unexpectedly, or inadvertently. And yet, you know, I couldn't tell you that Maharaji wanted me to do Devi Puja necessarily, specifically. It just happened that way, by God's grace. It's not like Maharaji ever said, "Do that! I want you to worship the Goddess!" But things were arranged so that it became inevitable, and that's often the way Maharaji worked.

When I think of Durga Puja, I think of Kali—bloodthirsty and the rest. But that's Bengal . . .

That's Kali Puja; this is Vaishnavi Devi. A different aspect of the Goddess. You can't even break a coconut in front of her. You have to break it off temple grounds and bring it in. Oh, Maharaji made it so that it was totally consistent with the principles of nonviolence. Now, there was a lot of animal sacrifice up in the hills, it's true. They do a lot of that stuff, and Maharaji wanted to discourage that—he wanted to bring in a more *sattvik* kind of worship.

Oh . . . that's interesting.

Sure, that's why he did it.

I always wondered about vegetarianism—whether it's accepted as an

important principle by the followers of Neem Karoli Baba.

He didn't give us any rules, actually.

But you did say he was trying to instill *sattvik* worship. Vegetarianism is part of a *sattvik* lifestyle, which focuses on life, purity, goodness, wholesomeness, and so on.

Right, but Maharaji's teaching—if you can call it that—left it open to the individual. It wasn't formal; nothing was formal. We weren't required to wear any particular type of clothes; he didn't initiate us into any mantras; he didn't give us teachings about meditation and chanting and life. That wasn't what he did; he did things very differently. For me, he's like the sun, just shining on everyone and everything. The plants don't need a manual on how to grow, but when you're in the sunlight, that's just what you do—you grow, like it or not. And that's what he is for all of us who had his association.

You see, all of us are exactly who we are—and he nurtured that. He never required us to be something other than what we were.

Now, on a certain level, there wasn't always a lot of love between his followers, because we weren't made into a homogeneous group of any kind. Not that making people into a single group necessarily creates harmony, as you know. But we were all disparate individuals, and so we saw things differently, but that's okay. We all share something that can never be taken away, something special. He loved us as we were, and he could see everything about us, too, which made his love really special—he loved us in spite of ourselves. He wanted us to accept ourselves for what we are, with all our shortcomings. He didn't want us to be anything else, thinking that we need to be good little boys and girls in order for God to love us. No. He showed us unconditional love, and what it really means. Not to think about what could be, or about what might be in the future . . .

So his teaching was really about a kind of "be here now" experience.

Well, it's like that Rumi poem, which says, "My whole life is composed only of this, trying to be in Your presence." This is our *sadhana*, our practice, if you will. You know, chanting is great; it's a very effective means to cultivate higher consciousness, and *asana* and *pranayama*—all of it is useful. But our goal is not to become great chanters; our goal is to be in the presence of that love. And he manifested that for us and he represents it for us. For this reason, our whole lives are encapsulated in our relationship with him, in our interaction with the guru and what he represents to us.

So, to understand that he didn't give teachings—and to understand that I don't chant because he told me to—is a very important thing, because motivation is everything. Well, listen, I didn't chant for a long time, for a lot of reasons. But when I did start chanting, I did so for what I think are the right reasons, you know, as far as that's concerned. And so I didn't run into a lot of the problems that a lot of other people run into, because chanting gives you a lot of energy. But if you don't clean your heart, the darkness gets in the way. It's personal work, and you can't rely on formal teachings, ecclesiastic authorities, or institutions. It's you. And you can see what happens in institutions and with people who think in terms of groups. People wind up getting harder and harder, and their pride gets more subtle, and their egos get in the way. But it's very subtle, and he was aware of that. You can't build a house on quicksand—sooner or later it's gonna sink.

Before you said that you didn't chant for a long time, and for many reasons. Can you share some of that?

Oh, I was just messed up. [Laughter]

In what sense?

Just depressed, unhappy. When he left the body, I kind of . . .

Went into a depression.

Very terrible time, for many, many years. I mean, I was chanting with people, on and off, with the people who knew him from the old days. But for me, it was like rubbing salt in a wound. It was that painful. I couldn't take life in his absence.

It's a hard day when one's beloved teacher passes; you feel tremendous pain. I experienced that, too, with Prabhupada.

I'm sure, yeah.

Where did you find solace?

Mr. Tewari, the Tewari family, devotees of Maharaji. I spent many, many years with them after he died, particularly that family. They really adopted me and took care of me.

Do you want to talk a little about that?

They were lifelong devotees of Maharaji; they were great saints, actually. Mr. Tewari was a secret *yogi*; not too many people knew that side of him. He was headmaster of a school—a schoolteacher.

What was his name?

Mr. K. C. Tewari—that's how he liked to be known—and his wife, and they were both extraordinary beings. They showed me that love was possible between human beings, that there was caring and goodness, without any expectation of return. I saw this on a daily basis, because I spent lots of time with them. It was different than just going and meeting for a little while and feeling great; this was day after day, for many times months at a time. I just moved in with them and traveled all around India with them.

Did Maharaji ask them to watch over you, or it just happened?

No, it just happened . . . But, you know, I can see his hand in everything.

Did they have biological children?

They had children, sure, and I'm still close with them. They both passed, but I'm still close with the kids. Two boys and a girl.

That's interesting . . .

Oh, yeah. I wouldn't have made it without them. They were very loving, nurturing; they really took care of me.

So, let's backtrack a bit—you were going to talk about your dark night of the soul. Maharaji asked you to return to the States in '73, and he passed around that time, and you went into a state of depression.

I just moped around and did odd jobs and all kinds of things. Well, there were two turning points for me. One was 1984, when I went back to India. At that time I was severely depressed; I mean, I was really, really bad off. I wouldn't say I was suicidal, but I didn't want to live. I was at the bottom.

You couldn't see purpose in life . . .

No. Because when Maharaji died, I thought I had lost my only chance to ever be happy, because being with him physically was the only thing that ever worked for me. So when he wasn't there, what could I do? I was helpless. It was that bleak.

So, in '84 you went back to India . . .

Right. Eleven years after he died, I went back . . . and he came back to me. I walked into that room in Kainchi, where I had spent time with him, and I was hit by a thunderbolt, and . . .

You saw him or you felt him?

I felt him, but intensely. I didn't see him with my eyes. I was hit by a thunderbolt—that's what it felt like—and I fell down on the ground. My heart just exploded—it exploded in my chest, and I wept. In the blink of an eye I saw everything I had done in that whole eleven years, from the moment I had heard he had died until that moment there. Time lost meaning. It all went past me like the frames of a movie, you know, click, click, click. And I saw everything I had done, and also why I had done it.

But more importantly, I saw that I had built a wall around my heart. I would not let myself feel. I was pissed off and I was angry and I was ashamed, thinking that I had betrayed him. But then I saw that he was right there with the wall of my heart, in the wall, on both sides of the wall; the wall meant nothing to him. I saw that he hadn't really left me, and I was feeling all this stuff I wouldn't previously let myself feel. And then I saw that I could take this wall down, this external wall, and let him stand in its place.

I just had to look at that stuff; I couldn't pretend it wasn't there. And I knew it would all start to go away. So I was in ecstasy. I mean, let me tell you: I never, ever had that kind of experience before that day, or since. It was total. It was like, "Ah, okay. Let's show some mercy. Let's let the kid live. BOOM!" You know, like that. [laughter]

Wow, so that was a life-altering experience.

Absolutely, because I recognized that I could be happy, that I hadn't blown it. There was a reason to live and all I had to do was to pay a little attention—and stuff would start to change.

So that took you out of your pain. And then you moved toward kirtan more intensely. Why don't we talk a little about kirtan?

Okay. I'm just going to tell you the way I see it and you can put it in any context or leave it out of the book altogether.

My first glimpses of real kirtan left a deep impression in my heart. There was stray contact with kirtan early on, as I mentioned, but it really happened when I was in India for the first time. One night, I was walking around the lake, in this mountain town I was living in, Nainital. As I passed by a small temple, I heard this chanting coming from inside, and I was completely blown away. I had never heard chanting like that—there was such intensity, such joy. There was no distraction, no sadness—it was just *right there*.

Ananda, bliss.

Totally from that other dimension, from the spiritual realm. They were giving 100%, you know? It was rock and roll, in the sense that they were having a great time. And yet it was worship.

Was it amplified?

No, it was just inside this little temple. And I actually walked in and they let me sit down and, you know, it was just extraordinary. I had never seen that kind of intensity, and I knew it was holy stuff—it was in a temple. Now, the temples on Long Island are quite a bit different, as I'm sure you know. [laughter] People mope around and groan and . . .

[In a Yiddish accent:] "Oy. Vy do I have to be here?!"

Right. [laughter, and then, also in a Yiddish accent:] "Vy? Vy? Vhat is dis? I gotta go home!"

Well, this kind of spiritual intensity just wasn't there while I was growing up in America, at least not in my neighborhood, and so when I saw it, it was like the lights went on. I just went, "holy shit," so this is what spirituality can be like. And right from that moment, I couldn't get enough of it. Whenever I heard it, I went to be with it, like a magnet. I wanted to sing, from the heart, like them, and of course I wanted to learn all the words and everything.

What were they chanting? Do you remember?

I think they were doing the "Hanuman Chalisa," as a matter of fact. It was a Tuesday—funny how you remember some things—and I was just blown away.

Going back to your background on Long Island—was it a secular Jewish family, religious, or . . . ?

Yeah, Reform Judaism, I guess. As Surya Dasa says, "I'm Jewish on my parents' side."

Right, right. I've heard that. [laughter]

Anyway, once I heard that emotional kirtan, coming from that temple, I just sang as much as I could—I would search out people and sing with them, anywhere and everywhere. If people were singing, I'd try to join in. If they were good, I'd try to emulate what they were doing . . .

Any people stand out in your mind, people that were really doing it, like specific *sadhus* or such? Do you remember where you derived your thirst for kirtan?

I think the greatest influence on my chanting, the genesis, came from these Hare Krishna guys from Vrindavan. Maharaji would have them come up to Kainchi and spend quite a bit of time with us—spring, rainy season, summer, and fall. And they would sing Hare Krishna around the clock, from four in the morning until about eleven at night, every day.

Were they part of ISKCON?

Not ISKCON, no. But they were definitely from the Gaudiya Vaishnava Sampradaya. They were all properly initiated and all that, but they weren't part of ISKCON. In fact, they were all Indian guys. Besides, this was in 1970, and so there weren't many ISKCON people in India yet. I think they started to arrive during that same year and just after that. That's when they started showing up in Vrindavan.

Interesting. So your initial inspiration for chanting Hare Krishna came from Mahaprabhu's side, from the Gaudiya Sampradaya.

It was these particular people. What impressed me so much was their total absorption—they didn't seem interested in any other kind of gratification. In fact, this *was* their gratification! They didn't want to do anything else. This was how they were spending the rest of their lives, chanting the name. That's it. They weren't in any hurry; they weren't going anywhere; they weren't trying to get anything. They were simply chanting the name, totally present. And they were gonna be chanting the name for as long as they could. They didn't have plans to become movie stars or to do anything else in life. Breathing, eating, sleeping—this they *had to do*. But singing—this was their life. This is what they *wanted to do*.

Of course, I learned more about them as individuals later on, and I saw that they had other sides to them, too, and some of them were not as holy or pure as I had initially thought. But my first impressions—and certainly something that was a genuine part of them—were simply this: that they were in this for the duration. They weren't chanting to get anything else. They weren't trying to make a career for themselves as singers; they weren't after fame, money, women.

Like Chaitanya Mahaprabhu's famous verse: "O almighty Lord, I have no desire to accumulate wealth, nor do I desire beautiful women, nor do I want any number of followers. I only want Your causeless devotional service, birth after birth."

Beautiful. That was it. Many of them had left all that already. They were older guys, and many of them had had families, children already grown, and now they were just devoted to this chanting. They were now spending whatever days they had left with the holy name. And to sit with them was a beautiful commitment, a total experience. The channel didn't change every half hour, if you know what I mean. The show wasn't over in fifteen minutes.

They weren't looking at their watches, waiting for the next thing to do. This was it!

There was nothing else. You didn't have to look at any schedule because they were singing Hare Krishna now, and they'd be singing Hare Krishna in eight hours. So you could just immerse yourself in it, just sit in it and watch the truth come out.

Were they doing Bengali *bhajans*, too?

No *bhajan* at all, only *maha-mantra*. But they used diverse melodies, all kinds, from everywhere. They used stuff from shows, film music, and traditional stuff, too. Whatever melodies they had around they used for the *maha-mantra*, which is quite interesting. Because that's what I do now. And that's where I get it from, I guess. But the melodies I have come from New York instead of Bengal. [laughter] So that's the difference.

It was wonderful to be accepted by them, and they really did accept me. I know this because I sat in with them a lot, and we sang together with great joy. Not so much when Maharaji was in the body, although we did sing with them. But afterwards, when we would go back to the temple, they were still there, years later. Every season they would show up and they would sing. At that point, I started singing a lot more, and with greater intensity. You know, when the guru is in the body, all you want to do is look at the guru, to bask in his presence. I mean, you don't want to do any *sadhana*, even if they say to do *sadhana*, which he never did. Our whole *sadhana* was just staring at him.

Ah, yes. This is the classical dichotomy between *vapu* and *vani*, the guru's form and the guru's sound. On one level, devotees are attracted to his form, naturally. But higher still is the sound, the truths that emanate from his lips.

But, yes, I know what you mean. The same thing happened in ISKCON. When Prabhupada was on the planet, everyone just wanted to be around him.

Sure. That's the way it is. The guru embodies this spiritual energy, the presence of God. Who wouldn't want to bask in that?!

But here's what I find interesting: A lot of your attraction to chanting came from those Gaudiya Vaishnavas.

Absolutely.

And it's interesting that, today, the Hare Krishnas respond to your chanting, too. There must be some connection . . .

They do. They seem to like it.

And when I hear your kirtan, I also get a sense of this—the "I don't have anything else to do" mood—as you described with those Bengali *kirtaniyas*. It's very patient, calming, with a "this is just what I do" vibe.

Yeah, well, it's true. I don't have any agenda. I just want to be there, to immerse myself in the chanting. Every night is different, the group is different, and the chanting goes where it goes, and that's it. It tends to come together, and it goes off in its own direction, and I'm there for the ride. I'm not running the show—I know that. There's a divine energy that enters into the picture. I'm just kind of . . . I don't even know what I'm doing, to tell you the truth.

You're an instrument.

I guess so.

What about philosophy, like correlation between kirtan and prayer, any thoughts on that?

Well, you know, Ramana Maharsi says that our true nature is a state of invocation. Invoking that presence and being in that presence is what life is really all about. Beyond that, I don't know much philosophy. Sometimes, I come upon writings that resonate very deeply with me.

Anything come to mind?

There's this quote from Sri Ramakrishna, where he says that each and every repetition of a revealed name carries an undeniably sanctifying power, and even if the power of the name is not experienced in that moment, it still has an effect. He says it's like a seed being blown by the wind and lodging between the tiles of an old house. Over the seasons, coming and going, the roof kind of disintegrates and the seed is able to take root. And the roots further encourage the disintegration of this house. He said that that house is the conventional mind, and the conventional view of who we think we are.

Profound.

Very profound, yes. That's when I realized that Sri Ramakrishna is pretty cool.

Yeah. In some ways, he was overshadowed by his disciple, Swami Vivekananda. But they both certainly had something to offer.

You know, basically, I feel that Westerners don't need any more concepts — we have enough concepts. I feel what we really need is experience, and we need true experience. We don't need to be creating some kind of fantasy life for our emotions to hide in, which is what I think most people do. Kirtan breaks you out of that. Whether you're hiding behind your work, your family, your conception of self, your religion — it doesn't matter. A true experience — a kirtan experience — can help you break free.

Because God is already present. He's there in His name and He's there all around us. God came before us, He's prior to us, and He's more real than we are. So any fantasy concocted in our minds, any construct from our mental fluctuations, is simply more illusion. And if we can directly experience the ground of our being, the depth of our being — and this what happens through the chanting of the name — we can rise beyond all that.

What do you focus on when you chant?

I'll tell you what I don't focus on. I don't think about a blue boy with a flute when I sing to Krishna. Instead, I think about supreme love, about the essence of reality. Isn't that what Krishna is all about? I don't say that the images, the forms, the personality, don't have meaning. Krishna is who He is, and I'm not denying that. But the underlying truth speaks to me more directly.

When I chant, I don't think about Shiva sitting on some mountain and having three eyes — I think of that presence, that being, and that truth of ultimate reality. For Westerners, especially, this is more to the point. Why focus on realities that are beyond our comprehension? I say, focus on what you know, on what you can relate to. That's a much better starting point.

When people say to me, "What do the names mean?" I say, "I don't know. I'll tell you when I'm there, and then I'll know." Until then, I'm just dreaming, like the rest of us. We don't need to make it real by defining it or by articulating some complex philosophy — it's already real. If anything, *we're the ones who aren't real.* We think we're who we think we are. C'mon, what's real about that? It's just another thought, another illusion. Where is that going to be after we take our last breath? We don't want that. We want reality. We want God.

If you want the Lord to live in your heart — or to dance on your tongue — you have to make a seat for Him, you have to clean the place up. And that's the hardest thing to do. That means we have to be honest with ourselves, about our greed, our jealousy, our lust, our anger, even our self-hatred. We can't pretend that these things don't exist because they're running our lives, at least for most of us. And that's the great mystery of the name, the power of the name. It turns us upside down — it gives us perspective and leverage.

That's what chanting the name does for me, and that's where

I feel it's bringing me and has brought me so far. So, I don't feel it's necessarily Indian, I don't feel it's American—I just feel it's human. Anybody can do it at any time, and they don't have to know anything first. You don't have to be initiated, you don't have to believe anything—you certainly don't have to have any faith because faith will come from your own experiences, after chanting. You can only know when you know—not when someone tells you—and that happens from your own experiences, from your own effort. Your own effort to receive the grace, because it's all grace, anyway. All this is grace. Everything. Love, life, existence. It's all the grace of God.

That would be a fitting ending for the interview, but I want to hear about your recordings, about how you founded a record company and all that.

Oh, yeah. We started a record company, Karuna/ Triloka Records. I started that with Mitchell Markus . . . It was just something else to do . . . I mean, really, we started the company to give Jai Uttal a forum, to make demos for him, and then his manager didn't want demos. So then we started a record company so we could record him, and we recorded his first records.

He's very good.

Yeah, Jai's great.

But how did your own recordings come about?

Well, I had started singing down at Jivamukti in New York on Monday nights whenever I was in town.

What year was that?

It was in 1994, late summer. Earlier that spring I had been lounging in my apartment and, right then and there, I just knew I had to start singing with people. It was like an epiphany.

You lived in the city?

At the time I had an apartment in the city, yeah. And I was just hit by the realization that I needed to start singing with people who didn't know me. I couldn't just keep doing kirtan with people from the old days. I had to put my ass out there on the line, in front of all kinds of people, or I would never be able to clean my heart; I would never be able to reach these places of darkness, places I had to access and get this stuff out of there. So I forced myself to go down to Jivamukti and asked David and Sharon if it was okay that I sing there. They said, "Sure," and so I started doing it. And after doing that for awhile, and seeing that people liked it, I thought I should make some kind of recording, even if just as a calling card. I realized that I was just reaching people in New York, but if I made a calling card, and people got to know what I did, then I could get invitations to go other places.

So that's how it started. And now it's . . .

So the first CD was just a calling card. I mean, that's the way I looked at it. There was no concept of forging a career. I wasn't even charging a fee at Jivamukti. I would just go and sing — there were no donations or anything. In fact, I never, ever charged anything at Jivamukti, until we started doing the bigger nighttime things. But when I would go down on Mondays I never charged, not for years and years.

I had expenses, though. I mean, I had to get there, so then I started charging a certain amount of money and splitting it with the yoga centers, just to offset my expenses. And so it was through "One Track Heart," which started to sell at yoga classes, that I made some money. A little bit. But word began to spread, and by the time the second CD came out . . .

You know, that first CD, I can barely listen to it. I hear so much in my voice, and what was behind my singing. I say to myself, "What were you thinking? What was that? Shut up and sing." You know, it's really hard for me to listen to it, although there are some very beautiful things on it; some of it I really like. But other parts are a little too calculated, and I can hear it; I can hear my mind at work, my desires.

You hear your ego?

That's right. I hear my wants — I hear need in my voice and I hear hunger. Then, by the second CD, I felt differently. I was in a different space . . .

I wanted to transmit the joy of the way kirtan is done in India. Over here, for many people, it's a burden, a chore. People in the West generally don't have that same innate happiness. They think, "Oh, I have to chant now. This is good for me, so I'll do it." They see it as spiritual practice and they do it . . .

Begrudgingly.

Begrudgingly, right, because we hate to do stuff that's good for us. So that was in my head at that time. But with "Live on Earth," all I wanted to do was sing, and then Rick showed up — so all I had to do was sing.

Yes, the Rick Rubin connection. Before that, can you tell us just a little more about your CDs up until that point?

My second album, "Pilgrim Heart," came out in 1998, with a guest appearance by Sting, who sang on the tune "Mountain Hari Krishna" and played bass on "Ring Song." Cool, huh? Then came the double CD, "Live on Earth . . . For a Limited Time Only" in early 2000. So things just kept snowballing. It all happened so fast, a lot of kirtan. All grace. "Breath Of The Heart" was released in September of 2001 on the new Karuna imprint. This is where Rick Rubin came in, and the album included a kirtan choir of fifty people — with really good musicians — both Eastern and Western.

Okay, so how did Rick Rubin come on the scene?

Rick started coming to kirtan when I was in LA, and I went up and said "Hi" and we had dinner together . . .

You recognized him?

Sure. And we went out to dinner, just hanging out, you know, and I leaned over and said, "I've got to start thinking about another

CD." So he responds, "You gotta do live." So I said, "I just did a live CD." My double live CD had just come out. But his response was quick. He said, "It doesn't sound live." Next conversation, and we went on from there. Didn't pay much attention to it.

The next day, there was a message on my phone. He had called me as I was driving up to Santa Barbara to sing. Later, I got the message, "Hey, it's Rick — I have some ideas about the live record-ing. Here's what I think we should do." I called him right back and said, "Rick, you said, 'we.'" That's when he said, "Yeah, I want to produce it."

"Oh, okay." [laughter] I would never have asked him, but I kind of knew that would happen. I had a feeling, but I still would have never asked him. And he just wanted to do it — so it was beautiful.

He has an attraction to kirtan?

Oh, sure. He loves to chant; he's totally into it, as well as being into Slipknot, you know. I mean, he's an extraordinary and diverse kind of guy, into Johnny Cash and Tom Petty and . . .

But for me he was great. All I had to do was sing. Because Rick had a way of hearing. He had a way of knowing what the artist wanted it to sound like, a way of knowing what it *should* sound like, and being able to get that on the recording. He's really a genius. So I did the next two with him — "Door of Faith" was the second one I did with him, and on that one I basically wanted to share some of the prayers that I had known all these years and had been singing just to myself. I wanted other people to become aware of these prayers. I thought it was a good time to do that. I wasn't up to getting a whole group together and doing the whole production at that time, so "Door of Faith" is very quiet and very deep in its waay. And then the compilation came out — "The Greatest Hits of the Kali Yuga," with the DVD, and then "All One," which consists of various versions of Hare Krishna. That's it — only Hare Krishna.

Also, I've been singing the "Hanuman Chalisa" for over thirty years, and that's the newest CD, "Flow of Grace," which was released in March 2007. This was released as a CD and also separately with an accompanying book. It goes deep into the glory of Hanuman, the embodiment of devotion, service, strength, and compassion. We did other CDs and DVDs, too. But that's the gist of it. Hopefully, we'll go on and on.

For more information contact:
www.krishnadas.com

*Y*AMUNA DEVI

In late 1966, when Joan Campanella was in her mid-twenties, she went to New York for her sister Jan's wedding. Though Jan had written her several letters saying that she was taking "lessons" from an "Indian swami," Joan could not have been less prepared for what greeted her in New York.

Coming, as she did, from an upper-middle-class family in Oregon, she was shocked to find that the swami's world had engulfed her sister's life, even to the point of his being priest and cook at the wedding.

He was then known simply as "Swamiji," but he would soon be called, "A. C. Bhaktivedanta Swami Prabhupada" — the guru who would eventually change Joan's life.

Her sister's wedding was a new birth, of sorts, introducing her to Indian culture and vegetarian cooking — and to the phenomenon known as kirtan. "The wedding was my Waterloo," she said. "I became deeply interested in what Swamiji was saying. And his kirtan rocked my world." Six months later she became an initiated disciple, receiving the name "Yamuna Devi." For the next seven years, off and on in England and India, the Swami personally trained her as a kirtan leader and as one of his personal cooks.

Significantly, in 1968, prior to her Indian sojourn with her spiritual master, Prabhupada sent six disciples — Yamuna, her husband, and two other couples — to London. They worked well together and were especially tight as a kirtan singing group, named "The Radha Krishna Temple."

At that time, George Harrison of the Beatles was also interested in Eastern spirituality. It was meeting with the Radha Krishna Temple group that became pivotal in his turn toward Gaudiya Vaishnavism, or the Hare Krishna Movement.

In the summer of 1969, before the break-up of the Beatles, George produced a hit single — "The Hare Krishna Mantra," performed by George and the devotees of the London Radha Krishna Temple. Yamuna's voice was at the helm, making her the first American to lead a kirtan on a popular recording in the West.

Soon after rising to the Top 10 or Top 20 on the best-selling record charts throughout England, Europe, and parts of Asia, the Hare Krishna chant became a household word — especially in England, where the BBC featured "the Hare Krishna Chanters," as they were then called, on the country's most popular television program, Top of the Pops. And in all of this, Yamuna's voice was center stage. In 1971, the Hare Krishna single was included on a full-length Apple LP, "The Radha Krishna Temple" album, which did well, but not as well as the single.

Over the last few decades, Yamuna has concentrated more on writing than on recording or leading kirtan at events, though occasionally she does so. Instead, she keeps her love for chanting the holy name vibrant by doing kirtan several hours a day, morning and evening, with friends and loved ones.

✳ ✳ ✳

Yamunaji, this is quite an honor—you are credited as being the first American to record kirtan in the West.

In the early 1960s, the Smithsonian Institute released a few chants from India, and the Bauls of Bengal, too, released a couple of albums in the mid-'60s, mostly their own songs—not call-and-response kirtan.

Prabhupada released his "Happening" album in 1967, and while his voice was the focus of the recording, the LP came out with the help of Western devotees on various instruments. But in 1969, the first non-Indian voice appeared on a kirtan record, and it was yours. And produced by George Harrison, no less! But before we get into all that, let's give our readers a little background. Who were you before you became Yamuna Devi?

I was Joan Campanella, but don't ask me too much about her.

[laughter] Well, maybe you can tell us at least a little about Joan—when she was born and what growing up was like for her.

Ah, the birthday—May 19, 1942. I was born in Butte, Montana.

Until age five, I lived in a log cabin on the outskirts of Butte with mother Mary Lee, Aunt Agnes, and my little sister, Janice Marie. While mom and Agnes worked day jobs, my sister and I stayed at our Italian grandmother's house. Activity at gram's was work centered—gardening, laundry, fire-tending and cooking. With no live play friends in our down time, we created imaginary ones and spent time exploring the woods nearby. Our unknown father never returned from World War Two.

At age six, Aunt A. moved to San Francisco and we three moved to Klamath Falls, Oregon, to live with relatives: Aunt Edna and Uncle Dean. Again, mom worked full time. Edna owned and ran the Normadean Dance Studio, which became a second home for us kids. With seven days of ballet class each week, I showed promise, evidently enough to win summer scholarships, when I was only nine and ten. These allowed me to study under Harold Christensen at the San Francisco Ballet Company. It was assumed that after graduating high school, I would be joining the famed SF corp de ballet. It never happened.

I know you went to school in Oregon. How did that come about?

When I was eleven, mom married Bob Oslund, a lawyer, and the family moved to Salem, Oregon. At that time, my mom stopped working, spending more time at home and golfing at the Salem Country Club. Two years later, Bob joined the firm Georgia-Pacific, and moved us to Lake Oswego, a Portland suburb. I stayed there until I graduated from Lake Oswego High School.

That fall, I attended the University of Oregon in Eugene, but I dropped out in my freshman year. That's when I moved to Portland to live on my own. For two years, I worked a night job to pay rent and took pottery classes at Portland State College . . . and calligraphy classes with Lloyd Reynold, much renowned in the calligraphy world, at the Portland Art Museum.

I really got into the pottery stuff for a while. Two years later, I further honed my skills by attending a summer workshop with Bauhaus-trained master-potter Marguerite Wildenhain at Pond Farm in Guerneville California.

Sounds like that was going to be your career.

Yes, definitely. At the sassy age of twenty-two, I became co-owner of "The Pot Shop" — a pottery and calligraphy establishment on Upper Grant Avenue in San Francisco's happening North Beach.

And I guess you got involved with the whole hippie scene . . .

Well, this was a bit prior to that. I fused in with the local North Beach beatnik scene, which later morphed into the hippie scene in the Haight. I rejected middle-class American values, explored alternative literature, politics, philosophy, and spirituality, especially in the form of Zen Buddhism. I frequented local book and music hangouts: City Lights Bookstore, the Hungry I, Coffee Confusion, and the Coffee Gallery, to name a few.

Okay, so I assume this led to your interest in kirtan and . . . Well, how exactly did all that come about?

When I was in my mid-twenties, my sister Jan invited me to attend her New York wedding — now paired up with my ex-Portland jazz musician friend, Mike Grant. For some months, both had written me about taking "Sanskrit and music classes" from an Indian holy man they called "Swamiji" or "the Swami." On short notice, they asked me to rush to New York to "represent the family" at their Indian-style wedding. So I wrapped up things within a week, and took off on my first plane trip ever . . .

Okay, let's talk about your spiritual background before you met "the Swami," who, of course, turned out to be A. C. Bhaktivedanta Swami Prabhupada, the spiritual master of the Hare Krishna Movement.

Well, I was baptized a Catholic and grew up Catholic. But the experience of my confirmation, first confession, and first communion were disappointing. At a young age, in my heart and in silence, I rejected Catholicism as "real" uplifting spiritual practice. This is not to say that the tradition doesn't have anything to offer, or that I didn't realize that there must be something to it, at its core. But I didn't have any genuine role models, and that's critical when you're going to embark on a spiritual path.

So you traveled East.

Well, only inwardly, at first. In my early twenties, I was exposed to Zen Buddhism while studying calligraphy under Lloyd Reynolds. Reynolds was a genius teacher who inspired by example. He lived what he taught, and inspired by action and words. In due course, I began to read about, then study, what I could of Zen Buddhism.

Shortly before the scheduled wedding, Jan and Mike and nine others were the first Western students to take formal initiation from "Swamiji," thus becoming his disciples. Jan was given the spiritual name Janaki, and Mike, the name Mukunda.

I'm interested in your meeting with Prabhupada. You met him ostensibly because you were attending your sister's wedding, but Krishna had other plans for you . . .

He was the first truly spiritual person I ever met. It was life altering. I was twenty-five at the time—in September of 1966. I flew to New York City to attend my sister's wedding. It was here that I met him, the Swami. One moment in his presence, and I knew I had met a genuinely holy person—wise, kind, and pure. Though he was Indian by birth, I envisioned him on a par with an outstanding Vatican Pope. That, and maybe more.

Can you recreate the scene for us? Do you remember specifics?

I recall the event in some detail. Within an hour of arriving in New York, I was whisked off to a lunch meal—one routinely cooked and served by Prabhupada in his apartment. When I entered the room, Swamiji, as he was then called, was passing out Indian flat breads. Physically small and almost Gandhi-like frail, his golden skin was shining in the afternoon sun. He was shirtless and barefoot, wearing only a saffron lower robe.

Though seventy-one years old, he moved with grace and agility. As we came closer, as we moved toward him, he smiled and his watery brown eyes twinkled. Then he welcomed and embraced me before uttering a word. When at last we did have a verbal exchange, I knew I was in the presence of greatness.

My exchange with Swamiji during the meal is a long story. In short, the vegetarian food was called *prasadam*, and it was unlike anything I had ever eaten — nothing remotely like my mom's attempt at Indian fare, or like my own, for that matter. Nothing like Indian restaurants, either. It was an entirely spiritual experience. In India, this is considered a part of one's devotional practice — the food is offered to God with love and prayers, and the remnants are purifying. It's a yogic form of eating.

These dishes — the ones we ate that day — made up a meal varied in textures, colors, and flavors. There were juxtaposed samplings of sour, sweet, salty, even bitter tastes. Vivid color from golden-yellow split pea soup to creamy white yogurt, tomato-glazed mixed to earth-toned char-flecked wheat flat bread *chapatis*. As I ate, Mukunda explained that this was vegetarian, temple-style Indian cooking, the recipes centuries old. This was all clearly "wowie-zowie" by any standards, as was the Swami who cooked it.

So the wedding and the *prasadam* lunch was your introduction to Prabhupada, but how is it that you stayed on, became a disciple, and even started cooking for him? And then you sang kirtan on that early Apple record, too. Let's hear a little about how all of that evolved.

After lunch, that first day, Swamiji asked if I would assist him in cooking the wedding feast the next day, and I agreed. That day, I spent seven hours sitting in one place making only one of the thirteen dishes on the menu — deep-fried, potato-stuffed pastries called "Aloo Kachori." My assigned task was to make batch after batch of medium-hard pastry dough and seasoned potato filling, then stuff and shape *kachori* pastries. Swamiji deep-fried them and single-handedly prepared the other twelve dishes. It was not until after the wedding ceremony that I first sampled the feast called kirtan — the chanting of the holy name.

Ah, yes, the feast that is kirtan. Well put. So after the wedding, Swamiji—Prabhupada—led the chanting . . .

Yes, at the end of the wedding ceremony, Swamiji looked at the married couple and guests and said, "Now, kirtan." He picked up a pair of hand cymbals, closed his eyes, and established a simple one-two-three beat. Quickly, other cymbals and instruments joined him with the rhythm.

Then the Swami began chanting the *maha-mantra* – Hare Krishna, Hare Krishna, Krishna Krishna, Hare Hare/ Hare Rama, Hare Rama, Rama Rama, Hare Hare – in a simple melody. Soon other voices followed, singing along with him, in call-and-response fashion. When I looked around, I noticed that I was the only person not chanting kirtan. I decided to give it a try, to join in.

I listened to the order of the words until I got it, and then I chanted, first slowly and then with more confidence. It immediately felt good. No lyrics to remember or instruments vying for center stage. Just a rag-tag group of near strangers chanting a simple melody, following a simple rhythm and the sixteen-syllable mantra consisting of only three words – Hare, Krishna, and Rama.

Obviously, you didn't know what you were chanting . . .

And it didn't matter. After getting lost in the chant for maybe five minutes, awareness of my surroundings slowly faded. I felt very comfortable chanting and lost any sense of self-consciousness – I just stopped thinking about peripheral things. I felt myself becoming calm, centered, peaceful. I lost track of time, along with my list of things to do and not to do. Whoa – chanting kirtan felt cool, very cool.

When the kirtan ended, I looked at my watch. Twenty minutes had passed. I was sorry to see the kirtan end, but ready for the *prasadam*, the feast. And the next morning and the following night I could join kirtan again. I remember thinking, "This is something that could become habit-forming."

Around the time you joined Prabhupada, in the fall of 1966, *The East Village Other*, a New York counterculture newspaper, ran a one-page

item about the movement. The front page shows a photo of "Swamiji" leading kirtan in Tompkins Square Park beneath the banner headline, "Save Earth Now!" You remember? Below the photo is the full Hare Krishna *maha-mantra.*

The article was written by a guy named Irving Shushnick, a reporter with no particular interest in Eastern spirituality. But he seemed to really catch onto the idea that kirtan was at the heart of Prabhupada's method. Here's how he quoted Prabhupada: "The kirtan," says Swamiji, "is as natural as the cry of a child for his mother. It is a meditation of body and spirit through the senses. It is feeling the presence of God and crying out to Him for help."

I remember that. Really, really wonderful! And it's true: Kirtan is our birthright. It comes from deep in the soul—it's a crying out to God, like a child cries out to its mother.

Tell me—are there certain kinds of kirtan you prefer over others? And what are your realizations about kirtan in general?

Though kirtan is pleasing any time and any place, certain kinds of kirtan hold a special appeal. At this time—in my life, now—I greatly relish kirtan when experienced chanters get together for long sessions and leave their ego at the door. This allows kirtan to go deep, run powerful, and flow spontaneously. This allows the magic of kirtan to unfold, and to increase our taste for it.

Does good kirtan rest on numbers? No. You can experience good kirtan any time, any place, in any circumstances. Might be only two, or two hundred or two thousand voices—numbers don't matter.

Are instruments a concern? I've experienced incredible kirtan when the chanters only use their hands as rhythm instruments, and great kirtan with select expert musicians playing varied instruments. Kirtan depends on feeling and personal effort; you get what you put in; it has no hard or fast rules.

Do you have a favorite scriptural passage about the holy name and kirtan, something that personally inspires you?

Yes, there's a quote from the Vaishnava teacher, Bhaktivinode Thakur, who, in turn, is quoting the *Adi Purana.* Here it is in full:

There is no vow like chanting the holy name, no knowledge superior to it, no meditation which comes anywhere near it, and it gives the highest result. No penance is equal to it, and nothing is as potent or powerful as the holy name.

Chanting is the greatest act of piety and the supreme refuge. Even the words of the Vedas do not possess sufficient power to describe its magnitude. Chanting is the highest path to liberation, peace, and eternal life. It is the pinnacle of devotion, the heart's joyous proclivity and attraction and the best form of remembrance of the Supreme Lord. The holy name has appeared solely for the benefit of the living entities as their lord and master, their supreme worshipful object and their spiritual guide and mentor.

Whoever continuously chants Lord Krishna's holy name, even in his sleep, can easily realize that the name is the direct manifestation of Krishna Himself, in spite of the influences of Kali-yuga.

Beautiful. Well, that kind of sums it all up, doesn't it? At this point, let's get into your 1969 recording on Apple Records, which is touted as the first kirtan record in the West with a non-Indian leading the chant. How did this come about?

Zoom back in time to 1968. I'm one of a party of six—a family of close friends—that Srila Prabhupada sent to England to start the UK ashram. When we arrived in England in the fall of '68, we performed kirtan anywhere we were invited, calling our merry band, "The Radha Krishna Temple." Each one of us remembers the Apple Records/ Beatles/ George experience of '68 through '70 differently, because we each experienced it differently.

Here's a simple outline from my vantage:

One of Prabhupada's disciples, Shyamasundar, met George at an Apple function, and they immediately connected as friends. George was a follower of Maharishi Mahesh Yogi, been to India, and experienced kirtan. He mentioned that he had heard our kirtan and liked it. At that initial meeting, they set up some options for sharing the holy name.

Some days later, George snuck into one of our evening kirtan sessions at the Arts Lab—a happening spot at the time in London.

Another time he visited our ashram for *prasadam* and kirtan. These short kirtan experiences led George to invite us for some long sessions at his house. These were delicious kirtans—several hours long and intense—followed by *prasadam* feasts. These kirtan experiences inspired George to personally produce an LP and single featuring the Radha Krishna Temple. They were released and promoted through Apple, including Apple-sponsored tours and concert events.

Can you flesh this out a bit? I'm sure readers will want more details about how you first got to know the Beatles. How did The Radha Krishna Temple, the band, get so close to George?

Initially, to get the Beatles' attention, we daily delivered mouth-watering apple dishes to Apple Studios in London. We did this regularly for some weeks, and when we missed one day's delivery, reception at Apple Studios requested us to resume—employees on every floor were starting to anticipate their daily apple treat, including the Beatles themselves, and now they missed it when we didn't show up.

A few days after this incident, through a friend, one of the members of our kirtan group, Shyamasundar, attended an Apple press event, and when George saw his Indian dress, he pulled him aside to speak with him. The two of them immediately connected as kindred spirits and determined that they would meet again soon. This meeting was the event that led to George's lasting friendship with members of our initial Radha Krishna Temple kirtan group.

And it developed from there.

Yes. George invited the group to his house, where we spent six hours chanting together, and we invited George and Patty to our Betterton Street warehouse, where we spent long hours chanting together. These kirtans eventually led George to produce our records.

Where did the recording take place?

At Abby Road studios. Our first session took place just after the

Beatles had wrapped up one of their own sessions there. Paul and John hung around in the background; only George took a hands-on role.

George had a way of tapping into each of our strengths and making them better. He was a genuine, likeable person—and in spite of, or despite his, fame—a gentle man, and a terrific record producer. This manifested in many ways, particularly with how he worked with our group of non-professional musicians.

Well, Mukunda had been a professional musician . . .

Yes, he was the one exception. Mukunda was the only professional musician in the group—previously a jazz pianist—and he acted as our arranger on the "Govindam" cut of the LP George produced, which became quite popular. It's still used every morning at Krishna ashrams throughout the world. George worked closely with Mukunda on that cut.

Tell me more about the group that worked with George.

Initially, there were six of us in our Radha Krishna Temple Group: Shyamasundar played *sarangi*; Mukunda played *mridanga* drum; I played *harmonium* and most often led kirtan; Janaki, Malati and Gurudas played percussion, especially *kartals*.

When we recorded our first 45 hit single, the group increased with several more devotee voices. By the time we recorded "The Radha Krishna Temple" LP, the group further increased with more devotee musicians: Yogeshwar on drum, and some vocals; Tamal Krishna on flute; Harivilas on *oud*—to name a few. On the "Govindam" cut alone, George added his own guitar; jazz-man Billy Preston's organ; and sounds from the London String Quartet. Srila Prabhupada eventually called that particular track, "A symphony of Krishna Consciousness."

Now, on the *maha-mantra* 45 single—which, again, became a hit in 1969—you were the lead singer, and I had heard that it was George himself who selected you to do that. How did that come about?

Why did George select me to be lead singer? Only he knows. He once commented that I had an expressive and naturally strong voice. I've always felt I sound like a bullfrog, but that's another story. [laughter] He further suggested that I become a solo artist on Apple.

Oh, why didn't you do that?

I would have never even considered it at the time. It was an unappealing notion to me, as it would have taken time away from my service as head priest to Sree Sree Radha London Ishwara, the deities of Radha and Krishna at the London ashram. In any case, it happened not.

As an aspiring devotee for over forty years now, I have never identified with any occupation. Though I sang on two released records with Apple in the late 1960s — the *maha-mantra* single and the LP that came after it — and penned three cookbooks in the late '80s and early '90s, and taught around the world, I feel I am not a singer, author, or teacher. I just engage in these activities in the course of exploring the deep culture and practice of Gaudiya Vaishnavism — that is really what my life is all about.

I'm familiar with your cookbooks. How did you get into writing those? What prompted that?

Well, I was Prabhupada's cook, as I said, and I had collected tons of recipes traveling around India with him. Ultimately, I was inspired by what I learnt from him about cooking, and I decided to further hone my skills in that area. This led to the publishing of my cookbooks.

Award-winning cookbooks! I've looked into the critical response to your work, and it's all quite favorable. Especially notable is *Lord Krishna's Cuisine: The Art of Indian Vegetarian Cooking*, which is like an encyclopedia of food and Vaishnava lore, with 680 recipes of regional Indian cuisine.

E. P. Dutton originally released the book in 1987.

Not to embarrass you, but I'd like our readers to know that that book

won three prestigious accolades—two awards from the International Association of Culinary Professionals, first as "best Asian cookbook of the year," and second as overall "best cookbook of the year." The third award was "The Benjamin Franklin Award in the 'Best Cookbook' category." That's pretty impressive. And then your second cookbook—*Yamuna's Table*—won the 1992 James Beard Award as "International Cookbook of the Year." Our readers should know that you've written other cookbooks, too, that you occasionally teach cooking classes around the world and even opened your own cooking school. So you've been busy.

All this is true, but as I said, I don't identify with any of these things, just as I don't consider myself a writer, a singer, or a teacher. I'm just an aspiring devotee.

What you are is a lover of kirtan. That's quite clear from the way you sing. That original Radha Krishna Temple album is still one of my favorites.

"Lover of kirtan." Well, I can't deny it. Kirtan is the easiest way to control the mind, and, ultimately, the only way into the higher realm of Radha and Krishna—the ultimate kirtan in the spiritual world. Such perfection, I'll admit, is the cynosure of my life, and I know it can be obtained through attentive, pure Krishna kirtan.

For more information contact:
yamunadd@gmail.com

SHYAMDAS

Shyamdas, born Stephen Schaffer, took the long journey from 1960s Jewish hippie to authorized representative of a well-established Vaishnava lineage – the Vallabha Sampradaya. Having lived in India for more than thirty-five years, he fully imbibed the culture and teachings of this esoteric tradition and now shares it with the rest of the world through kirtan.

Originally traveling to the land of the Ganges on a personal spiritual quest, he first met Neem Karoli Baba and then His Holiness Goswami Prathameshji and other lineage stalwarts, who offered him direction on his life's path. Soon given the name "Shyamdas," he diligently studied classical Indian music, as well as Sanskrit, Hindi, Braj-bhasha and Gujarati. Using his language skills, he has written and translated more than twenty books on the yoga of devotion (Bhakti-yoga), particularly as seen through the eyes of the Vallabha Sampradaya.

He now specializes in the mystic devotional poets of North India and is a master of bhajan and kirtan. Sharing his knowledge at workshops and yoga retreats in the United States, Europe, and India, Shyamdas has sung with Sting, Mike D., Paul Simon, and played for Madonna. Accompanied by his musician wife, Tulsi, who plays the pakhavaja drum, he weaves together songs, stories, and bhakti teachings in the spirit of ancient India's ecstatic bards, such as Vyasa and Tulsi Das.

Shyamdas' CDs convey his diverse musical and devotional experiences, evoking the traditional, ambient sounds of India's countryside and city temples. "Chant your way to mystic India and the secret dwelling places of Radha and Krishna," he says. And his CDs can easily help to get you there.

"Beloved Chants," his first professional CD, is a breakthrough in kirtan recordings. He is here joined by accomplished Western kirtan musicians Krishna Das, John McDowell (piano and African drums), Ty Burhoe (tabla), Steve Gorn (bansuri flute), and Benjy Wertheimer (esraj). The work was co-produced by Shyamdas and John McDowell, composer of the "Born into Brothels" soundtrack and acclaimed percussionist of "Speaking the Mamma Tongue." Background vocals by Tulsi and Sharon Gannon.

Then came "Sweet Radhe!" (2005) These kirtans explore various moods of union and separation, ecstatic celebration and intense longing – all in relation to the ultimate divine lovers, Radha and Krishna. Also included are three tracks of sweet love poetry by the sixteenth-century poet, Rasakhan. Shyamdas sings on all tracks, plays his signature harmonium, and engages his handy recorder as well. He is accompanied on the CD by Naren Budhakar (tabla), Joe Veillette (guitar) Tommy Be (percussion, keyboard, bass), and Arundhati (harmonium and vocals).

"Cool Dual" (2006) is a live, double-CD of sacred chant and recorded lectures, documenting exactly what Shyamdas does in his workshops and kirtan performances around the world. The work is aided by a number of friends and well wishers: Tulsi (pakhavaj drum), Tommy Be (kanjira), Adam Bauer (bass), and Ananda Ashram's Bhakti Immersion Weekend attendees (support vocals).

His most recent CD, "Songs of Sweetness," is largely comprised of traditional Sanskrit chants, accompanied by the versatile hands of Arjuna on tabla.

✳ ✳ ✳

I am pleased to interview someone affiliated with the Sri Vallabha Sampradaya. Mantras come down through such lineages, and Vallabhacharya's immediate disciples were especially known for their kirtan.

I assume that readers want to know some background on people who do kirtan, and so I usually begin by asking each interviewee their full legal name, birth date, where they were born, and something about the environment of their youth.

Sure. So my legal name was Stephen Schaffer. Born February 11, 1953 in New Haven, Connecticut.

Okay, and what was it like growing up? Was it a religious family or what?

It was kind of like yours: Jewish. It wasn't very religious—it had more of a secular vibe. There was some synagogue, but not much. I didn't even have a Bar Mitzvah.

No Bar Mitzvah?

No.

I guess my family was a bit more traditional, then. My mother insisted on Bar Mitzvahs, though her religious sense didn't go much beyond that. Okay, was there any spiritual learning in your early life, or did that all come much later?

No, there was something there in my youth, but it was unusual. It certainly wasn't prompted by my Jewish upbringing or through my exposure to Western religion. You see, ever since I was a kid, or rather, since I was a young boy, I was mystified by this dark, young adolescent who often appeared in my dreams and sometimes even seemed to be present, right there before me.

Oh, interesting.

And I had absolutely no clue what to call him—no idea what his name might be. Or if he was real. I was even sent to a psychiatrist because of this. I didn't have the good sense to keep my mouth shut, and so people naturally thought I was crazy. But it was a vision, a blessing. It wasn't quite *sakshad darshan*, or a direct viewing of Krishna, with flute, peacock feather, and all the rest, but it was close.

That's amazing. So there's some image of a darkish form, but it was unclear. Now you look back, and it's got Krishna written all over it. But why were you given this vision? Were you a pure-hearted kid, or was it a carry-over . . .

No, I certainly wasn't pure, but I believe it was a carry-over from a previous life, impressions from a past birth. The image wasn't clear, but I knew it was a young boy; I knew that. Maybe twelve years old. Sometimes I associated him with an older cousin, because I was a little kid at the time, and I didn't understand what was happening. But it wasn't quite a perfect fit—it wasn't my cousin. All I knew was that this wasn't ordinary. There was something perfect about this young lad, and I knew he wasn't like the rest of us.

Fascinating.

Now, this was way before any of us were doing yoga. This was in 1960 or something like that—so I'm about seven or eight. There was no Krishna movement in the West. It was just this image that would come and go. Like a presence.

So your parents took you to a shrink.

They kind of took me to a shrink, yeah. Probably for a number of other reasons, too.

[laughter]

It was only when I was a bit older that I started to make sense of it. But when I was a kid, and I didn't have a sense of what was spiritual, or what wasn't—it was just this weird sensation that I was being followed by a beautiful, dark-hued youth. Not always, but from time to time. Then, as I got older, I became interested in Eastern thought, and things started to gel. I read the book, *Be Here Now*, which many of us read at the time, and a whole other world started to open up.

Let's back up a little bit. The dream was just a few times? Or was it . . .

No. It wasn't really a dream. Well, it did manifest in dreams, too, but it was more in my waking state, and I could feel the presence of this divine kid. It was this thought and this image that remained in my mind, pretty often.

Was that for your entire youth or did it just come and go? How frequently did it occur?

It would come and go.

Into your teenage years?

Mmm . . . maybe until I was eleven or twelve.

Then it subsided?

Then I think it turned into something else, for a couple of years.

What did it turn into?

I don't know, chasing girls?

[laughter] So that became the next fascination, as it does for most teenagers. What about music? It was the hippie era, no? Did you get into music like most of us?

Well, yeah. I was always into music. It was a thing that I excelled at. I played saxophone. I had taken serious piano lessons. I was in a band.

Playing keyboards?

No. I played saxophone and I sang as well. And I was very into athletics. I was a super jock, the state champion wrestler when I was in eighth grade—but I was champion for high school level.

That's cool.

I was a skier, too. I was good at athletics and terrible at languages. Couldn't learn, could barely learn English. I got special permission from a psychiatrist that I didn't have to learn a second language in school. It's odd that I eventually became a linguist, of sorts. I'm just a weird guy, I guess.

Well, aren't we all. So, alright. You were a jock as opposed to a hippie?

Oh, no. I was a hippie, full-blown.

But you were also a jock.

Jock-hippie. First jock, then, afterwards, hippie-jock, then hippie, and then, afterwards, very quickly: *yogi*.

Let's talk about how that evolved, how you became a yogi. Let's jump into that.

Well, as I was mentioning, when I was around fourteen or fifteen, I started to read. There was a book called, *The Master Game*. Then I slowly slipped into *Autobiography of a Yogi*, and that led me to *Be Here Now*. And that hit me very strongly — the whole notion of the search, and mystic India, and Maharaji — Neem Karoli Baba. So I started to do *asana*, reading *Be Here Now* very carefully, too. Soon, I started to have dreams of him.

Of Neem Karoli Baba?

Yeah, of Neem Karoli Baba. At this point I was maybe seventeen. I started to have dreams, and he told me that I should come to India.

Told you directly, through a dream.

So that's what I did. I had a girlfriend. She was many years older than I was, and we made some money selling artwork, because I was an artist as well.

Oh, you were an artist, too? What kind of art?

Well, at that point, I was selling watercolor paintings . . .

Realistic, impressionistic . . . ?

Sort of realistic. I would basically paint them and they were printed. It was not your highest level of creative expression, but it did allow me enough income to go to India. I was sort of thrown out of my home at age seventeen.

Hmm? Mind if I ask why?

Irreconcilable differences. I was supposed to be on the lawyer/ doctor track and that just wasn't me.

You were more of a musician/ painter kind of guy.

Right.

Okay. So you went to India because Maharaji came to you in a dream and told you to go. You did actually go to India, and what were you looking for? Were you looking for him specifically?

Yeah. I was looking for something very specific. Actually, I was looking for a couple of things. First of all, I was looking for Maharaji. Then, on top of that, I had a real, existential, theological question that was burning my heart out. And it was this: Was Brahman, or Absolute reality, *nirguna* or *saguna*, that is to say, in the ultimate analysis, is God without qualities and impersonal, or is He the Supreme Person, full of ecstatic qualities? Was it a wisdom path, where you meditate and merge into an amorphous Supreme, or was it about personal relationship — a theistic path of *bhakti*, or devotion? I don't know why I was so possessed by this singular question. At the time, I didn't know that it was *the* question, the one that sages had been debating in India for the last 1,500 years.

But the question is natural for those of us who were reading those books in the '60s, because you're reading everything from Alan Watts and D. T. Suzuki to the Upanishads, which is coming more from the *nirguna* school of thought, and then you get into the *Gita* and the *bhakti* poets, which is *saguna*...

Right. Well, I didn't actually read any *bhakti* material, not at that time.

Oh, you didn't?

No, because there really wasn't too much available. Obviously, ISKCON and Srila Prabhupada had released their books by then. And there were others, too, no doubt. But I wasn't familiar with them. I didn't have interest in reading those books — I was more into the yoga stuff and the Buddhist stuff. Still, I was very concerned about getting an answer to these questions.

What year was this?

1972.

Okay. So what happened when you got there? Did being in India answer your questions?

Well, what happened was I went with a whole group of Neem Karoli Baba followers to Istanbul, and a bunch of us traveled overland. We went to Afghanistan and Pakistan—you could do that back then. Finally, we ended up in India and went directly to Vrindavan. I think I stayed in Delhi one night, but my destination was Vrindavan, the land of Krishna.

And your theological question . . .

Along the way I started to get answers, even before I arrived in India. When I was in Kandahar, Afghanistan, I had a massive *kundalini* awakening—this is when I was doing *asana-yoga*. It scared me so much that I vowed to never do another *asana* as long as I lived.

What was the experience like?

It was like being plugged into twenty billion volts of electricity, pouring through my body, and Maharaji appeared to me, too. So my spine opened up and I truly felt I was going to die. It was so blissful and so painful at the same time. I guess it was clearing up some subtle energy, burning away lifetimes of karma, so I could make a proper entrance into Vrindavan. It follows the chronology revealed in the *Srimad Bhagavata*, too, which I later found out—about thirty years later.

You see, before Krishna gave the *gopis* and the *gopas*, His cowherd friends, vision of Vaikuntha, His eternal realm, He first showed His divine light, His effulgence. It was a first step. Having cleansed them of all karmic impurities by immersing them in His white light, He then brought them out of it, out of the abode of liberation, which made them qualified for *lila darshan*, or the vision of His eternal realm. Now, they are eternal associates, of course, and I am just . . .

You're creating a parallel between your experience in Afghanistan and the *lila* of the Lord's associates.

I'm only putting this together for the first time right now.

But it makes sense. I see the correlation. By way of analogy, you might have something there.

I would say so. I mean, it happened to me just before I entered Vrindavan, a few weeks before. So I think there's some meaning in that. Anyway, at that point I was just not interested in doing *asana* anymore, because I was just too afraid of having that experience again. But on another level, I also understood that it was a very profound thing. It was the grace of guru, the grace of Hari, and so I moved on. But it didn't answer my question, about *saguna* and *nirguna*. That would come later.

But before we move on. There's another parallel that comes to mind. In the *Bhagavad Gita*, when Krishna shows His Universal Form to Arjuna. In that particular episode, Arjuna was also frightened. He was given a profound spiritual experience, but he wanted instead to see Krishna's original two-armed form.

Oh, of course, yes, yes. That's the *virata-rupa*, the Universal Form. It does have certain similarities, yes. This was more truly *nirguna*, though. This was a formless experience, a magnificent energy, a white light. With the Universal Form, we still have a variation on *saguna darshan*—it's a vision of Krishna as *jagat*, as the cosmos, with everything coming out at the same time. So it's not exactly *nirguna*. You'll see where I'm going with this.

Okay. So then you go straight to Vrindavan. Did you go right to Neem Karoli Baba's ashram or did you explore Braj?

I was with the Western followers of Neem Karoli Baba, and I was quickly blessed with his darshan in Vrindavan. We also went to stay with others at a *dharma-shala,* called the Jaipuriya Bhavan, where all the Westerners were staying. Then I went out wandering around Vrindavan on my own, on the *parikrama* path, and I passed a Nimbarka ashram, right on the banks of the Yamuna River. It was a place called Shyam Kuti. It's about a mile and a half down the *parikrama* from Maharaji's ashram.

So a very traditional holy man from the Nimbarka Sampradaya came out and started speaking to me in Hindi. Remember, it was my first week in India, so I didn't understand a word he was saying. Now, there was a man who lived upstairs, right near where we were talking, and the holy man called him down. Almost immediately, this man, who was also obviously quite saintly, greeted me and quickly invited me to live with him. He gave me a Krishna mantra right off the bat. He said, "Recite this mantra: 'Sri Krishna is my refuge.'" He just took me in. He seemed to be a wonderful person, and it turns out he was from the Vallabha lineage.

You know, the prior couple of weeks had brought me such amazing experiences, even before I went to India. So this just seemed like more of the same. It was part of a larger program that I was definitely interested in following. So the next day, I brought my backpack and I moved in with this Vaishnava saint.

What was his name?

Mangal Das. He was a Gujarati and a great devotee of Krishna. It was right after I met Maharaji in the flesh for the first time. I moved into Shyam Kuti and moved away from the other Western followers of Maharaji and, as fate would have it, I didn't have much contact with Maharaji's Western *satsang* until 1985. This was God's arrangement, no doubt, because it afforded me a different type of experience. I saw life from the Indian side of things. But I did see Maharaji himself on a number of occasions. And this is where the answer—if you can call it an answer—started to make itself known.

The question about *nirguna*, or formless reality, a formless divinity, versus *saguna*, or God with limitless qualities. How did the answer come about?

The answer came about after I moved in with Mangal Das. One night, as I was resting, Maharaji appeared to me again, for a moment, and then gave me a *darshan*, a viewing, of Sri Krishna. It was as bright as a million suns. I mean, not like the *kundalini* experience, which in relationship to that *darshan* was insignificant. The blades of grass, where Krishna was standing, were more amazing than a billion *kundalini* experiences. But this time I wasn't afraid because it was in a different context. It was intimate and personal. It wasn't like Shyamdas experiencing the scary infinite through a *kundalini* awakening. This was Krishna's sweet grace upon me for no specific reason. It was causeless, something I knew I didn't deserve—something I could never obtain on my own, with any amount of meditation. It was clear. This was something that comes only if God wants to give it—period. So I had a glimpse of that truth that is Bhagavan Sri Krishna, the personal Lord, and it was so absolutely clear to me—the importance of His divine personhood. At that point, I hadn't even read the *Bhagavata*. I was not familiar with Krishna-*lila*, really.

So, concisely, what was your realization? How would you summarize the revelation?

I realized that formless divinity, or *nirguna* Brahman, is just one of the elements of Purushottama, or Hari, or God. It's like the effulgence of His bliss, a light emanating from His form—that's the simple truth of *nirguna*. It's a small part of His glory. The source, ultimately, is Krishna. This entirely spiritual, transcendental person is at the core of everything, and all other spiritual realities are ultimately subservient to Him. I would have to add that this is not something I would really teach to anyone, unless they were really interested in it, unless they were ready for it. Some people just don't want to hear this.

I understand.

And, anyway, *nirguna* Brahman is just fine. If you can merge yourself into absolute reality, then go for it, although it says in the *Gita* that this is a really difficult accomplishment for embodied beings.

So you had a glimpse . . . and this glimpse came to you by the grace of Maharaji?

Yes. But it was a very clear *darshan*, coming directly from God. And it wasn't just a dream. It wasn't just in my heart. It was . . . you know . . .

Tangible. It was something substantial.

And it was something that can't be conveyed. I only later realized what I had experienced.

But here's my question. This life-altering vision came through the agency of Neem Karoli Baba, correct?

So it seems, yeah.

So then my question is this: Why did you pursue the Vallabha tradition rather than becoming a follower of Neem Karoli Baba?

Well, in fact I did become a follower of Neem Karoli Baba. The Vallabha tradition is along those same lines, as you'll see. It's this fantastic way of living, with knowledge, which just continued to teach me and educate me as to what I was . . .

Are you saying that what you got from the Vallabha tradition and what Neem Karoli Baba teaches are somehow non-different?

Non-different. Absolutely.

Oh, okay. That's interesting.

Maharaji was a Vaishnava saint. He really was. Unconventionally Vaishnava, no doubt, but Vaishnava nonetheless. Was he tantric? Was he Buddhist? No, he was Vaishnava. This might not be evident on the face of it, but if one knows something about the tradition, one can see it.

Yet if you talk to the mass of his disciples, they would never describe him like that.

That's because most Westerners have never studied his tradition. They arrived, they spent a couple of months or even years with him, and he blessed them. He brought them further. He gave them a lot, you know, but he left it at that. He didn't necessarily define what he did for them.

But if you look at it through the eyes of the tradition, what did he give them? Vaishnavism. When they were there, when they were with him, what did they do? They ate *maha-prasad* and they chanted Hari-nam, they chanted the names of Krishna and Rama. They followed Ekadashi fasts. There were no onions or garlic in his ashram. So? It was a Vaishnava ashram. Maharaji had two books that he read, which he sourced from. One was the *Bhagavata Purana*. The other was the *Rama-charita-manasa*. Everyone chanted the "Hanuman Chalisa": They always chanted, "You will all be born in the eternal realm of Rama."

Incredibly interesting.

Yes. And so I can't help it if many of the Westerners didn't know what he was trying to give them, that it was a form of Vaishnavism. You know, when Maharaji left his body in 1973, they were there for a year, some maybe for two or three, whatever. They weren't there for very long. Almost none of them spoke Hindi, and no one studied the literature. I can't say, "No one." But I would say there were very few Westerners who knew where he was coming from. By and large, they weren't interested in understanding why Maharaji spoke about Rama and Hanuman and Sita — and all with an emphasis on Vrindavan. It's all Vrindavan. Maharaji himself was a Braj-bhashi. He spoke Braj-bhasha. Before leaving his body, he ran from his ashram in the hills, where he was staying, so he could leave his body in Vrindavan. This is Vaishnava. He was with Banke-Bihari, the deities there, almost every day. He was a total Bhakti-marg devotee, the path of devotion.

But why is it, then, that so many of his followers seem to lean toward Buddhism, and they seem to latch onto the *nirguna* conception, too, don't they?

Good question. Right. People say this: "Oh, most of the Maharaji Westerners are like Buddhists." Some of this comes from Ram

Dass, who took many of the Westerners to Buddhist meditation retreats early on. For this and other reasons, many of the Western followers took their own impersonalist and amorphous forms of spirituality and foisted it onto Maharaji. He allowed for all forms of spirituality to manifest around him and did not push any particular practice on anyone.

Now, Maharaji left his body in 1973, and I stayed on. I was very curious to know what this was really all about. It matched my experiences with Mangal Das, who was part of an ancient Sampradaya, or lineage. So I followed the natural course of investigating *bhakti*, which is what Maharaji was also teaching.

This is enlightening, because I understood Maharaji in an entirely different way. I never heard about this Vaishnava connection.

I think you might have been somewhat misled about him. Most of the Westerners didn't understand his connection to Vaishnava *dharma*. To see that, you had to know some Hindi and also a bit of Sanskrit. Then you have to study Vaishnava doctrine. If you do, the connections are very clear. Otherwise, you're just going on feeling, on something intangible. Maharaji was and is always more than people think he was.

Was Maharaji able, willing, to accept every type of person? Yes. Did he help anyone in any type of practice, according to their inclination? Yes. Ultimately, though, was Maharaji a *bhakti* teacher? Of course he was. Did he have total attachment to Vrindavan? Yes. Did he teach a certain non-duality? Yes. But was he from the Mayavada or Shankara tradition? Absolutely not. He taught non-duality and duality as well—which is Vaishnava teaching.

See, now I find that interesting, because some of Maharaji's followers appear to espouse what I consider a purely Mayavada doctrine, emphasizing the formless nature of reality.

And yet they have intense attachment to Maharaji's form, don't they. [laughter]

[laughter] Right, right.

That's very Vaishnava to be attached to form like that. Mayavadis reject all form. Maharaji's followers love his form and are very attached to it. Their love for their guru is quite exemplary. That's Vaishnava.

Yes. Okay, let's move on with your personal story . . .

So I stayed on in Vrindavan, and I took the instruction and the vision seriously. As I continued on the path, I found Pushti-marg, the lineage of Vallabhacharya. Here was the perfect teaching, the perfect Sampradaya. You see, I started to learn Hindi; I learned Braj-bhasha; I learned Sanskrit and Gujarati; and I started to read, all the while engaging in practice, in kirtan and *sadhana*. After that, I started to translate, and I've spent thirty-five years now, investigating the nature of *bhakti* and Bhakti-yoga.

I see. You informed yourself about the tradition, and so you were able to see Maharaji from a different perspective, with some measure of balance, and also in relation to other devotional traditions.

Exactly. And this knowledge is now coming to the West. The modern-day Western *yogi*s and people who just took the teachings superficially — they're starting to catch on. It's starting to take a turn now, which is of course the subject of your book. They'll ultimately find that kirtan is central. They'll move on from *nirguna* to *saguna*, and kirtan will be an important part of that.

That seems to be the course of things. We're moving in that direction, aren't we? But let's hear more about your involvement with Pushti-marg and how that came about.

Well, I had returned to the States for some time but decided I couldn't live without Vrindavan. So I came back and I started to live again with the same *sadhu*, Mangal Das. He said we should do a Braj-yatra, a *parikrama*, a pilgrimage around Braj. So we did. This was in 1973. I started off with him, but I left him as we moved on. I'll explain. He had been telling me for some time about this great teacher, from Pushti-marg, that I have to meet — His Holiness Goswami Prathameshji. He was head of the first seat in the Vallabha tradition. But I was never able to meet him, for one reason or another. Anyway, Mangal Das and I went to Jatipur, on our pilgrimage, where Goswami Prathameshji had his headquarters . . .

Near Govardhan.

Near, yes. There are seven seats in the Pushti-marg and he was head of the first. So I was anxious to meet him. We went there a couple of times, but he was a hard man to find. He was never there. But when we went there for the pilgrimage, we met him. For many reasons that I won't get into here, I was ready to move on from Mangal Das, and so Krishna led me to Goswami Prathameshji, which was extremely fortunate for me. And that began another stage of my *sadhana,* where I spent at least twenty years with a leading figure of the Pushti-marg lineage. With him, I found total absorption in divine sound, in music, in classical music. With Dhrupad and Vedanta and Braj-bhasha. He was a master of everything. He was an incarnation in the lineage.

Did you start getting more into kirtan at this point or no?

Oh, yes. Pushti-marg, actually, does classical kirtan. We sing in classical *raga*. I'm one of the only guys who bring in those aspects of kirtan in the West. I sing in several kirtan styles, including pure Pushti-marg *raga*. It is kirtan that is sung in classical *raga,* using ten, twelve, fourteen or sixteen beats. Of course, this classical Dhrupad singing is beyond the scope of congregational Western chanting. But I've been starting to employ it as a teaching mode in my workshops. I also bring in teachings from the *Bhagavata,* and also from the saints, from Sri Vallabhacharya as well as from his followers, the Ashta Chap — the eight poets.

Yes, talk about the Ashta Chap poets a little, the early *kirtaniyas* and the songwriters in the Sri Vallabhacharya line.

Well, my guruji, Goswami Prathameshji, is a master of Dhrupad singing, a master of Braj-bhasha. He was born in Braj, so he spoke Braj as his mother tongue. And he's coming in the line of the Ashta

Chap. We're going back to the early 16th century, even the late 15th century, now. The Asta Chap were these eight premier Krishna poets, and they were the direct followers of Vallabhacharya and also the followers of his son, Sri Gusainji. They composed an ocean of devotional literature, of poetry, which was sung, back then and now as well. It's called kirtan, and they were called *kirtaniyas*, actually. I started to study their material, under my guruji, and I try to carry on in that line in my kirtan today.

So while you were studying with Goswami Prathameshji, did you keep up relations with Maharaji's people?

Well, at this point, Maharaji's Western *satsang* had more or less left India, except for a few people. Most went back to the West, but I stayed on. So I lost track of them for some time. I grabbed onto a different part of Maharaji's *lila*—I saw Maharaji's program of being the *dasa* of Hari, the follower of God, not merging into God but rendering service to Him. In a word, *bhakti*. I liked this. I liked to worship Hari and to take assistance from His saints, and this is what brought me to Pushti-marg, the path of grace. But most of the Western devotees in the Maharaji ashram went in a different direction. So Ashta Chap kirtan wasn't on their radar. I'm not judging anyone. Everyone is on the journey, and they go in their own way, at their own pace. Hari has unusual plans for all of us.

That's right.

My path was steep. I was the only Westerner that lived in the little village of Jatipur, and I didn't see another Westerner for years, basically, except for my friend, Assim Krishna.

I knew Assim as well. He was initiated into the Gaudiya tradition. For years he lived in Braj and became quite close with Shrivatsa Goswami at Radha-raman Temple.

That's right. Alan Shapiro was his Western name. Several years my senior, and we were great buddies and we hung out a lot. I even met Bon Maharaj, his initiating guru in the Gaudiya Math, and we went together to meet Srila Prabhupada, who I met only once or twice.

A lot of people don't know this, but Assim had been with Maharaji before going to Bon Maharaj. I didn't know him back then.

And you? Where does your story go from here?

So I became a kirtan singer, actually. I became a *kirtaniya* in the Vallabha tradition. I used to sing with the guys in the temple. I kept singing and singing, and then, one day, the main singer at the temple had to go somewhere, and so I became the temple singer.

Wow. A temple kirtan singer—in India. That's where you gained the experience necessary to do what you're doing now. You can teach workshops in the West because you *lived* kirtan amongst those who make it their lives.

His Holiness always used to tell me that, "You will be teaching in the West. You will have a thousand children." He used to joke with me like that.

Actually, my return to the West happened like this. You see, I came to India thinking that everyone does Ashtanga-yoga, and I was amazed to see that very few people were doing any *asana*.

Right.

I was in Braj, which is not an *asana-yoga* place. So one day I was walking around in an area that I normally don't go—it was between Raman Reti and Banke-Bihari—and I see this Western guy doing some advanced yoga positions. So I was amazed. I walked up to him and said, "Whoa, what are you doing?" And he said, "I'm looking for Maharaji's ashram."

"Well," I told him, "you found the right guy. Who are you?" He said, "My name is Eddie." And we became friendly—I brought him over to Maharaji's ashram, and we got to know each other really well. So one day he said to me, "You know, you should come to New York next time you're back in the West." At that point, I was spending several months each year in the West. This is going back almost twenty years now. And he says, "You should lead kirtan there, and you should share your experiences at the yoga center, a place where I teach—Jivamukti."

So you did?

So I took him up on his idea. When I came in that year, I started to sing at Jivamukti Yoga Center. This was something that no one else had really done up to this point. Singing in yoga centers was not happening. I started it back then, and there were three of us: David, Sharon, and Eddie, and my infant son, sleeping on the floor. He was maybe one or two.

What's your son's name?

Mr. Deva. [laughter] So I started leading kirtan. I would teach a bit, too. It started with three or four inquisitive people, went to five, and then we were getting sixty or so people. We did it every Monday night. A few years later, Krishna Das came by, and he said, "Shyam, this is great!" I said, "Well, KD, I'm just doing kirtan." He said, "This is great. I should do it, too." So KD also started doing kirtan there — at Jivamukti — and made the program I started even more popular.

Then I helped arrange for Jai Uttal to come to New York and we engaged him in the same process. Of course, he loved it — and the people attending the kirtan loved him. He said, "Great! I want to do it again!" And Bhagavan Das — we got him there, too. So that's how we started to sing in yoga centers. All of us. People from ISKCON were chanting Hari-nam kirtan, Sankirtan, in the streets many years before, so this was nothing new. But I decided that the yoga centers would be an interesting place to do this, because, yoga, really, is about linking with God, and the best way to link with God is through kirtan.

What type of kirtan did you do back then? I know that the Vallabha line especially emphasizes Lila-kirtan, but that can get a bit complicated, using Dhrupad methods and classical music. So you chanted Nam-kirtan, right? Just the names. You must have done, like, "Jai Rama," or "Hare Krishna *maha-mantra*."

Yeah, Hare Krishna, and Jai Rama Jai. I experimented. You're correct — I decided that the classical stuff was too much for a Western audience, so I simplified it all. One of the songs I used to do a lot was from the Nimbarka lineage: *shyama gori, nitya kishori, pritam jori sri radhe* . . . beautiful stuff. Also, we did other mantras, like, "Govinda Jaya Jaya, Gopala Jaya Jaya."

I kept it focused on Krishna, Rama, and so on, because, as Tulsi Das warns, "If you focus on a single thing, you attain everything. But if you worship everything, you get nothing. When you spread your devotion out too thin, you can't find devotion anywhere." So I chanted only the names of Hari and avoided becoming too "New Age," where people say "all is one" but don't firmly believe in anything. I mean, there *is* a certain oneness between God and everything else, no doubt, but this can be taken to ridiculous extremes. The authorized lineages teach that it's important to have an *ishta-deva*, a focus on a particular aspect of God, and it has to be very clear. With such focus one can make spiritual advancement. If not, it's very difficult . . .

And so you teach this focus by giving talks and also in your kirtans. Eventually, your kirtan at yoga centers snowballed into making CDs and conducting workshops . . .

Yeah, so I started to do kirtan in yoga centers and, early on, Krishna Das and I used to lead retreats. We led a retreat at the Ananda Ashram. This is before he even had a CD out. We'd each lead half the kirtan. He told me, "No, I don't teach—I just sing." So he would do kirtan and I would do kirtan, and I would also teach. Bhima was on the drum.

Great *mridanga* player, huh?

Incredible. I'm in awe. So, anyway, KD and I—and, slowly, others—brought kirtan to many yoga centers. I also spent a lot of time translating and writing books on Bhakti-yoga. I write about one book a year. You can check them out at shyamdas.com. As the kirtan movement matures, people are becoming more interested in knowing what the devotional process is all about.

Right, which kind of brings me to the next question. Can you talk a little bit about the philosophy of kirtan, what it means, what can

one hope to get from the experience. and where should it take your consciousness?

The thing about kirtan is that anyone is able to do it. You can do it from pretty much any platform, because it will benefit you regardless of what you're doing. If you're going to look at the real motives behind the original *bhakti kirtaniyas*, it was very simple. It was to attain love of God, which, of course, is also the goal of yoga—to link with the Supreme.

Kirtan, ideally, is not really done to attain something. If you do something with that kind of motive, you're bringing it down a notch. That motivation nullifies the higher purpose, because what you imagined you would like to attain is just a small portion of what the thing really is. So if you approach it without any motive, then your chances of receiving something even greater will naturally increase.

But that's a tall order. I mean, unless you're pure, how do you do something without motive?

You can aspire for that. You try to bring yourself into that pure state of consciousness—to chant without any personal desires, to only chant for the Lord's satisfaction. The chanting itself is for purification, too. You see, chanting is two-fold. It's a purification *sadhana* and it's a reward. They are identical. I think that when you see that the means and the reward are identical, it puts you in a non-dual state where you stop judging things. You become more equal-minded, forgiving, and you develop humility. When you see things equally, you become compassionate. We want to have compassion for all beings, deep down. And chanting does that—it brings us together. It allows us to understand our essential oneness but with a respect and appreciation for our differences as well.

By prolonged chanting we can actually experience what the holy names really mean. Actually, all *shabda*, all sound, is Brahman. But the holy names of God narrow it down—they're like concentrated nectar! By chanting the names in the way the sages have taught us, we can grab onto something really special. But we don't have to make some overbearing endeavor. We should just chant—everything else will come naturally. God is merciful and it's all in His name. If we just begin the process, it will take us into realms we can't even imagine. That's the power of kirtan.

For more information contact:
www.shyamdas.com or www.sacredwoods.net

PATRICK BERNARD

Now a resident of Montreal, Canada, Patrick Bernard's name is virtually synonymous with New Age music and the healing effects of kirtan and devotional song.

Born in Algeria in 1952, he and his family moved to France when he was a child. In his teenage years, he began to travel the world, wandering like the yogis of India. At twenty-one, he met A. C. Bhaktivedanta Swami Prabhupada, founder of the Hare Krishna Movement, and although he accepted the Swami as one of his teachers, he did not stay in ISKCON for long. While Prabhupada remained in his heart, he eventually met a second teacher that would further change his life, setting him on the path of devotional music: Swami Shridhar Maharaj of the Gaudiya Math. With the blessing of his two gurus, he embarked on a kirtan crusade through the medium of New Age music.

Consisting mainly of original compositions, his music focuses on mood and emotion, attempting to evoke meditative states that are conducive to spiritual practices. His rich recordings use sacred chants – mainly from Sanskrit, Latin, and Hebrew – as a foil for contemporary music, using high-tech synthesized multi-choral progressions and numerous acoustic instruments.

His unique blend of soothing instrumentation and soft, melodic devotional chanting serve as a perfect adjunct for any healing practice, including meditation or yoga.

Over the last decade, his CDs have consistently achieved high praise, winning awards and even achieving Gold status in certain music circles. He was the first Canadian ever to emerge on Billboard's *New Age listing.*

In addition to his more than sixteen CDs, Bernard recently released a full-length book about the effect of sound on consciousness and environment: Music As Yoga *(Mandala Publishing, 2005). He also recently opened his own recording studio, Devi Communications, Inc., and offers concerts, workshops, and private sound massages at his own wellness center, "The Providence."*

✳ ✳ ✳

I listen to your material a lot. Although you don't usually do kirtan —call-and-response—on most of your CDs, you're clearly pointing in that same direction, and you're coming from a kirtan background. As with all the other *kirtan-wallahs* in this book, I want to begin with some simple background. Just some basic facts—date of birth, where you were born, anecdotes from your childhood, and so on.

I was born in Nigeria, South Africa. It was a French colony during the 1950s, when I was coming of age. I was born February 2, 1952. It was a big cultural household at the time, a lot of diverse ideas, with my mother an outspoken French existentialist and my father a "freethinker."

The environment was quite strange, surreal, because at the time Algeria was at war—we had a civil war around us. So things were really difficult, because of the war atmosphere. It was a battle between the Arabs and the French.

It must have been like living in modern-day Iraq.

Well, I saw bodies, dead people. That affects you, if you see that at a young age.

You actually saw dead bodies?

In the streets.

Hmm. I can't even imagine it . . .

So I was always asking my mother, "What goes on after death?"

No wonder she was an existentialist . . . [laughter]

Yes, and she always answered that death was the end. When people die, that's it—finished. But I had problems with that answer. I remember when I was very, very young, I thought that my mother was missing something here, that she couldn't understand something basic about life. I didn't know why, but I just felt like she didn't get it, that she missed a fundamental truth about who we really are. I knew, instinctively, that if life—the energy that separates us from dead matter—exists at all, then it must exist always. I just knew that energy can't be created or destroyed. Of course, I didn't think about it in those terms. But I felt it.

You intuitively sensed that there was something more to life.

Yes. At the same time, my home life wasn't dark—it wasn't all about the war, about death. Not at all. I was surrounded by music. Jewish music, Spanish music, Egyptian, from Libya, Italy, music from Bali, Morocco, Tanzania . . .

That certainly sounds like a wonderful variety of influences.

Yeah. Many traditions were living together in harmony. In that sense, Algeria was a special place. Christians, Muslims, Jews—and they had a lot of magical healing practices that I was exposed to, from central Africa. It was really a beautiful place, too. Of course, there's the mystery and great calm of the Sahara.

The Sahara Desert, yes. And what kind of school did you go to?

My school was Jesuit.

Ah, you went to a Jesuit school. They're known for their thorough education.

Yes, because my family was quite rich, I attended that school.

Did you study music at all, when you were young?

Not really, though I did later, when I went back to France. In school we learned French and Arab languages at the same time. That was interesting.

You learned about Arabic culture and Islam then?

Yeah. But you know, it was a colony, so you can't even imagine the pressure. After the war, we went to Paris and Normandy. Then I had my first inspiration to play guitar, so I did. And I studied piano and composition as well. I was twelve years old at the time. When I was thirteen, my interest in music really blossomed.

That was probably in the mid-'60s.

Yes. That's right.

So, the hippie thing was starting. Did you get into that?

Well, sure, to a degree. Music was quite an important part of the countercultural milieu, with Bob Dylan and other thoughtful poets and musicians. I was attracted to that. The counterculture's reaction to the war in Vietnam, especially in 1968 — I was part of the revolution instigated by the students in Paris. At the time, I was in a university in Normandy, near Paris, and I was studying philosophy.

Do you remember any of the philosophical systems you studied?

Yeah, I do, but quite frankly, I wasn't satisfied with any of it. I liked Greek stoicism to some extent, but it, too, had severe limitations. Too much asceticism.

Yes, in Greek philosophy, balance came later, with Socrates and Plato. Tell me, did Plato interest you? Some of his ideas are traceable to India.

Also, yes. I was very impressed by his memories of Atlantis, actually. I was looking for that kind of magical perception — people who could see alternate realities. I was interested in alchemy. In fact, I was reading Fulcanelli.

The French alchemist from the nineteenth century.

Yes, you know Fulcanelli? He was a master.

But when did your interest with the East come into being? How did that develop, or is that much later?

Later, because after the French students' revolution, I went to Amsterdam. I dropped out and stopped my study. I didn't want to be a student anymore. We wanted to change the system—all the young people at the time, from my generation, saw the way things were heading, how our parents were making a mess of things. For example, we saw the dangers in atomic energy and nuclear power. It was being abused by our parents' generation, and we knew it. Instead, we proposed some alternative programs, including wind energy and tide energy and solar energy. But we lost. No one would change. And I was really a bit depressed about all this. So I went to Amsterdam during the psychedelic years—enjoying peace and love while looking for a pure state of consciousness.

So that was your stint with sex, drugs, and rock and roll?

Yeah, sex, drugs and progressive rock music, because it was not really rock and roll at the time, at least not for me. It was more progressive rock, like Genesis and . . .

King Crimson and such?

King Crimson, of course. Gentle Giant, and all those kinds of progressive rock bands.

It was a more sophisticated kind of rock, with elements of jazz and classical music.

Yes. And while in Amsterdam, I met quite a lot of people from India and Nepal and Tibet. So my interest in Indian music and philosophy began at that time. Back then, Amsterdam was like San Francisco, you know.

Yes, it has a history as a progressive city.

But after a few years in the psychedelic environment, I just gave it up. I saw that, in an ultimate sense, it was as superficial and as vacant as the mainstream culture that it was trying to replace.

So I moved on. At that point, I was just looking for God. That's all that mattered. I gave up my guitars and my records, everything. Because, you know, I was fascinated by the personality and teaching of Jesus. I was enamored by his total commitment and his absorption in the spiritual realm.

Can you expand on that a little bit?

First of all, I felt a lot of anger against the Roman Catholic Church, which even today still espouses a politic and sectarian program absolutely opposite to what Jesus said to the world in his time. So I was reading everything I could about the real Jesus and his teachings. I was more drawn to the healing part of his teachings, which is an important part of it.

You mean the mystical powers and such?

Not really. It was more about being in harmony with nature. In Europe, we have a huge esoteric movement, with many books being published in French and other languages about the real Jesus.

Are you referring to Jesus's connection to the Essenes?

Yes.

Okay. Many people are unaware of that connection.

Yes. This is something that is usually overlooked by the mainstream, but it's extremely important. It shows his love and his concern for his fellow man, and it shows the power of purity, and the urgency of living close to the earth. And, more or less, this is why I am doing the music that I do now. There is definitely a search for harmony, for complete harmony, absolute harmony, which is a very important element of health.

Right, if the body is in harmony, then health will follow . . .

Exactly.

Disparate elements working together—in life, as in music also.

That's one of the things I try to convey with my music. But let me not rush ahead. At that time, in Amsterdam, I was reading Paramahamsa Yogananda and Krishnamurti and others, like everyone else. But I just wasn't satisfied with that stuff. It never seemed to go deep enough.

You were rather eclectic then—drawing from Jesus, the Greeks and Indian philosophers.

Yeah, that's about it. I was interested in others, too, of course, but that would be an accurate summary. After Amsterdam, I traveled quite a bit. I wanted to see the world—but all the time looking for truth, looking for God. I was intrigued by world cultures, and how different people expressed the same truths according to their respective cultures and languages. I was also interested in musical expression, and how it varied from place to place, from country to country.

You were playing mainly guitar at this time?

Yes. I was playing guitar.

Keyboards, too, or no?

No. Just guitar. And then, after some years, I went back to South Europe, where I just decided to walk.

Walk?!

Yes, like the *yogis* of India. And I did walk for quite a long time, usually barefoot, with no money. I ate only what people gave to me, sleeping under the stars.

Like a real *sadhu*.

Like a madman, too. Chanting the prayer of the heart. You know what that refers to: the prayer of the heart?

You mean the Jesus prayer? "Lord Jesus, son of God, have mercy on me."

Yes, but in French. This is what I did all day. I didn't have a guitar anymore, either.

So, you were living simply, close to the earth, searching for God. And you were praying, calling out to Jesus to help.

Intensely calling, begging to be in his company. I was looking for an answer, for a direct connection. I was also looking for a guide, a spiritual guide, but I wasn't interested in any of the popular gurus circulating at that time. I went to see so many different masters . . .

When did it finally come together for you? Apparently there was some satisfaction with the teachings of Jesus, but you were dissatisfied with the church. So where did you . . .

Well, one day in the south of France I met two wonderful, spiritually minded persons; their names were Madhavendra Puri Das and Mandakini Devi, a married couple. We went to Geneva together. They were disciples of A. C. Bhaktivedanta Swami Prabhupada.

That was your introduction to ISKCON.

Yes, it was in 1975. They gave me many books about Vedic philosophy, the *Bhagavad Gita*, the first edition of *Srimad Bhagavatam* and *Sri Isopanisad*. I was overwhelmed with the depth of knowledge.

Did you find these books answered your basic questions?

Very much, very much. Here's where I learned about *yukta-vairagya*, how real renunciation is not merely the rejection of the material world but rather learning how to use the things of this world in a spiritual way—to spiritualize matter through divine service. This is the primary principle of Bhakti-yoga, the yoga of devotion, the yoga of love. So this spoke to me on a deep level.

I also responded to the idea of Brahman, Paramatma, and Bhagavan. This shows us that God can be understood in impersonal terms, as Brahman, at least on a rudimentary level; more advanced is the Paramatma stage, which is localized personhood—God as He appears in every atom and in every soul; and finally Bhagavan, which is all inclusive, God proper, the ultimate person, with whom we can have an intimate and personal exchange of love.

So God is both impersonal and personal. This really made sense to me. Why have that constant inner debate about God's nature, asking ourselves whether He is a person, like theistic traditions teach, or impersonal, the way the monists teach? Why can't He be both?

Indeed, if He's perfect and complete then it would seem to make sense that He *must* be both.

Precisely. It was beautiful. The realization was so beautiful. And I got that from the scriptures, and from Prabhupada's profound elucidation. But it wasn't something pushed on me. No. When I read it, I found that it was like a flash of light. Something went off in my head, and in my heart; it uncovered sleeping wisdom, something that had been lying dormant for many births. So it was already inside of me, just waiting to be reawakened.

And so where does kirtan come in?

The transcendental vibrations of the holy names. Actually, I was already chanting Tibetan and Christian prayers, as I said, especially the prayer of the heart. This was also a form of kirtan. So, when I started to read Vedic texts and the Puranas and the *Gita*—it was an easy transition, in a sense. I took spontaneously to the chanting of the *maha-mantra*, because it was so familiar; it was what I was doing all along, but now it was more intense, more to the point.

I love the chant: Hare Krishna, Hare Krishna, Krishna Krishna, Hare Hare/ Hare Rama, Hare Rama, Rama Rama, Hare Hare.

I also liked the feminine aspect of the mantra: "Hare," which is a form of "Radhe." In other words, God is not only masculine, but He also has a feminine aspect, a feminine counterpart. This, again, speaks to His perfect and complete nature—He must have both male *and* female dimensions to be complete.

That's what really attracted *me* to Vaishnava philosophy too. Radha and Krishna—the two sides of Godhead.

Radhe. This is the feminine aspect of the Absolute, and the compassionate aspect, the aspect of service, of grace.

Radha Dasyam.

Radha Dasyam. Exactly. Yes, which is service to the divine energy. And so music came back into my life, almost miraculously, when I was given the service of producing records to broadcast the message of the *Bhagavad Gita.*

Oh, really?

I was in France, working with ISKCON under the jurisdiction of Bhagavan Maharaj.

Bhagavan. I remember him.

He gave me this service. "Okay," he said, "you're a musician, so you should write songs about Krishna."

So, wait, let's backtrack a little. You went with those two devotees and they helped you develop spiritually. Did you join the ISKCON ashram after that?

Yeah, I joined. They introduced me to Srila Prabhupada. He went to France and London in 1976, and when I saw him, I said, "Well, that's it. He's the guru, the light of my life."

And you eventually received the initiated name, Prahlad?

Yes. Then, after that, when I went to see Shridhar Maharaj, he gave me second initiation, as a Brahmin priest. Prabhupada had left the planet, and I started to take guidance from Shridhar Maharaj.

You see, I never stayed in one temple. It was difficult for me. My life in the Hare Krishna Movement was actually a beautiful experience, but at the same time, I couldn't fit in. I was creative, and I needed some leeway, some ability to express myself in different ways . . .

Because you're an artist.

Yes, and I couldn't limit myself in the way ashram leaders wanted me to. You see, really — and I speak to you frankly — I strongly feel that the teachings of Bhaktivedanta Swami Prabhupada were misunderstood, at least by some of the movement's members. Many of the disciples understood the letter but not the spirit. Anyway, that's my opinion. That's the way I saw it back then, and I still see it that way. The ISKCON devotees are, by and large, beautiful people, and they are doing important work, but some of them just don't get it. That's all I'm saying.

I would express it a little differently. I would say that perhaps some of them didn't get the full import of Prabhupada's teachings. I mean, there are certain things that they *did* understand, like the the value of the holy name, the urgency of developing one's spiritual dimension, the importance of distributing sacred vegetarian food, and so on. But I agree with you that there were certain things that they missed. By and large, they neglected to apply the teachings with a necessary sensitivity. They missed a larger, loving aspect. Not all of them, only some.

Some of them also missed the universal aspect of the philosophy, which is hard to miss, really. It's right there in the scriptures and in the writings of the predecessor gurus, like Bhaktivinode Thakur and others. Prabhupada writes of it often, too.

Actually, at its core, ISKCON is teaching Sanatan Dharma, or the essence of religious truth. Prabhupada wanted to convey the universal science of God consciousness. But some of his followers were inadvertently turning it into another sectarian religion—"my" religion as opposed to "your" religion. Prabhupada wasn't like that.

I like one incident, when Prabhupada was on TV in San Francisco. I think it was in the mid-'70s, and he said on TV, "There is no conflict between the Koran and the Bible and the Vedic literature." He said also that sincere Muslims can be counted amongst the Vaishnavas and that the Koran is a holy scripture. So this sense of universal spirituality is there in the philosophy, even if some of the members don't quite get it.

Yes. I must say, however, that ISKCON is really changing. The bulk of the devotees work hard to correct previous wrongs. It's a growing process, isn't it? They're maturing like everyone else. And they've come a long way.

I'm really glad to hear that. And when I joined ISKCON, to tell you the truth, I was happy — it was a great time in my life. It was then that my music came back to me.

You mean when Bhagavan Maharaj engaged you in making records? Can you talk about that a little?

He gave me the instruction to produce records, you know, for the Sankirtan devotees. The records would contain Krishna Conscious songs — kirtan and more popular, Western-sounding music — and then the proceeds, whatever money came in, would go toward maintaining ashrams and printing Srila Prabhupada's books.

We had the "Change of Heart" example in America. So we wanted to do the same in Europe.

Oh, Mangalananda's album, aka Michael Cassidy. That album was something, wasn't it? His work is a good example of contemporary kirtan—he'd write beautiful and accessible rock or folk songs but with a God-conscious message. And he'd often incorporate Sanskrit mantras, especially the *maha-mantra*, with call and response. Really great stuff.

Yes, the "Change of Heart" record was very, very beautiful. So I did three or four records along those lines in France, and then because Bhagavan became too much for me, I went to see Jaya Tirtha in London. You remember Jaya Tirtha?

Of course.

Yeah. So I went to Bhaktivedanta Manor, in England, and because I was a musician, I did the same — I produced a few records for the London ashram.

You know, I remember one song—I think it was one of yours. It was called "Vrindavan," with French lyrics. Beautiful track.

Yes. I was working with Havi Das at that time.

Havi! Yes, yes. He's a good friend of mine. Very popular in South America—both as a *kirtaniya* and in popular music.

Oh, he's a great musician! We did some interesting music together. We did the "Night and Daydream" album and one called, "Adventures of the Great King Rama." Stories, music, kirtan. It was a contemporary way to convey the holy name, and the records sold well throughout Europe. But, of course, we're going back many years.

Right. I remember there's a wonderful cover on that Rama album.

Yes, the floating stones, and Rama and Hanuman looking so bold and beautiful. Anyway, Krishna kept giving me my music back. That's the point.

Now, why did I give up music in the first place? This is something we should briefly explore. It happened because I was looking for God. And when I found my path, what did I find? Music. So, there's a lesson. We cannot renounce. Or, at least, we should renounce maturely. In other words, there's no need to give up music. But, there *is* a need to advance spiritually. And when one advances spiritually, one will naturally engage whatever one does in God's service. So that's what I learned from my earlier years on the path.

This also relates to the teaching of Shridhar Maharaj. He used to say that there are two obstacles: exploitation and renunciation. So, before, I was doing music in the mood of exploitation, for sense gratification, and to fulfill non-spiritual desires. Then I gave it up to look for *moksha*, liberation. But through the teaching of the *Gita*, I learned that renunciation can also be an obstacle. So in the middle you find balance, which is dedication, Bhakti-yoga, or devotional service. So my service was to dedicate my music to the glories of God. I was very happy attempting to do that.

Yes. And was it after Jaya Tirtha that you went to Shridhar Maharaj?

Not right away. No. I went to Quebec, Canada. There I met Kirtanananda. And we did a few records for the devotees there. But the interesting thing in Canada was that I did a few records with mantras, which was a bit different than my earlier endeavors. You see, I was mainly writing my own God-conscious songs in French. But now I was focusing on authentic mantras.

Like the *maha-mantra*?

The *maha-mantra* and a few others, like the *Sri Isopanisad*. And this was a revelation for me. It was like, "Hey, wow, I should do *this* instead of writing French songs . . ."

I see. The previous albums were mainly English or French songs.

Yes, when I went to Canada, I did my first real Sanskrit material. I was chanting "Om Namo Bhagavate Vasudevaya," "the Hare Krishna *maha-mantra*," and, of course, "Om Purnam Adah Purnam Idam" from the *Sri Isopanisad,* among others. The title of the album was "Exile."

Exile?

You know, like in "the exile of the soul . . ."

I see. And then?

And then I went into a difficult period.

What year was this?

Maybe 1980, or thereabouts. I was having difficulty with the institution, the leaders of the ashram. And it was a time of deep questioning for me, too, personally. So I decided to go out on my own, and to do commercial music again. I did some New Wave. It was a musical movement coming from Great Britain. New Wave, a kind of Pop-Rock music. I did that in Montreal, Quebec, with great success. My material went to number one in some areas.

Fantastic.

In less than two years, though, I was again disenchanted with the commercial atmosphere. So then I went to see Shridhar Maharaj in Navadvip, near Calcutta. That was a turning point in my life.

You were fortunate that you had a place to go—you went to a genuine *sadhu*.

Yes. He saved my life. I went to India and took shelter of my second spiritual master. In a sense, Srila Prabhupada gave him to me; that's how I see it. It was quite wonderful, because Shridhar Maharaj was really a poet, a philosophical poet, and that's what I needed at the time.

A poet. Yes, he was.

He was living in a beautiful little ashram in Navadvip, on the bank of the Ganges. It was like a dream. The realization of the holy name went deeper. In such an environment, you can really let it in. Also, that's when I discovered Chaitanya Mahaprabhu, in a deep way, because in Navadvip you can visit all those places, the historical places, where Chaitanya Mahaprabhu lived and sung, almost 500 years ago.

I remember, in 1984, I went to all of the South Indian areas that were visited by Mahaprabhu. It was very special. You become drenched in the theology of the holy name. Of course, Navadvip, where Maha-prabhu spent his youth, is even more special.

Navadvip, yes—a magical place.

So you went there and spent some time with Shridhar Maharaj.

Yes. Actually, he gave me faith again. He showed me the potency of Vaishnava *sadhana*, especially the practice of the holy name, and everything came back in a deeper way. I again understood the philosophy of God and His name being one. That He and His name are nondifferent—but now it struck me with renewed force. I really got it this time.

Yes, the Vaishnava teaching on this is really something special. In this world, a thing and its name are different. That's relativity. But on the Absolute platform, a thing and its name are one. This is why you can actually associate with God by chanting His name—He's present in the sound.

Yes. This is a very important spiritual principle.

The named one (the *nami*) and the name (the *nam*) are nondifferent.

It's actually explained in great detail in the writings of Jiva Goswami.

The named and the name are one.

Yes.

So, that brings us to kirtan. When you chant or when you listen, you are directly in contact with the sweet Absolute.

I love that expression: "the sweet Absolute."

Sweet Absolute. That was Shridhar Maharaj's expression.

Although there are many manifestations and aspects of God, you can only think of Krishna when you hear "sweet Absolute."

Yes. And Krishna is a musician. He plays flute.

That's a beautiful image, isn't it? He calls us all back to spiritual world through His sweet flute music.

So Shridhar Maharaj gave me his blessings to carry on with my music, but he said, "Don't do it in the mood of exploitation, because if you approach it in that way, you will bring trouble. So don't do music in the mood of exploitation. But, on the other hand, don't go toward the side of renunciation. Don't renounce. Krishna gave you the ability to understand harmony; so you do it, but you do it for the glory of His name."

You don't chant to become God, and you don't chant to look for anything else: Just chant in the mood of dedication. That means in the mood of service, in the mood of love. The real kirtan singer doesn't ask for anything, not even liberation. That's the important teaching of Shridhar Maharaj. The singer is the servant of the name. When he chants, he serves the name; he chants in the mood of divine service.

Yes, this is an important point.

So I am trying to carry on with this mood. I consider myself a servant of the name.

So Shridhar Maharaj gave you his blessings and you went back to the

West. Then you started producing CDs that have become incredibly popular.

Yeah, my first CD "Atlantis Angelis" had "Jaya Radha Madhava" on it. That was important for me.

Good, yes. I think at this point we should talk specifically about your CDs and how you got into making them.

Okay. There are a lot of things to say about that, but first of all, at this time, nobody was singing in Sanskrit. I mean, at least in the New Age arena. We had Kim Saur. She was singing a little Sanskrit, which was unique. At this time, there was no Krishna Das, no Deva Premal, nothing.

So when you started, no one else was doing it, hmm?

And I must admit, some ten years after that, when I saw that devotional singing in Sanskrit was becoming a trend or a fashion, I was quite surprised.

I guess you were one of the people who instigated that.

In a way, yes, I was a pioneer.

Well, I'm glad you did it! [laughter]

So, when I began, I didn't want to use known melodies. I wanted to create new ones, with new intervals. Do you know this word, "intervals"?

Interval, like "in-between"?

"In-between." It's a very important concept in music.

Oh, I know what you mean: It's like, in painting, they speak of positive and negative space. Same in music: It's not so much the notes you use, but also the notes you _don't_ use. It's the use of taste, of space in between the sounds . . .

Wonderful, yes. That's what I mean by intervals. It's very important. In contrast, many Sanskrit singers today use a lot of loop.

I'm not quite sure what you're referring to.

Loop machine. Anyway, it's a different technique. But the idea of creating new melodies, new techniques, and new intervals—that was significant. I wanted to break with some of the established traditions, because we are trying to speak to a new generation, with new ideals and new directions. So the sounds have to appeal to them, to speak to them, to reach out to them—where they're coming from, where they are, and where they're going. This is why I wanted to create new melodies. And I knew that some traditionalists would criticize me for that, and they did . . .

But you know what's funny about that: the *bhakti* poets in the 15th and 16th century, like Sur Das and Tulsi Das—they did the same thing. They broke from the traditional Vedic mantras and did it their own way, for the people of the time.

Exactly.

Actually, the transcendental sound is purifying, and if you convey it properly, it will have the desired effect, whether you contemporize it or present it in a traditional manner.

How true. But everyone has to move in the directions that God sets out for them. And I had my vision, my approach. Basically, I used intervals in my music to create specific effects in the minds and bodies of my listeners. And if you can have a specific effect in their minds and bodies, then you can affect their consciousness.

I do this independent of the holy names—it's more in the music of my compositions. For example, on my first CD, during "Jaya Radha Madhava," I used the C-G interval.

The C-G interval?

Which is a C, you know, the first note of the scale? And G. E, F, G. So, it's a fifth. You find this interval in Brazilian music, and in Japanese, also. The quality of this specific interval, C-G, is a kind of transmutation, in which the listener is stimulated in various ways. It opens the creative potential, allowing the mind a certain freedom, extending the mind, which brings inner joy.

So, it's a sort of a *raga*, allowing different emotions to arise.

Yes, in a sense. Each *raga* brings with it a specific effect. And in music, each interval elicits that same thing, releasing inner emotions in the mind and in the heart.

Right, right.

So, to sum up: What is an interval? An interval is the resonance of a musical space created by two notes. Each interval has a different vibratory contract. Sound has the power to do that, if it is handled properly.

This is good. Now, specifically about your CDs, could you talk about some specific titles . . .

"Amor Immortalis" was an important CD for me. As on "Atlantis Angelis" and "Solaris Universalis," I tried to use my vocal style to evoke the divine. Of course, as you mentioned, my material is not really kirtan in the usual sense — most of it is not call-and-response kind of music. But it *is* kirtan in that it is glorification of God. On the "Amor" CD, I'm supported by my own guitar work, but I also use ethereal orchestration, with harps, strings, and so on.

"Love Divine" is more directly in the tradition of Bhakti-yoga, with devotional music in a bit more traditional style. I try to use healing sounds, especially soothing, melodious vocal chanting. The Sanskrit mantras are a special focus here and are meant to be purifying and health-giving.

But why don't *you* describe some of my other CDs? I don't mean to put you on the spot, but you said you listen to them, no? [laughter] I feel strange talking about my own work.

Well, I'd say "Shamanyka" is something of a departure, with more of a down-to-earth, tribal feel, right? But I really like it. The tracks have the Vedic mantra material as a basis, but there are also Native American chants, from the Sioux and other tribes. There's also one traditional African chant, which is really cool, and an Islamic-Sufi tune. I especially like the Hebrew Kabbalistic song, called "Adonai." So there's a sense of non-sectarianism here that I really respond to.

How am I doing?

This is great. Keep going! [laughter]

"Supreme Moment" is an interesting CD, too. It seems like a retro-spective, in a sense. It revisits your devotional past, and all of the enlightening experiences you've gathered over the years. You can hear it in your voice.

There are others, too, but I think your readers will get the gist.

Anyway, I really appreciate your work, but a lot of it is somewhat abstract or obscure. You'd think it would be over most people's heads, and yet it sells well, doesn't it? Why do you think people have responded so nicely to your CDs and to your music in general?

This is a very difficult question. I think it's because they can feel something. When they hear it, something opens up for them, and it feels nice. You see, in my music, I try to incorporate the mood of self-lessness that I learned when chanting the holy name. If the names, the holy names, are heard from a genuine *bhakta*, a pure devotee, like Shridhar Maharaj or Swami Prabhupada, it is far more effec-tive than hearing the same mantra from an ordinary *yogi*, or from a person who is simply aspiring on the path. Of course, I'm no pure devotee, but I'm trying to create a parallel idea here: You see, because I really believe in my music and because I try to heal with my music and to convey a certain sense of purity, people benefit from the sounds I send out to them. It has to do with intensity of purpose. Hearing from a disbeliever doesn't have the same effect.

And if it's really bad, it's just entertainment, at best. Don't mis-understand me: There's nothing wrong with entertainment. Every-thing serves a purpose. But it's all a question of degree. On the lowest rung is plain entertainment; after that, there's music with a message; and then there's what I do—I offer music that heals and carries good vibrations, sometimes spiritual vibrations; and then, above what I do, is the sound conveyed by pure devotees—that is the highest kirtan, and the most effective kind of music. All sound vibration can be entertaining, but some go deeper than others. A pure devotee's kirtan is the highest, because his or her purity comes through in the sound, permeating all physical, mental, and intellectual layers of existence — and touching the soul.

For more information contact:
www.patrickbernard.com

$\mathcal{B}$HAKTI CHARU SWAMI

*His Holiness Bhakti Charu Swami,
a native Bengali, was born in 1945
and spent most of his early life in
urban Calcutta. In 1970, he left India to pursue higher education in
Germany. While there, he became aware of the profound wisdom of the
Vedic literature and developed a renewed interest in India's spiritual
heritage. By 1975, he returned to India in search of a spiritual master.
After an intense and disappointing search, he found what he was looking for: In 1976 he found his eternal spiritual master, His Divine Grace
A. C. Bhaktivedanta Swami Prabhupada.*

*At their very first meeting, Srila Prabhupada gave him the assign-
ment of translating his books into Bengali and made him his Secretary
for Indian Affairs. Within only a few months, Prabhupada gave him initiation into the Gaudiya Vaishnava lineage and soon thereafter awarded
him the order of sannyasa, which made him a swami.*

*Bhakti Charu Swami eventually fulfilled the mandate to translate all of
Prabhupada's books into Bengali, consisting of more than fifty volumes.
Subsequently, he became a member of the Governing Body Commission of
the International Society for Krishna Consciousness (ISKCON) – which
is that organization's chief managerial body – and served as its Chairman
in 1989. He is now also one of ISKCON's initiating spiritual masters.*

*In 1996, the Swami embarked on a major project: "Abhay Charan" –
a 104-episode television mega-series on the life of Srila Prabhupada. This*

was produced in conjunction with Indian National Television and was successful throughout the subcontinent. At present, he oversees several projects in Ujjain, India, where, as of February 2006, he completed construction of a beautiful temple in glorification of Lord Krishna.

✳ ✳ ✳

Maharaj, your accomplishments are many, but you are also known for your sweet singing and, of course, you were immersed in Bengali culture from early on.

Well, I was born in Bengal, in a Hindu family. At an early age I was exposed to Indian classical music. So I was very fond of music and naturally developed a taste for it. However, I was not really exposed to kirtan, nor did I recognize its spiritual significance, until I came across my spiritual master, Srila Prabhupada.

My grandfather was a Vaishnava, but my father did not continue with that tradition—at least not strictly. In those days, India was consumed by British influence. The trend was to follow the powers that be. Most of the native Indians didn't give up their Hindu culture, but there was a tendency to become Westernized . . .

So your father adhered to a Vaishnavism of sorts.

There was hardly any real Vaishnavism in his way of life. It was severely Westernized, to my understanding.

Let's begin with your birth name and birth date.

My birth name was Kishore Kumar Das, and I was born on the 17th of September, 1945.

Okay, so you're originally from a Vaishnava family, even if it was somewhat secularized because of British influence. Is that what you're saying?

Yes. My father was a product of British education, and that made a difference.

Did you hear kirtan in the house as a child?

Not so much in the house. Sometimes we'd have some home programs, and we'd invite some prominent kirtan singers, just to hear their performance. But that was just for the sake of music. There was hardly any awareness of its spiritual importance. We were more inclined towards Indian classical music, and modern Indian music in general.

Dhrupad?

Yes, that sort of classical music, highly sophisticated vocal music. Not so much Dhrupad but more the modernized classical trend. Like Khayal, Thumri, and music like that.

Ah, the semi-classical tradition from the north . . .

Yes. Due to its pronounced Muslim influence, classical music in the north took a different shape, and traditional Indian classical music, which was originally meant for glorifying the Lord, was taken to the royal courts of the Muslim kings, for their sense pleasure. Not only music, the entire Indian culture became affected in that way.

And in my family there was always an appreciation for Indian classical music, as I was saying. I was exposed to many great classical musicians, like, for example, Bade Gulum Ali Khan, Amir Khan, Salamat Ali Khan, Najakat Ali Khan—and many were virtuosos on classical instruments, like Alauddin Khan, Ali Akbar Khan, Vilayet Khan, Mia Bismillah, and so on. Actually, now that I reflect on it, I realize that most if not all of them were Muslim. Of course, there were many Hindus also, like Ravi Shankar, Bhimsen Joshi, D. V. Paluskar, A. T. Kanan. But most of them were actually from Muslim backgrounds.

Why is that? Why do you think Hindus didn't develop their musical traditions in the same way?

I would imagine it's because musicians, the entertainers, in Vedic culture, were considered *shudras*, or lowborn. That's how they were identified in ancient Indian culture.

So, they were seen as taking music away from its original intent in glorifying the divine.

And that's why they were looked down upon. However, the Muslim kings patronized them, and they gave them honor and respect, whereas, in the degenerated Hindu society of later times, they weren't treated with dignity, and therefore they converted. And even if they came from Hindu families, it was easy for them to be converted, because they didn't really know the culture.

And the Vaishnavas—real, practicing Vaishnavas, doing authorized kirtan—were not so prominent. To be frank, in the name of Vaishnavism, many unscrupulous people were indulging in such abominable activities that the Vaishnava tradition was not accepted by the educated, cultured, and affluent members of Hindu society, at least not at that time. It was more of a poor man's culture, so to say.

You're speaking from experience, from when you were growing up in Bengal.

Yes. Unfortunately, I was not exposed to the teachings of great Vaishnava *acharyas* like Srila Bhaktivinode Thakur. Nor was I exposed to Srila Bhaktisiddhanta Sarasvati Thakur's mission at that time.

Right. That came later.

Of course, many people at that time were. But my family was not fortunate enough to come across their teachings and receive that great spiritual wealth. At that time, what was going on in the name of Vaishnava culture—outside of Bhaktisiddhanta Sarasvati Thakur's movement—was extremely distasteful. The *sahajiyas* and the *apa-sampradayas*, that is, cheap imitators and concocted lineages, these were more prominent, and this is what the average person thought Vaishnavism was all about.

So the cultured and educated Bengalis, at least, didn't want to identify with them.

Yes, and as a result, most cultured people, at that time, didn't take kirtan seriously, because it was seen as kind of cheap—the people who were practicing it and promoting it engaged in such repulsive and promiscuous activities that refined individuals preferred to not have anything to do with it. They developed a natural distaste for whatever these so-called Vaishnavas did, and as a result of that, they failed to appreciate real Vaishnavas and the most profound spiritual music in the form of kirtan. And some of these groups had incredible musical talent, but a part of their culture involved a tradition wherein a man had to run off with another person's wife.

That's an accepted part of some of these particular Vaishnava sects?

That's right—to elope with someone else's wife. This was part of their so-called religious practice: To truly comprehend Radha and Krishna's divine love, you have to have an affair with someone else's wife.

That's incredible! But I'm sure that not all practitioners in these groups would take it that far. I don't know how a tradition could be sustained with such behavior. You're talking about a few . . .

Right, I'm talking about their tradition in the extreme, but that's how degraded it became. In the name of following Sri Chaitanya Mahaprabhu, they were indulging in all kinds of abominable activities and that's why cultured Indians didn't want to identify with Vaishnavism as such, at least in Bengal. In other parts of India, their influence may not have been that prominent. But in Bengal, it was a serious problem.

And it was Srila Bhaktivinode Thakur, in the 19th century, who gave it back its real shape and credibility. He explained the true meaning of Chaitanya Mahaprabhu's teaching . . .

This must have been a very difficult job . . .

Oh, yes, it was an incredibly difficult job. And despite his immense work, many of these deviant sects still exist. So this is largely what I found growing up in Bengal.

And then you went West . . .

Right. But I want you to know that although I was exposed to numerous *sahajiya* traditions, these deviant sects, I never really took it seriously. I was never really interested in that kind of thing. But I would sometimes hear their kirtan at night, especially when I was in Tripura, at my uncle's place . . .

I would hear it from neighboring houses. In the evening, people would sit together and chant the Hare Krishna *maha-mantra*. It was quite alluring. It was the same kind of tune that Prabhupada brought to the West. That was how I was actually exposed to kirtan.

At the same time, I saw it as just some music, some prayerful music—I had no philosophical understanding at that time. Still, it was simple, sweet, and now I can see that I was attracted to the holy name, even then. But I wasn't ready for it and, again, it had those negative associations.

So let us now jump ahead to where you arrive in the West and you get reintroduced to kirtan.

Right. Many of my friends were going West for higher studies, and I also decided to go. My plans were different, though. I planned to travel with one of my friends—his name was Prasun. Prasun Sarkar. Later, after being initiated by Srila Prabhupada, he became Sarvabhavana Das. He and I decided to do it in a different way, not by flying but by traveling over land.

And why travel the long way, by land?

At that time—we're talking about 1968 to 1969—we became interested in hippie culture. We read books like *On the Road* by Jack Kerouac and listened to music by Bob Dylan, Joan Baez, the Doors, the Rolling Stones, and we wanted to do what young Americans we're doing in general.

We also noticed that many Westerners, especially Americans, were coming to the East, to India, traveling over land, hitchhiking, and so on. That's what initially gave us the idea, but we would go in the opposite direction.

[laughter] Westerners were going East and Easterners were going West...

In those days, we weren't able to travel through Pakistan, and so we took a boat to Iraq. From Bombay to Iraq. And we went to Basra, and then from Basra to Baghdad. In Baghdad, we decided to split up, to travel separately. You see, in Baghdad, we met a group of young Iraqis. They were extremely friendly and we were having a wonderful time with them. Sarvabhavana wanted to stay on for another week or so, but I decided to push on. So we split. We planned to meet up in Munich, where we had some friends.

After that, I traveled on my own and ended up in Hamburg. I had some relatives there. When I arrived in Hamburg, it was a different scene altogether. My cousin was a very successful man and quite conservative. He couldn't relate to what I was doing and tried to convince me to change my ways. Sarvabhavana, too, somehow arrived in Hamburg a few weeks later.

While we were there, we reflected on our experience thus far. To some degree, we saw the futility of sense enjoyment—that no matter how much one engaged the senses, no matter how much one tried to squeeze pleasure out of the material world, it always seemed lacking. One always wanted more. We observed how all these young Americans, hippies, whose families knew the height of materialistic affluence—they were all renouncing in their own way, making a statement about the negative aspects of Western culture, about the values of their parents. In other words, our travels had given us certain realizations about life and people.

It opened you up to Vedic wisdom, prepared you for what was yet to come. Given your background in India, it must have been especially interesting to you...

Oh, very interesting. That was perhaps the most important, most formative year of my life. At that time, too, in Germany, my cousin conveyed certain ideas to me about life, and about thinking long-term, not with words but with his eyes. When I looked into his eyes, I could see that he thought I was wasting my life. He was married to a German girl, and it was clear that he couldn't relate to what I was doing, just traveling, living on the road, without direction . . .

You were in your mid-twenties at this point?

Yes.

He probably wanted you to get married and to live a more conventional life.

Actually, he mainly wanted me to continue with my studies, to go back to school. I stayed a while and tried to adapt to that kind of life, but the die was cast. Despite its accomplishments, I realized how empty Western culture actually was—both the conventional kind and even hippie life, with its superficial rejection of the Establishment.

At that time, I made many friends in Germany. Most of them were actually Americans. They were exchange students from the University of Dayton, in Ohio. There were five or six of them, and we became very close friends. We stuck together because, initially, my German was pretty shoddy; so I had difficulties communicating with the indigenous people in their own language. And for this reason, too, my friendship with these exchange students from America naturally developed.

What school are we talking about?

The University of Hamburg. I was supposed to study chemistry, but I didn't really pursue it. In fact, most students, it seemed, were just there to dodge the draft. There was a lot of apathy in the air, and people just wanted to have a good time.

So, at this point in your life, it seems, you were at a turning point. You were seeing through the glimmer of Western culture, although initially you admired it. You were also looking at life in general and wondering what it was all about.

Yes, right, and that led me to an appreciation of my own culture, my Indian heritage. I began to see something authentic, something traditional, of lasting value. And as I looked more deeply at

my history, the history of the Indian people, their profound literature and spirituality, I became proud. I would even speak to my
friends in the West and try to convince them about the profundity
of Vedic culture. But, of course, to substantiate that, I had to know
my culture, the origins and the details.

Right.

So, it was then that I really got into the Vedic literature. I read
everything I could get my hands on. I remember one of the first
books that interested me along these lines was a book by an English journalist traveling in India. His name is Paul Brunton.

**Yes, I'm familiar with his work. He was a British philosopher who inter-
estingly, lived among the *yogis*. His legal name was Raphael Hurst.**

I didn't know that. Anyway, Brunton's book, the first one that I
read, was *A Search in Secret India.* That book was my initial contact, helping me to understand how rich Vedic culture actually
is. That was just mystical India in general, of course. Not Vaishnavism per se.

But in terms of overall Indian spirituality, I liked Brunton's
books quite a lot. He gets into the philosophical aspect of it, which
is fascinating, especially for where I was coming from at the time.
In fact, most of the books I found at that time were influenced
by Shankaracharya's impersonalistic ideas. And so you had this
mix of devotion to a personal deity and impersonalism—it was all
quite perplexing.

**But at least it enhanced your awareness of the existence of the soul
and of alternate realities beyond this material world.**

Exactly. But then I reached a point where I realized that now I had
to go back to India. I realized that I needed a bona fide teacher. So
I returned to the land of my birth, but with new vision.

**There's a certain irony here, isn't there? Paul Brunton, a Westerner,
awakened in you a taste for Eastern spirituality . . .**

Yes. That's right. Whatever the case, I specifically went back to search for a guru. And, I must tell you, this was very, very disappointing, at least at first. I had read enough to know what was genuine and what wasn't. I had good intuition, too. I was looking, but I was a skeptic. So finding a guru was not an easy feat for me.

From a distance, you might find many who seem to be *sadhus*, saintly, but when you come close—watch out! [laughter] Many of them are like "Vedic Hippies," just smoking pot, hashish, and what have you, just having an easy life. So I was quite disappointed. And I also met with so-called spiritual leaders, people who were well known and had clearly attained some spiritual status, but when I spoke to them I could see that they really didn't have it—their understanding of spiritual truth was lacking. If you read the Vedic texts and look for the qualifications of a bona fide guru—these people just didn't have them, no matter how holy they might have looked, no matter how they might have positioned themselves as spiritual adepts. When people speak, you can generally see where they're really at.

Yes, at least you get the sense that something's missing.

Pseudo spiritual masters simply can't satisfy your thirst for spiritual life, your inquisitiveness. And so that was actually a very difficult phase in my life. I pretty much gave up my search, concluding that if I was meant to have a guru, then let *him* come and find *me*. It was around that time that I came across Srila Prabhupada's *Nectar of Devotion*.

You found it in a bookstore?

No. Sarvabhavana had already joined ISKCON, in Germany, and he came back to visit, to tell me about it. I heard that he had joined the Hare Krishnas, but, at that time, I didn't think that he was really serious about it. I thought that he was just fooling around, really. Mainly because, up until that point, he had never given me the impression that he was spiritually inclined.

So Sarva joined and I didn't think much of it. I thought, "Okay, it's another path, another approach . . ." But when I saw him, after he became a devotee . . . he was totally transformed. I really appreciated the change: He became more serious about spiritual life, more confident about what he was doing, and yet he also had a humility and a sense of his place in the greater scheme of things. He also didn't preach to me, which I really liked. He would just visit and we would spend time together. He would tell me what he was doing and leave it at that, never suggesting that maybe I, too, would benefit from his path . . .

Sometimes closely-held beliefs are difficult to convey to friends.

That's true. I think that's why he kept it light. He also just wanted to let it take its own course. He knew it would evolve on its own. In this way, we used to visit the temple in Calcutta together, too. It was very light-hearted and friendly.

One day, while at the Calcutta temple, I wanted to purchase a copy of the *Bhagavad Gita*. But for some reason we couldn't access it, we couldn't get to the store. Maybe the person with the key was unavailable. So I said, "Why don't you give me any book, whatever you have on hand?" And so the devotee there gave me *Nectar of Devotion*, Prabhupada's summary of Rupa Goswami's *Bhakti-rasamrita-sindhu*. This is the complete science of Bhakti-yoga.

From the very first page, an entire new world opened up to me. Clearly, this was what I was looking for. All of a sudden, a door opened with all kinds of information. A door opened to another reality. This had such a wealth of data, about God, about how to develop a relationship with Him . . .

I was totally fascinated by this one book, by its depth and comprehensiveness. That night, I read it until the early hours of the next morning, when I fell asleep. And then, when I woke up, I immediately began reading it again. I think for that entire day — I just read. You know, *Nectar of Devotion*, at some point, after the first section, when you get into the second, it becomes quite complex. And I was unfamiliar with a lot of the terms and concepts. But I couldn't stop reading. Although most of the book was over my head, I just kept going, like an addict. And that second night, I had a dream of Srila Prabhupada.

At this point, you hadn't met him yet in person ...

And yet still I had a dream about him. I saw him as if he was sitting on a throne. In those days, I didn't know the term, *vyasasana*, or the seat of the spiritual master, because in India, the *sadhus* generally don't sit on an elaborate seat. They just sit on simple seats. But Prabhupada was sitting on a throne, and there was a brilliant glow around him. And that vision of Srila Prabhupada filled my heart with a wonderful realization: I had found my spiritual master.

The experience was that intense?

Yes, and I didn't do anything; I didn't ask any questions; I didn't even try to speak to him. It was a vivid dream. All I did was offer obeisance to him.

How did you know what he looked like? Was his picture on the book or something?

I think so. Yes, the image of him came from the picture on a book, or something I had seen at the temple. In any case, that dream made quite an impact—I decided to offer my life to Krishna, to His song, to kirtan, to Prabhupada and the spiritual quest.

You know, when I was reading *Nectar of Devotion*, I was imagining myself doing all the things described in the book—like a devotee in Vrindavan goes to the temple, he visits all the temples. So I did that in my mind's eye.

Actually, that's a type of *lila-smaranam*, or entering spiritual pastimes through meditation.

Right. I didn't know that at the time, but I was picturing myself doing all those things. And this increased my excitement, my initial enthusiasm.

After the dream, I asked Sarvabhavana where Prabhupada was, telling him that I wanted to meet him. He replied that Prabhupada was in America at the time. So I asked when he'd come back to India, and he said that Prabhupada generally returns in the winter.

This was late summer, or autumn, so I thought that I might

travel to holy places associated with Krishna and Sri Chaitanya Mahaprabhu, preparing myself, purifying myself, until Srila Prabhupada came back to India. Then, upon his return, I would meet him and surrender myself to his mission. This is what I wanted to do.

What year was this?

That was in 1976.

Calcutta, 1976. Okay. So Achyutananda was there. Great *kirtaniya*!

Yes, Achyutananda was there, and I knew him well. Oh, he led great kirtan. And he was one of the first Westerners to really capture its spirit, the authentic spirit of kirtan. He used to give such wonderful classes, too. He knew Bengali quite well and . . .

So, this is where you were exposed to kirtan.

Right. I became really immersed at this time. Jai Sachinandana was there, too. And, of course, I loved Srila Prabhupada's kirtans. This was my real exposure. I used to like Bhavananda's kirtans as well, although he is not generally known for kirtan.

To be frank, although I was not much of a singer myself, my exposure to Indian music made me a bit cynical about the way some devotees used to chant. Their kirtan was generally too passionate for my tastes. In fact, I used to think that I would never be able to lead a kirtan myself, because it was usually so passionate and loud. I'm more inclined to softer, gentler forms of expression, even if most of ISKCON, especially at that time, liked these loud, passionate, demonstrative chanting sessions.

In due course, though, I started to lead kirtan as well, because I instinctively knew there must be other kinds of kirtan, those that were more prayerful, as opposed to these more overwhelming outbursts of emotion.

More like *bhajan*?

Yes, you might say that. *Bhajan*, and even more mellow forms of kirtan—or more melodious kirtan. You find it goes on more now.

ISKCON now has both kinds of kirtan, which is good. I guess as devotees mature, they develop different ways and methods of presentation.

Well, when you think of the Gaudiya Vaishnava tradition, Narottam's Garan-hati kirtan is slow and melodious; it begins that way and then it gradually builds up. So you would be more inclined to that.

That's more in Dhrupad style. But, yes, that's what I like.

In our remaining time, can you talk a little more about kirtan? I know this is actually the center of your current practice and also the main theme of your recent temple, opened in Ujjain.

The way I understand it, kirtan is actually a prayer to the Lord. Originally, those prayers were very personal, when initially composed. And then they take on more general expression, and anyone can chant it. But, early on, these were confidential prayers, like the mantras in the Vedas, where they are not open to the general public. Those mantras—like Gayatri, for example—were meant for meditative chanting, but they were circumscribed, only for special clientele, so to speak.

Now, Chaitanya Mahaprabhu came to give a different idea. He gave the *maha-mantra* openly, saying it was for anyone and everyone. So, for the first time, such mantras became public. And it was presented as being both for personal meditation and for loud chanting, which enabled practitioners to share it with others. The loud chanting is generally known as Nam-sankirtan. This refers to congregational chanting, many people getting together—the more the merrier—to glorify the name of God. This makes it even more effective, more powerful. That is the *yuga-dharma*, the method of spiritual practice for this current time period, called Kali-yuga, as taught by Chaitanya Mahaprabhu.

He explained that people in this age are not qualified for any other yogic process. They won't be able to meditate; they won't be able to perform sacrifice; they won't even be able to worship the deity of the Lord in the temple. What to speak of worshiping the deity, they won't even be inclined to go to the temple. That's the state of this age, the condition of this age. Therefore, Chaitanya Mahaprabhu inaugurated this Nam-sankirtan—a simple process —allowing everyone to get involved in this chanting of the holy name of the Lord.

So that is the origin of kirtan in our present age. After that, Mahaprabhu and his followers spread it throughout India. For example, in the following generation, great teachers, like Shrinivas Acharya, Narottam Das Thakur, Shyamananda Prabhu, and others took this movement further with newly developed chanting styles and traveling Sankirtan parties. They were preaching through music and storytelling. People in those days were a bit more refined, in a sense, than people today. They could sit together, day and night, just hearing descriptions of Chaitanya Mahaprabhu's pastimes, the descriptions of Krishna's pastimes. They were cultured, able to relish transcendental topics through drama, music, and so on.

Yes, this was the age of Padavali kirtan, spiritual song and narrative melded as one.

This is how it started, and as a result, Mahaprabhu's movement spread like wildfire. Great devotees traveled throughout the countryside, expressing the Lord's pastimes with sophisticated forms of song and dance, with dramatic performance and other developed artistic presentations. Because it was a cultural presentation, it was patronized by powerful kings and other influential individuals. Therefore, this is seen as the golden age of the Sankirtan movement.

But then, gradually, there was the inevitable decline. Kali-yuga, the age of quarrel, will not be cheated out of its due, and deviation began to manifest. In the name of following Chaitanya Mahaprabhu, other *sampradayas*, lineages, with compromised teachings, started to introduce all kinds of deviant concepts, as I mentioned earlier. In the name of spiritual practice, they started to introduce illicit behavior, extremely gross and degraded sense gratification, which is against all decency and all yogic principles. But what's worse is that they started to gain in popularity, and they became more and more prominent. You see, the deviations began in a simple way, with apparently well-intended spiritual practitioners, but then the divergence becomes more and more serious, causing the practitioner to stray from the Lord's real purpose and teachings, and it inevitably degenerates into gross sense gratification. People then use it to rationalize all sorts of illicit activity and non-spiritual behavior.

You don't hear about such groups in the West, although even many yoga groups and Western branches of Eastern thought are subject to their influence. In order to follow the disciplic succession of Lord Chaitanya Mahaprabhu strictly, one should avoid these *apa-sampradayas* or illegitimate cults or pseudo spiritual communities. They were Vaishnavas. Or they started out that way. But then deviation occurred. When that happens, one is cut off from the current of divine knowledge, losing the potency of the authorized lineages. There are sincere souls in all groups, no doubt, but, historically, this is how deviation developed.

And so that's why, by the time you were reaching adulthood in India, Vaishnavas appeared compromised, and you had little attraction . . .

It was compromised, yes, and because of this, people naturally had a condescending attitude toward Vaishnavism. First of all, as I mentioned, it was a poor man's culture, for the uneducated. It didn't seem refined or dignified, and as a result, Sri Chaitanya Mahaprabhu, at least for a time, was totally disregarded. The Supreme Personality of Godhead Himself, in the form of Sri Chaitanya, came to Bengal and the Bengalis were totally unconcerned about him. What an unfortunate state of affairs.

As a result, Mahaprabhu's mission, his teachings, were practically lost. Oh, there were moments of hope, no doubt, moments of glory: Vishvanath Chakravarti was a great mystic and poet, and Baladeva Vidyabhushana wrote his commentary on the *Vedanta-sutra*, and people had to take notice. But the essence was largely gone, at least among the mass of people.

Then came Bhaktivinode Thakur, and he worked hard to revive the culture, to show what it really was. And then Bhaktisiddhanta Sarasvati, who institutionalized it and gave it more formal shape. And then Srila Prabhupada came and gave it a global dimension, spreading it all over the world. Prabhupada's mission, as I see it, is continuing on in the form of ISKCON. It is through ISKCON that this mission is going to spread, to continue to spread, and that will happen chiefly through the holy name. So, it begins with kirtan and it ends with kirtan.

That's good, but now let's talk a little about the philosophy of kirtan, how chanting affects people's consciousness, and so on.

Okay. Well, consider the idea of sound. There are different types of sound. First of all, there are two types in particular: meaningless sound and meaningful sound. For example, the bell rings, the gong sounds, you drop something on the ground. This produces some sound but it doesn't convey any special meaning. It's just sound. However, some other sounds convey specific meaning or give a concrete idea — like when I say "water," that sound gives you some idea of a substance. These are sounds that are generally called words. In this way, through sound, one perceives an entire world, not only of objects but of emotions and feelings. And this is extended through literature, poetry, songs, music, and so on.

Now, beyond this material world, there is another reality — the spiritual reality or the spiritual sky. The information of that reality also comes in the form of sound and that sound is called mantra. Through mantra one becomes elevated to that spiritual nature from which mantra originates. As one meditates on that sound vibration, spiritual reality becomes manifest to that person — and he or she is actually transported to the spiritual realm.

The mantra, which is generally known as Gayatri, has three aspects — *bija*, which is the seed of the mantra, *nam* or the identity of the personality of the mantra, and finally *nyasa*, or the method of meditating on the personality of the mantra. As a matter of fact, mantra quickly purifies the senses and spiritualizes them, and as a result, one becomes eligible to perceive spiritual reality and go back to the spiritual sky.

In the Vedas, there are innumerable mantras, but there is only one *maha-mantra*, or the greatest of all mantras. This mantra has the greatest power to reveal the Supreme Personality of Godhead in His most sublime form—and it enables one to develop a loving relationship with Him.

Narottam Das [the medieval Bengali poet] says it's "imported" from the spiritual world.

Imported from the spiritual world, right. That sound vibration is not generated from the world of three dimensions. It comes down from that other reality. And according to the purity of the chanter, the spiritual world unfolds—it becomes revealed to him. The purity of the chanter is important. That's why Prabhupada used to say, "We must hear the chanting of the pure devotees of the Lord." That's because if the person is not a devotee of Krishna, if he is not pure, his chanting won't have the desired effect. It might sound nice; it may even instill some inner peace. But it won't bestow love of God, which is the real fruit of chanting. For that, one must hear chanting of the holy name—true kirtan—from the lips of a pure devotee, or from one who has heard from a pure devotee.

So that's how the sound vibration actually brings the message of the spiritual sky down to the material world. It creates a bridge for all those who find themselves in the world of matter—you might say that it acts as a conduit to the spiritual world. So that's the basic philosophy of chanting the holy name. One must get it in disciplic succession and hear it from a pure devotee. That's the first thing.

The next thing is that one must also be pure oneself, one must try to develop his love for Krishna, practice austerity, and live a good, *sattvik* lifestyle—that's another prerequisite to get the most out of chanting. In addition, the involvement of many individuals also makes it effective. When many people get together and chant, that is called Nam-sankirtan. The more that people participate, the more effective it's going to be. That's why Prabhupada was so emphatic about spreading his movement all over the world. In this way, we can all help each other taste the holy name. You see, the word *sankirtan* literally means, *samyak kirtan*—"*complete* glorification of the Lord."

Does this imply that regular kirtan is somehow incomplete?

No. Nothing is incomplete when it comes to spiritual matters. I would say that what we are talking about here is really about being complete and being even *more* complete. [laughter]

Kirtan refers to chanting the blissful glories of the Lord, which is of course totally spiritual and the recommended process for this age. But there's a way to do this even more effectively — to engage in *complete* glorification of the Lord — and this involves many, many people getting together and chanting as a group.

I see.

This phrase *samyak kirtan* has another connotation, too — one that is even more intense than chanting. This other connotation is that everything belongs to the Lord and must therefore be utilized in His glorification. That is actually the higher concept of Sankirtan. You can see it in the lives of Bhaktisiddhanta Sarasvati and Srila Prabhupada: They actually embodied this *samyak kirtan* ideal by using everything to glorify the Lord. You see, that's the ultimate spiritual principle: Everything belongs to Krishna and must therefore be used in His service or glorification. That's real kirtan.

ISKCON's ultimate mission is to bring that aspect of Sankirtan out into the world. Chanting the holy name of the Lord, congregationally, is certainly important, but even more important is using everything in Krishna's service.

So *Samyak* means "complete." Everything belongs to Sri Krishna. Therefore, everything must be utilized in His service. "Whatever belongs to my master, I will use it for his pleasure, for his glorification. That is its proper use." So that is the full understanding of *samyak kirtan* or the absolute glorification of Krishna, the Supreme Personality of Godhead — not just to use some sound, some words, to glorify Him but also to use everything at my disposal in His service. That's obviously a more complete form of glorification.

That's an extension of kirtan, then, isn't it? It's even an extension of Sankirtan.

That's an extension of Sankirtan, yes.

It reminds me of what Bhaktisiddhanta Sarasvati called the printing

press. He called it the *brihat-mridanga*—or "the big drum." Why? The sound of the printed word can be heard all over the world, whereas the ordinary drum is heard for only a few square blocks. So the larger kirtan of book distribution is . . .

It is the greater kirtan. That's right. He called his press the *brihat-mridanga*. He considered how to spread the holy name of the Lord, to spread his master's glory, and one of the best ways to spread it is through books.

Prabhupada used to say, "I am using everything. People they say, why is a *sadhu* getting involved in these things? Why is a *sadhu* traveling around the world? Why is a *sadhu* having all these facilities and becoming involved in so many complex material arrangements? The bottom line is, it's all for the glorification of Krishna." That is the ultimate consideration of Sankirtan.

Actually, it was with this understanding that I embarked on making spiritual movies, because I felt that it was in the mood of our teachers, our holy predecessors, who used every possible means to spread the glory of the Lord.

Well, it's easy to see how movies could be an extension of kirtan. Like books.

Exactly. It's the medium for communication. Whichever medium presents itself, according to time and place, that's what we'll use. That's a real *kirtaniya*. We are using tape recorders, cassettes, CDs, cameras, computers—they're all an extension of kirtan.

You see, kirtan ultimately means glorifying the Lord. How we glorify Him is up to us. And this glorification is an expression of our love for Him. First through words: Chanting—"Hare Krishna, Hare Krishna, Krishna Krishna, Hare Hare"—is actually a prayer to Krishna. It means, "O all attractive Supreme Personality of God–head, please allow me to love You, allow me to serve You." Or, as George Harrison sang, "I really want to see You, I really want to be with You, my Lord . . ." This is the *maha-manra*—to pray to the Lord, to humbly ask to be engaged in His service. And then we do kirtan through action.

But first comes chanting. And when we chant or sing this kirtan, whether by ourselves or collectively, it should be done as a prayer. We must offer all our love to Him, fully recognizing His love for us. He has given us so much. He is taking care of us in so many wonderful ways. He is going with us wherever we go, in all forms of life. He is always with us as the Supersoul, in our heart of hearts. And as we become aware of this fact, a spontaneous love for Him naturally grows in our hearts, and we, just as naturally, want to express that love through all our words, through all our prayers, and through all our actions. That is the real kirtan. That is Sankirtan.

For more information contact:
www.bhakticharuswami.com

DAVE STRINGER

The Los Angeles Times *referred to the experience of chanting with Dave Stringer "a departure from ancient kirtan. Stringer's performance shaped the experience into a far more compelling musical encounter." He has been widely profiled as one of the most innovative artists of the new American kirtan movement in publications as diverse as* Time, Billboard, Yoga Journal *and* In Style.

Stringer's sound marries the transcendent mysticism of traditional Indian instruments with the exuberant, groove-oriented sensibility of American gospel, and he is regarded as one of the most accomplished singers in the genre. His work creates a modern and participatory theatrical experience, using as a basis the ancient traditions of kirtan and yoga, which are open to a multiplicity of interpretations and accessible to all.

Initially trained as a visual artist, a filmmaker, and a jazz musician, Stringer's formative experiences with chanting occurred when film-editing work brought him to the Siddha Yoga ashram in Ganeshpuri, India, in 1990. A subsequent period of residence at the ashram laid the foundation for his continuing study of the ideas, practices, and music of yoga.

Since 2000, Stringer and an extended family of accompanying musicians have toured both North America and Europe tirelessly, developing new venues for music and expanding the audience for kirtan. He has introduced chanting to many seemingly unlikely cities and, through his repeated visits, has been instrumental in the development of a number of *thriving local kirtan communities. He has also served as a volunteer who teaches meditation and chanting to inmates at a number of correctional facilities in the United States.*

An articulate and engaging public speaker, he probes the dilemmas of the spirit with a wry and unorthodox sense of humor. Stringer frequently works in tandem with masters of Hatha-yoga, creating related music for workshops led by John Friend, Shiva Rea, and Gurmukh, among others. Of particular note has been his friendship and collaboration with yoga teacher Saul David Raye, with whom he has realized a number of CDs.

Now based in Los Angeles, Stringer has also produced varied recordings with other significant World Music artists, including Azam Ali, Vas, Axiom of Choice, Rasa, Suzanne Teng, Shaman's Dream and the Open Door Orchestra. Chanting artists Donna De Lory, Suzanne Sterling, and Girish first began their careers in the genre after spending time in Stringer's performing and recording ensembles. His voice also appears on numerous soundtracks, including the blockbuster film "Matrix Revolutions" and the video game "Myst." The CDs he has produced under his own name – "Brink," "Japa," "Mala," and "Divas & Devas" – are favorites in yoga studios throughout the world.

✳ ✳ ✳

Let's begin with some background: where you were born, family situation, and so on.

Okay, the obituary thing.

[laughter] Yes, exactly.

I was born in St. Louis, Missouri. I grew up in Chicago, and in Milwaukee, Wisconsin. My mother's a Midwesterner, and my father's from the deep South. On my father's side, many of my family are religious fundamentalists.

What denomination?

Baptists and Jehovah's Witnesses. Evangelicals. On my mother's side, we're from Mennonite stock, later becoming Presbyterians and Lutherans. I would say, when I look through my family tree, that there's clearly a deep sort of spiritual searching that seems to be going on.

Siblings?

I have a younger sister and a younger brother. My sister is a year younger than me; I guess we're what they call Irish twins. She and I taught each other to sing, basically. She has a gorgeous, gorgeous voice, and she mostly sings in the church. She's not by any means conservative. The thing about growing up in Wisconsin is that what you encounter there is the religious left, not the religious right. They're all Lutherans. They're all Swedes and Norwegians and Germans, and they come from a whole different religious tradition—in marked contrast to my father's deep Texas roots.

Okay, So, let's move on to early spiritual memories. Was there a fascination with the East from early on, or was it primarily Western spirituality?

Well, my father's Baptist background and my mother's Presbyterian background had them looking for an alternative and both of them had kind of left where they came from. They ended up settling on the Lutheran church.

I guess the opening chapter of Dave's spiritual life began in the backyard of our house. I'm about four years old, or five, and I'm playing ball with my father, who was trying to teach me how to catch a baseball. The more he throws baseballs at me, the less I am able to catch them. This reached a point where suddenly I'm just frozen, stunned, and can't even move. My father is so angry and so frustrated at my inability to do what he wants that he burns a baseball right between my eyes. Like, you know, right into the pineal. He just flattens me, and I lay there, on the ground . . .

You mean he actually threw it at you?

Yep. He threw it right at my head.

Oh, God.

This is important later on. I don't want to complicate this story with our subsequent relationship, but, I'm like five or something and I fall to the ground, crying. My father comes over, kind of looks at me, snorting derisively, and walks away, leaving me with a bloody nose on the grass. My mother comes running out to look after me.

I can't believe this.

Yeah, that's how it started. I love my father very much and have done a lot of *sadhana*, spiritual practice, with him over the years. But in that moment, I'm lying on the ground, stunned. Now, while there, I experienced an amazing flash of light that occurs when you get a baseball thrown at your third eye.

Right. [laughter]

But that, squared with what I was contending with, led to a certain realization. Here was a force that I thought was loving, and yet, he had visited something entirely unloving on me. It revolutionized my conception of reality. It left me to pick up the pieces on my own, but it also brought me to a new level of awareness. At the same time, another loving source came to my rescue — my mom. Somehow, this dual experience, of love and non-love, made me question the nature of being, and I asked for the first time in this life, "What is the soul?"

How did that connect with the soul? Was it like, "Who am I really?" Was it that kind of thing?

"What am I doing here? What does this all mean?" That was the first time I remember asking those questions, because I was in a place of pain. The world had initially seemed to be a place of love. But then idealism ended. I saw another side of life. And everything kind of opened up. You see? A force that had created me, and appeared to love me, also dealt a blow to me. How was I to reconcile a force that was both loving and fearsome? So, in a sense, my father came to represent, I guess, a kind of Shiva energy — the destroyer. Initiation by drama, by impact, through something that involves struggle or pain. And it does say something true about the universe, but it's not the whole truth. There's also . . .

Vishnu—the preserver. There's the positive, nurturing side of reality.

Both are valid. I finally came to a point of honoring my father for opening me up to that other side. That wasn't his intention, of course. But he had his own issues, and we've worked through that. In the end, he showed me that life is a balance, that it's got two sides.

Nevertheless, this is a tough lesson for a five year old. But it brings to mind the Chinese word for "obstacle," which has a dual meaning—it also means "opportunity."

Exactly. So, for me, that kind of experience embodies the dual nature of reality. And it sparked initial thoughts about the soul and spirituality.

My next spiritual memory brings me back to when I was nine years old. I'm in Sunday school and I was given this Bible, and it was like one of those things comparable to your first communion or something like that in a Lutheran church. They inscribe it, "On this day..." You know the drill. I remember sitting in Sunday school, thinking, "I don't relate to this. I don't relate to this outer God. I don't relate to this vengeful God. I don't relate to this judging God." And I still have that Bible. Now here's the interesting part: In the back of the book, I wrote, in my nine-year-old hand, something vulgar about the church. It was a common obscenity. And then, you see, I crossed it out, and under it I wrote, "Excuse, please."

In a sense, here was my declaration of independence from a system of thought that was going to tell me what to believe. On the other hand, in asking to be excused for my emotional response, I was also asking for redemption or forgiveness. Those are really loaded Christian words, I know. But there's a mood in there, like a step back and a step forward. And sure enough, I found myself, even in my teen years, circling around Christianity.

If you grew up in the Midwest, at that time, there were certainly Jewish people, but not much more religious variety than that. Actually, there were Lutherans, there were Catholics, and there were Jews. That was my neighborhood. There weren't Muslims. There weren't Hindus. And so everything had to be, at least for a time, found within the context of the Judaeo-Christian tradition. If I were going to find anything, it would have to be from within those parameters.

And there were certain things I liked about the Judaeo-Christian tradition. The passionate Christ appealed to me, but the judgmental God of the Bible, well, no. It sounded like a mafia God to me. It's like, "You see what I've done for you? If you don't obey, if you don't worship me, I'm going to mess you up. I'll take it all away. I mean business." That never really squared with my own experience of what love should be, must be. So, after that, I found myself trying to find God in the mystics, as it were. I mean, when you're eleven years old, or whatever, people don't say, "Hey, here's the Christian mystics; read this." But you eventually find it on your own.

Sure.

Later, my father had a copy of a Gnostic text, specifically one translated by Elaine Pagels. I read that at some point, probably when I was in junior high, and that started to open up another aspect of Christianity. Here you learned to take on Jesus's qualities and to become like him — that was the path.

There's also *The Imitation of Christ*. I found that, too, when I was in high school.

Yeah, yeah. And, actually, I was blessed when I was a teenager: My church had this young 27-year-old pot-smoking pastor, the assistant pastor, who was the youth minister, of sorts. He presented an entirely different picture of Christianity, emphasizing service and compassion. So we ran a little coffee house in the church, and folk singers would come through. We would do musicals, your usual gospel stuff, and Jesus Christ Superstar and stuff like that. Inevitably, I would play Judas.

This was the 1970s. You know, post-Vietnam, take-all-the-drugs-you-want '70s. So I got a much broader view of Christianity at this point, which, in a sense, has sort of stayed with me.

Let me ask you a question here. You were talking about the vengeful God of the Bible, and that you were attracted to the compassionate nature of Jesus. Now, I was going along the same road, the same line of thinking, when I was younger. But then what happened, consistently, was that I encountered Christians who said, "Jesus is the only way." Although the personality of Jesus still rang true for me, there was this exclusivist Christian idea, even amongst very, very liberal Christians. They seemed to say that unless you surrendered to Jesus, you were going to go to hell. So I would always wonder, "What about people from before Jesus's time? Or people from other lands?" I wondered about them. Were they all destined to hell, simply because they didn't know Jesus?

You're right. This troubled me back then, too. It troubles me now. But the teachings of the East helped me with that, and they actually helped me reclaim Christianity. Because to say, "Jesus is *the* way" — that's a bit misleading. I read it more like the Taoist would: Jesus is "The way." And if you find "the way" — however you find it and whatever it means to you — you have found Jesus, in one form or another.

Oh, I see.

I find congruence there. The way of the Christ *is* the way of the Tao — it simply means the way to the Truth. Finished. It's not meant to be sectarian. We are free to seek the company of teachers and the example of teachers that can show light on that way, and we have to walk this path ourselves. This is true Christianity, or Hinduism, or whatever. Call it what you will.

One thing I still have a tremendous problem with, though, is this idea of needing to be saved. In fact, the whole idea of sin is a bit strange, isn't it? Well, I can reconcile sin in terms of *samskaras* or *karma*. Okay, we did something in the past, and the fruits or reactions await us. Fine. And I can see that, yes, we come into this life with a set of tendencies, and we have to deal with them. If that's sin, then okay. But I don't like the way the word is used, how spiritual leaders tend to use it to manipulate people; so I won't generally use it. There's something more important than sin: There's a sense of whether we're on the way or we're not.

True. I agree. But, at the same time, we should be consciously aware— we should take stock and notice if our activities are pulling us away from our spiritual path. In this sense, we need to avoid "sin."

Of course. Sin, as you say, refers to those things that pull us away from grace. And so, yes, we should avoid sin. But this idea of a reckoning, if you will, of some God that's up there with a check sheet, keeping score—that doesn't work for me. The other thing is related to sin: this need to be saved. My experience now in meditation and yoga and chanting has to do with immanence, the presence of God—I guess you can call it the perceived presence of the Soul, the Atma, or whatever. But there's this sense of an intelligence, a presence of love that exists from form to form, but that's not bound by form. With such a beauty permeating our being, I don't know that I need to be saved. I know that I need to work toward cultivating my awareness of that transcendent being, and that if I am to be saved—if we're still going to use that word—it's in developing my capacity to deliver myself to that supreme goal. Grace is required, no doubt. My free choice involves making the necessary effort to shift my awareness—to be in alignment with ultimate reality. I must act. I can't wait for being saved. No. I must save myself.

Yes, it's not just about faith but about exerting some effort. In fact, the Bible says, "Faith without works is dead." But perhaps the idea of being saved originally applies to the guru principle—the idea of meeting someone who sets you on the path and who gives direction.

Right. I believe that. Again, when Christ says "only through Me," he has to be referring to a general principle. It's what I now see as the guru principle.

In fact, Jesus was the guru in Palestine, 2,000 years ago. If you look at that New Testament verse—"No man comes to the Father except through me"—it uses an extremely present-tense form of the verb. The Greek word is *erketai*, which means "can presently come." In other words, at that time, and in that place, Jesus was the guru. But most people don't read it that way; they prefer an exclusivistic Christianity.

Interesting, but, yes, the guru for that time, and others arise as the need presents itself. But the important thing is this: Only through that guidance, through that awareness, will you find eternal life or wake up to that aspect of your nature, which has, in a sense, always been here, will always be here.

Well, that's certainly a more mature understanding than usual . . .

Right. And there are Christians who come to exactly these conclusions. They're usually the mystics. Unfortunately, Christianity has barely tolerated its own mystical tradition. In fact, the Church has systematically silenced them, often for political reasons. Islam has a similar attitude toward its Sufis. That's just the way of things in this current age, the Kali-yuga.

Chanting is a big part of that mystical tradition. All religious scriptures talk about the efficacy of chanting, but it's downplayed in the more conventional forms of religion. It's the mystics who seem to give chanting its due. So, let's begin by hearing about your introduction to the mystical East.

My initial encounter with things Eastern was when I was kid, when I was twelve. I got into a discussion with a Hare Krishna guy in the airport in Miami.

Gee, I wonder if it was me.

Really?

Well, it's not beyond the realm of possibility.

Ah. I would say my motivations weren't entirely spiritual. I was at a point in my preadolescence in which things that pissed my parents off had tremendous positive value to me. Talking to a Hare Krishna guy while waiting to change planes was probably just a calculated way to upset my parents.

[laughter] Right, right.

So he was talking to me about the *Bhagavad Gita*, which, honestly, I'd never heard about until that point, and we were actually having a kind of interesting discussion. My parents got really upset . . .

They were right there with you?

No, they were a little ways down. I had wandered off a bit. Then, it was like, "Where is he? Where's David?" And when they turned around, they saw me talking to a guy with a shaved head and an orange robe. So it was like, "Oh, no!" You had to see them: They're waving their hands and everything, trying to get me away, and suddenly I realized I had to go. So I took the *Bhagavad Gita* and ran off with it. In effect, I basically stole the *Gita* from a Hare Krishna guy when I was twelve. You know, in the yoga world, we say that everything you do incurs a certain amount of karma, and I look back and I say, "Steal the the *Bhagavad Gita* when you're twelve, and you're doomed to read it when you're twenty-five." In fact, even to finish working that one off, you may have to spend the rest of your life chanting Krishna's name. [laughter] So that was planted right there, in my life, and I actually did read through it a little bit at that time. It sat on the shelf for a very long time, sort of sleeping and unfolding.

Like a time bomb.

A time bomb, yes. So there was that experience, and I guess as a musician I was attracted to Eastern things, too: For example, a lot of the George Harrisonisms, you know, were really some of my favorite tunes. Even when I was a kid — when I was nine, I taped George Harrison's *Within you, Without You* on an old reel-to-reel with a splicing block. I cut it up into a bunch of pieces and put it back together in a kind of random, different order, creating a sort of otherworldly sound. This technique is known as "musique concrête." But those things—mystical, psychedelic, Eastern—appealed to me then in a way I couldn't really explain at the time. Eastern-tinged music touched me in a really significant way. I was exposed to that early on. I went to summer camp for a couple of years, in fact, where the chaplain would lead the hymns with an interesting instrument: the *harmonium*. [laughter] Right. I remember thinking back then, "One day I gotta get one of those," which indeed I did.

From here did you move on to a more pronounced interest in India and things Eastern?

Well, I didn't, actually. This is the funny thing. I ended up in India not because I wanted to go there. There was a point at which I put all things spiritual down—it wasn't for me, and I was sure of that. I moved to Hollywood to work in the film industry. I continued to be a musician, though . . .

What did you play?

Well, I studied with the jazz singer, Eddie Jefferson, for a little while as a singer. I'd pick up other instruments, too, and I'd really get into them, like xylophones and accordians—I played in a number of ensembles with these instruments. I played in Gamelan orchestras, where we played in basically two tunings: *sléndro* and *pélog*, which are five and seven degree scales that don't really conform with Western scales at all.

I made experimental films, too, creating soundtracks with basic musical forms, electronic techniques, tape manipulation, oscillators, and so on. As I think about it, I got a job as a film editor when I was still in college. I was 19—I just needed a job and I wandered into a production agency. Because I had been a musician they felt they could make me an editor. Go figure. So I became an assistant film editor for some time and Francis Ford Coppola happened to come through Madison, Wisconsin, while I was going to school there, to make some political commercials. The short version: They were looking for people to come in and help and I ended up working for Dean Tavoularis, who was Coppola's art director at the time—I became his assistant. That got me some connections in Hollywood and ultimately I got an internship at Columbia Pictures Studio for a summer, which had me moving out to California. I went back there with a whole gang of friends after college, mostly intent on making a living in the film industry.

Where did you go to college?

The University of Wisconsin at Madison, which is sort of the Berkeley of the Midwest. I mean, Madison's tremendously wide open for a city of its size. It's a very cosmopolitan place. Anyway, I moved out to Hollywood with a lot of my peer group from college and we started working in the film industry. I still had ambitions as a musician, but it seemed wiser to be making a living doing something that people actually paid me $2,000 a week to do—I could get back to the music later.

True.

So that's the background, and because of that I spent much of my mid-20s devoted to the world of sense pleasure. That was my life, and spirituality was very far away. Now, I had my initial contact with yoga because I had a back problem that wouldn't go away. Some friends started practicing yoga in Los Angeles in the 1980s and said I should come. So I went, and it helped my back. I was really indifferent to the "OM" part of it, the chanting, the metaphysics. I was ensconced in Hollywood life and couldn't care less about the spiritual stuff. Guess what? I was also very depressed at that time. A couple things happened. As much as I was engaging the sensual world, I was also extremely weary of it. Hollywood was not really serving me in my quest for meaning. I was enjoying, but I felt vacant—nothing really mattered. But Hollywood was cool. Ultimately, believe it or not, I came to see it as a great and holy place.

Hollywood?

Yeah. People come to Hollywood with all kinds of expectations— fortune, fame, self-fulfillment of a certain kind—and are generally greeted with nil. And so you say, "I want," and the universe says, "No." You try to control the timing of things, and you simply have to wait. In the face of all your attachments and desires, the universe says, "no," and you spend a tremendous amount of time staring at the void. You have all of your needs and wants and ambitions—along with stark refusal from the universe.

The doors of Hollywood open sometimes to those who are more or less desire-less, and also to those people who are incredibly driven and ruthlessly ambitious. Ultimately, of course, there's a price. But so you spend a lot of time staring at the void, at emptiness and disillusionment, and ultimately you start to ask those questions again: "What am I here for? What does it all mean?" There are a lot of people dealing with that in Los Angeles and I think this is one reason why yoga is so popular there, why it is one of the epicenters of things yoga right now.

That's an extremely interesting take on the Hollywood experience . . .

Well, it's true. People have a lot of time on their hands, often with more money than not. Or even without money, it's a place where you really have to stare into yourself and ask what all this means. So many of the things that Hollywood offers turn out to be specters, *maya*, illusion, and you have to contend with that, and also, in turn, with yourself. So there are a lot of spiritual opportunities there, underneath the surface. And I have met many, many, very spiritual people in Hollywood, all trying to come to grips with this paradox of seeing beyond the illusion. But at the same time, they're working to create it. That's the paradox. But I found, pre-India, my world had kind of collapsed. I was so depressed I couldn't get off the couch.

Sounds serious. This was no doubt a turning point.

Yes. Somewhere in the mist of all this I had a compelling dream: I was moving at high speed through a formless void. Strangely, there was little visual imagery in the dream, and there was no sound. There was almost no content. I really can't describe it. But I felt myself moving extremely fast and somehow the universe around me was endlessly branching out. There was a thunderclap and a sort of lightning bolt at the base of my spine, and an electric current surged upward in my body. My head and heart exploded into this ball of white light. I woke up feeling intense love, with everything, and I felt myself to be in great intimacy with everything. It was like the whole world was somehow part of my being. In every direction I saw that there was nothing but love. There was complete oneness.

That's a bit different than a baseball zeroing in on your head.

A little different, yeah. [laughter] I didn't want to move from that spot—from the place where I attained that awareness. There was a problem, though—I couldn't hold onto it, and I fell back asleep. In this same dream, a grandfatherly voice appeared and gave me this little blue spark. It seemed to be the smallest thing in the universe and yet it contained everything within it. He gave it to me, and he said, "Meditate on this," and then he went away.

A spark?

A spark, yes, a little glowing blue thing. It was big and little at the same time, inconceivably. He said to meditate on this, and I didn't really know how. I had been to a few yoga classes at this point, and so I sat and tried to meditate. But it really didn't work. Now, that grandfatherly voice . . . it was like some sort of guide that just appeared to me. So I maintained a relationship with the voice, at least in my head. Some time went by. I'd been invited on several occasions to meet a number of spiritual teachers and I refused. But some friends of mine eventually became involved with Gurumayi Chidvilasananda of the Shaivite lineage, traceable to Swami Muktananda and, before him, Swami Nityananda. I'd been invited to meet her. Actually, I'd been invited to meet Swami Muktananda in the 1980s, before he took *maha-samadhi* [passed away], but I wasn't into it.

So a friend of mine had become involved with this ashram, and she befriended someone there who had been a longtime devotee and was told that it was time for her to leave the ashram—to go out and make a living for a time. She—this ex-ashram person—had been editing videotapes and things for the Muktananda organization in India, and when she came to Los Angeles she was given my name as a contact, somebody who might be able to help her get a job. So she called me up, using the name of our mutual friend. As it turned out, I was able to help, and I got her some work. So that was fine. A few months later, she called me up and said, "Hey, do you remember me?" I did. So she said, "You know who Gurumayi is, right?" I said, "Yeah, and if you're going to ask me to come have *darshan* with her, you should know that I've been asked 500 times. The answer was no then, and it's still no."

But that wasn't her intention. "No," she said. "It's not that. They need someone to go to India to make some films for them. They asked me if I knew someone who could do the job, and I sat down in meditation to see who might be right. And you appeared to me as the person who was meant to go." I was a bit surprised—and suspicious. I responded like this: "Well, that's really an interesting way of getting a job. It *is* a job, right? I don't have to join the ashram or anything like that. They're hiring me to go to India and to do some work for them, and that's that." She said, "Yeah, why don't you just talk to these people." I did just that—I rang up some of their representatives in New York, but the money they offered kind of sucked compared to what I was accustomed to. So, initially, I turned the job down. There were a few other things brewing in my life at that time, too, all of which I was counting on as coming through. But a few months passed and nothing else materialized, and now I'm dead broke. So I had a brief moment of clarity. I began to ask myself: "Hey Dave, you ever been to India?" The answer came quickly: "Ummm . . . no."

"What do you think the odds are that you'll ever get another job in India, paying you to go there?"

"Well, probably kind of minimal."

"Well, you need a job now, dontcha?"

"Well, yeah."

So I called them up, and I said, "Hey, is that job still open?" They said, "Well, yes it is, but we needed you to go some time ago and, as it now stands, you'd have to leave next week," I said, "Hmm. Well, okay, I can do that." And once I committed to it, I stood by and watched how a million things came together, almost miraculously, with hardly any effort at all. They worked out the visa thing for me as well as a bunch of other stuff. I mean, in a week I was on a plane to India.

Amazing. How long did you stay?

Initially, I was there for four months.

Did you go with someone?

I met one of their representatives in New York, changed planes at Kennedy, and he met me there, and . . .

I mean, to go to India without any knowledge of Indian culture can really be a trip. That's why it's good to go with someone who knows the region.

Somebody from the ashram came with me and took me around. We flew from New York to Bombay, where we went to the ashram in Ganeshpuri. When I got there, within hours of arriving, they showed me to my room and I fell asleep. It was a very long flight, of course, and I was extremely tired. And so I fell into a dream. Actually, this dream was almost identical in every way to the dream I had had several years before. The only difference being that before it was like a bolt of lightning at my spine; this time it appeared that a snake was uncoiling in my spine. At the same time, the same burst of light, the same feeling of love everywhere, intimacy with the universe—it was all there again. Some time after that, a few hours later, I was taken to meet Gurumayi, and she laughed and laughed and laughed. She seemed to know something that I didn't. Her laugh was saying, "Look how long it took you to get here and look what you had to go through to reach this point." I looked at her, and I was not expecting an encounter with a guru to be like this. She's a beautiful woman, full of delight and just laughing and laughing, always laughing. I said, "Well, Gurumayi, I had this strange dream a few hours ago and . . ." She looked at me straight in the eyes and said, "snakes, snakes," and she started laughing again. Amazing. Then I look up, and there's a picture of Swami Muktananda on the wall. I look at it and I say, "That's the guy! That's this grandfather dude who showed up in my dream." She wasn't surprised.

How did you know it was him? You didn't see him in the dream, right? No form.

I knew. It's funny how you know those things. I didn't see him in the dream; he was just a presence. But I looked up, and there he was. I just had that feeling like, "Oh, there he is again."

And I looked back at my life at that time, realizing that in some ways even my disbelief, my resistance – all this stuff brought me to this place. It *had* to be like that. I didn't want yoga. I didn't ask for it. I wasn't seeking it, and yet, in some way, I was heading toward it just the same. So there I was, and now I was all lit up with this expansive feeling of ecstasy. I just wanted to hang out there and see if I could remain in that place forever. For me, this brings to mind the *Bhagavad Gita*, which begins with the doubt of Arjuna. That's actually very powerful for me. Christianity kept asking me to have faith, but I didn't have faith. Along comes yoga, and it says, in effect, "Start where you are – start with what you have." The doubts of Arjuna speak to most people today. We're not coming from a place of faith, not really. At least I wasn't. I was on the battlefield and I didn't want to fight; I had given up. I went for a life of illusion. I could see how I had been searching through that lens, and I could see how yoga was going to use everything I had in this process.

The job, as it turned out, was not for me. It didn't work out. They wanted an online editor, and they got an offline editor. So in effect, they'd hired the wrong guy. The funny thing is, I had this astonishing spiritual experience upon arriving there – so, on another level, I *was* the right guy. So there was much consternation about all of that, and they tried to figure out what to do with me . . . I mean, I was there. Anyway, they gave me talks by Swami Muktananda and Gurumayi, usually discoursing for an hour or two at a time. They wanted me to edit them down.

They gave you audiotapes?

Videos and old film footage. They asked me to go through the material and cut each topic down into fifteen-minute versions that would be suitable for showing to beginners, which I was. So for the first four months that I was in India, I spent each day listening to Swami Muktananda and Gurumayi talk about their realizations regarding the philosophy of yoga, quoting from the Upanishads, later scriptural sources, and other stuff too. I digested that information and edited it into fifteen-minute packets about varied spiritual topics. It was a tremendous gift that I was able to sit there and basically absorb Eastern philosophy. And more than that: Not just listen to it, but process it into little packets, which increased my understanding of it. In the meantime, I'm going through all kinds of spiritual changes and I just wanted to stay in India. I couldn't think of any good reason to go back to Hollywood at that point.

I understand. And they were paying you for this, correct?

Yes. They were quietly depositing each paycheck in a US bank account for me. After some time, I realized I had plenty of money to just stay in India. So I did. Instead of editing, they gave me some *seva*, some service, to do in the ashram. They had a school across the road. They told me to go teach at the ashram's school, which I wasn't really qualified for, but in some ways it was perfect. I found myself with a bunch of eight and nine year olds, with no set curriculum. I could more or less just invent the teaching schedule, and the classes.

Were they Indian kids or Western kids?

Indian and Western. So the instruction was actually in English. At the school, there was an old *harmonium*. I had come to India with a couple of Western instruments, not really knowing what I was going to do in my spare time. I brought a little Appalachian dulcimer, which is portable, and this little Chinese accordion, which is also very portable. Initially, when I was in the employee phase of working in the ashram, they didn't really invite me to the chants. All that stuff was going on, but I wasn't a part of it. I think if I had been a seeker there, somebody would have taken me by the hand and said, "Hey, this is this, this is what is going on, this is what it means." But, no, I was there on business. On some level, I was free to kind of ask questions or not. And so the chants would be going on, either kirtans or classical *bhajan*, but there were also everyday text chants, where various *gitas* were sung as part of the ashram discipline.

By various *gitas* do you mean *gitas* from the *Bhagavata Purana*, or the *Gita Govinda*, the *Bhagavad Gita*?

Yeah, all of it, as well as various *stotrams*, traditional songs, etc. So there was a vast amount of textual material that was being chanted. I would by and large hang out across the road from the ashram and listen. Just listen. I learned how to play some of the kirtans on my accordion or on my dulcimer. It was only when I started working at the school that I actually kind of jumped into the kirtans in a systematic way. There was an old *harmonium* there, as I said, and the kids knew a lot of kirtan, a lot of traditional kirtan. We would sing every day before school, so, in effect, the school children taught me how to chant the kirtans. The ashram had an official strategy on how that was done, but at that time I wasn't really invited into it. I mostly chanted with nine year olds. That's how I really discovered kirtan.

Were you inclined to it right at the beginning? Did you like the sound of it, the feel of it?

Yeah, that was the thing. From the very beginning, I found the ashram music fundamentally compelling. I didn't think, "Oh, this is weird." I found it really beautiful and it affected me in a way that was totally Other—it was beyond mind and beyond understanding. I also found that I could memorize Sanskrit very easily, as if I already knew it.

Without studying the language? Just through the songs?

Yeah, I could just memorize the verses, so I found I was able to chant quite easily. Even without knowing the language, it still had an effect on me. I guess this is important still, because my way into kirtan was not as a seeker, not as a devotee. It just happened.

It happened organically, in a spontaneous way.

Right. So, here I am. I don't think of myself as a seeker of things Eastern, and yet I just found myself in a ringside seat, you know? It's interesting, though—musically, I had been writing things in that vein, even before going to India. Now, looking back, it seems as though I was trying to create mantras on my own. But these were clearly baby steps, the fledgling endeavors of a newcomer, carrying on from some past life. I would sing "wordlessly," if you know what I mean, and, more than writing songs, per se, I really loved to sing without words. Scatting, humming and vibrating incoherent sounds. So when I encountered mantras for the first time, I realized that I had in some ways already been in a process of trying to discover them within myself. They seemed very familiar. All of a sudden I was exposed to a whole tradition of music, of singers who were in some ways like me. What I was trying to do was to use sound that would transport me beyond my mind.

Okay, so, while in India, I encountered real mantras, and not only did they seem very familiar to me, but they were also intoxicating to sing, delicious to sing. They're liberating to sing. And since I was sitting in the middle of it, I started to discover the meanings of the mantras, the meaning of these obscure sounds. I began to learn that in Indian history there was a long tradition of songwriters, ecstatic poets, who went around singing of that experience. The *bhakti* movement itself is a very interesting phenomenon in that it was amazingly democratic, theologically. *Bhakti* poets told us that love itself was equally present in everyone, and that no priesthood, in the end, could ultimately be the arbiter of that. It was revolutionary, especially at that time, in Medieval India.

They were teaching simple mantras to people who were by and

large uneducated, even though many of the *bhaktas* themselves were educated and came from noble Brahmin families. They renounced all that and went around singing their ecstatic hymns of love, often for crowds of people who were from lower castes. Some of these poets and spiritual leaders, of course, were from these lower caste families themselves.

They broke down the boundaries, and they opened up the tradition for everyone.

Right, they broke down those boundaries, first by refusing to recognize the caste system, which permeated India, as it still does. Actually, it took enormous courage—their message was that God's love was not constricted by those categories.

They were reminiscent of Jesus in some ways, weren't they? He's like the ultimate *bhakta*.

Exactly! They're saying, "Look inside yourself! Cultivate ecstasy in your own being! Do this first for yourself and, by that, you are in effect doing it for the whole world. The world is affected by your vibration. Yes, you can memorize the Vedas, but that's not going to take you there. You need more. You need love. Cultivate this experience in yourself." For me, especially given my history with Christianity—that was a very potent message.

And so I also started writing kirtans, like the *bhakti* poets. At first, I felt guilty about writing such things. Most kirtans are traditional, written by adepts, and they are passed down by serious practitioners. People would tell me, "Oh, this one is very old and it was handed down," etc., etc. The implication was that somehow these were all written already, you know, at a more sacred time, and there was no need to write any more. "How dare you try to write them yourself."

Tradition gave them some authority.

Right. But when I encountered the tradition in a deeper way, I realized that these singers were inventing the songs; that's what they did. In their ecstasy, they were inventing the songs, and the fact that they had done it then did not in any way mean one could not do it now. There's a similar phenomenon in Christianity, where 2,000 years ago, Jesus's time, is idealized—that was the time to be alive! But really we're here now. We need to bring this into the modern era. That's what the *bhakta* poets were doing in their day. It's useless for us today to act like a *bhakti* movement from the fifteenth century; we need to adapt it to modern times.

When you talk about the devotees who wrote songs way back when, are you talking about devotees like Surdas and Tulsidas, people like that?

Absolutely. Mirabai. Yes. But also, thousands of nameless *bhaktas* who came up with some tune that caught on. Everybody started singing it, and eventually the song survives the singer.

And all of that material was based on the Vedic tradition as well as on personal experience.

Right.

And so if you know the tradition and you're having your own experiences, why not write original songs today, in modern language, that really speaks to people, to our contemporaries?

Exactly. I started to do it and I soon found that people liked it—the songs actually worked! It's interesting that when you're writing a kirtan, in the instance of its inception, it's a very ecstatic process. The best things I've ever written took all of maybe two or three minutes. It was just sort of there. Now, for those listening to the kirtan, or taking part in the chanting, their appreciation will be commensurate with their realization, with what's going on inside of them.

I can see that. If one is *rasik*, that is, a cultured listener, one can feel the *rasa* and the *bhava*—the feeling and emotion—of what you're trying to get across. But someone who's not spiritually cultured, might not.

Right. There have been times when I'm trying out a new kirtan and the crowd would sing it back differently. I feel myself thinking, "No, it goes like this!" But they'd sing it back, and they'd be like, "No, it goes like that."

As an artist, in some ways, I also had to pry my fingers from the process — to avoid trying to control it and instead allowing myself to serve it. That's a process that's still unfolding, the process of seeing the kirtan as an act of surrender.

It's an art. One has to learn to see kirtan as give and take. The people responding to your chanting are as much a part of the process as the person who writes the songs and the person who's leading.

Right. It's like the universe in miniature. In kirtan, everybody, in effect, is at the center of the universe, theologically and experientially. What you do has a direct impact on what happens around you. If you really get into a kirtan, you can experience that — trying to surrender to a bigger and more expansive consciousness than the one we're ordinarily limited by. But everybody's both leading and following, in terms of our relationship with the divine and with love itself — we come to see ourselves as both leader and follower.

It's a _mandala_. It's circular.

Correct. It strikes me as being enormously significant — yoga and religion ask us to open up in this way. But I'll tell you, traditional systems can close you down just as much as open you up, depending on how you approach them. When I was in India, at the ashram, they had a very specific way that they liked to do kirtans, and you departed from that at your peril. My instincts as an artist were pushing against this. I saw virtue in it, but I also saw virtue in doing things my own way.

This is always a difficult thing. When an artist, especially, joins a spiritual movement, they tend to run up against this wall. They're asked to do things in a traditional way, and then their creative sense says, "But we can also do it this way, too, and in that way." I guess the trick as an artist is in seeing the virtue of the tradition and adapting it without losing its essence.

Exactly. But if you're too inventive, you're almost always put on a trip. In my case, I spent a lot of time singing in choirs. Where I was coming from, to sing harmony, for example, was an expression of great bliss. Still, they'd accuse me: "That's your ego!" And I'd be like, "No, that's my bliss. It's your ego that's telling me not to do this." So we would go back and forth.

But the evidence you gave, and I think it's legitimate, is that one *can* do this. That's in fact what they were doing in 15th- or 16th-century India. They were coming in the tradition—respecting their predecessors, whether Vaishnava, Shaivite, or Shakta—and yet they weren't just singing things from the Vedas; they were making up their own songs and their own melodies and their own ways of doing it.

That's right.

So it's definitely legitimate. I think the only question is this: Exactly *who* has the right to create or to invent? Who can write kirtans on behalf of their tradition? This would be the one bone of contention, I'm sure. Maybe they would say you have to be accomplished in your particular practice before you can assert your individuality, before you could presume to create on behalf of the divine.

That's what I came to; I surrendered as long as I could. I kept trying to be a good boy and to do what they wanted me to, and it was not without attainment. I saw the message in it. The idea that the singer surrenders himself to the song, that the artist surrenders his own needs to the effect of the experience — these are all important things to know and to appreciate. One needs to realize, "Look, it's not all about you."

Right.

But water will always seek its own level. You can't stop it. People have to use the talents God has given them, right? That being said, if an unqualified person starts his own kirtan, it will lack juice; it won't have that spiritual potency. So, buyer beware. I continue to struggle with that. Once their rules were removed, I still found that there's an inherent *dharma* in the chant that you can't depart from. It's like, this is what the chant wants. I boomerang when I work against it and I'm ecstatic when I'm there, when I'm going with the flow. So let's see where it goes.

Let's backtrack a little at this point. So, you were in India becoming more involved in the Siddha Yoga tradition of Gurumayi. Did you take initiation in that tradition?

I didn't take *sannyasa*. I didn't become a monk or a swami. But I received initiation in that I was given what they call *shaktipat*.

Shaktipat, right. The transferal of spiritual powers by touch. And did you get a name?

You know, it's interesting, I went up and asked for a name and Gurumayi said, "You already have one." I said, "What?" She said, "Dave. It means God."

Oh, right, Deva, the Sanskrit form of it.

Right, as in Gurudev or Mahadev. I really wanted a spiritual name, though. [laughter]

For our readers: Could you briefly define Siddha Yoga?

Siddha Yoga is based on Tantra and Kashmir Shaivism, which are non-dual traditions. The directive of Siddha Yoga is very simple: Look within yourself to find God. With focused intention, become established in this loving and ecstatic awareness. In the light of this consciousness, open your eyes and heart to the world.

It's not an easy matter, of course. In the experience of *shaktipat*, you are able to glimpse what feels to be the truth of your being, and you understand that everyone has the potential to see this within themselves. But you can't hold onto this experience.

Yes, in Vaishnava traditions, they say that the bliss of the impersonal Brahman usually leads to fall down, because the soul thirsts for interpersonal relationship. The idea of being one with God has certain limitations, but impersonalists tend to ignore these limitations, and they identify with God. This identification cannot stand. Along these

lines, the *Gita*, in the beginning of its Twelfth Chapter, advises theism as opposed to monism, or worship of a personal divinity as opposed to an amorphous void. Krishna says that it's difficult for personal entities—like us—to maintain any kind of relationship with a nonentity, or an abstraction, even if it's a divine abstraction. He therefore asks Arjuna, and through Arjuna, each of us, to enter into a relationship with Him—people will interact with people, not with concepts. That's why, yes, for the impersonalist, for the person who identifies with God, it's difficult to maintain spiritual realization.

But it can be accomplished. It requires a great deal of practice, or *sadhana*, to maintain this awareness at all times. The dishes still need to be done, sure, and the trash still needs to be taken out. You can't spend all of your time chanting and meditating, So you of necessity start to look at everything you do as a kind of spiritual practice. As you do this, your can start to see God in everyone and everything.

It is most especially difficult to see this when you are under intense pressure, when you are in the grip of your own attachments and disappointments. The genius of the ashram environment is that it models the world in such a way that you have to accept responsibility for your own spiritual progress, and it uses arbitrary and capricious situations—and, often, difficult people—to accomplish this. On one level, it's a kind of cross between an encounter group, a mental institution, and a minimum security correctional facility. Which sounds terrible, but the effect is that you start to see yourself reflected everywhere. Heaven or hell—it turns out to be pretty much your own call.

I understand. Really, you get out of religious institutions what you put into them. They can act as a conduit to the divine. Or they can foster your stagnation. It's up to you.

The fact is that such movements are made up of people. All kinds of people come to all kinds of movements. You might see it like this: There's a clear source, or a clear spring of water that erupts from the earth, and people cluster to drink from it. Now, even if the water itself is pure, the people drinking from it might not be. So spiritual organizations are composed of people in progress, people on a spiritual path. That's already a good starting point.

I agree.

I think the question is this: "What can this person or group teach me?" Without them being finished in their process, is it possible in *my* process that they can be uplifting, that they can take me further? By extension, if this world is not finished or if it appears to be imperfect, can it not, nonetheless, teach me? Is it not, in a sense, my guru?

Right, very good. It brings to mind the Eleventh Book of the *Bhagavata Purana*, where one finds a list of twenty-four gurus—in addition to a perfect master—who can help us along the way. These are creatures and aspects of nature from which we can learn, like the earth, air, sky, fire, pigeons, pythons, the sea, elephants, fish, and so on. For example, air blows on both sweet and foul-smelling things without any discrimination or preference. From this, the spiritual aspirant should learn how to live in the world, unaffected by the dualities of life, like joy and sorrow, and by the objects of the senses. In this way, air is to be seen as a sort of guru.

Beautiful. That's fantastic.

It's along the lines of what you were saying . . .

That's great. I'm glad to hear that it's grounded in tradition in that way, too.

Okay, but let's bring it back to kirtan. How did you become a well-known Western *kirtaniya*?

Hmm. Well, let me begin by saying that I had artistic conflict with Siddha Yoga. It became difficult for me to continue doing music in their temples. At the same time, a yoga studio in Santa Monica, California, called Yoga Works, began wanting to offer kirtan on a regular basis. This would have been in 1997. They asked me to come and start leading a Sunday night kirtan.

How did they know about you?

Someone had visited a Siddha Yoga center and had heard me sing. So they asked for me—they were looking for somebody and so I said I would do it. At the same time, I began to teach meditation in the prison system.

Can you talk a little more about that?

I was doing weekly *satsangs* in two such places, mainly: Terminal Island Prison, which, I know, is a bit of a chilling name, and in Chino, too. Terminal Island is a federal prison and Chino is a state prison—both in Southern California.

There's actually people doing meditation in prisons all over America; yoga is big behind bars. That's a whole other story. In fact, I did a kirtan once at Folsom Prison, you know, as in the Johnny Cash record, backed by an inmate rock band. It was really great. So I was beginning to do this outside of the spiritual organization that fostered it at the invitation of different people. It necessitated a change of tone. You can't talk to people who are incarcerated in that sort of flowery, spiritual organization-type language. They just don't buy it. The point is to get them to participate and to have an experience. You have to change your tone and your terms.

I look at the diversity of my various teachers in this—school children, ashram people (keepers of the *dharma*), and incarcerated ex-drug offenders. All of these people have taught me ways to look at kirtan and various ways to approach it, too. I have to say, chanting in prison is quite a liberating experience. [laughter] Liberating both because of what inherently happens when you're chanting and in the sense of exploding your preconceived concepts.

You mentioned three teachers—the children in India, the ashram people, and the prisoners—but actually the most important one is the fourth one: the Paramatma, the Lord in the heart. Right? From within you, you were getting guidance that helped you sing kirtan.

Oh, yes, of course. Of course. That's ultimately the primal one, the essential one. I guess, just as you said, there's the perfect teacher and then there's your dog. You can get the same thing from both, in a sense, at least if you know how to access the divine. It comes from within.

But then in the yoga studios, people weren't focused on a particular teacher or a particular tradition, not for the most part. In the yoga studios, I had to make this open to anyone, without considering whether you were, say, a Shaivite, a Vaishnava, or a Shakta—or just a person who wants to feel good about themselves—without regard to whoever your primary teacher may or may not be. Many of the people who came had just been practicing yoga *asanas* for some time and had heard that chanting was a way of deepening their practice. They wouldn't necessarily know anything about it.

So I consciously brought myself back to where I was when I was a beginner. In effect, standing across the road from the ashram, listening to the chant, I realized that I was affected by the chant without knowing anything about it. I guess what I'm saying is, as a kirtan leader, I've put my trust in the sounds, in the experience itself, and said, "First you give people the experience, and you let the inherent stuff affect them in the way that it does. After that, let their own interest take them further."

When I interviewed Krishna Das, he said something very, very similar: "Have faith in the chant, in the sound of the chant." He just chants with people and allows the spiritual potency to do the rest.

I do that, too. Yes. But I feel like I'm trying to function on several levels here. I have also found that if I don't explain what the chants mean, at least on some level, people spend the whole time wondering what they're chanting. And then they miss the experience. So I do offer an explanation. The deities evoked in the mantras, for example—I try to explain them in general terms: "These are different aspects of the way we encounter the divine, or love, or whatever name you want to put to it. This one evokes its fierce and terrible aspects; this other one its compassionate aspects; its ability to move through obstacles, etc." I try and put it in those terms, and often I even use Western, almost scientific language.

That's good. People need a basic idea, at least. Then they can chant in a more comfortable mindset. The mantras can do the rest.

Right. This is where, in a sense, as a Westerner, I'm finding my way into this, too. The Western scientific methodology says, "Gather your facts, gather your experiences, and draw your conclusions from that. Can someone else come to the same conclusions through the same experiment?"

This is what makes something a science.

Exactly. So what I'm saying with kirtan is, "Okay, don't believe in it. Let's drop that part of it. How about if you just sing these mantras? Tell me how you feel right now. Now sing these mantras. How do they make you feel? Did it shift the way you felt? What happened to you during the process of chanting?" In this way, they can see the science of chanting in action.

"The science of chanting in action": This brings us to your CDs. Let's devote the remainder of our conversation to what you've personally done with kirtan on your commercially available works; let's talk about your approach to the practice of chanting. You might mention some traditional kirtans that you like, but mainly your work, what you've done.

Well, this draws on my background as a jazz musician, by way of group improvisation and all that. I mean, the melody is defined, the mantra is defined, but in the tradition that I'm coming from, the chant speeds up. Like this kind of wave develops: it starts slowly and then each time it comes around the speed of the chant increases incrementally. So you can end up chanting it two, three, four times the speed that you started with.

It sounds like certain forms of Bengali kirtan, which also start slowly and then build up to a crescendo.

There's actually an entire art and science to doing that. Certain drummers are very expert at that and so purely from an arrangement standpoint, it's going to come around again. The idea is to both advance the narrative in terms of shifting the arrangement slightly, so it has compelling interest, musically, but never to leave the space OF the kirtan, if you know what I mean. So you want to keep people in the pocket of it, in the bubble of it, in the space of it, but you want to shift it slightly. So this can mean the drummer slowly changes rhythms, or the cymbal player starts playing with a different accent. In my case, I add harmony to it, with multiple layers. I will tend to play with fairly large ensembles, too. I'll often have six or eight musicians accompanying me, and so we've developed a whole kind of art of Western kirtan — the bass player comes in, and the bass player drops out. The violin player doubles the melody, the violin player creates a counter melody. An electric guitar player may play something spacious and then all of a sudden, something chunky. I've found that kirtan as a form is allowing me to quote from a lot of traditions of the world. So we're able in the space of a single kirtan to morph from a traditional Indian ensemble into a funk band and then into a bluegrass band and back again. This is what you'll find on my CDs.

How would you define a good kirtan? What are its hallmark signs?

A good kirtan is indisputable. Everyone involved can feel it. Now *that's* science, to go back to what we were discussing a moment ago. Experiment and observation. You engage in kirtan, with full heart, and it gets a particular result. If you can repeat that experience with some certainty, then that's what science is all about. That's the science of kirtan.

And then the music stops. That's science, too. It's so intoxicating to sit there with a group of people and to not move, to scarcely breathe. Time has stopped. Desire has stopped. Mind has stopped. If even only for a fleeting instant, to sit at the edge of that stillness is just such a profound thing. If without believing it, it has the capacity to take you to that place, then something's really happening. So if you add a component of intention to it, *then* let's see what happens.

So a devotional attitude can help?

Intention always helps. But people have to start from where they are. That's fine. All I can do is show up and sit down and start chanting. Beyond that, I have to trust that the practice itself is what's powerful. I'm just there to serve it; I'm just an instrument in this thing. In that sense, it lets me off the hook—it has increased the depth of my heart because it asks me not to posture. It asks me not to pontificate, not to take myself too seriously. If anything, I tell jokes. I found a way to do that. Since we're often sitting cross-legged when we chant, in a lotus position, or in a facsimile thereof, I guess you'd call me a "sit down" comic. Sometimes I tell stories that are meant to put some light into the thing, some laughter into the experience, to say, "You know what? We can be spiritual without taking ourselves too seriously." I just want to invite people into the process, to share with others the beauty and magic of kirtan.

For more information contact:
www.davestringer.com

**RAVIDA DAS**

Dravida Das began his career as an English editor for the Bhaktivedanta Book Trust in 1975, a service he continues to the present moment. From 1983 to 1989 he was part of the team that produced the last six 1,000-page volumes of His Divine Grace A. C. Bhaktivedanta Swami Prabhupada's magnum opus: an English translation and commentary on India's prime jewel of Vedic wisdom, the 18,000-verse Srimad-Bhagavatam (Bhagavata Purana). *He also helped produce the revised version of Srila Prabhupada's nine-volume* Caitanya-caritamrita *during 1995-96 and* Krsna *from 1994-95. In addition to his editing work, he teaches Bhakti Yoga classes at Los Angeles and San Diego ISKCON centers.*

As a result of this immersion in India's ancient spiritual literature, Dravida developed a love for the Sanskrit language, and especially the elaborate Sanskrit prosody of the Bhagavatam, *portions of the* Caitanya-caritamrita, *and other* bhakti *literature. He also developed a taste for the devotional poetry of the Gaudiya Vaishnavas, especially those chanted in complex meters. His expertise and unique abilities in this field have garnered for him international acclaim as a modern-day individualist in the kirtan world.*

✳ ✳ ✳

Okay, let's begin with your background.

My given name is Thomas Stephen Doliner. I was born on Long Island, New York, USA, in December of 1947, into a lapsed Jewish family. I had one brother, five years older. There was no real religion in my upbringing; if anything, I guess I would say my faith revolved around communism — this is what I was brought up with.

My parents idealized the Soviet Union, and my father was active in leftist politics — he was involved locally, at least during my early years, and nationally earlier in his own life. I remember standing on the street as a kid on Election Day and handing out buttons for Adlai Stevenson. We were lower middle class in that my father had trouble finding a decent job because of McCarthyism.

Let me ask: Was it a happy childhood? I mean, it sounds almost as if you were forced into early adulthood. [laughter]

No, not really. It was basically happy. Normal school and play. I was always pretty good in sports. I had my share of friends.

Around the house music was quite important, but it was almost always folk music. And it was, again, usually, songs from the left — "This land is your land, this land is my land" — Pete Seeger, Woody Guthrie, and later Joan Baez, Bob Dylan, and the rest. Also, jazz and a little classical, too. But I never liked rock and roll. My father taught me recorder at five or so and I became quite expert at playing the little flute. Later I played clarinet in grade school and high-school bands and orchestras. I also took up the Western transverse flute. I had a highly developed sense of rhythm. (In his youth, my father had been a drummer in a summer band in the Catskills.) This musical training and rhythmic sense would help me to take easily to the chanting of various Sanskrit mantras, when I took up my search for God.

What kind of schools did you attend?

Schools were average suburban public schools of the 50s and 60s. I was always the head of the class or near to it, and had little time for sports — a little tennis. In high school I gradually became more and more involved in the civil rights movement and the anti-Vietnam War movement.

Oh, that's interesting. Can you talk a little more about that?

I marched on Washington in '64 and '65 and gradually became attracted to Thoreau's and Gandhi's ideas of nonviolent non-cooperation. I planned to turn in my draft card soon after going off to college—I went to the University of Chicago with a full scholarship. This was in 1965, at the age of 17. Since I expected to be incarcerated for draft resistance, I lost my impetus for study.

So what did you do at school?

I hung around with lefties on campus and read books like Dostoevsky's *Notes from the Underground*. Camus and Sartre were other favorite authors. So I fancied myself a principled existentialist—like Sartre, the resistance fighter in World War II. Though the hippie years were starting in 1966, when I dropped out of college, I was totally into the lefty politics antiwar cohort of the youth movement. I didn't even like the Beatles! No spirituality, no religion, no yoga. But I do recall my fascination with Indian music when I first heard a Ravi Shankar album in 1965.

How did spirituality enter your life?

My father's political activities somehow gave him clout with the local draft board, and so although I did turn in my draft card he was able to get me a 4-f deferment. By that time I was a little more reluctant to go to jail, so I accepted it and started a period of drifting from one menial job to another—just sort of floating. In 1968 I went back to school, at NYU.

I took a philosophy 101 course there, trying to figure out what this crazy life is all about. Didn't find much help in the philosophy course. Around this same time, too, I became deeply involved in the antiwar movement and moved into an apartment on the Lower East Side, just a few blocks away from the then New York Hare Krishna temple at 61 Second Avenue. (They had recently moved from their first New York headquarters.)

What about your music? Where did that fit in?

I still liked to play, which now took the form of jamming on a western or eastern (bamboo) flute with the Puerto Rican and black drummers in Washington Square Park or Tompkins Square Park. I would frequent both parks—it was just fun, with a lot of people and all kinds of things going on.

I occasionally saw Hare Krishna devotees chanting along St. Mark's Place, the main drag of hippiedom on the Lower East Side. But I still thought they were kooks at that point. It would be three years before I took an interest in *bhakti*, and before I realized what the Krishna movement was all about. However, the one rock song I was attracted to at the time was "My Sweet Lord"—Harrison's song. I didn't know exactly why, but at the end the chorus sings the Hare Krishna mantra, and I felt as though it was calling out to me, beckoning in some way.

What was the turning point, though? Was there a bridge, of sorts? Was yoga the connection?

Very much so. Yes, that was a big influence. In 1969 I became seriously ill with hepatitis—I just wasn't taking care of my health, you know, poor diet, staying up late. I spent a month in the hospital in July of that year, and I remember seeing the televised first moon walk from my hospital bed. When I got out I stayed at my parents' home and rehabilitated. It's then that I started practicing Hatha-yoga, purely as a way to regain my health.

Soon I was traveling into Manhattan to visit one of the yoga studios there. The first was Yogi Gupta's yoga studio in the fifties on the East Side. Amala Bhakta Das (then known as Shiva Prema Swami) was in charge. I began the standard *asanas* and began to change my diet to vegetarian. I remember a meditation class in which we chanted a Sanskrit mantra. We didn't learn the meaning, but we were chanting it again and again, and I was attracted to the rhythm and the sound of the chant. This was the first time I chanted a mantra with Krishna's name in it—Pundarikaksha was the name we chanted. It means "One who has lotus-like eyes."

About this time I also read *The Way of a Pilgrim*, a story of a Russian Christian ascetic who learns to chant the "Jesus Prayer" — "O Lord Jesus, son of God, have mercy on me, a sinner" — constantly. I was fascinated by the adventures of this pilgrim as told in the book. This is the first time I encountered the idea of repeating a spiritual sound or prayer over and over as a mantra. Later, the idea of *japa*, chanting of the holy name on beads, naturally followed.

So, I guess like most New Yorkers, you were juggling your work—because you had to make a living —and your spiritual path.

Right. Well, I did have a job at this time — this is 1970-71. So, yes, it's true. I was working as an inhalation therapist in a hospital on Long Island. This allowed me to have my own apartment, where I lived alone and would practice Hatha-yoga. I was naturally following certain principles at the time — I was avoiding meat eating, intoxication, gambling and illicit sex, not because someone told me to do it but because it just seemed right; it seemed like it would situate me in the right mindset to achieve my by now burgeoning spiritual goals.

I left Yogi Gupta's place and started going to Integral Yoga on the upper West Side, and later on West 13th Street or so. I was also visiting the Ramakrishna Mission on the East Side, around 94th Street. At Integral Yoga I remember picking up a little booklet on the Hare Krishna *maha-mantra*. Swami Satchidananda's guru was Swami Shivananada, one of whose ashrams was in South Africa somewhere. Apparently he had instituted the nonstop chanting of Hare Krishna some time previously, and this booklet was a commemoration of the 25th year of unbroken chanting. There was one essay after another on the glories of this particular mantra. I got inspired to make the Hare Krishna mantra my meditation mantra and started chanting it systematically, a couple of rounds a day, and trying to chant as much as possible the rest of the day.

I picked up a *Gita* at the Ramakrishna Mission, basically just a translation, and would read it at work in the hospital. The description of the modes of nature and the evils of birth, old age, disease, and death were being played out in front of my eyes—right at my place of work! I even tried to chant and to "project" the energy of the Hare Krishna mantra a few times when patients were dying before me.

So you were getting more and more serious about the spiritual pursuit . . .

Yes, though it was really gradual. And here's what happened: In the spring of 1972 I had been working a year at the hospital and got a week's paid vacation. I took the opportunity to go on a yoga retreat with Integral Yoga people at a convent school complex in the Connecticut countryside. It was great. I read *Be Here Now*—didn't everyone at that point?—kept silent for a week (that was one of the rules), became a vegetarian, did a lot of yoga and *pranayama*, and heard my first kirtan: It was "Jaya Ram, Sri Ram, Jaya Jaya Ram Om." The whole chorus of about 600-700 young people was singing this mantra in a big hall near the end of our retreat. I felt ecstatic. I did a lot of Hare Krishna chanting and meditating on that retreat. I distinctly remember telling one of the young *yogis* as we got on the bus to return to the city that all you need to do is chant Hare Krishna.

The chanting moved you, but were you studying the accompanying philosophy at this point?

I incorporated a few practices into my life and reading was one of them. When I returned from that yoga trip, I tried to take up a raw food diet. It was tough. I was always making juices and eating fruits and nuts. I still lived alone and was going into the city all the time. The leader of the Ramakrishna Mission was the successor to Nikhilananda Swami, who had written a popular edition of the *Gita* at the time. By the time I saw him, around 1972, he'd had a stroke and could only silently sit at the table, with an attendant. But the young yoga master who succeeded him was quite something.

I was attracted to his lectures on the *Gita*, and I started going in on Sunday mornings and doing service and hanging out at the

Mission on 94th Street. Soon I was invited to the "insiders'" lunch, and I could see that this *yogi* wanted me as a disciple. He definitely had some mystic powers—he told me things about myself, such as the fact that I worked at a hospital, that I hadn't told him. Now, someone could have told him about my job, but I saw that he had some inner awareness, or at least that he seemed to be able to read minds. He was a serious *jnani* [on the yogic path of knowledge] and an impersonalist, too—minimizing the form of God and talking about merging into the Supreme. He taught that *bhakti* is for the sentimental masses; the higher practice is *jnana* and Brahman realization. But by that time I had done so much chanting of Hare Krishna that I was naturally attracted to *bhakti*. The Ramakrishna Mission was very eclectic, and if you wanted *bhakti*, they had books for you. I bought their *Uddhava Gita* translation and loved it.

Then I met an Indian expatriate engineer at the Ramakrishna Mission. He was a Rama-*bhakta* and loved to tell me stories from the *Ramayana*. I had a car and he didn't, so on Sundays after the afternoon program at the Mission he suggested we ride together to the Hare Krishna temple in Brooklyn, and then I would drive him home to New Jersey. This is how I first met the devotees. I was attracted, but the kirtan and Deities and all the "noise" were a bit much at first. Of course, the *prasadam* [sacred vegetarian food] was a big attraction, a real challenge to my all-raw mucusless diet. I remember buying a *Teachings of Lord Chaitanya*, one of Prabhupada's books that gives a thorough background on *bhakti* and puts impersonal philosophy in its place, to say the least.

I see. So you were gradually moving from impersonalism and Brahman realization to personalism and devotion to a personal God.

Yes. Soon it was March and there was a big Gaura-purnima festival in the Krishna temple—which began with a Sankirtan party in Central Park. I took part in that, and when I told my "guru," the *yogi* at the Ramakrishna Mission, about it, he was dismissive and even offensive to the devotees. He was trying to break my faith in them, to bring me closer to him, but he had just the opposite effect. I began reading Prabhupada's book on Lord Chaitanya and abandoned Nikhilananda's *Vedanta-sutra* commentary, which I'd been dipping into.

From reading *Teachings of Lord Chaitanya* I became convinced of the philosophy and soon joined the movement, ISKCON. I was happy to find a place where I could chant the Hare Krishna mantra to my heart's content.

After joining ISKCON and immersing yourself in kirtan, did you develop a taste for particular *kirtaniyas*? Were there people who stood out, whose styles and techniques you preferred?

My early influences in kirtan where the luminaries in Brooklyn at the time: Bharadvaja, Vishnu-gada, Jaya Sachinandana, Santosh, Dhira Krishna, Nanda Kishor. I remember my first Ratha-yatra—in Philly in 1973—with Vishnujana Swami leading the kirtan. I danced the whole way and was never more blissful. I felt it was a spiritual breakthrough for me.

In New York we did Hari-nam, street chanting, for three hours a day for most of the first year I was there. Chanting and dancing were my favorite activities. Also at this time I began chanting the verses of the *Bhagavad-gita* and became very attracted to the Sanskrit language as a vehicle for poetic expression. I was memorizing verses by the first week I was in the temple. You remember, I had a musical background, with a strong rhythmic influence from my drummer father and the drummers on the Lower East Side—there was a very pronounced jazz background here, all of which sublimated into an attraction for chanting the verses of the *Gita*, the *Bhagavatam*, and especially the *Caitanya-caritamrta*, when the latter began to come out in '74-'75.

Preferences in kirtan style?

I have no special preferences for kirtan style. The main thing is the *bhakti* of the chanter. I like a simple melody that everyone involved can pick up and follow without too much trouble, and a solid percussion section. I have a special affinity for B. B. Govinda Swami's kirtans, complete with the sax player.

How would you describe your philosophy of kirtan, indicating the relative importance of head and heart, how mantras and/or the holy name have an ability to purify and to aid in spiritual advancement?

Well, I can tell you how it impacted my life: I was adrift, alone, and sinking fast in the early 70s when I came in touch with the holy name of Krishna. I began chanting and, thankfully, I came into contact with the devotees, where I experienced kirtan full force in the Brooklyn temple — and all that chanting healed me.

Lord Chaitanya says *namnam akari bahudha nija-sarva-shaktis tatrarpita:* "The Lord has countless names, in which He's invested all his energies." And we hear from the *Padma Purana, abhinnatvan nama-naminoh:* "The Name and the Named are not at all separate." So when you chant you associate with Krishna — and that's the most purifying and uplifting thing in existence. My years in the Brooklyn temple were saturated with a lot of kirtan: *mangal arotik* in the early morning; three hours of Sankirtan out in the streets, pretty much on a daily basis; evening kirtan back at the temple — or, on Saturday nights, a couple of hours of *"maha"* Hari-nam in Times Square.

From the beginning, my heart leapt when I heard the *kartals* and *mridanga* strike up. My awareness was also infused with *Teachings of Lord Chaitanya*, as I mentioned, and Prabhupada's other books. The real experience of bliss in kirtan, the opening of the heart to affection for Krishna and His devotees, my sense of mission in life — my whole life was transformed and it was all due to the power of the holy name.

Really, I don't have a separate philosophy of kirtan. The basics are obvious: the most important aspect is the purity and *bhakti* of the chanter. There are so many kirtans out on tape or CD now, but my overwhelming preference is still Srila Prabhupada's kirtans because of the pure *bhakti* that comes through. I listen almost exclusively to Srila Prabhupada's kirtan.

Sankirtan, or congregational chanting, is a combination of meditation, glorification, and prayer. The first thing is to hear. I'm convinced that not enough emphasis is placed on the need to "just" hear the words, the syllables of the mantra. If we just think "Hare

Krishna, Hare Krishna . . ." as we're in kirtan, if we've focused the mind fully on the thirty-two syllables of the mantra, the name can work His magic on our consciousness. This is the "yoga" part of Sankirtan, so to speak.

In addition, we should feel exuberant in our glorification of the Lord. If we're not, we're doing something wrong. In the temple, I like to feel that the Deities are hearing our glorification of Them and are pleased — and out on Hari-nam, outside, there is added bliss because you're glorifying the Lord to the masses and trying to attract them to Krishna. This is so special. It has to be experienced to be understood.

Finally, the kirtan is also a prayer to Krishna to lift us up and reinstate us as His servants. We've fallen from that condition, and chanting brings us back — it reminds us of who we really are in the spiritual realm. It cures us of our spiritual amnesia. Meditation, glorification, and prayer — it's a complete package of transcendental absorption for head and heart.

Since you're so well versed in the ancient texts, are there any scriptural passages that you particularly like, or poetic stanzas that emphasize chanting or kirtan?

Oh, there's so many! Here's one from an anonymous author that I really like [Chants Sanskrit and then translates from memory]:

> *Of sweet things, it's the sweetest you will taste at any time;*
> *Of things that bring good fortune, it's the perfect paradigm;*
> *Of things that purify, it purifies most powerf'lly;*
> *The Holy Name of Sri Hari is surely all that be.*

Or, there's another great one:

> *"Sri Krishna, the Personality of Godhead, who is the Paramatma [Supersoul] in everyone's heart and the benefactor of the truthful devotee, cleanses desire for materialistic enjoyment from the heart of the devotee who has developed the urge to hear His messages, which are in themselves virtuous when properly heard and chanted."*

I can feel the purification going on when I chant. I feel closer to Krishna; I feel His love expanding into my heart. Here are another couple of favorites:

> "Those who drink through aural reception, fully filled with the nectarean message of Lord Krishna, the beloved of the devotees, purify the polluted aim of life known as material enjoyment and thus go back to Godhead, to the lotus feet of Him [the Personality of Godhead]."

> "O my Lord, persons who smell the aroma of Your lotus feet, carried by the air of Vedic sound through the holes of the ears, accept Your devotional service. For them You are never separated from the lotus of their hearts."

> "Descriptions of the Lord spoken by those who are free of material desires are the right medicine for the conditioned soul undergoing repeated birth and death, and they delight the ear and the mind. Therefore who will cease hearing such glorification of the Lord except a butcher or one who is killing his own true self?"

These verses and countless others like them form the intellectual background to the chanting of the holy name. At the same time, these verses are part of that glorification and the transcendental purifying sound itself. They themselves are *uttama-shloka* — transcendental, topmost verses.

In addition to such verses, are there other suggestions you could give that might enhance one's kirtan experience?

Well, I've found over the years that kirtan is enhanced by chanting various Sanskrit verses embodying obeisance, prayer, descriptions of the Lord and His associates, etc. The great thing about chanting these verses, if you do it right and understand the meaning, is that (1) it fully engages the intelligence, which has a tendency to fight the pure holy name at times and yield to distraction, and (2) it puts one in contact with the aesthetic element of Sanskrit poetry, thus filling out the mantra experience. That aesthetic element is really the beauty of Krishna Himself embodied in the sound vibration of these descriptive verses.

It never fails for me that if I just chant some of the verses I've memorized about Krishna in Vrindavan, or any verses from the *Bhagavatam* — and there are quite a few — I feel blissful. I feel reciprocation from Krishna, and this encourages my chanting.

Going back to your question about my "philosophy" of kirtan, I think I can best summarize it by recalling the five verses from the *Bhagavatam* that Srila Prabhupada quotes in his *Markine Bhagavata Dharma* poem — *Bhagavatam* 1.2.17-21. These verses describe how Krishna Himself cleanses unwanted things from the heart of His devotee who relishes hearing *krishna-katha*, or subjects about Krishna. Krishna is referred to in the next verse as Uttama-shloka — "He who is glorified in the best of *shlokas*, or verses." I know that for sure — so many *shlokas* by Rupa Gosvami and others provide us with an abundance of beautiful poems about Krishna that we can memorize, chant, and relish. The process is one of purification, and Krishna is doing the purifying from within our hearts. Through such chanting, one rises up to the mode of goodness, becomes fixed in devotion, experiences happiness and feels clear, bright, and pure; eventually the process clears all doubts, karma, and attachments, and one comes face to face with God. All from participating in kirtan, from hearing and chanting the Lord's names, qualities, pastimes, etc.

Let's hear a bit about your own involvement in the professional kirtan world and how it led to producing CDs and other publicly accessible material on kirtan.

I don't know about "the professional kirtan world." I started making recordings of scripture in 1985 and selling them in *ISKCON World Review*, which was a newspaper that was primarily read by ISKCON devotees but also by Indians outside of the movement and by others in the yoga community. Gradually, I recorded the *Brahma-samhita*, *Krishna-karnamrita*, *Chaitanya-chandramrita*, some poems of Rupa Goswami, *Mukunda-mala*, *Bhagavad-gita*, and various other works. These were then copied all over the world and are now available on MP3. My recordings with the Temple Bhajan Band, headed up by Sura Prabhu in Los Angeles, began about seven years ago, and this is purely voluntary work, with the profits going to ISKCON and the Bhaktivedanta Book Trust.

What would you say is your unique contribution to kirtan? When I hear your tapes and CDs, I notice a distinct percussive style that I really like, odd meters and things of that nature. It's kind of like scatting and using other jazz techniques that, surprisingly, really work when applied to kirtan.

Hmm. My "unique" contribution, as you call it, might be my strict adherence to the Sanskrit sounds (*chanda*), the pronunciation of the verse. Along these lines, my jazz and improvisation background nicely dovetails, as you've noted. The wonderful, intricate meters Sanskrit is capable of in the hands of masters like Rupa Goswami, Bilvamangala Thakur, Krishnadas Kaviraj Goswami, and other great teachers in the Gaudiya Vaishnava line is pretty much unknown in the Western world, even in much of ISKCON. (Go to http://www.templebhajanband.com/, and listen to number five ("Namaste") for a good example of what I'm talking about.)

I try to bring this incredible use of Sanskrit to light by using authentic, traditional meters for chanting their songs, and the prose, too. But I often adapt the melodies, and that's why it might sound a little different than what most people are accustomed to.

Could you give a more detailed idea of your style, just so readers can get a clearer image of what you're talking about?

Sure. Well, rhythm is said to be more of a "universal language" than music in general — and music is pretty universal. In my own experience, I certainly found rhythm to be special, too. The interesting thing in jazz — although most people probably wouldn't think about it in this way — is that its improvised melodic and harmonic creations are woven on the framework of a rhythmic base. Also, ideally, you're supposed to feel the raw emotions of the artists expressed directly in real time through their improvisations. There's something similar going on with the sages and their compositions.

There's a difference in that Sanskrit verses are carefully composed; it's not about improvisation. But the rhythmic element is there, and I like to create my own little melodies around those rhythms to bring out the sublime meaning of the verses. Of course, I would be remiss not to mention that jazz is usually saturated with the lower modes of nature—such as ignorance and passion, feeding off of desire and materialistic pursuits—and so it doesn't generally uplift the soul toward God. But the Sanskrit verses from scripture always do. They're coming from a different stratosphere altogether, a different plane of existence.

Now, there are countless mundane works in Sanskrit as well, but my exposure has always been to the transcendental literature. (It's interesting that one of the last jazz compositions I listened to before embarking on the spiritual path in earnest was John Coltrane's "A Love Supreme." This work in fact helped turn me toward God; I'd been totally atheistic before that. Now I get all the jazz I need from B. B. Govinda Swami's saxophonist! A love supreme, indeed!)

Anyway, regarding my own style, it's hard to convey exactly what I'm talking about without an audio sample. But take Chap-ter Thirty-five of the *Bhagavatam*'s Tenth Canto, for instance. This whole chapter, which comprises the *Yugal Gita* of the four *Gopi Gitas*, is in Svagata meter, which means "welcoming." It appears in the form of $-\cup-\cup\cup\cup-\cup\cup--$. In this scene, the *gopis*, who are the superlative cowherd maidens of the spiritual realm, are welcoming Krishna back to the village of Vraja, even as they're singing of Him cavorting in the forest during the day—they're anticipating His return.

If you try clapping this meter, you'll see that you can walk to it or dance to it. If you take the trouble to learn this chapter and chant it with concentration, it's a great meditation on Krishna, and you can begin to perceive the emotions of the *gopis* as they await the return of Krishna from the forest. You can enhance the experience by reading Prabhupada's comments in his "*Krsna book*" or the commentaries of Vishvanath and the other great teachers in disciplic succession. Over and above this, as Srila Prabhupada has pointed out, the sound itself is purifying even without understanding the meaning. The scriptural Sanskrit is infused with transcendental potency. I don't know how to elaborate on that. You have to try it — try chanting it and you'll see its effect on your consciousness.

Now, while chanting this chapter, the regular 4/4 rhythm of the lines gradually begins to break into quicker eighth notes at the beginning, if you will. We get ∪∪ ∪ – ∪ ∪ ∪ – ∪ ∪ – –. This indicates that the *gopis'* hearts are beating faster out of excitement as Krishna's return becomes imminent.

In Canto 10, Chapter 31, by contrast, we have a "complaining" meter — Krishna has abandoned the *gopis* after the initial meeting in the Rasa dance. This is the famous *Gopi-gita*, the songs of the *gopis* in separation from Krishna. The meter is called *kanaka-manjari*, "golden bud." It goes like this: ∪ ∪ ∪ – ∪ – – ∪ – ∪ –. That it's basically a complaining meter is confirmed in Section Ten of Rupa Goswami's *Ashtadasa-cchandah Stava* ("Eighteen verses summarizing Krishna's Vraja pastimes"), when he uses it to describe Krishna's stealing of the *gopis'* garments.

So it definitely works; there's a science to it. But there are limits to how much you can explain these things intellectually. And this is especially true when you start to try to quantify or intellectualize emotions or other "heart" parts of the kirtan, which is really what kirtan is all about. How to describe the aesthetic/spiritual pleasure of chanting Rupa Goswami's *kanaka-manjari* verses or the verses in the Tenth Canto? How does all of this relate to my jazz background? I don't know; maybe not much. But the kirtans, *bhajans*, and chanting of mantras have fully satisfied my desire for music. It's all sublimated into hearing and singing and chanting these transcendental sounds.

Can you tell our readers about your new approach to kirtan—the multimedia project you're working on?

Yes, I'm really excited about this. I'll tell you how it started: Some time ago I felt the need to put some of my favorite verses into English poetry. The chanting of the Sanskrit verses was all well and good, and I would never give it up, but I found that it's very rare to be able to impart to devotees the desire to get into chanting fine Sanskrit poetry. The learning curve is too great for most people. So I thought I should try to create some English versions so I could share the meaning in a poetic way. Then, having access to the Bhaktivedanta Book Trust archives of digitized paintings, I had the idea of doing slide shows with the poems and adding kirtan for a whole multimedia experience.

Modern Westerners really need as many sensory inputs as possible to become absorbed in transcendence. So I bought a projector and a portable screen and learned PowerPoint and started compiling "shows" consisting of Sanskrit and Bengali verses with poetic translations interspersed — adding Krishna paintings or Deity shots. Usually we chant a few rounds of Hare Krishna on beads between verses while viewing a pastime or Deity shot.

I think we can develop a kind of user-friendly Lila-kirtan here — like the Bengali style of reciting Krishna's pastimes in song, as opposed to Nam-kirtan, which is a song made up of names only. We can give modern Westerners poems or songs in English, Harinam, Sanskrit verses (or not), and slide shows of illustrations, making it all really accessible. It's unlimited. It's a full multimedia program. And it works! I recently did it with the eight beautiful verses of Lord Chaitanya at the New York Ratha-yatra festival on the Sunday night after the procession, and people really liked it. It was a success. So I think a lot can be done with it and I definitely plan to develop it in the future.

For more information contact:
www.unlimited-resources.com/dravida.html
or www.templebhajanband.com

$\mathcal{S}$NATAM KAUR

A practicing Sikh and Kundalini Yoga teacher, Snatam Kaur is a singer and musician of increasing world renown.

Attending Mills College in Oakland, California, she received a bachelor's degree in biochemistry. After college, she studied kirtan in India. Specifically, she went to the Punjab, where she situated herself near the Harmandir Sahib, also known as the Golden Temple, in Amritsar, which is considered incomparably holy in the Sikh tradition. There, she began studying kirtan under her mother's teacher, Bhai Hari Singh.

Today, her music mixes Western melodies with Indian rhythms and moods, using mantras from the Kundalini Yoga tradition as well as her own Sikh-inspired lyrics.

She frequently tours the United States, Europe, Canada, and Asia, where she is well known as an accomplished kirtan singer.

On her recent "Celebrate Peace Tour" (2007), she was accompanied by Guru Ganesha Singh, Manish Vyas, and Ram Dass Khalsa. Her CDs, released by Spirit Voyage Music, include "To Heaven and Beyond" (2000); "Prem" (2002); "Shanti" (2003, which was a World Music Grammy finalist); "Grace" (2004); "Mother's Blessing" (2005, performed with Prabhu Nam Kaur, Snatam's mother); "Celebrate Peace" (2005); and "Anand" (2006)

✳ ✳ ✳

I want to begin by saying that I was surprised by how prevalent Sikh kirtan happens to be at this time. Normally, one associates kirtan with Hindu traditions. But if you google the words "sikh kirtan," or even just "kirtan," it's amazing how much specifically Sikh material comes up. Kirtan is really an integral part of Sikhism.

Absolutely. If you study the Sikh tradition—its texts, its culture, its people—kirtan permeates the Sikh lifestyle.

Maybe we could begin by getting a few hard facts out of the way: Your birth name, date of birth, where you grew up, and those kinds of details.

Okay. My birth name is Snatam Kaur Khalsa.

That was your birth name?

Yes. I was born in Trinidad, Colorado on June 19, 1972.

Was it a religious family?

Actually, my parents were practicing Kundalini Yoga at the time, and they were practicing a yogic lifestyle.

Vegetarian?

Right, vegetarian along with other yoga principles. They were considering whether or not to become Sikhs at that time.

What kind of *kundalini* were they practicing? Were they followers of Shivananda Swami? Charles Leadbeater, of the Theosophical Society, was a big proponent of Kundalini practices, too. Were your parents into Theosophy?

No. They were practicing Kundalini Yoga under the guidance of Yogi Bhajan.

Okay. Can you tell a little about Yogi Bhajan, who he is and what tradition he represents? First, let me just briefly summarize for our readers who are unfamiliar with Kundalini: The word literally means "coil." Kundalini practitioners believe that Kundalini energy is coiled like a sleeping snake at the base of the spine. In order to awaken this

energy, one can practice Kundalini Yoga, a series of physical and mental exercises combined with chanting, breath work, and meditation. When the Kundalini energy awakens at the base of the spine, it rises up through the spine to the top of the head to create a state of bliss, physical health, deep awareness, and joy. Okay. So, Yogi Bhajan . . .

Sure. Yogi Bhajan came to the West to share the science of Kundalini Yoga. But there were those who felt that the practice should be kept confidential. So some people said, "No, you shouldn't share it with anyone," because it was traditionally passed from master to student. He responded that, "Kundalini Yoga is for the masses; it's meant to heal people." So he came West.

Was he a master?

Yes. He mastered Kundalini Yoga at the age of sixteen.

So, I'm not following. How is that a break with tradition? If he's a master and he's giving it to new people—isn't that how the tradition is passed down? Isn't that the system in India?

It was traditionally taught from one master to one student.

Oh. I see, and he wanted to do it in a more broad-based way, reaching a lot of people at once.

Right. He wanted to make it available to people in general. So that's how he started, and he started just teaching Kundalini Yoga mostly to young people. You know, the youth of the `60s. And it was really good. I mean, he helped save a lot of people's lives, actually — people who were going down the path of drugs and who were moving along without direction. He gave them an alternative.

I see. What year did he come to the West?

In 1969.

Was he affiliated with the Sikh tradition?

Yes. He began by teaching people Kundalini Yoga and meditation, and many people were just coming to practice the yoga and the meditation and that was fine. But some people were also inspired by his lifestyle, his Sikh lifestyle. So he gradually taught about the Sikh lifestyle as well, and my parents were definitely into that—they were inspired to become Sikhs. I was born during that transition period. My parents were becoming Sikhs.

I see, and what was their background? Were your parents Christians, Jews. . .?

Before that they were Jewish.

Both of them?

Yes.

Okay, so you were born into this rich spiritual background. Your parents were seekers and on the verge of embracing Sikhism.

Right. Both of my parents were musicians, too.

Oh! That's interesting.

My mother has a beautiful voice and sings, and my father plays flute, so it was a very musical house to grow up in. And the music was a real foundation for the Kundalini Yoga and Sikh lifestyle. In the practice of Kundalini Yoga, there's quite a bit of mantras and music . . .

Mantras?

Oh, yes. In both the Kundalini Yoga and Sikh lifestyle, mantra and music are at the core . . .

But let's not jump ahead. Where did you go to school?

I lived in Trinidad, Colorado and then I moved to Long Beach, California, and I lived there as a young child, from about two to five. We lived in a beautiful house across from the ocean. We'd often go to the ocean and practice morning *sadhana*, meditation.

What did that consist of?

It consisted of doing *Jap-ji*, which is sacred reading. *Jap-ji* means "meditation of the soul," and it's written by Guru Nanak, the first

Guru of the Sikhs. It's quite a beautiful work, actually, that's studied and translated by people in India of other traditions outside of the Sikh tradition. That's because it's universal in nature. We did *Jap-ji* every morning and then Kundalini Yoga, you know, for about forty-five minutes, and then we chanted for about an hour.

Were you an only child?

Well, I was an only child for awhile, until I was about seven. But I grew up in an ashram with a few other children.

So it was an ashram environment; it wasn't just your parents and you.

That's right.

Yogi Bhajan. Now wasn't that called the 3HO temple or something?

Yeah, it's 3HO: Healthy, Happy, Holy Organization. We lived in a 3HO ashram in Long Beach. There are ashrams all over the country, and throughout the world, but that was one of the early ones. It's no longer existing in Long Beach.

I see. So that sounds like a happy childhood: there was music, there was yoga.

Right. I was told that during the *sadhana* part, when I was a child, I'd be sleeping next to my parents. But when it came to the chanting, that's when I sat up bolt right.

Ah, so you were attracted to the chanting even then.

My mom said that I used to sing all the time.

Were you into outside music at all or was it mainly spiritual music?

Well, of course, at home it was mainly spiritual music—that's what I was exposed to. We then moved to Sacramento . . .

Another ashram?

This is when I was six. No, we were there as a family. I guess our home was an ashram, but it was just my family living in Sacramento. I attended the Waldorf School.

Can you tell me a little about that?

It's connected with Rudolf Steiner, promoting a form of education that tries to integrate practical, artistic, and intellectual elements into the teaching of any and all subjects. Learning is interdisciplinary and coordinated with "the natural rhythms of everyday life." It emphasizes that children, especially, should learn music when they're young—that children should be taught more through art and music, at an early stage, and as they get older and older, that's when science and other subjects should be incorporated.

Don't misunderstand: We did a lot of math and everything like that, too, but it was more through imaginative stories. It was a very creative, artistic type of learning environment. So when I was in second grade, I was given a choice to learn an instrument. All the kids had to choose between a violin, a viola, or a cello, and so I picked the violin; and I learned to play my chosen instrument in school. Then we had regular singing as a part of the curriculum, too. I also learned the recorder. My parents were really supportive of all this, and it was great. They got me a little violin and separate lessons as well, so I could get real good at it. At this time I was studying classical violin, so I guess we could say I was exposed to other kinds of music.

Any contemporary music? Pop, rock, jazz, blues?

Not when I was growing up. I got into that later . . .

Okay. Now you said at first you were an only child and then another child entered the family?

Yes, when I was seven, my brother was born. That was wonderful for me because I was really ready to have a little brother. That was a really wonderful time in my life.

Did your brother take to the spiritual life as well?

He did. When I was eight, or a little older, my parents got a divorce. My father stopped being a Sikh at that time. In fact, I so loved my father that I tried rejecting Sikhism, too, for a couple of years.

How old were you at that point?

I was almost nine. It was a pivotal time in my life, because something called within me, "I want to be a Sikh, I want to do this." I was pretty young for such yearning, but there it was.

Your mom was still a Sikh.

My mom was still a Sikh, but she was letting me make my own decisions about it. People ask me, "How did you become so devoted?" and I kind of want to talk about this point in my life because it's when I really made a decision inside myself—it's something from deep in my soul. I can't really describe it. But I made that internal decision, at that time.

I was living with my father, who had stopped being a Sikh, and I really wanted to be one. So it was a challenging time for me. In the end, what happened was, through the family court process, my father got custody of my brother and I went to live with my mother. My brother was actually raised in a Jewish family.

It was during this time that I really started to practice on my own, developing my own morning *sadhana*. Ever since that time, I've kept the discipline of doing a morning meditation. It wasn't about my parents doing it—it was something that I wanted to do, for me.

Did you go to college?

I did. Well, let's see. I started off practicing as a Sikh on my own—just a few years before high school. My mother remarried at that time; she in fact married a guy who used to be the manager for the Grateful Dead.

Oh, really?

Yeah, so that was fun. We were able to get backstage passes and I went to some of the Grateful Dead concerts. That exposed me to the concept of writing your own songs and your own music. I started taking up the guitar at that time. My stepfather, Sat Santokh Singh, founded an organization called "Creating Our Future." This was a youth organization to help young people organize peace activities in our community on a local level.

So because he had started it, I was a part of it also. We had these weekend retreats for teenagers at our house. That's another way my musical sense expanded, because we were engaged in all these activities, teaching kids how to organize peace events, how to reinforce awareness of such things, and in the evening we'd gather together and play music. That's when I got out my guitar and started playing music — that's when I wrote a few songs, too.

Folk songs, or . . .?

Right, folk songs, in English. So that's how I grew in that area. I had been growing in the Sikh lifestyle, and learning the Sikh way of music. When I was six-and-a-half, though, we went to India.

Ah, I should have asked about that.

Yeah, we went to India and spent a lot of time at the Golden Temple in Amritsar. We also took a trek up to Hemkunt, which is a temple up in the Himalayan Mountains.

Oh. Gurudwara Hemkunt in the Himalayas—isn't it one of the holiest places for Sikhs?

Right, it's a beautiful temple up in the mountains; it's at a really high elevation, with a lake that people dip into for healing and an experience of union with God. It's considered Holy Water.

So, we were doing a lot of music at that time. My mother and father were actually playing music as we were touring all the different temples. In India, people looked to us as American Sikhs; they had a kind of awe and inspiration toward us, because we were Westerners actually embracing their religion.

At that time, I met Bhai Hari Singh, who had been teaching my mother kirtan. I spent some time with him as well. He wasn't teaching me kirtan at that young age, but I was embraced as part of the family. Later, after I graduated from college in 1995, I went back to India on my own and had an opportunity to study with Bhai Hari Singh myself; so it was a cycle of completion. My mom had studied with him and then I studied with him later. But my mother was the real inspiration and teacher in my life because we went through many things, material and spiritual, together.

She was your first teacher, I guess.

Well, yeah, definitely. We went through quite a lot together and I know that the divorce was painful for her and so she really gravitated towards kirtan as a comfort . . .

Kirtan as solace.

And she really shared that with me, just through her example. But also she would talk to me about kirtan in a real, down-to-earth way. She would talk about how kirtan is everything—how it soothes and calms and how it excites and evokes passion for God. In the Sikh tradition, our kirtan is in the form of Shabads, which are essentially sacred poems or recitations.

I guess it comes from the Sanskrit word for sound: *shabda*.

Right. But in the Sikh tradition, Shabad means, "without the ego." So what we're talking about here, basically, is expression without ego. When we sing a particular Shabad, if it is done in a state of devotion, humility, awareness, and without ego, we call upon the energy of the Guru who originally composed it or recited it.

So she would teach me different Shabads, and we would sing them together. We would talk about the different elements of each Sha-bad, and she would say, "This Shabad came to me, the energy came to me, and this is what it means to me," and we would go over each of the words. She would say, "This is what this word means, and that is what that word means." She was so passionate and excited about it. She would spend hours and hours looking at each Shabad and studying its meaning. She transferred that kind of passion to me through her own example.

I see. She gave you a passion for kirtan and she taught you how to take shelter in kirtan in times of stress.

Right, definitely. And then she also taught me to see the kirtan as an infinite source of bliss. The way that she would translate one Shabad, she would have five meanings for one word that she'd looked up in three different dictionaries.

Thorough.

She said, "Translating these Shabads is like finding the meaning in your own heart." She would say, "This is what it means to me. You can find your own meaning." To this day, I have my dictionaries, and when I look at a Shabad I really sit down and try to discover newer and newer meanings.

It's not that I have to intellectually understand the words—although that's certainly a part of it; but it's more feeling what the words mean within my soul. Now, if I spend the time studying before I chant, which is ideal, then when I'm chanting the words just become a part of me. So I don't sit there and think, "This is what the words mean—this is what I'm singing." It's not conscious awareness; the idea is to make it a part of you, like second nature.

Of course, it's helpful to know what the words represent, what they mean, and so on. But that's not really what it's all about. It's about experiencing the divine.

Yes. It's really about letting the divine flow through you.

What is her name, your mom? I don't know if we got that.

Prabhu Nam Kaur.

"Prabhu Nam." That's a great name. It's like "the master of the name."

Nice. In our tradition, *prabhu* means "light" and *nam* or *nama* means "the name."

Prabhu also means "master." So, "master of chanting the Name." Like the Baal Shem Tov in the Hasidic tradition—his name is Yiddish for "the master of the holy name."

Well, she has been a wonderful teacher to me.

She's still living?

Yes. We just recorded a CD together, which was a really beautiful experience. It's called, "Mother's Blessing."

That sounds wonderful. Let's see. So where do we go from here?

Well, I was thinking about going into the Sikh tradition of kirtan, much more specifically, because I can teach it to you like my mother taught me. [laughter]

Yes, let's start with a little history about Sikh kirtan.

I would love to. In the Sikh tradition, as you probably know, there were ten living masters or Gurus. The first was Guru Nanak, who was born in 1469. Each one of the Sikh Gurus had a gift or an aspect or quality, which contributed to this beautiful diamond of teachings that exists for us today. Each one of them lived and had a beautiful contribution so . . .

Are you going to speak about each of them?

Do you want me to?

That would be good. Just something brief, for our readers.

Okay. Guru Nanak was the Guru of the Aquarian Age, because he was basically the founder of the Sikh religion; so he created something new, in a sense.

Some say that Sikhism is sort of a blend of Islamic and Hindu beliefs. Would you agree with that?

Well, no.

I would like to hear your perspectives on this.

Sikhism is a very pure tradition, and it is an accepting tradition. So, in that sense, yes, it accommodates the earlier traditions in India. But it's quite a unique thing, and it's original with Guru Nanak.

The essence of Sikhism begins with the teaching of Guru Nanak. His first words were *ek ongkara*, which means "God is one," the Creator of all, and within all." Guru Nanak taught this basic concept, and that the caste system was off, that people could practice side by side with each other, that it didn't matter what caste they were in. So this was an incredibly new concept for that time in India.

Right, revolutionary.

He really just taught that the way to attain God is through chanting His Name. He broke away from all the secondary teachings.

Now, I don't know if you're aware of this, but around the same time as Guru Nanak was someone named Sri Chaitanya. He's considered the father of kirtan as a form of yoga. And there's a medieval, Oriyan text, from the sixteenth century, called the *Chaitanya Bhagavat*; it's written by Ishvara Das. This work mentions Guru Nanak meeting with Sri Chaitanya, saying that they danced and chanted together at the Ratha-yatra festival in Puri.

Wow.

Right. And Chaitanya, too, taught non-sectarianism, and he broke down the barriers of the caste system, and so on. So there was something brewing in India at the time . . .

Well, that's interesting, because Guru Nanak traveled on foot with Mardana, his companion, who played the *rebeck*. They did kirtan all over. I'm sure in Puri, too.

The *rebeck*? That's that bowed instrument, usually with three strings, right? I believe it's kind of like a violin.

It's beautiful, and it makes wonderful music. Mardana was a master of this instrument, accompanying Guru Nanak throughout India. They would travel from town to town and village to village. Nobody knew who this Guru Nanak was—people would hear by word of mouth that a saintly person was coming and they would receive him with great respect. He would teach through the spoken word, but he would also do some of his teaching in song, where he would sing in an ecstatic state of bliss. So it was a kind of magical combination of words and music, taken from his experiences of bliss, just singing to people about God.

Do you know what language he spoke?

He taught and sung in the language known as Gurumukhi, which has evolved to the modern-day language known as Punjabi. Guru Nanak started out in what is now Pakistan, and he traveled in areas of Northern India, mainly. There's this wonderful little map showing his footprints throughout the subcontinent, southern India, Saudi Arabia (specifically Mecca), China, and even areas of Tibet. There's a place in India where you see his shoes—these old wooden sandals, you know? You get a sense of a real, living person when you see those shoes.

He and Mardana traveled profusely, and to this day there are temples all over India in honor of Guru Nanak's initial visit there. He brought the experience of chanting God's Name and the experience of the light of God within to many people in many lands. People would come and sing with him, and that, so to speak, was the beginning of the Sikh religion. For me, Guru Nanak is a great inspiration. As I travel all over the world, I remember his message and feel his spirit with me.

Who was the second Sikh Guru, after Nanak?

Guru Angad. Guru Nanak chose Lehna, his disciple, as a successor rather than one of his sons, which was the usual tradition at the time. Bhai Lehna was named Guru Angad and became the second Guru of the Sikhs. He is said to have mastered and embodied the quality of devotion and he really taught that to his Sikh followers. Angad means, "limb," like the limb of a tree.

Yes, again from the Sanskrit: *anga* means "limb."

The next guru was Guru Amar Das. He and his wife began the tradition of the free kitchen, where before he would allow anyone to see him, they would be asked to go and eat a meal cooked in the holy vibration of the Guru's congregation, or Sangat. Sometimes this meant a *raja,* or someone of royal descent, someone like that, would come to see him and he would say, "You need to go eat first," and the *raja* would have to sit next to one of the beggars who had also come to receive the Guru's *darshan.* So the free kitchen continues to this day and it's part of our practice, where we come together for our Gurudwara and sing together.

What does Gurudwara mean?

It means "gateway to the Guru." It usually refers to Sikh temples but it can also have a more general meaning. It's a place where we congregate and sing and gather as a community, where we make prayers and engage in a sacred reading from our scriptures, which I'll get to.

I see. Okay.

So, that's Guru Amar Das. Guru Ram Das was the fourth Guru, and he was the Guru of healing and miracles. It is said that he would go out on the streets at night and wash the feet of lepers, giving them medicine and otherwise taking care of them.

Engaged Sikhism!

He also established—under the direction of Guru Amar Das, who told him to do this—the Golden Temple and the nectar tank, which the Golden Temple sits in the middle of, like a lotus. He began that project . . .

What's a nectar tank?

Well, we call it a nectar tank because it sits in the presence of the Gurudwara, where sacred songs or Shabads are sung—we feel that the essence of that nectar goes into the water. People come and drink from the tank, for purification and blessings.

I see. They give "tanks" for their blessings.

[laughter] There are actually a number of stories of people coming to this nectar tank and being healed. That was really the essence of Guru Ram Das. I'm talking about all these Gurus as if they lived in such and such a time, but for us, these Gurus are very much present. We call upon their presence by reciting the sound current or the Shabads.

That's really the essence of Sikh tradition, especially in relation to kirtan—each of these Gurus gave their sound current or their spiritual expression through the sacred words of the Shabads, and now we partake of those sacred words. Really, the technology or the practice of it is simply this—by reciting these same words that these Gurus recited, in the same mood, you come to embody their spirit or their essence within you.

Each one of them composed sacred songs, used sacred words in a particular way, and it's a very beautiful thing. And they were human beings, like us. Guru Ram Das had a family—the Sikh Gurus had families; they lived in this world. So the Shabads, because they came to them in their human body, in human expressions, they speak to your human senses. Their Shabads are thus relevant and can touch us on a very deep level.

Who were the other Gurus?

Guru Arjan was the fifth Guru. He was the first martyr of the tradition. He was the one, in fact, who compiled all of the earlier Gurus' teachings into one book, known as the *Adi Granth*. The text was completed in 1604, so you get a sense of when Guru Arjan lived.

He is said to have embodied the quality of being able to sacrifice. There was pressure on the people of India at the time from the Mogul rulers to become Muslim. Guru Arjan was seen as a threat and was therefore killed after undergoing unspeakable tortures. People were being killed by the thousands, just for the sake of conversion . . .

. . . to Islam?

Right. That's why Guru Hargobind, Guru Arjan's son, took up the sword to defend freedom and justice. Because of this, in the Sikh tradition, we have the saint aspect, which is Guru Nanak, and we also have the warrior aspect. So, he was the sixth guru.

And then there was a time of peace for the Sikhs and the people in their region, just after his reign, and the next Guru was Guru Har Rai. This was a Guru who really communed with nature. He had this quality of nurturing, and peacefulness, and caring for animals and plants. He emphasized the loving side, the accommodating side, the compassionate side, of the Sikh tradition.

You would think, then, that vegetarianism would be a part of Sikhism, although usually it's not.

Well, from my perspective it certainly is. Religions are complicated, at least people make them that way, and so all kinds of deviations set in. But, in principle, vegetarianism is very much in line with Sikh tradition.

But most Sikhs wouldn't agree, would they?

I think they would. Actually, most Sikhs would vouch for vegetarianism. But a small number—unfortunately, including a number of scholars, and that's how a lot of people find out about the Sikh tradition—would deny the vegetarian connection. Still, most Sikhs understand that compassion for animals and an awareness of physical, mental and spiritual health is a necessary part of Sikhism.

Oh, I see. Good.

Let's move on. Guru Har Krishan, the eighth Guru, was a five-year-old boy who became Guru. His basic message—obviously influenced by his age—was that no one is too young or too old to be enlightened. Age was not a factor, he taught, in Guruship. He was known for his miraculous ability to heal people as well.

And then the ninth guru was Guru Tegh Bahadur—he is known as a true master of meditation and contemplation. He taught that all of the treasures of life will come to you, if you can sit still and be in your true nature. You don't have to chase after things. At the end of his life, many people living in the Guru's region, including a large groups of Hindus, came to him asking for help, as the Mogul rulers were becoming increasingly aggressive in their conversion attempts and many people were being killed. Guru Tegh Bahadur went before the emperor and said, "If you can convert me, then you can convert all of these others." Of course, this didn't happen. But it cost him his life—he died for the religious freedom of others.

His son, Guru Gobind Singh, was a master warrior, and he created a resistance to the Mogul rule that eventually shook the empire of its hold on India. He personally trained his army, many of whom were farmers and common villagers looking for freedom. Guru Gobind Singh was also a poet, with beautiful songs. One of his poems, entitled "Jaap Sahib" gave his warriors courage, and they would recite its rhythmic verses while in battle to maintain their strength and their edge over the enemy. There are many magnificent writings from Guru Gobind Singh, characteristic of the Sikh lineage, and he is the tenth guru.

When he was on his deathbed — this is the beginning of the eighteenth century — numerous followers were saying to him, "Who is going to be the next Guru after you?" Guru Gobind Singh replied, "The next Guru is going to be the *Sri Guru Granth Sahib*," which is a collection of the sacred writings of the previous Sikh Gurus and other enlightened masters of the time from other faiths, such as Shek Farid from the Muslim tradition and Kabir from the Sufi tradition.

A distinction should be made here: You previously mentioned the *Adi Granth*, which is a name often applied to the *Guru Granth Sahib* as well. But the *Adi Granth* is really only the portion of the *Granth* that Guru Arjan compiled in the 1600s, which you already mentioned. Since the names of these books are often used interchangeably, we should point out that the context in which these names are used is crucial, so one knows when the entire work is being referred to or, alternatively, just the earlier title.

Right. The *Adi Granth* was established by Guru Arjan, the fifth Guru of the Sikhs. When Guru Gobind Singh gave the Guruship to this sacred body of writings, he made a few additions, and then gave the name, the *Sri Guru Granth Sahib*. But the more important thing here is that Guru Gobind said, "The Guru resides within the *Sri Guru Granth Sahib*." For me, it's hard to even say "sacred writings," because they're not merely writings; the *Sri Guru Granth Sahib* is more like a form of energy, and a beautiful energy, at that. What's more, these scriptures became our Guru from that point forward.

So there are no Gurus today, in the form of people?

The *Sri Guru Granth Sahib* is our Guru. Within the sacred words that it contains it's a living embodiment of the energy of our Guru. As a part of my own personal practice, whenever I have questions, I go to the Guru and I "take a reading" and the answer comes forth like a living presence. I wish I could describe to you what actually happens. It's very magical and beautiful for me.

It's part of our daily practice: After we do our daily meditation, we take a reading. It's called a Hukham, which literally means "command." Each Hukham is usually a single page or more, depending on which section you choose. A Hukham is read when a child is born; a Hukham is read when somebody passes away; a Hukham is read when people get married. It's like a guiding light for us, an important part of our practice, where we gather together with the *Sri Guru Granth Sahib* presiding. In a Sikh Gurudwara, it sits on a sacred altar in the focal point of the room.

Kind of like the Torah in the Jewish tradition.

Exactly, the scripture is often wrapped in beautiful, opulent cloth, and it is celebrated with enthusiasm.

I'm thinking about this tradition of seeing scripture as Guru. You know, traditionally, in India, the Guru-disciple relationship is seen as a back-and-forth experience. Fledgling devotees tend to have practical questions in their everyday practice—and they might have interpretive problems when it comes to scripture. For example, how do we know if we're properly understanding sacred texts, or if we're misinterpreting them? There are many possible readings of a given scripture. That's why a certain "back-and-forth" with the Guru was deemed necessary. There was a check and balance system: Guru, *shastra*, and *sadhu*—the teacher, the scripture, and the holy people. If one of these is out of kilter, then one's interpretation is to be considered suspect. Also, the Guru should be able to choose whether or not he or she will accept a given disciple, just as much as the disciple chooses who will become their Guru. You see my question . . .

That's a good question. In the Sikh way of life, we are not initiated by anyone—it is a self-initiation. When the light awakens within, and one feels connected to the Guru, as it exists in the *Sri Guru Granth Sahib,* there is no question. It has happened for me and for many others. It is a soul connection, where you just know you've found the right path. It is true that there can be different interpretations of a text, as you say, but in my experience these teachings are so true, that no matter how you interpret them, the truth can be found, in the same way that one turns a diamond in the light, and you see many different colors.

We do, however, have a check and balance, too. Our Guru gave us the power of community. Guru Gobind Singh said that wherever there are five Sikhs of the Guru, there the Guru is. In times of need, we gather as a community either in this formation of five, or even more is okay, too. With our collective consciousness, we resolve issues and dissolve duality as it can occur on the spiritual path. We are a simple people who have been taught to earn by the sweat of our brow, to give of our earnings to people in need, and to love and respect each other and all of humanity as the creation of God. But most importantly, we have been given the vibration and sound current of our Guru, and empowered to live with our Guru in our lives and hearts every second of the day.

And in this way, we sit in the presence of the Guru, which exists within the vibration of the Guru's Shabads. All of these Shabads come from the *Sri Guru Granth Sahib.*

So it's singing—we're kind of back to kirtan.

Right, back to kirtan. In our practice, we seek to bring the presence of the Guru into our own heart through these Shabads, through the recitation of the sacred words.

And a lot of the words involve the holy name, like Hari, Govinda and Krishna.

Exactly. If you go into the *Sri Guru Granth Sahib,* you'll see a lot of the Shabads are poems. They're about the joy of singing God's name, the gifts of glorifying God. It's really an entire text devoted to the praise of singing God's name. Now, in the *Sri Guru Granth*

Sahib there are thirty-one *ragas*. All of the Shabads are assigned a specific *raga*. This was the work of Guru Arjan.

How would you define *raga*, by the way?

In the technical sense a *raga* is a specific collection of notes, a specific scale. In a spiritual sense, *raga* is an avenue to God through a mood or a feeling that those particular notes create. As human beings we have many different avenues towards union with God, and we have different emotions or feelings. In the Sikh tradition, and perhaps in any musical tradition, we say that these feelings are good and natural, and instead of shutting them down, we embrace them and sing the Shabads with that feeling, with that love.

The appropriate feelings were set down by Guru Arjan. And then they are replicated with similar emotions . . .

Exactly. And the feelings are set forth, but not required. Not everyone sings in perfect *raga*. In fact, these Shabads are available to anyone with feeling—some of my best teachers have been people who sing completely out of tune. It's more about the . . .

Emotion.

Right, the emotion and the essence, or the experience of the Guru within you when you recite.

Purity.

The purity. Yes. Kirtan is essentially about capturing that purity. It's about sweetness and love as manifested through sound. For me, it's a gateway to God, and the experience of God, through the medium of sound. I've learned that when I chant these sacred words, it not only changes how I'm feeling inside, but it changes the vibration around me—it affects others, too. So when I chant kirtan in my recordings and at concerts, I really think about that. It causes an internal change, no doubt, and it changes the world. I especially know what happens to me every time I chant, every time I tune into that energy.

And when you do, it's good for you and for everyone who hears you.

Right, and I encourage others to pick up on that as well. When I do kirtan with my local community, and during our concerts, I really encourage people to sing along because I know it's not just about them sitting there and watching me sing. "Oh, what a lovely voice." Or "See, she's playing that *harmonium* so nicely today," or whatever. It's about the practice—of them also benefiting from those sacred words and having that experience. I feel that my job, if I were to say I have a job, is to inspire people to sing these sacred lyrics and to have that experience I know to be so real and true. I really feel that within the *Sri Guru Granth Sahib*, within the practice of the Sikh tradition, we have sacred words that have an incredibly healing effect that can heal anyone of any path. I've experienced this in my own life on a very personal level, going back, as I mentioned, to my parents' divorce.

I saw the miracle happen. My father, who stopped being a Sikh, came to one of my concerts and really enjoyed it. We were able to connect in a way that was impossible for many years. I feel that the sound touched him in a deep way, and also allowed me to open my heart. To me, all of the healing that comes from the Shabads is precious, and so I've taken it as my mission to share this sacred sound current with people of all faiths, because I've had many experiences of the powerful healing that inherently lies within each sacred recitation.

For more information contact:
www.snatamkaur.com

$\mathscr{K}$ARNAMRITA DASI

*Born and raised in American ash-
rams, Karnamrita Dasi began studying Sanskrit, Braj-bhasha, bhajans,
kirtan, and classical Indian music at
an early age. Spending much of her time in Vrindavan, India, she is as
much Indian as she is American — and her music reflects this fusion in
an almost mystical way.*

*Even as a child, her ashram teacher taught her to chant numerous prayers
from India's Sanskrit scriptures, which set the stage for an entire life of
divine sounds and mantras.*

*Then, in 1998, her mother passed away, but not before urging her to
devote her life to* bhakti *and the music it ushers forth — her mother asked
her to sing and to make singing the core of her soul. By that time, she had
studied Sanskrit and sung* bhajan *for well over twenty-five years. Still,
she wasn't sure she could satisfy her mother's request, at least until she
received proper training.*

*That same year, as she took her mother's ashes to India, her love for
Krishna directed her to a devotional life centered on classical Indian music, in the style of Dhrupad. By providence, she came upon two teachers who would change her life: Pandit Vidur Mallik and Tarun Krishna
Das. These teachers guided her through four years of meditation and vocal
training. Indeed, this would lead to the fulfillment of her mother's desire.*

She eventually recorded a landmark CD — "Dasi: Prayers by Women."

This CD is a personal offering of devotional prayers dedicated to the female saints of India. Filled with haunting harmonies, Karnamrita's soulful, velvety voice blends with mandolins, violins, sarods, sitars, *pianos,* harmonium, mridangas, tablas, *and other instruments to bring together the heart of India and her own Western homeland. Her music brings to bear her classical training and the heart of kirtan as well.*

✳ ✳ ✳

Jai Karnamritaji! Your mother joined a spiritual community soon after you were born and raised you in an ashram environment. So, you're a bit unique when compared to the average *kirtaniya* today, since you were actually raised with kirtan.

Right, I suppose you can look at it that way.

Let's begin with your legal name.

Well, as far as I'm concerned, my legal name is Karnamrita, since that's what people have called me all my life. It's not like I got it when I discovered Sanskrit or something. [laughter] I mean, if you try calling me by my legal name, I don't think I'd respond too quickly . . .

[laughter] Okay, well, why don't you tell me something about your background.

I was born in Boise, Idaho, and I have a younger brother. I don't know much about my father. He wasn't present while I was growing up. My mother was born in California, but her parents were from Idaho, and she was raised there.

And were you into music as a kid?

Very much so. In our community, where I lived with my mother, kirtan was a huge part of our everyday experience. My mother brought me there when I was just a toddler, so I can't say I remember the first time I heard kirtan. I sort of just grew up knowing that it was normal to sing for four hours a day in Sanskrit. [laughter] And, in that regard, kirtan, singing, community spirit — these were normal things for me. Especially as a child I loved the freedom that singing and kirtan allowed me to feel.

So you were raised in this environment until you were a teenager?

Right. Those were my early years of kirtan — and, believe me, there was *a lot* of kirtan!

Those were formative years. Who did you hear back then? Were you listening to Vishnujana Swami and people like that?

Definitely. It was Yamuna and Vishnujana — they were my childhood heroes, if you know what I mean. We didn't have television or radio, so live or recorded kirtan was pretty much it.

When I think of my own heroes as a kid—from Spiderman to James Bond to Jimi Hendrix—what a contrast to yours! You probably didn't realize that your influences were special.

Hmm, yeah. You don't realize it at the time. When I grew into my teenage years, I'd sneak out and listen to George Harrison and Chrissie Hynde. I found old tapes in someone's basement and it was just cool to be rebellious. [laughter] But aside from that, until I was about sixteen, I had only heard kirtan. Music *meant* kirtan or *bhajans*, at least to me. I didn't even know that other music existed until I was a teenager.

You didn't hear outside music?

No. And I wasn't really interested. Kirtan was and still is on many levels the most beautiful thing to me. It's a magical feeling of being connected — to the universe, to the self. Even now that I know many forms of music, my favorites are usually devotional Sanskrit chants — kirtans of all different kinds.

How interesting. So you were weaned on kirtan and you felt satisfied, without the need for exploring different kinds of music.

Yes. As I mentioned before, kirtan was a huge part of the ashram atmosphere; where I was, people took their spiritual practice seriously. It wasn't until I left the community — going out on my own, to public high school — that I was really introduced to Western culture, including its music. And then it was a somewhat strange trying to fit in.

I could see how that would be so, but could you give some examples?

Well, for instance, I noticed that the first few times I told anyone I was raised in an ashram . . . people just didn't know what to make of it.

You went back to Idaho?

Yes. I went to stay with my mother's family. I wanted to experience life outside the ashram, to check out public school and to experience another way of life.

When I arrived in Idaho, I started going to a regular high school. And, as I was saying, I found that I was somewhat socially backward. I mean, I felt like I was starting out in grade school or something. But remember, too, that I was at that very awkward age — I was a teenager. It was a strange time in terms of finding my identity. "Who was I?" The other kids would talk about what was going on, you know, like popular TV shows and such, or they would talk about their favorite rock stars and radio stations — and I didn't have a clue as to what they were talking about. One time I went with my cousins to Church camp, and for the whole bus ride up to the mountains, everyone on the bus sang, "Flintstones, meet the Flintstones . . ." and all these other TV songs. And for the first time, I was without any song. I really had so much to catch up on.

I guess there are two ways to look at it: (1) You were divorced from Western culture, both its positive and negative aspects; or (2) as part of an ashram, you were given access to a alternate way of living that, while separating you from the usual pleasures of day-to-day Western life, afforded you a special way of being, one that was infused with spirituality. Actually, as your life went on, you ultimately experienced both, didn't you?

Yes, that's true. But at that time, I was just acclimating myself to another world, which was very interesting. It was a bit of a challenge—a lonely one, sometimes. You know, you feel sort of isolated and left out in many ways. Of course, now—and in the big picture—I'm grateful for my early years in an ashram environment. It gave me a whole life of music, a foundation for understanding sound vibration, meditation, kirtan, and the importance of community. So many things. But I'm just describing for you the transition period, and like all transition periods, it was a bit difficult and alienating at times, especially compared to what I was used to.

Understandable.

I was going home every day from school with my cousins; they would help me in my studying and in catching up on a lot of different subjects that we didn't cover in our ashram education. And at the same time, I was catching up socially, too. This included hearing rock music and becoming familiar with pop culture, with "new" instruments, like the guitar. [laughter] Well, the guitar was new to me anyway, and it sure seemed like people played it on every song. [laughter]

[laughter] Did you become wayward? I mean, sometimes, when people try to catch up— if they feel backwards and want to fit in—they might start doing wild things.

No, not really. I caught up relatively quickly, and I've always been practical; I think I've always had a pretty balanced sense of right and wrong.

That's commendable. So no drugs, then? If you don't mind my asking.

No. I didn't feel the need. You see, there were so many things that we didn't have in the ashram, that the whole experience was sort of like being on a drug. It was certainly a new experience every day. There were so many exciting things to experience and learn in my new life—and I'm talking about, good, positive things—that everyday routines were exciting enough. Really. Some days it was like overload. Just learning and experiencing regular life was so stimulating in itself.

And then you went to college?

Yes, and I studied there for about a year and a half. But when my counselor told me it was time to adopt a major, I realized that I didn't know what I wanted to do. I felt as though I had not experienced enough of my own life, my own individuality, to know that. First, I had a rather uncommon and isolating experience at the ashram, and then I was introduced to America through a pretty conservative Idaho town—I knew there was a huge bridge in the middle of the two, and I was sure there was a lot beyond both. So I decided to take some time, to experience that space. I decided to travel, and to experience life, finding out for myself what direction I'd like to take—from a practical level, not a theoretical one.

And singing? When did you realize you could sing?

Oh, back in the ashram—as a child I knew that I loved singing. Which of course didn't necessarily mean that I *could* sing. A lot of people like to sing, but that doesn't mean that other people are going to like it. [laughter] I just sang because it felt good—because it had a special altering effect on my consciousness and it kept me connected to myself in so many ways. It was always my companion. And it just so happened that people liked my singing.

But I'll tell you something interesting: Long after I had left the ashram, my cousin and I were in her car one morning driving to high school, and she happened to turn on the radio. Well, I was really happy because I knew the song, and I naturally started singing. We were in her little VW bug, and she said, "You know—when I turn on the radio, I do it to hear the radio, not to hear you." And I had this really interesting realization. Her words didn't hurt my feelings, but I just realized, "Oh, not everybody likes my singing, like they did in the ashram." So, literally, for ten years I stopped singing. I just completely stopped and . . .

Well, your singing in the ashram was a different kind of singing.

Yes, when we sang, it was not just singing for the sake of singing. It was devotional, and in that way we were sharing sounds and prayers with each other, sounds that brought us to a communal and spiritual place. It was a way of connecting as a community, with ideas, feelings, and spiritual friendship. . . . You know, I'm talking about the things you feel when you chant that are absolutely impossible to express in words. [laughter]

You see, in my class—I was always in the oldest age group of girls, and the best in Sanskrit class—our teacher often asked me to sing the prayers; she had me lead the call-and-response singing, the kirtan. I think that's when I initially developed my singing.

That's important background.

Yeah, and we chanted a lot. There were all the prayers that we recited before we ate breakfast, each day. We would all sit in a big circle, and while we looked on as breakfast was being made, and eventually served in front of us, we would chant the entire *Brahma-samhita*, from beginning to end. That's seventy-two full Sanskrit verses! We eventually memorized them, the verses becoming so familiar that we could rattle them off like Sanskrit rap stars and have them all finished before the food was cold. I still have those mantras memorized in my head today, even though I haven't really chanted them since I was fifteen years old. Sanskrit has a way of really finding a place in your memory, and eventually capturing your heart as well.

Brahma-samhita? Those mantras are complex, too. You chanted them in the original Sanskrit?

Oh, yes. In the original Sanskrit. And before we ate dinner, we would sing the entire *Isopanisad* as well.

Sounds beautiful, if also rigorous.

So we became pretty musical, early in life. We really got to know Sanskrit well, too; it was a part of our daily regimen. Sometimes we would memorize verses from the *Bhagavatam* or other texts. We really had a lot of variety. And to add to that, our morning chanting was three hours long—so you could say we did a lot of chanting. [laughter] My mother was so proud of me as a Sanskrit student that she used to bring me her favorite verses, and I'd memorize those as well.

What was your mother's name?

Kunti.

I see. And Karnamrita means "nectar for the ears." That's a beautiful name, especially considering who you are and what you do.

Well, at a very young age, I was given the name to commemorate my time in the ashram—sort of an award for making spiritual vows. It was like an initiation ceremony. My mother had this wonderful friend, Radhanath Swami, who was also like an uncle to me as I was growing up. After the ceremony, he came up to me and asked: "Do you like your name?" And I said, "Sure. I guess so." To me, it was just so overwhelming being part of this ceremony that I hardly even thought about my new name: Karnamrita Dasi. I knew that *karn* meant ear, and *amrita* meant nectar; so I knew it related in some way to chanting. But I didn't think much about it. He then asked if I knew what the name meant. I told him that I didn't, because it felt like he was going to tell me something special about it. So, he started walking next to me, and told me the meaning of my new name. But it didn't dawn on me until years later how this name would become so significant to my life.

In recent years, I asked Radhanath Swami how he knew so much about my name, since so few in the community were competent translators of Sanskrit, and I also asked him why he was so curious about whether I liked the name or not. As it turns out, he was the one who chose the names for all initiates that day. And I'm happy with that; I have a deep love and a high regard for him.

I know him, too. He's the genuine article—a real *sadhu*. Anyway, to backtrack to our earlier discussion, what happened after you went ten years without singing or chanting? What got you back into chanting?

Well, it was a long path getting back to chanting. But, basically, I traveled around the world, backpacking, for a few years. Starting in 1994, for about three, four years, I was just traveling, going throughout Europe, North Africa, Australia. It all really started to gel when my old girlfriend, Purnima, phoned me up and said, "You should come to India." I responded, "No, I was there in 1991 and I really didn't like it. I'm just not ready to go back."

What didn't you like?

To be honest? The pollution, the garbage, the noise, and the crowds . . . it was just a bit much. Maybe I was set up for something else, though. Growing up in the ashram, we would sing about the beauty of Vrindavan . . . the birds, the waterfalls, the bees, the peacocks. And so I had preconceptions about what it would look like. India was built up in an idyllic way, from every point of view. So, the first time I went to India, in 1991, I was pretty disappointed. What could possibly live up to those grandiose descriptions we were given as children?

Right. You were expecting something else.

Instead, there were taxis honking and chaotic traffic everywhere, *rickshaws* and people mixed up like a moving sea, and endless pollution. Where were all those colorful waterfalls and honeybees and peacocks?

You quite naturally had an idealized Vrindavan in your mind's eye, and then you saw what India really looks like. Prabhupada once addressed that. He said, rather poetically, that, when we are in conditioned life, we have a patch made of material ingredients blocking our eyes, and when we lift that patch with our devotional practices, we can see the true, spiritual Vrindavan in all its glory. In other words, you have to really *want* Vrindavan to penetrate its external covering, and when you do, you can see what Krishna sees.

Well, when I went there I was pretty shocked. But Purnima was living in a completely different kind of India. She told me, "If you come and stay with me, you'll see India from another point of view. Give India another chance." Her father was working in South India and living a bit more connected to the indigenous Vedic culture, and it was much more peaceful—the atmosphere was more *sattvic*, gentler, and cleaner in general. Later, I traveled around India for about a year by myself, on second-class trains, just meeting the villagers and learning the language. I'll tell you, it was quite exciting being a woman and traveling alone in India.

Did you learn Hindi or Tamil or . . . ?

Pretty much Hindi, yeah. In the South they don't speak much Hindi, just their mother tongue and English, so it was easy there. I learned to communicate well with them in several languages. And then in North India it was really Hindi with a bit of English. Now, my Hindi wasn't the best; it was broken, but people understood me. And I would sit in the trains and listen to them sing—and sing and sing—until like five in the morning. There were little kirtan groups that would come on the train; there were kids that would come on, too, and do little acts, little dramatic performances. But music and singing was so prevalent—it was just everywhere. It was like the villagers would get on board and perform all sorts of music and dramas, or sell their goods, and then after a while the next village flavor would board. I really got to feel the pulse of India by traveling this way.

Yes, it's quite something. I traveled that way, on a train, all over South India, and up in the north, too, in 1984.

Then you know what I'm talking about. I could see something special in all this—I could see that there were no boundaries in the community. They all seemed connected to each other, to speak a common language through music. That was what I was looking for, what I wanted to see. These people just shared what they had, whether it was inspiration or a talent—and very often they would even share their little lunch boxes, too.

Did you visit many Western ashrams in India?

No. I was trying to find the real India; not from my mother's point of view, not as filtered through a particular devotional community, not from books. I wanted a non-biased, fresh perspective from my own experience with the people and the land.

You wanted a more objective experience.

Right. I had to search for myself, because my mother brought me to her ashram when I was young, and it was her choice. So this was a point where I had to embark on that journey myself.

Entirely understandable.

One day, Purnima said, "Why don't you come to Vrindavan; it's Kartik — the month of celebrating Diwali and all the folk festivals of Braj." And I thought to myself, "Well, okay, I'll go for Kartik, but that's it." So I traveled up north and I went to the ancient temples of Radha-raman, and Banke-bihari — so that I could feel their tradition and their relationship to Krishna. I wanted to experience it in a very natural and cultural way. I wanted to experience the spirit of the indigenous tradition.

I guess your mother's ashram seemed non-traditional because of its Western ambiance, even though her ashram, as I understand it, was a legitimate part of the Gaudiya Sampradaya . . .

Yes it was, but it was connected to my background, too, which is something I wanted to get away from. I wanted to experience the tradition in its original, natural setting, away from the institution and the people I grew up with. Anyway, one night I happened into one of the temples in Vrindavan, and a friend invited me to come see this traditional folk performance. Some villagers were going to be performing an all-night devotional drama with classical music and dance. They do these remarkable three-hour performances, with classical music, on Krishna's daily activities, and that night it was the full moon and they were performing the Rasa-lila. It's considered Krishna's special night in Vrindavan, where He dances with each of the cowherd girls of Braj (the *gopis*). As I said before, it was the full moon night of Kartik, which is a very special and devotional night for the people of Vrindavan. So I went, and — wow — was I blown away. I had never seen or felt anything like this in my life.

Where was it? Do you remember any of the specifics?

It was at a place called Jaipur Mandir, in Vrindavan.

And do you remember the name of the troupe?

It was Swami Fateh Krishna's troupe. They were amazing. The power, the feeling, the emotion. After the performance, my friend who had brought me there offered to take me backstage to meet all the actors and musicians. I declined. You see, the performance took me out of this world, transporting me to a realm of bliss. I really felt something magical had happened to my spirit and I didn't really need to go and talk to the actors or musicians. I wanted to stay in the meditation and joy I was experiencing.

My friend insisted. He said, "Well, it's an opportunity you'll never really have again — nobody usually gets to go back there. " I thought about it. Maybe I should have gone, but instead I told him, "Look, I just saw something that was so real for me, so connected. I don't need anything more. I certainly don't need to meet the actors — by being here, I experienced everything. That was all I needed." Besides, I didn't want to know more about them as people. They had shown me who they were *spiritually*, taking me higher than they possibly could in any other way. I didn't need to have a conversation with them — it had already happened without a word. Sometimes, the truth behind the drama is such a disappointment. You know, like once they take off the crowns and the make up . . .

They'll bring you down.

Well, I was a little afraid they might just want to talk about America or practice their English, which is typical in some of the smaller villages. And I just wanted to stay in the space they had created in my consciousness and heart. I didn't want that interrupted. And I felt, "That performance was beautiful; it was magical for me — it was all I needed. Period."

And then my friend said to me, "Okay, one nice tradition is that, at midnight, after the performance . . . you go and do full *parikrama*, circumambulation, of Govardhan Hill." That means walk barefoot a full twenty-seven kilometers around the base of the sacred hill, Govardhan. So there we were, on the full moon night, walking side by side with thousands of other barefoot villagers, singing and occasionally stopping to take chai from a villager who would prepare it right there on his makeshift firewood stove. Finally, around four in the morning, we heard these intense bells ringing as we came up to a very sacred bathing place called Radha-kund. It wasn't until after sunrise that we left there. That night, I had a full immersion, a real concentrated focus on Braj, on Govardhan, on Radha—it was a special night, to say the least. And it affected my consciousness in a tremendous way . . .

How could it not? You're there on holy ground, witnessing a re-creation of Radha and Krishna's most intimate pastime, and then you go to Govardhan, trekking a great distance, around the entire hill. You watch the sun rise at Radha's lake. If that doesn't absorb your consciousness in something transcendental, what will?

[laughter] It was just magical—there were these angelic bells and countless people and images, all reflected in the water, with the full moon and . . . It was like, when you're so touched that you can't speak, you can't express what that feels like . . .

You were stunned . . .

Stunned, and touched. And I was so in the moment, right there at Radha-kund, I found something within my heart. I found what I was looking for, without even really looking. It was a new day, in more ways than one. I felt like I had entered a new space.

What would you say you found there, if you had to articulate it?

I just found all the pieces—they finally fit together. And it didn't feel like there was any effort involved. Hmm, you know, your question is a really good one, because I hadn't thought about this in a long time. I guess I would say that my whole life finally made sense. I saw what Krishna was doing, allowing me to be born to a mother with devotion; spending my early life learning about *bhakti*; chanting mantras and experiencing a yogic lifestyle; experimenting with life outside the ashram; and, by grace, coming back to India and finally being able to sing again. It all came together. I could feel the grace that was guiding me.

I understand. Everything made sense. . . . But back to Radha-kund: So when you were there, at that sacred spot, you could say that, in a sense, you found Krishna?

I feel like that. Between 9 PM and 7 AM the next morning . . . that night I found Krishna. [laughter] I found His beauty. Considering that the actual meaning of the name Krishna means "Full Beauty," yes, I found something totally beautiful.

[laughter] And He found you!

Yes! And the interesting thing was this—I found Him in a whole other context. It was something different from what I was raised with. I mean, it was the same Krishna, of course. But it was Krishna beyond the ashram, beyond the limited perspective of one group of people. And it was beautiful to see it. I could feel from the villagers that He was real. Sometimes, the *bhakti*, the connection to Krishna through the heart, is more apparent in the love of His *bhaktas,* and on this day that truth was the major factor of my transformation. Seeing their love for Him was powerful, convincing, and believable.

I see what you mean.

I could fully feel that Krishna was actually born here, in Vrindavan, thousands of years ago, and that the Brijbasis saw Him as a villager from their village. And I could see and feel why that was important: It enabled them to have an incredibly intimate relationship with Him. When they sang to Him, in Hindi, it was very personal and heartfelt.

Many times I noticed that the poems the villagers sang in the temples address God with the phrase "TUM," which shows familiarity. In Hindi, you usually address an elder with respect, by saying "AP," but here, in Vrindavan, when they spoke to their God, to their Lord, they used the more familiar term of addressing Him —"TUM." It was so endearing to watch them sing, to feel the intimacy. You see, when I got to understand Hindi, it revealed to me that they're not afraid of God but rather that they feel very familiar and close to Him. You get the sense that He's their best friend. I'd never experienced such closeness with God anywhere else.

Right.

So I started to frequent the temples in Braj, Radha-raman and the others. Especially Radha-raman. I heard the devotees there singing songs, right in front of Radha-raman, and they were calling Him TUM. I had never experienced that before . . . but I saw where it was coming from, so far beyond fear or awe and reverence. It was a very close love. And I had never experienced that kind of mood toward God in the West. In Christianity, as far as I could understand, there was this sense of awe and deep respect . . . sometimes even fear. That's okay, for sure. It's a step toward God. But it didn't seem to go as deep.

So you did have some contact with Christianity . . .

Well, I had been introduced to Christianity through my mother's sister, and I had heard so much in Church about hell and about God striking you down. It was frightening, sometimes, to think that God might do that to me. But here I was, watching how the Brijbasis, the local Vrindavan people, weren't afraid of Krishna! They were certain He would never strike them down! They felt that He was their friend. It was a very special thing, a different side of worship.

Aha. I see, I see. Well, to be fair, all religions have their awe and reverence side, it's true. But they also have their more sweet, intimate side. The Christians do have Jesus, you know . . .

That's very true, for sure. But what I saw here was different from anything I had ever seen. I saw Krishna from a Vaishnava point of view, and it didn't have any of the usual religious fear attached to it. These people were grounded in simple love, with an intimate deity. . . . Some of them even considered Krishna to be their child. They sang songs to Him telling Him to wake up from His nap—they'd sing that the milk was hot and ready for Him, and that it would get cold if He didn't wake up on time. That's the sort of intimate love I'm referring to.

I see. It sounds to me like you went through a transformation from *vaidhi* to *raganuga*. You shifted from an awareness of the "awe and reverence" aspect of the Supreme, or, from a structured "rules-and-regulations" type of *bhakti*, to an appreciation of a more spontaneous variety of devotion, which focuses on the sweet Absolute—Krishna. This can happen when in proximity to advanced devotees, or simply from being in Vrindavan.

Yes, and I could now see that Krishna belonged in my heart, in all of our hearts. It became immediately apparent. He didn't belong in the rules and regulations. I could see that so clearly.

Right. It's not forced; it comes by grace and only by grace. That's the *raganuga* realization.

Well, I had been taught this as a child, but this was the first time I was seeing it practiced—and it was a new revelation for me. Because many institutions, it seemed to me, usually don't emphasize this heart-over-head dimension. Rather, many of them focus on the rules and regulations. And when you grow spiritually, you become aware of this other side of *bhakti*, usually on your own. This experience in Vrindavan really opened me up to it. True devotion doesn't live in your head—it lives in your heart.

Exactly.

And I felt like, prior to that, I was living in my head. It was what I was taught. Now, focusing on the rules and regulations is a necessary place to start, I guess; it's a good thing, but it's not all there is. Like when you're new at any art, you follow the rules, but after a while you don't have to follow a recipe anymore. Suddenly, there is an intuition and a connection like you've never felt before.

Absolutely.

And these people in Vrindavan knew that it was all about the heart, that it wasn't in the head, you know? It was simple for them: "I have a personal relationship with God, and of course He's my friend, and He wants me to cook for Him and to make Him clothes and get Him new jewelry on His birthday — and bathe Him in milk and honey and on and on." These are the things the Brijbasis did with their time, and I could see that God was really a part of their everyday life, in every way. I guess being born in Braj will do that for you.

Certainly.

And so I really and sincerely rediscovered Krishna in this intense mood of intimacy.

Okay, so now you're at Radha-kund, you discovered Krishna—but how does all of this interconnect with your emphasis on kirtan? Is that when you went back to your singing?

Well, this was a beginning, for sure, since so much of music begins with the condition of the heart. I felt that Vrindavan was getting my heart ripe, so to speak; so that my voice could express what was sprouting inside of me. I used to listen to a lot of music in Vrindavan, a lot of live music in the temples and on the streets. I was around it all the time, and it was enthralling, moving, in so many ways. There were entire ashrams of widows who would sing for hours a day, and I loved the blind *bhajan* singers who sang out on the streets in Loi Bazaar. . .

Aside from the obvious sincerity of feeling, was it technically good?

Well, not to everyone's ears . . . but I would say, on a deeper level, it was technically great. It was fulfilling, it was infused with *bhakti*. Sometimes I would go and sit at the widow's ashram and just listen to them sing. A lot of them sang off key, it's true, but somehow it didn't matter. There was just so much substance in their singing. Their hearts came out in their voice.

It's said that Bhaktisiddhanta Sarasvati would often engage his spiritually advanced but less musically qualified kirtan singers in leading kirtan just to make a point. He would get them to lead because he wanted his disciples to see that it's not about musicality but rather about devotion.

Yes, I've heard that, too. So between listening to the Braj widows and hearing all kinds of kirtan, classical musical performances, the music of the folk troupes, and so on, I developed a full appreciation and affinity for Braj music. You know, I actually went and followed the Rasa-lila troupe around India just to be close to this music and to stay in the mood of it all the time. I did that for a couple of years while studying in Braj.

So it was like an obsession. You were totally absorbed.

Yeah, I guess you could put it that way. I watched every *lila* in terms of kirtan and dramatic performance. I saw the *lila* of Radha and Krishna, the *lila* of Chandravali, the *lila* of Govardhan, the *lila* of Mahaparabhu. Everything I knew as a child, that I had learned at the ashram, from *Bhagavatam* and *Chaitanya-charitamrita*—it was now coming to life. I was watching—along with upwards of 10,000 people in the audience—and experiencing in three- and four-hour devotional shows, complete productions with costumes, lights, stage, classical music, and so on. And it was all in the context of their own personal love—it was like they knew Mahaprabhu, the same way they knew Krishna. You have to experience what it's like to hear 10,000 people sing kirtan at these shows. It can transform the heart. Just the sound vibration alone is amazing, otherworldly.

I can imagine.

So I was reintroduced to the entire spiritual galaxy of my youth. But now I saw it within a distinct personal and cultural context. And as I have said before, this was important for me. My childhood ashram didn't integrate the cultural part that much. How could it? Being a product of the West, it naturally had limitations in that area. I mean, there were certainly individuals who were able to get the essence of the culture, even though they cultivated their Vaishnava practice in the West. They were able to do it because, in essence, it's a spiritual phenomenon. It's not Eastern or Western. But it's more difficult to do in the West—to imbibe the culture of Vaishnavism. That was my perception. In any case, the Western ashram did introduce me to so much of what I would now learn in a different way, enabling me to appreciate this next level of experience.

But back to your love of Braj music.

Right. Well, I was pretty much living in India, I had my own apartment there in Braj, and I would study music or practice or in some way be listening to music throughout the day. It was quite unconscious a lot of the time, since India always has music going on in every market, in all the bazaars, restaurants, cars, streets. It permeates the atmosphere. You find that there's a loud speaker or a musician doing their thing just about everywhere. Anyway, in the summer, when the heat was way more than most people could handle, I would leave and find work in the West.

Then, in the summer of 1997, I remember getting a life-changing e-mail message. I was in Australia and my mother wrote to me, telling me that she had cancer. She said she would like me to come home. I knew it had to be something serious, because she never asked for anything or made a big deal of things. Never. So for her to ask me to come home from traveling, which she knew I loved so much, I knew that this was serious. And so I came home and took care of her for a year.

If you don't mind my asking: What kind of cancer did she have?

Breast cancer.

She didn't catch it early then . . .

No. Actually, when she first felt a lump she had a test done and the office read the reports wrong, telling her it was only a calcium deposit.

It's so unfortunate when such things happen.

For a long time she didn't know that, and so it just kept growing . . . But my mother dealt with it like a true saint. She made a
point of letting me know that she saw this as Krishna's blessing.
She didn't want to get into any kind of lawsuits or anything like
that, though people kept recommending that she do so. She just
said, "I don't want to go after anyone, blaming doctors, or fate, or
whatever. I accept this for what it is. I don't want to pass from my
life with that sort of negative consciousness around me." So I took
care of my mother, and when she passed away I took her ashes to
Vrindavan and I put them in the Yamuna River.

Did you have any people there to help you through this?

Well, by now, of course, I had a family, of sorts, with the Brijbasis,
and so just being in Vrindavan again was like being with many loved
ones, with an extended family. I flew to India with her ashes alone,
and when I got there I took in the love of Swami Fateh Krishna's
family, some of my mother's devotional community, as well as that
of my dear friend Padmanabh Goswami and his wife.

**For those who don't know: He is the head Goswami or priest of what
is arguably the main temple of Vrindavan, known as Radha-raman.**

Right. And by Radha-raman's grace, that is the temple where I eventually studied and sang while living in Braj. More on that later.

I went back to India mainly to bring my mother's ashes to the
Yamuna, which is traditional for the soul of a Vaishnava, secur-
ing their next destination after death. At that time, it just so happened to be Kartik in Vrindavan again, and so many people who
knew my mother—dear friends from the West, along with Brijbasi
friends—were there to celebrate the festivities of the season. So I
wasn't really alone. It was here that I met one of my best friends. I
saw this girl sitting on a *rickshaw*, and eventually I was introduced
to her. She had come to spread her brother's ashes in the Yamuna,
just as I was bringing my mom's. She was raised in an ashram in
Canada and we were about the same age.

Kindred spirits.

We became extremely close friends. She was a large part of my healing that winter in Vrindavan . . .

What's her name?

Krishna Devata. We were both struggling with our loss, grief, and confusion. We were unable to just enjoy Vrindavan as we had before — *sari* shopping, playing with the animals, roaming about, walking to the river, and so on. Both our lives had just been dramatically changed, and, because of this and because of our similar background, we understood each other, more than others could. She was a blessing, specially sent to me at that time. No doubt. I think we were blessings to each other.

The harsh reality of material existence was there, but Krishna gave you a buffer.

It was certainly a harsh reality, yes. And she was and is great in so many ways. We took our days pretty slowly, and we stayed in a lot. But after some time, we got kind of stir crazy and decided we needed to get out a bit more. So we went out and found this *rickshaw-wallah* one night, and we said to each other, "Let's go out every evening and discover something new — let's find out something about Krishna that we didn't know the night before."

Yes, I can see how that would be healing.

It was the only thing we could do to feel real and excited about anything again. We desperately needed to look into what our lives were all about — what was being given to us, what our paths were trying to tell us. We knew that Krishna was trying to come closer, to make His presence known in our hearts and in our lives. We had just lost people very dear to us, and we were raw, feeling things very deeply.

So we told this *rickshaw-wallah*: "Please stop by every evening at 5PM, just before the evening darshans at the temples — each night we'll go to a different place." We let him choose which temples we would go to. So, the first place he took us to was the nearby Mirabai temple. It was special, different from the other Braj temples I had been to. In the inner sanctum, there was a courtyard that was filled with ivy and flowers, really beautiful. It felt very much like a garden, with that earthy and "alive" atmosphere that gardens tend to have. We took darshan of all the Mira images that lined the courtyard and then the *pujari* came out from the altar area and began telling us all about Mirabai, where she was born and her life story.

On the way out, our *rickshaw-wallah* said, "Okay, now I'll take you to the next temple," and he took us to the beautiful, old temple of Radha-raman, which we sort of knew, but only in the daytime. Since it was now evening *darshan*, we didn't know what to expect. Upon entering the temple, we saw at the back of the room, there were these musicians singing and playing classical instruments, and we found that the music compelled us to sit and listen, in a meditative way. We were spellbound. We couldn't even think of leaving. The music was so powerful, it was overwhelming.

After some time, we actually went up and sat on the platform right next to the musicians. We were just drawn to get closer and closer, to be next to the music. It felt like a safe haven for our hearts, unlike anything we had found thus far. We sat there for the next two or three hours, and from that day on, although our driver took us to many different temples, he would always drop us off at Radha-raman at the end of each evening. We would stay there until the temple closed, just listening to these kirtan and *bhajan* musicians.

Did you meet the musicians? Did you learn from them?

Well, one day, the main singer—Tarun Krishna Das—said to me, "Who is your music teacher?" I guess he wanted to know why Krishna Devata and I were so interested in the music and how we could sit so long just listening and listening and listening. "Well," I said, "I don't have a teacher." He responded quickly, saying, "Come to Jai Singh Ghera at 5 PM tomorrow for class."

When he saw that we were interested, he explained the back alleys behind the old temples, giving us shortcuts to his Guruji's Dhrupad class. So we went. After a while, we started taking classes with him privately; Krishna Devata was learning *tabla* and I took classical vocal lessons.

I'd go in the evening, taking regular classes with my Guruji, Pandit Vidur Mallik. I sat amongst many other students who studied with him, and it was here that I was introduced to Dhrupad. Pandit Vidur Mallik was one of Dhrupad's living masters, and his patience and loving nature and especially his smile made me feel as if I had found a healing salve for my heart. He had come from Allahabad to Vrindavan to teach — and to spend the golden years of his life on holy ground.

So you studied with him, or with Tarun Krishna . . . ?

Well, I eventually learned from both of them. But in the beginning I was training with Tarun Krishna Das, who was one of Pandit Vidur Mallik's senior students. He would repeat for me the lessons that Guruji taught in class, so that I could gradually understand what he was saying. I was learning the ABCs of Dhrupad, from the ground up . . .

I've read that Dhrupad is the origin of kirtan, at least stylistically.

Well, Dhrupad is actually the original classical music of India. It's the classical underpinnings. Although it has developed over the centuries, traditionally they try to keep it pure. For instance, when Dhrupad musicians perform, they use only the traditional instruments, such as *vina, pakhawaj*, etc., that originate in India.

I see, so they don't use *harmonium*, for example.

No, not usually, and not the *tabla* either. Just the ancient traditional instruments of Bharat. Our Guruji's classes focused mainly on singing, though. So, I was following this very, very ancient method of learning how to sing. There's something about Dhrupad singing that's unexplainable. When you sing, you focus, you meditate on pure notes, and you can enter a place of pure sound vibration.

You're going to need to explain that. [laughter]

When you practice Dhrupad, you focus mainly on the breath, and on the purity and simplicity of the sound quality. There are usually only a few words that are sung within a long composition. It's a meditation. And so you really, really experience sacred sound in a way that is unlike any other musical style. It's said that if you can do Dhrupad, you can do any other form of classical Indian music, because Dhrupad demands that you go into a very thoughtful meditation of breath, rhythm, and of course sound vibration.

So they taught you techniques for doing this?

Yes. I studied that way for about six years . . .

You were determined.

I would come and go, and I wasn't always there for an entire year. But six years coming and going, I was studying . . .

And your friend continued to study too?

No. She moved back to Canada and then to the States. But we still celebrate our music together and we're still very close friends. I went back to India without her and, as I said before, I would travel out of India in the summers to work in order to pay for my studies and living expenses. I needed to have this music — it felt like it gave me a reason to live. It was the thing that brought color, and feeling, back into my life — the loss of my mother was at times intolerable.

You were very close . . .

Yes, we were extremely close, and we became especially close just before she died. And, significantly, at the end, she told me that she wanted me to sing — that's what she wanted me to do with my life. At first, I didn't really consider what she said; I never imagined myself as a musician or an artist. Actually, I didn't want that kind of "struggling" life. Even as a kid, I noticed how artists always seemed plagued by so much trouble — whether it was their emotional state or their financial instability or whatever. But, after my mother was gone, I found that when I sang, it felt like she was close by. She was very much present and alive whenever I sang, and so I began to seriously think about her request.

After a while, it became obvious that music was a natural way of life for me; in fact, it became a loving obsession. After playing around with it, I decided to take it to the next level. I decided to seriously study how to sing. I mean my mother wanted me to sing, but that didn't mean that I knew how to do it, not really. So I decided to study seriously. And Dhrupad really fit perfectly, because it got me involved with vocal training on a very serious level, and it healed me internally. I realized that devotional music left me speechless, and made me feel totally complete. When I was in its company, I didn't feel fractured anymore—I felt like everything in my body's cellular structure lined up in harmony. I felt at peace.

Well put. Now, you were studying the classical aspect of spiritual music, Dhrupad. But did you bring the *maha-mantra* or other usual kirtan mantras into the picture?

In Dhrupad, they have something called a *bandish*, which is like a fixed composition. You see, Dhrupad is done only in Sanskrit or in Braj-bhasha—the local dialect of Vrindavan—and is only done in praise of Krishna or other aspects of divinity. Traditionally, it is sung in the temples. That's how traditional this is—it's not meant for entertainment, or for crowds and concerts. It's meant for yoga —real, genuine linking up with the Lord. So it's really that meditative in nature.

In big temples, like in Nathdwar, for example, where the deity of Sri Nathaji resides, they sing for Him, offering Dhrupad music to Him. And it goes on from generation to generation, with very famous Dhrupad artists passing down their techniques and styles. There's not many Dhrupad masters still living in the world, and it's a very difficult thing to study, to do properly, so it's becoming somewhat of a dying art. It requires tremendous training and many, many years of practice.

So how does this relate to my question about the *maha-mantra*?

Well, the point is this: When they sang, it wasn't necessarily the *maha-mantra* as such, but it was these old Braj-bhasha and Sanskrit texts, like maybe one verse that they would sing over and over, lapsing into a profoundly meditative state while doing it. But they would often focus on one long note to enter into it. [She sings an example of Dhrupad] You know, they could focus on one word, and they could make you feel that word in a thousand different ways. So, the *maha-mantra* is not generally used, but the idea of sacred mantra and repetition is definitely there.

Were these words from sacred texts, like the *Gita-govinda* or the *puranas*, or something like that?

Yes, they definitely used texts from the ancient Sanskrit sources. It comes from traditional Braj-bhasha or Sanskrit. That's the point.

Okay. Who are some of the people that inspired you when you started doing this, besides Tarun Krishna and his teacher?

You mean when I was in Vrindavan?

Yes, or just over the years—people that inspired you in kirtan.

Well, I would have to say that one of the first inspirations was Yamuna. You know, when I was a kid, we listened to her recording of *Brahma-samhita* every morning, and I was just amazed by her voice and the feelings she was able to transfer. She was definitely a huge inspiration. Yamuna and Vishnujana were my initial influences, when I was very young, and they've remained very active influences even to this day.

Vishnujana was special. Yamuna, too.

I wish more people knew about them. I think they're amazing. Now, when I was in Vrindavan, much later, I was definitely influenced by my Guruji, Pandit Vidur Mallik, the local Braj folk songs, and the classical troupe that I followed for many years. Besides that, I have to tell you, even the *rickshaw-wallahs*, beeping their horns and shouting, "Radhe! Radhe!"—these were influences, too. The sounds of Braj . . . what can I say? . . . They feel ancient, like eternal sounds. You have to experience them to know what I mean. And that's why this next album that I'm working on right now is focusing on "Returning to Vrindavan." I wanted to express my indebtedness, musically and devotionally, to this special, sacred village.

It just has such a unique quality; it's clearly spiritual. When you have sensitivity to these things, you'll know. You'll step foot in Vrindavan, and you'll know. For me, when I went there, it felt like I had come home.

Right. I know. Let me tell you a funny story along those lines. The first time I went to Vrindavan was in 1979. A close friend and I were going for the first time, and we were in Mathura. So, it was late at night, and we got in the back of a wagon or a bullock cart, or something like that, and we were galloping along to Vrindavan, on this country road. This is the middle of the night, and we are dead tired from travel. We had been traveling for days to get to Mathura, as a stopover before heading on to Vrindavan, and now here we were—on the road to Vrindavan! All of a sudden, I smelled something really familiar, and I said to my friend: "Yadu, do you smell that?" He said, "No, what?" I said, "I don't know where it's coming from, but I know this smell— it's _so_ familiar." And then his eyes opened wide, pointing to a sign on the road: "Look over there!" We read the sign together: "Town of Vrindavan." [laughter] It freaked us out, because it's just like: "Right, I recognize this smell because now I'm truly home." It was like the Twilight Zone: "You've just entered a space not of sight or sound but of mind. Your next stop—the town of Vrindavan."

[laughter] Exactly. Yeah! It's like you're obviously picking up from where you left off in some other life. And so you just recognize Vrindavan, all its sights, sounds, smells, even the market madness.

It's so true!

That's wonderful that it came to you through your sense of smell. At least one of the senses will always give you some indication that you know this place.

Right. Well, the other thing we need to discuss is how you came to sing as you do today and record your first CD.

I was often invited by my teacher to sing in the evenings at Radha-raman. This was such an honor. So, at Radha-raman, I would sing with him. Now, there's a part of me that didn't want to sing. I just wanted to listen. I mean, I felt unworthy, for one, but also, I just loved listening to him and to the other musicians there. I wanted to take in the sounds. I could understand why *shravanam*, or hearing, comes before *kirtanam*, or chanting. The sacred sound enters through your ear, and it goes inside the core of your being; it goes into your heart, permeating your full existence. It's roasting, percolating—it's warming up inside of you, getting ready to come out with the flavor of your own *bhakti* . . .

Nicely worded.

And when it finally comes out of your mouth, when it comes out in your own voice, it's the culmination of all you've been through; it's coming from all the different *sadhus*, all the different teachers, all the different musicians that you've heard over lifetimes. I remember looking at the faces of the pilgrims and guests at Radha-raman Temple, and, sometimes, they looked more beautiful than Radha-raman Himself. I could feel that, through their company, through their prayer and inspiration, I was truly connecting to *bhakti* on so many levels.

What's that? The devotees looked more beautiful than Krishna?

Well, because they reflected Krishna, and they embodied love for Krishna, which is so intense. Often, their expressions of love and prayer led me to something deeper than I could have experienced on my own.

Oh, I got you, okay.

So that's when I really started singing at Radha-raman. And I kind of knew then that I would eventually record some of my own music. But gradually what happened is this: I decided that I wanted to go back and finish my degree. Superficially, it was a bit of a detour, but not really—because it certainly enabled me to do my music, as you'll see. I enrolled at Antioch College in Yellow Springs, Ohio. I chose Antioch because every other semester you're required to leave the formal environment of the campus and classrooms, and go study and work outside. You can also do your own projects and receive credits for it. And so my project was returning to India every other semester to continue studying and to gradually record an album. That's when I recorded "Dasi." I went to India and started recording the album there but finished it in Los Angeles with a dear friend, who helped tremendously.

I see. Okay, and one last thing. Could you conclude with just a brief idea about the philosophy of kirtan?

Well, that's a vast subject. I would say that the key elements of kirtan are devotion, humility, and love. Kirtan is a calling out to God that resonates with a soft heart, and it has a universality about it that you don't find anywhere else. If you chant the names of God with a loving and open heart, all the secrets of the name come out to you. Like a shower or a waterfall, it pours its grace into you. That's what Sri Chaitanya said. Humility and love break down your internal barriers, and the name can come into your heart. The only thing that stops it is our own internal barriers. However, there are external barriers also, such as identifying with these bodies, and that can stop us from truly appreciating the spiritual nature of the name.

This seems like an internal barrier as well. Why do you distinguish this as external?

Well, all barriers are ultimately internal, though some have external implications, manifesting in the external world more than others. The bodily concept of life is more of an external barrier in the sense that it impacts on our external identification: black, white, rich, poor, male, female. It's an internal misconception that deeply affects us in our external life. That's one reason I tried to focus "Dasi" on Vaishnavis, or female devotees—it's about women who saw through these illusions because of their love of Krishna. When we can see beyond these bodily identifications, we can absorb fully the nectar of kirtan.

For more information contact:
www.karnamrita.com

ESHAV DAS

A professional musician for roughly 35 years, Keshav is now a kirtaniya *of considerable renown. Hav-*
ing recorded with Krishna Das on the Triloka label and performed with
Jai Uttal, Shyamdas, Alice Coltrane, Jeff Buckley, Narendra Budakar,
Rakesh Prasanna, Ayub Khan, Gulam Mohammed Khan, Dave Stringer,
and the Dervishes of Masjid al-Farah — Keshav gets around.

One of his greatest accomplishments to date is his CD, "Barefoot in
the Heart," comprised of seven beautifully crafted kirtan songs.

Guests on the recording include bansuri player Steve Gorn as well
as Stephen James (a student of Ravi Shankar for over twenty years) on
sarod and Indian violin. Krishna Das shares his vocals on two tracks
and kirtaniya Gandharva Sauls contributed some bass. First chair violinist from the Peking Classic Opera Company of New York, Wang Guo
Wei, was on hand as well, playing Er Hu (the two-string Chinese violin) on a traditional Bengali bhajan.

On his CD, Keshav sings with the Krishna Caravan — a talented group
of bhajan singers from both the Neem Karoli Baba satsang and that of
Ammaji. Today, he focuses on his privately owned East Village music
establishment: Keshav Music Imports, which he opened as a service to
musicians — particularly kirtan musicians. Unlike large companies that
purchase instruments sight-unseen over the phone, Keshav and his crew

fly to India personally, at least three times each year, to purchase hand-picked items for resale in the States. In addition, he eschews middlemen, allowing him to offer the best possible prices for his customers.

Keshav Music acquires most of its select instruments from DMS Music of Old Delhi. It also imports fine one-off pieces purchased in the Rabindra Sarani, Lal Bazaar District in Calcutta, famous for its harmoniums and tablas.

✳ ✳ ✳

So who are you? Surely, you weren't born Keshav Das.

That's right. The name on my driver's license is Christian Frey. Born September 10, 1952. That, of course, pertains to the body.

And where exactly did this body come into being?

In Freeport, Long Island.

Big family, small family?

Only child . . .

Did you get into music early on?

Yeah, I started playing guitar when I was nine or ten years old. You know, typical American kid listening to the radio . . .

Alright, so this is mid-60s?

Let's see . . . I got my first guitar in 1961 or 1962, and I was listening to Peter, Paul and Mary, folksy stuff like that. And I went to a very unusual school—it was based on an English School called Summerhill, run by a guy named A. S. Neil, and here in the States someone sort of tried to create an American version of it. I was exposed to a lot of really interesting stuff there, stuff that most ten-year-old white boys don't get exposed to. I was listening to Coltrane, Leadbelly, Miles Davis . . .

This was an American counterpart to an English school?

British school, right.

So why all this black jazz and blues?

Well, because the staff were all basically ex-beatniks, you know, and folkies. Really avant-garde artist types. *Johnny Get your Gun* and *Naked Lunch* were like required reading there. This is before the whole hippie thing. The word *hippie* didn't exist yet. This is pre-Beatles. But this was clearly a countercultural kind of place. So I got exposed to all this jazz and blues—Mose Allison and all that kind of stuff. I still actually have albums that people gave me back then, more than forty years ago. I still own them.

Hmm. You've held onto them for quite a while.

They're really precious to me. But I was exposed to a lot of blues and stuff. . . . This was folk blues, basically. You know, John Lee Hooker and Reverend Gary Davis Jr., and that kind of material. So I basically started out playing slide and ragtime blues, and so on. So that was my beginning. Then, of course, a little while later the Beatles happened; before that, rock and roll was all about the Philly sound; it was all black music, growing out of the blues.

Like Chuck Berry and . . .

Chuck Berry. Oh, yeah, totally. And the Philly stuff was big. A lot of dance music came out of Philadelphia, because this was pre-Motown, when Motown really didn't have a big presence. And then the Supremes came on the scene—that's when everyone got hip to Motown. But before Motown it was the Philly sound.

So, pretty progressive kid growing up in the pre-hippie era, influenced by happening music, dance music, stuff with rhythm.

Yeah.

Getting into music, the sounds of the era. I can relate—I had similar interests and sensitivities, though maybe a little later. And then the hippie thing happened and you got into that?

Yeah, all the typical American rock bands, and the British stuff that everyone was exposed to. It took over. You know, the Beatles,

Dave Clark Five, Rolling Stones, Dylan. You know, I knew just about every Dylan tune by heart! He was really a profound presence, especially back when I was in school. Everybody was just crazy for Bob Dylan. And, you know, especially when you're a kid, when you're that age, music, I think, really affects you — so much more profoundly than it does when you're an adult.

Right. Well, you're more raw, more open to things.

Yes. I mean there's just something special about youth. I rarely get that experience today, no matter how good the music is. It seldom has the magic, the impact it did when I was a kid.

The other thing was that Dylan wasn't just singing, "Ooo, Ahhh, Baby Baby." He really spoke to us, about our deeper concerns. He was saying stuff that was very easy to understand, even for a ten- or eleven-year-old boy. It was fundamental — truths that resonate with all people, I think. Anyone can understand the significance of all these social issues . . .

At least on a rudimentary level.

Yeah, I mean, I understood racial prejudice, black injustice, the excesses of the bourgeoisie. And I understood his sense of humor, lyrics that could easily have been just taken for nonsense — and of course a lot of it was simply "clever" — always provocative to a young mind. Stuff that got you thinking . . .

Did you get into the harder stuff, like from the Yardbirds to John Mayall . . .

Absolutely. Yeah, the Yardbirds. I mean, Jeff Beck has always been a guitar hero for me — a musician's musician. John Mayall didn't do it for me.

But he always had great guitar players with him . . .

Oh, of course. Peter Green, Clapton.

So you were into Cream, Hendrix, and stuff like that?

Oh, absolutely, yes. You know, I had an endless stream of garage bands, playing in Queens, making a little money here and there. We did all the usual covers of Cream material, Vanilla Fudge, and on and on.

Actually when I was fourteen I worked at the Village Theatre, on 2nd Avenue and 6th Street, which later became the Fillmore East.

Oh, I didn't know the Fillmore had previously been another place ...

I worked there after school, as a stagehand, and sometimes I also worked as a door person. I did whatever they needed, just so I could see all the famous bands. It was great.

This is when it was the Fillmore East?

No, before it became the Fillmore. I only went to the Fillmore once or twice when it actually opened ...

So the earlier venue had popular bands there ...

Oh, yeah. Sure. I mean, this was a place that had traditionally been one of the old Yiddish theatres, where people would go to see movies, and in-between features there'd be a live show, and Baggy Pants comics and hootchie dancing. It closed down for some years, and then, just when the hippie era was really unfolding, a guy named Roger Elson took it over—that's when I started working there. Over time, I saw the Doors there, and Cream and Derek and the Dominoes, Blue Cheer, Sly Stone, Carla Bley, Procol Harum, Leslie West—both in "the Vagrants" and later in "Mountain" ...

I thought that by the time Derek and the Dominoes and those bands came ...

Derek and the Dominoes must have already been the Fillmore— that's probably one of the two times I ever went to the Fillmore. I just resented these San Francisco guys taking over, you know? This was basically an East Village institution. It was a crazy, wonderful place, but not without its problems. Even with all the craziness behind the scenes at the Fillmore, it was a much more tidy, conservative operation than the Village Theatre.

The Village Theatre was badly run because the owner was a big druggie and did a lot of really weird stuff to people. For example, he hired these bands and then refused to pay them. Because of that, the musicians would wind up in jail, because they couldn't pay their hotel bills. So it was a really nutty place. Otis Redding played there, Wilson Pickett played there, the Who — oh, so many great artists. As a fourteen year-old kid, I really appreciated having that opportunity; I got exposed to a lot of amazing stuff. It broadened my consciousness, as they say.

And I was reading a lot of interesting books at the time, too. The guy who wrote *Steppenwolf*, his book on the Buddha . . .

Herman Hesse.

Herman Hesse, right. *Siddhartha*. I remember reading that one when I was like eleven years old, and I have a very specific memory at the school where I was going at the time — there was a laundry room in the basement, and I used to go there to have some quiet, a place to read. And I did, I read that whole book in the basement, in the laundry room.

So you started cleaning up your act in a laundry room. How appropriate! [both laugh] Would you say that this particular book was pivotal in your spiritual quest?

I don't know. I certainly liked what it was saying, about the journey, about questioning, about life. It definitely planted a seed, you know, for wanting to see India.

I see. Okay.

It's funny, a year after reading the book, I didn't remember much of the story — but I remembered Hesse's vivid images of India. I remembered the *sadhus* and the descriptions of ancient, much-traveled countryside. I thought, "Gee, I'd like to see that." But when you're eleven years old, you don't have much hopes of realizing your dreams, at least not right away. It's not like, "Oh! I'll just keep saving my nickels, throw some peanut butter sandwiches in a sack and hitch-hike to Benares."

So that planted a seed, but basically you involved yourself with the usual activities of childhood.

Yep, the usual stuff.

So how would you say the spiritual/ India thing really caught on in your life?

Well, it began with my early years. And it was Western religion. You know, my mother was a Sunday school teacher, and she was *very* religious. I mean, she was one of *those* kinds of religionists — a bit fanatical. So, her whole Jesus hysteria really turned me away from religion. She sent me to gospel camps and stuff like that. I just had it shoved down my throat.

A Protestant denomination?

It was good old American Baptist stuff. Whatever church there was, whatever town one happened to be living in — it really didn't matter. She was really big on gospel churches, up until when she was very old. Late in life she moved to Washington and always went to the real holy roller churches, where people were testifying, falling on the floor, and speaking in tongues. She really loved the whole Baptist hysteria thing. It worked for her.

So you were kind of raised with this fundamentalist Christianity, and that caused some sense of rebellion . . .

Well, yeah. I saw some level of hypocrisy in American Christianity, and so it really turned me away from the teachings. You know, I just couldn't get behind people saying that "Jesus is the only way, and if you're not with Jesus you can't be saved." I would always ask, "Why are there still millions of people who never heard of him? And what about all the people who came before he was born? Come on!"

That was always my question, too. I think a lot of people react to that narrow, exclusivist philosophy.

If that's our concept of God, if He's that narrow, well, I'm just not buying into it.

So that was sort of put on the back burner for some time. But how did interest in Indian spirituality start to emerge in your life?

Well, in 1988, I decided to give up drugs and alcohol, essentially. And that really put me on a path, when I became committed to change. My wife died . . .

When did you marry?

We were together for almost thirteen years. And so when my wife died, that prompted a lot of questions, and not a lot of answers. So I was looking into different strategies of life and reading a lot of books. And at that time, maybe thirteen years ago, I started doing yoga at Jivamukti Yoga Center.

Now what brought you there?

Well, prior to my wife's death I used to ride motorcycles—I did it semi-professionally, you know, with a bit of road racing at all the major race tracks in the United States. I had a lot of injuries, causing intense stiffness in various parts of my body, and someone said, "You know, if you don't do some kind of exercise you're going to be a crabbed-up old man really soon." Another friend took it further. I was having a cup of coffee with an editor of a local magazine, and she said, "Do you want to go to a yoga class?" I said, "Sure." I agreed half because I wanted to do something for my body, and half because, well, I thought she was kind of cute— and I'll go along with anything once, or even twice.

Anyhow, I went to a class at Jivamukti and I just immediately knew by the time the class was over that I wanted to do this. So then I was doing yoga for awhile—not too long, maybe a month or two—and I started attending *satsang* on Monday nights. This consisted of David and Sharon, the owners of Jivamukti, and a couple of teacher trainees and two or three students. We would sit and read passages from various holy books, whether the *Bhagavad Gita* or the *Mahabharata*, or some Sufi material, or even the Kabbalah, whatever.

And then we would take turns at the end singing kirtan, which was very awkward because most of us were too embarrassed to

sing, especially David, David Life—he really didn't like singing.
He was the former owner of Life Café. That's how he got the name
David Life. His given name was David Kirkpatrick.

So that's how it all started for me. And it developed from there:
One Monday night they said, "Oh, we're going to have a real *kirtan-wallah* here tonight, so we don't have to embarrass ourselves."
When I heard this, I thought, "Oh, great. This should be interesting." And then this Jewish guy with glasses came in and started
to sing, and I thought, "This sounds a lot like the guy on that tape
they always play in class. What's his name?" And then I went
over to talk with this woman "V.V." who worked at the center, and
I asked her, "Who is this guy? Why doesn't he introduce him-
self?" And that's when she told me his name was Krishna Das.
I then realized that it *was* the same guy on the tape. At the time,
KD didn't actually have any CDs out, but he was one of several
Maharaji devotees who were featured on a compilation with Ram
Dass, put together by Raghu Markus. Anyhow . . . I was impressed.
It was the first time I saw somebody actually singing kirtan live.
And I really liked what he did.

So you heard Krishna Das . . .

It grabbed me right away. Now, at that time, prior to my wife's
death, I hadn't played music for about nine years. But then, with
this new awareness happening in my life, I decided that I would
play music again. But only for pleasure. I wouldn't play for getting a contract or being on MTV, no career stuff. I would just play
for release, for feeling good. So, anyhow, after about three or four
weeks of hearing Krishna Das—he came there kind of intermit-
tently—I gave him a copy of a CD that I played on. That's when
he encouraged me to play; and any time there's an audience I was
anxious to jump in; it was much easier of course when there was a
great "front man" like KD. More importantly, I think, was the desire
to be a contributing member of the *satsang*; to be "a part of."

What did you play there, guitar?

Yeah, and he liked it. He liked my vibe. So he invited me in: "Okay, sit in with me." I just joined in with simple things. I would play bells or the *ektar* for him. You know, that was the beginning . . .

So, through him you became involved with Neem Karoli Baba . . .

That's right. I remember it began with this one girl, a young *yogini*, to whom Krishna Das gave a copy of *Miracle of Love*, the book about Maharaji. Now, by that time I was already hooked. I mean, I had a strong intuition that Maharaji was going to have a big influence in my life. It helped that KD was so good at storytelling. He has a wonderful gift for bringing Maharaji alive to people who have never heard of him. So the following week, when that girl came to the Monday night kirtan, I said, "Oh, you got the book— how did you like it?" She responded by telling me that it really wasn't her cup of tea. So I asked Krishna Das, or KD, as we had started to call him by then, if I could borrow it. He said, "Oh yeah, well she's not going to read it; sure, you can just have it."

Now, what's the story behind that book? Who wrote it and how did it come to be?

Well, basically—and this is the short version—there were two guys. There was a guy named Chaitanya and another guy named Kabir Das. And what they did was this: After Maharaji passed away, after he left his body, they traveled all over India with a tape recorder, interviewing all the older devotees of Maharaji, both in India and in the States. It was a huge project. Ram Dass more or less "commissioned" them and they were thrilled to do all the legwork. Halfway into the project, though, Ram Dass seemed to lose enthusiasm; he didn't really seem willing to inject the project with much in the way of resources. But these guys were *sadhus*, after all, and Ram Dass respected that. So he continued to fund them—at least he gave them enough money to buy a little tape recorder and some batteries and some paper and pencils. These guys were truly living as *sadhus*, very modestly. Every day, they would take the batteries out of the tape recorder and put them on a rooftop to heat them up in the morning sunlight—just to get a couple more jolts out of the batteries. That's how broke they were.

And they traveled around doing all of this interviewing, with whatever little they had, and eventually they hand-transcribed all the recordings, transposing all the stories with pencil and paper— I actually now have photocopies of the original hand-transcripts and I am gathering and editing a new book of Maharaji stories. Anyhow, after all that hard work, it just sort of sat around for some time. Eventually, enough people bugged Ram Dass and he finally got the idea—he saw that people were really interested in something other than his first book. So he—with a lot of help— edited *Miracle of Love* and it became a huge thing, at least within a certain circle.

I can speak for myself: That book just totally blew me away. I'd been reading so many books, you know, from all the great *sadhus*, and teachers, of *dharma* and truth, in its various shades. It didn't amount to much, though. It was all like, "Oh yeah. This guy is interesting and has some great qualities, but . . ." It was always just an intellectual thing for me.

It didn't touch your heart . . .

No, it didn't. Nothing really did. And then I read *Miracle of Love*, and it was a totally different story. I'd be reading the book and the phone would ring, and I'd be on the phone talking to somebody, but I'd still be reading the book. And tears would just be streaming . . . and I'd say, "I've got to go," and I'd hang up the phone and fall on the floor crying. I was so in love with Maharaji. Just totally. Just so lost in him . . .

So you accepted him as your guru without ever meeting him in the flesh.

Never met him in the body, no. But his presence, even in the book, through all the stories—it was so strong. And at that point, too, I had already been to India, so the whole thing had deeper meaning for me.

Oh, how did that come about? You were going to Jivamukti and then you took off to go to India?

Right, well, yeah, because I was doing yoga and I had a huge stack of books next to my bed, you know, all the teachings, and various travel essays and histories of India. So I really wanted to experience the place. That's what happened, and I just took off without too much of a plan. I just went there and I traveled around. At one point, while I was there, somebody asked me about that Neem "Curly" guy—I didn't even know who he was. I thought, "C-U-R-L-Y." I even thought maybe he was referring to Sai Baba. Maybe they called him Curly, because of the big hair, the afro. So, when I first went East, I had no idea who Neem Karoli Baba was.

Did you have any ISKCON experiences back then, meetings with the devotees and such . . .

No, not really, not until I met Bhima-karma.

Ah, the musician.

Yeah. I met Bhima, actually, somewhere in the mid-1990s. It was right before Krishna Das's birthday, I remember. We met in a strange way, but we really clicked. I saw this young kid sitting on a subway car very late at night, going home, and I was leaving for India the next day. And he was playing with his *mridanga* drum—right there on the subway—even though the drum was in a case, a bag. Great player. Cool bag. So I went over to him and asked, "Where did you get the bag?" I thought it would make a nice gift for KD, for his own drum. That's when Bhima and I started talking, and I said, "Give me your phone number and I'll call you when I get back from India."

I did, and we made a real connection. After that, he was playing kirtan with me for about five months. He was so good. In fact, I kept bugging KD, saying, "You've got to hear this kid play!" KD, of course, responded as I knew he would: "No, I hate the *kohl*, because you can't tune it. I've got three of them in my closet. I'd rather just use a *tabla* player." But I was insistent, and so finally he said, "Alright, let's check him out . . ."

I remember it happened one night when our *tabla* player wasn't able to show up. So KD said, "Bring the kid in." KD wasn't really into it, but he didn't have much of a choice, since the *tabla* guy wasn't going to make it. Of course, as soon as he heard Bhima play, it just blew his mind. He said, "Oh, my God. You close your eyes and you think there's some eighty-year-old Bengali virtuoso playing here." But, nope, it was this skinny white boy playing like an angel.

He *is* a phenomenal player. But let's backtrack a little: You've been leading kirtan. . . . How did that whole thing start?

Well, I started because, at that time, Krishna Das was still working for Triloka; he was still producing other artists. He was very active as a producer in the record business. So he'd be off...

I didn't know that.

Oh yeah, sure. He was very . . .

I interviewed him and I asked him about other musical experiences. He didn't mention anything about this, or at least I didn't realize the extent of it.

Well, he was doing it, sure. We'd play on a Monday night, say, and he would run off to JFK, to produce an album in South Africa. And the next week he'd be back, and then he'd be off to Europe . . .

Was it world music or what?

That's right. Mostly, yeah. He was into African music, and a lot of Reggae, too.

But back to you . . .

Right. Well, it's interrelated. You see, sometimes he couldn't make it to Jivamukti, for our kirtan gigs, because he'd be out of town, as I was saying. That's when, more and more, David and Sharon would press their teacher trainees to sing. They'd encourage people to lead a kirtan or two. We were sort of replacement singers.

I remember there were two old *harmoniums* that KD had gifted to the center. So I would go into one of the empty classrooms whenever I got a chance, and I'd practice on it. It came easily to me, because I was sitting right next to KD week after week, and I was watching him. I had already played keyboard, so it wasn't that big a transition to play *harmonium*. That's how we started doing kirtan on Monday nights, when KD wasn't there, and how I started to lead the singing.

What did you chant?

Hmm. At that point I was just doing all the same stuff that KD did. So it was a lot of, "Shri Rama, Jaya Rama" or other Sita-Rama, or Devi chants, and also the various "Hare Krishna" chants — all the tunes that were on the old Triloka recordings. We would do some of Jai Uttal's material, and some other songs, traditional stuff. I wasn't really writing my own melodies yet.

When you went to India, did any *kirtaniyas* really knock you out? I know when Vaiyasaki went to India, he started recording all these old Bengali guys. Did you do that kind of stuff?

Absolutely, I made a bunch of recordings of old Bengali guys at the ashram in Kainchi . . .

That's Neem Karoli Baba's place . . .

Right. I made a bunch of recordings of these guys and people kept saying, "Oh, will you make me a copy, will you make me a copy?" Back then, I couldn't just cheaply reproduce CDs, like now, and cassettes took time and trouble. I didn't want to be bothered with it — everybody wanted them and it was just too time consuming. So what I did was, I edited all the best stuff of the Bengali *kirtan-wallahs* and put it on three CDs. I never did find out if most of my Bengali friends ever got their copies of the CDs or not, because they lived in these little funky villages in West Bengal — who knows if they ever got them. I did most of this right around the time my mother passed away; it was on Krishna Janmashtami, the appearance day of Krishna.

What year was that?

It would be . . . about eight years ago.

So that would be 1999.

That's right. So we decided to do a benefit for the Vrindavan widows, and we sold a bunch of the CDs to the Neem Karoli Baba ashram. We also sent out emails to all the people in my customer database, for Keshav Imports, and we took pre-orders. We printed copies for all these people — and there were many — and then all the money from the sales would be added to the money from the kirtan. And we gave it to the Vrindavan widows. It was mostly Shyamdas and I — there were others, but they just played for a short amount of time and left, because most people didn't want to stay all night. Anyhow, that was the beginning of our whole Vrindavan widows benefit, and we've been doing that every year in August.

Beautiful. For those who don't know much about Vrindavan's widows: In India, in many low-income homes, especially, women are customarily given a lot of trouble after the death of their husband. Some become menial servants for their in-laws—doing backbreaking tasks and sleeping on the porch. Some of the younger ones are forced into prostitution. Widows, with no money and no husband, have no rights or protection from local corrupt authorities, especially in rural India. They arrive every day by the thousands in Benares and Vrindavan to beg alms, hoping to die in one of these two holiest cities. Many take refuge in "widows ashrams," where they sing *bhajan* and kirtan, particularly the *maha-mantra*, from 5 AM until 9 PM, nightly. In return, they often get a cup of rice and some kitchen scraps, along with a place to sleep on the floor.

That's the scene, unfortunately. So we worked to establish a benefit for them — the Vrindavan Widows Fund. I started this charity in honor of my mother, who died, as I said, on Krishna Janmashtami.

Every rupee we collected was used to buy wholesale blankets, mosquito nets, warm shawls — Vrindavan and Banares, as you know, can get really cold in winter — and whatever the women tell us is most necessary. There are no "administrative costs," because all the people involved, like the "Friends of Vrindavan Project," who help out a lot, are strictly unpaid volunteers.

How did we get onto this subject of Vrindavan's widows? I forget.

Right. Well, I was telling you about the *kirtan-wallahs* I recorded. I condensed their material into three CDs, as I mentioned, and I sold them to benefit the Vrindavan widows — that's how we started talking about this. Once I really heard those guys play, I was totally knocked out. There was one guy: Ramkumar Chattopadhaya. Absolutely unbelievable. Here was someone who was continuing on with a musical career that began in a prior life. He was that good. He's a really one-of-a-kind Bengali *kirtan-wallah*. I would listen to his stuff, but I couldn't approach it. No way. It was so sophisticated, I couldn't even attempt to emulate it, you know? I wouldn't know where to begin.

Out of your league.

Exactly. But the guys who played at Maharaji's ashram were very accessible. I would get up every morning at 4 AM and do morning ceremonies with them. I'd also sit with them on and off during the day, and once you sit, hear it, watch it, listen to it often enough, it gets into you and then it's really not that hard to figure out how to play the stuff they're playing.

And these were mainly Bengali Vaishnavas?

Oh, yeah, absolutely.

It's funny. I realized when I was speaking to KD that his initial influence with chanting "Hare Krishna" came from Bengali Vaishnavas, and now I'm hearing something similar from you. Jai Uttal, too. It seems that the seed comes from Sri Chaitanya and that Bengali lineage—that's where the essential potency of kirtan comes from.

Well, yeah, that's the flow. It comes through that line. Krishna Das used to always tell a story about doing kirtan all night, and how all the young *kirtan-wallahs* would really show off their stuff, when it was their turn to lead the kirtan. They would play all their hottest chops, and sing all their most difficult *ragas* and really show off. And then this one old guy would get up, and his voice would sound like ten miles of bad road and broken glass and barbed wire and stuff like that. But, somehow, when he would sing, everybody would be in tears. That guy was still there when I came to India, for about four years he was there. He was a Bengali Vaishnava.

What was his name?

The head guy at Kainchi was Shyamsundar. That's who I'm talking about here.

By the way, how did you get the name Keshav?

There's a lady who was with Maharaji for many years — for something like fifty years — and she was a big part of his ashram up there. Her story — as it's been told to me — begins with a saintly woman who lived up in Nanital, and she had a young daughter. One morning, Ananda Mayi Ma showed up at her door and said, "Your little girl is not just a little girl, she is really something special," and wandered off. An hour later, Sombari Baba — I think it was him, or, anyway, some other famous saint from that region — came to her and basically gave her the same message. After that — like an hour later — Neem Karoli Baba showed up and said the same thing.

Now, her parents didn't say anything to her — they just wanted her to be a normal, happy kid. They weren't looking to turn her into a spiritual superstar or anything like that. So she got married, had a couple of kids, and was living a normal life. And then one day, she had Maharaji's *darshan* in her dreams; he infiltrated her consciousness. After that, she just went to her family and said, "Listen, you know I love you, but this is what I have to do." And she just took off to be with Maharaji, spending the next forty-five or fifty years with him; she was like his right hand. Of course, she's not one of these people who will allow you to glorify her in any way. If you were to suggest to her that she was in any way his lineage holder or successor, she'd shove you out the door in a hurry . . .

And what's her name?

Siddhi Ma.

So you met her and she gave you the name?

I met her in 1996 and she gave me the name Keshav Das. It was really funny, when we first met, she said, "Oh, I guess since you're a Westerner you want a name." I said, "Oh, yeah, that's right," and she said, "Well, I don't give names." So that was cool. What's in a name, right? But then she said, "If something happens to inspire a name, we can give you one. Don't worry." And she also said "See me at the end of Holi and we'll see what happens."

Later on, she told me that Maharaji had come to her in a dream and said, "Call him Keshav." And it felt really right for me; I liked the name immediately. But there was a part of me that was really disappointed it wasn't Keshav "Das." You see, I was hanging out with the "Das" guys — so I wanted to be a "Das" too. I didn't mention this to anybody, except to my friend, Jagadish. Eventually, what happened was this: A year later, we went up to Nanital to see Siddhi Ma for the first *darshan* at Durga Puja. When we walked in, she said, "Keshav *Das*, how are you?". . .

Oh!

And I didn't say anything. But when we came out, Jagadish said, "She called you Keshav Das." And I said, "Well, you know . . . they do know what's in your heart.

But I guess in that tradition, as in the Gaudiya Vaishnava tradition, the name sort of automatically implies a "Das," no? I mean, you get a name that is associated with a divinity—but it's not that you *are* that divinity. You're a *servant* of that divinity. *Das* means "servant." So that's the idea.

Of course. That's right . . .

I always wondered why Jai Uttal doesn't have the "Das" part to his name.

Well, his name was Jai Gopal, but back then it was common for people to use half of their Hindi or Sanskrit name and half of their Western name. Uttal was his family name.

Okay. The only remaining things to talk about are how your CD came

about and any major influences in kirtan that you want to talk about, or maybe your understanding of kirtan philosophy.

Remember, I was doing kirtan—and I still do it—just for the pleasure of doing it; I am not trying to make a career out of it. I was doing kirtan at a place in Staten Island, at a yoga center, and one of the people who studied there said, "Oh, I have a little recording studio and you could come in and do a CD for free; you can come in and we'll record it." So I got all psyched and I thought, "This will be a lot of fun." I called up all kinds of people—I called Krishna Das; I called up Steve James, who studied with Vasant Rai and Ravi Shankar for like thirty-something years—he was really an amazing player. Steve recently passed away.

What did he play?

He played *sarod* and South Indian style violin on the CD. And I called Steve Gorn, and various other people. I said, "Oh man, I'm gonna do a CD!" And we were really excited. So we showed up at the studio, and the studio was like the size of a small walk-in closet. The guy had an eight-track cassette recorder, the kind you would see in people's college dorms like fifteen years ago, for making demos. And I said, "Come on, man. Where's the real studio?" And he said, "Well, this is it." So we did it. We just went in and basically did the tracks with very cheap microphones—the equipment was about as low-tech as it could possibly be . . .

You got tremendous results.

Yeah. I mean, it was the spirit of the people, really. We had a lot of fun. We used all kinds of instruments. I had worked in Chinatown for about ten years—I used to work for this Chinese community group. So, yeah, I called the people I knew and I got this Chinese two-string violin. It was just a wonderful conglomeration of events, and people, and instruments, and talents, conspiring to make a really nice CD of kirtan music.

Now, the guy with the Chinese violin wanted to know what the song was about, to get the mood of the tune. It's on the morning Hare Krishna track, and so we had to explain it to him. It was interesting, because the guy spoke this really strange dialect, so we actually ended up having to use two translators. And imagine me explaining first what the Hare Krishna mantra is all about and then also explaining that it was this early morning melody, and all that that implies. But I did it. I explained to him that the melody we were singing was the one that they traditionally play every morning. The *arati* ceremony at Kainchi, to rise with the Lord — so there's the part where it goes, *"jago, jago,"* you know, "Wake up, Krishna; wake up, Krishna." It says, "Start the world again and give us life — bring out the sun and give us one more day to love you." So this is basically what we explained to him, and he had no background in this stuff.

Beautiful.

So we were explaining all of that to this guy who spoke this very strange Mandarin dialect, and he said, "Oh, okay. I like that; I can get with that." And basically he sat down and played his part straight through, without any editing, and we were all sitting there with our hairs standing up on our arms. So it really was a fun project, a lot of fun and done very quickly. We actually packed something like eighteen people into that small studio. We loved it, though.

What about the opening of the store? We should talk about that.

Yeah, sure. Basically, when I was playing with KD and traveling all over the place with him, everywhere we went people said, "Where can I buy a good quality *harmonium*? Or where can I buy a pair of *tablas* and not get ripped off?" So, there was nobody we knew that we could really recommend in the States, at least no one that had consistently good quality stuff, and so KD and I were playing around with the idea of bringing a few *harmoniums* in the country and selling them. Some other kirtan instruments, too.

We went to the opening for Jivamukti when they got their new place, the one on Lafayette Street. They had a big show with Sting and a lot of famous jazz musicians were there. So basically, after the show was over and all the musicians were sort of hanging

out in what they were using as a backstage area, KD told everybody, "My friend Keshav is going to India and he really knows
his stuff—he can hook you up if you want a sitar or *tablas* or *harmonium*; he's the man." And like, really, I didn't know what I was
doing. I hadn't a clue, not a clue. There was one *tabla* player, a
friend, who showed me some basics—how to tell a good drum
from a bad one, and so on.

Oh, great. [laughter]

So that was a big help. NOT. But other than that I had no experience as a businessperson. Still, everybody trusted KD so much
that they said, "Okay," and all these big musicians came over and
just wrote me checks. So, there it was: I had to go to India and get
quality stuff at good prices.

**What a responsibility! But you must have done a good job, because
you now have quite a reputation as an importer of kirtan instruments. And what about renting that place on Fourth St., in the East
Village? That's *the* center for imported kirtan paraphernalia. How did
that come about?**

Well, basically I ran the business for eight years out of my little studio apartment—right out of my own home . . .

Oh!

That's right. For eight years I was doing that out of a 12 x 13-foot
studio apartment—I was living on top of my instruments, literally. And after eight years of doing that, I got tired of sleeping
on a mattress on top of forty *harmoniums*! It was getting really
old, you know, with this little apartment where there was no sunlight and nothing but instruments in every nook and cranny. The
place was so crowded you could hardly walk in there, and I had a
constant parade of Indians from Toronto and Afghanis driving in
from West Virginia, and all kinds of folks showing up at strange
hours. I even had an unannounced visit from Ustad Vilayat Khan,
who'd come to pick out a *harmonium* for one of his favorite students. Eventually it dawned on me that there was enough of an

audience for Indian music that you could run a real business out of it.

Now, initially, KD was going to be my partner. We used to sit around at the Starbucks around the corner from Jivamukti and talk about having a little music shop. But then his daughter, Janaki, said, "Daddy, you know what I think—I *am* going to go to college after all." So, he said to me, "Well, I don't have any money right now." Anyway, he moved in the direction Maharaji sent him in, and his CDs do pretty well, and I moved in mine. The store is doing pretty well.

It's important to remember, the little pipe-dream that Krishna Das and I had wasn't so much to be in the Indian music *business* and to make a lot of money, but to have a little place where people could hang out on the tucket, drink *chai* and smoke *bedis*, and, you know, now it exists. And it is a viable business, too, which is great. People really appreciate it. It's a labor of love, and it paid off. Kirtan is here to stay, and, hopefully, so is KESHAV MUSIC Imports.

For more information contact:
www.keshav-music.com

DEVA PREMAL
&
MITEN

Jolantha Fries and Andrew Desmond are two spiritual seekers whose music, in their own words, explores the essence of love, devotion, and consciousness. Known by their Sanskrit names, Deva Premal ("Divine Loving") and Miten ("Friend of God"), respectively, they have produced almost a dozen CDs, either individually or as a team, over the last decade and have played privately for His Holiness The Dalai Lama, who described their music as "Beautiful, Beautiful music!"

Eckhart Tolle, author of The Power of Now, *describes their music as offering "a portal into Presence. As you listen, the sacred space that lies beyond the mind emerges naturally and effortlessly." Brandon Bays, author of* The Journey, *describes their sound as carrying "the listener into realms of ecstasy, bliss, and joy." Deva Premal, particularly, has been dubbed "the Enya of mantra."*

Cher, *too, appreciates Deva Premal and Miten, having used their version of the traditional Gayatri Mantra on her farewell tour, some years ago. She says of their release "The Essence": "It is my favorite CD to do yoga to. In fact, I drive my teacher crazy, because it's the only one I ever want to hear!"*

❋ ❋ ❋

Let's begin with some background. Readers would want to know where you're coming from and how that led you to kirtan.

DP: Well, I was born in Nuremberg, Germany. My father has been, and continues to be, a big influence in my life. He passed away recently, but he traveled the spiritual path ever since I can remember, studying yoga and holy texts, the sacred scriptures — always very disciplined, waking every morning at 3 AM for two hours of meditation. He also taught himself Sanskrit and introduced mantras into our family early on. In fact, when my mother was pregnant with me, they welcomed me into the world with the Gayatri Mantra, singing it throughout the pregnancy.

As I was growing up, my father devised exercises for my sister and me, in an attempt to help us to develop spiritually and to help us become more aware. For example, we were taught to say "OM" whenever we placed something on the table, and "Rama" whenever we switched on the light — not the usual kind of life-training for young German girls in the 70s! He was great, really, but certainly different than your average dad.

When I was a kid, all I wanted was to be "normal," but with a father like mine I really didn't stand much of a chance. We were vegetarian — to this day I still don't eat meat or fish — and I grew up without TV or any of the usual social dependencies.

Did you have any Western religious connection?

DP: At the age of nine, I developed an interest in Christianity and began saying the Lord's Prayer every night. I did this secretly at first, because I thought it might be forbidden in my parents' household. But my fears were unfounded. When they finally found out, they showed no sign of disapproval. They were absolutely supportive, even a bit later, when I asked to be baptized. I was always encouraged to be myself, and to have my own experiences. Anyway, just before the baptism, fate stepped in, you might say: My mother returned from India as a disciple of Bhagwan Shree Rajneesh!"

So that brings us to Shree Rajneesh. Miten, let's also hear some of your background before we go on.

M: The earliest part of my life, in London, which is where I was born, doesn't have the spiritual sparkle, shall we say, of Deva's. My story begins when I was a bit older. Just for background: I established a successful career in the late '70s and early '80s as a singer-songwriter in Europe, appearing as a "special guest artist" along with such acts as Fleetwood Mac, Ry Cooder, Randy Newman, and Lou Reed, among others. Opening for those guys was really my training ground, at least musically. I learned so much. It was preparation for what I do now. I learned how to meditate while playing music. I didn't call it that at the time, but when I look back I see that I was totally absorbed in the moment as I played those songs. I stood beneath a white spotlight that obscured everything from my sight. I was aware only of the sound of my guitar, and the feeling of my voice vibrating through my body and filling the auditorium. It was a type of high. I'm very grateful for those days and what I learnt from them.

Eventually I was offered a record deal of my own. I recorded, went on tour—it was an exciting life for a young guy. But I knew deep down that it would never sustain me. I remember I would close my concerts with a song I'd written called "Show me a Home." It was a song sung by an outsider who looked at the world before him in bewilderment and hopelessness. And the refrain kept coming back . . . "Show me a home where I can lay down my head, where there's music and laughter and the hungry get fed . . ." I was looking for home, for spirituality, for respite.

What I didn't know then—though I know it now—is that whatever you really wish for, somehow, it mysteriously comes to pass, in one way or another.

Meanwhile, the record company, the manager, and the publishers, were all getting nervous. They had invested a lot of time and money in me, and nothing much was happening. The line wasn't moving—not big time. Also, my family life began to fall apart. I was married to a really nice woman, and, in a sense, we had everything. My career was going pretty well—I mean, we had some money in the bank and a beautiful two-year-old son. But inside there was still this nagging question that wouldn't go away: Where is this "home" that found its way into my song? Where is the spiritual respite I was singing about? All I knew for sure is that it was somewhere else.

In due course, I left my family. It wasn't easy. We were all heart-broken. But no matter how hard I tried, I couldn't live in the wrong home anymore. Thinking back, I associate those times with pain, frustration, ambition, helplessness. It was clear to me that I needed to embrace a new set of values. Something had to change.

And then it happened, the way it usually does: Someone gave me a book called, "No Water, No Moon." It was a book by Bhagwan Shree Rajneesh. I'd seen some of his disciples in London. They were known as the "Orange People." I guess it was because of the red robes. They dressed in the colors of the sunrise.

At this point maybe you can give our readers some background on Bhagwan Shree Rajneesh, also known as Osho.

M: The external facts. [laughter] — the internal facts you'd have to experience for yourself.

Right.

M: Let me say first, that he was grossly misunderstood, by almost everyone — including us, his disciples!

Briefly, he was born in Kuchwada, Madhya Pradesh, India in 1931. His parents gave him the name Rajneesh Chandra Mohan and raised him as a Jain, the nonviolent religious tradition founded by the sage Mahavira around the time of the Buddha, 2,500 years ago. Actually, it goes back into prehistory, but it was systematized by Mahavira. Anyway, when he was twenty-one he attained enlighten-ment. At that time, too, he graduated from the University of Saugar with first-class honors in philosophy. Actually, he was a professor of philosophy at the University of Jabalpur for nine years. In 1966, he left his teaching post and established an ashram in Bombay. Then, in 1974, he left Bombay and set up in Poona where his ashram became the place to be in the '70s! As the word spread, seekers, travelers, (and others!) came from all over the world to experience his contro-versial meditation methods and his inspirational discourses.

He was not a stranger to controversy. In fact, he welcomed it!

He saw that the Western mind was fully preoccupied with sexual fantasies, and consequently created methods to help clear the mind so meditation could happen. Hence the term "Sex Guru!"

This was ironic, in fact, because he was actually helping people to rise beyond the sexual pull, into a world of peace and quiet. Some years later, he relocated to the United States, in Oregon— where he established an alternative, experimental society named Rajneeshpuram, which was eventually closed down due to U.S. government pressure.

In 1986 he was deported for (frankly, ridiculous) charges of violations of immigration law and eventually returned to Poona. He left his body on January 19, 1990, claiming he had been poisoned while incarcerated in a U.S. prison.

Do you want to say something about his teachings?

M: Osho incorporates almost every method that anybody ever used to gain enlightenment, but the technique he stresses above all others (meditation, in a word), is one in which you observe your own mind, its workings, its prejudices, its conditionings.

Doing this perfectly, he teaches, can lead to a state of "no mind" — where we are masters of our mind and not governed by it—which in turn leads to enlightenment. He suggests that one should embrace material desires, not artificially repress them. His teachings are deep, and as I have said, often misunderstood. He encourages celebration and non-seriousness as a path to enlightenment. Sincerity, as opposed to seriousness. This leads to a non-judgmental approach to life, a return to Innocence, but not naiveté.

I never knew I could feel such a deep sense of the joy of life, until I lived among his people in their communes.

Deva, Osho also played an important part in your life. Why not talk about that a little bit?

DP: I was ten years old when I began experimenting with Osho's active meditations. I just loved them. And, although I was quite young, I saw in Osho's eyes what I later realized to be unconditional love. I knew instantly that I would be his disciple.

I had to seek my father's approval to "take *sannyasa*," being underage at the time. Again, I received only encouragement.

Perhaps you can tell our readers about Rajneesh's form of *sannyasa*. The Neo-Sannyas tradition established by Rajneesh has little in common with traditional *sannyasa*, or renunciation, as practiced in India for centuries.

DP: Yes, it's different from traditional *sannyasa*, but when I became a Sannyasin it was still a life-altering commitment, not to be taken lightly. We renounced our previous values and concepts, merely by making the sincere commitment to live in the "Here-and-Now." It required daily meditation, the wearing of red and orange clothes, the constant wearing of a *mala* [rosary], and a change of name. I adopted a new name given to me by Osho: that's how I became "Deva Premal."

So once again I found myself being different from all my friends at school! But this time it was my own choice. From then on my life became centered on meditation. The mantras and all other spiritual practices from my childhood instantly fell away and were replaced with something that I felt I had discovered for myself.

I found Osho's community, and his techniques for meditation in particular, to be a great support as I moved through my school years. By the time I was seventeen I was spending as much of my time as possible in India at the ashram. And during the following years, I studied Shiatsu, Reflexology, Cranio-Sacral Balancing and massage.

And what about your meeting with Miten? You work well together.

DP: It isn't work! It's our life.

Yes, I met him in the ashram. Despite our age difference it just felt great to be around him, right from the very beginning.

I knew he was one of Osho's musicians, and I'd always enjoyed hearing him sing in the evening meditations in Buddha Hall. We laughed a lot . . . and still do. He wrote and sung the most beautiful songs—"English mantras," I called them. So when he began encouraging me to sing harmony with him, I didn't exactly need a big push! I had grown up with music, playing violin and piano. So the groundwork had already been done, to some extent.

M: I began reading Osho's words, and a voice inside me began whispering, 'This is it!' And by the end of the book, the whispering had become a wild, ecstatic song! There was simply no question. I became a Sannyasin as soon as I could, and eventually lived in Pune, India.

It happened that fast, almost overnight. And all these years later, my life as a Sannyasin still continues to amaze me. Not only are Osho's words incredible, but his methods are outrageous. For a year I did his "Dynamic Meditation" technique at 6 AM every morning, and his "Kundalini" meditation in the evenings. I felt like I'd been given a new perspective on how to deal with the issues in my life that were causing so much pain. It was like a second chance for me.

I was given the name "Prabhu Miten," which, when translated, means "Friend of God."

So your spiritual quest initially took you to Osho as well. But when did you realize the importance of sound and its significance on the spiritual path?

DP: We realized sound as a healing instrument during Osho's meditations. Especially in the Sufi Dance meditations, where you would sing to a stranger, looking into each other's eyes, and be in total recognition of who he/she actually is. You'd be singing heart-to-heart.

But it was the ecstasy — and sheer volume — of hundreds, sometimes thousands, of people singing the "Name" together that was so inspirational. There's really nothing else like it. The entire group becomes as one.

Also, in Osho's Nadabrahma meditations, while humming for thirty minutes, the mind seems to evaporate into stillness. Later, during the workshops we gave, we saw again how the singing voice can be used as a transformative tool. It can be harnessed as a spiritual weapon, in a sense, slashing all preconceived notions and illusions. It's that powerful.

Do you remember the first time you heard kirtan? What styles and techniques do you prefer?

M: There was a huge population of Westerners in the ashram, but not only. The Indian disciples were there, too, of course, and they would do kirtan. Fantastic! It was a highlight. We would all go to the meditation, because the energy was so high, so blissful. But it never influenced me as a singer though. I'm a songwriter and enjoy the play of my native language.

DP: I also heard kirtan for the first time in Osho's ashram in Pune. I lived there for a few years, and the communal singing was my favorite way of meditating. It touches something deep inside, stirs memories of something long forgotten.

I love kirtan, but I never had a desire to become a "kirtan singer," per se. I had a strong connection to mantras through my childhood and I love singing them especially together with Miten and with groups of people. We love to let go, giving ourselves fully to the singing.

I must say, though, that we don't generally use the call-and-response form of traditional kirtan. But we do enjoy harmony – it is one of my favorite ways to honor the Divine. I choose mantras that speak to my heart. Then I find beautiful melodies – sometimes they come to me with the traditional tune, or Miten or other friends will compose new ones.

When the melody is beautiful it makes it even more joyful for me to sing the name of God. I would call what I do "singing God's name," rather than chanting.

How would you summarize your philosophy of kirtan?

DP: When I sing, it feels like giving and receiving. I'm singing in praise of the Divine and giving thanks for all that I receive. On the other hand, it also feels like an invitation to the Divine – to come into me and to work through me, using my voice as a vehicle. So I receive the blessings through the singing. This is my way of prayer and of giving thanks.

The head has really little place in all of this. The words and melody go straight to the heart, and especially since they're usually in a language most of us don't know. We don't have any associations with them. And since the melodies are relatively easy to sing, we don't have to get into our heads—we can just flow with them.

But most of all, we play for the silence that follows the chant. The singing, chanting, is great—it's joyful, warm, profound. But when it disappears into silence, then the magic really happens. Without the silence, you get only half the picture. It's like the hook or the climax of a good story—when you come to that point of, "Ah, yes!" It's a kind of eureka experience.

The silence is there after the kirtan because it exists in the kirtan as well, but at that point it's imperceptible. Still, it's there. In fact, like the kirtan itself, silence exists everywhere. It just needs to be recognized, experienced, felt. This is a silence, by the way, that has great healing potential, if we give ourselves the chance to tune into it. It is not the silence of the graveyard—it is the silence of the Divine Spirit—alive, and pulsating with energy.

This is really the main reason Miten and I sing—to bathe in Silence. It's our nourishment. It's what keeps us going. For me there is nothing more precious than having sung with an audience, ecstatic with bliss, entering into the deep space that the mantra brings. It's so deep, that with closed eyes you can reach a place where you sense the higher quiet of inner being—it's as if "nobody" is there at all. No audience, no performer—all separateness dissolves. Of course, it's really the illusion that's dissolving, and one can then move on to higher reality, the reality of God.

M: Basically it's like this—everyone with any breath in their body can experience their inner divinity, their connection to God. Every breath is an opportunity. Put sound inside that breath and you have the potential to talk to God.

Every tradition, every religion, sings the praises of divine sound. In western culture we've mainly reduced music to entertainment—we sing our pain and our hurt and our lust, which is all real enough. But we rarely venture beyond that. We rarely seek the higher realities that can open up to us through sound.

Western music is mainly concerned with interpersonal relationships in the world around us. And that's legitimate. But what about spiritual relationships? What about our relationship with God? In general, music or chanting is there to make a difference in our lives. And once the devotional singing voice opens, the heart opens. And once the heart opens, the story's over — our connection with God is established.

How does this work? How does chanting mantras or sound vibrations affect our consciousness?

M: Simply chanting the sound AUM — and other mantras — has a powerful effect on the body/mind organism. The cells in our bodies start to resonate and percolate, the soul begins to celebrate — we're on the bus going home. That's why I'd say the singing voice is one of God's greatest gifts. Properly used, it can bring us to the ultimate liberation.

These sounds, these "mantras," were created through scientific inquiry back in the mists of time. Back then, the body was their technology, and many mysteries were uncovered through sound. During the process of time and civilization, these more subtle sciences became obscured . . . but they never went away. And today they are reappearing, and being recognized for the great healing potential they embody.

And you've got a part in that. Now, if you would, please discuss your own involvement in the "professional" kirtan world, and how it led to producing CDs and other publicly accessible material on sacred sound.

DP: It all began in 1992 with our Voice Workshops. Our focus was on singing as a healing process. Opening the heart through the voice, as it were. Miten and I had both been touched by the ashram Sufi Dances, and we wanted to share that sense of ecstatic space with others. So, we started with chants and songs we'd loved, and took it from there. It wasn't until much later that we realized we had accumulated enough material for me to make various CDs of our own.

Up until that point, Miten had released three albums of his own with devotional western songs. We released a CD of chants that I loved to sing. It was a natural, organic process.

And that's pretty much how my first CD came to be. We called it "The Essence". . .

That's a beautiful title.

DP: I grew up singing mantras. The Gayatri Mantra was my goodnight song . . . and I chanted other mantras while walking with my father. . . . It was close to home from early on. But it wasn't until recording "The Essence" that I really found my voice. Until then, I was more or less Miten's back up singer.

I mean, that was a beautiful job, as jobs go. [laughter] But still, it was important for me to find my own voice and my own song . . . my own expression, and Miten encouraged me in that.

The Gayatri Mantra, and "The Essence," opened this door for me. Apart from the Gayatri Mantra and Om Asatoma, which are both Sanskrit mantras, "The Essence" also included a chant from the Hopi people, a chant from the Yoruba tribe of Nigeria, a *bhajan* in Hindi and also an instrumental piece. I love singing sacred chants from different cultures, but mostly I feel drawn to Sanskrit mantras.

M: I feel our music is way beyond commercial record companies. They can't make heads or tails of it. It doesn't fit. In the beginning, we were open to the possibility of signing with a mainstream company, but we decided to take another route. We'd already had an uncomfortable experience with a new age record company that we didn't want to repeat.

So we went our own way — we produced our work ourselves, marketed it ourselves — and now we've sold over 600,000 albums.

Pretty impressive. It's a kirtan revolution, as they say.

M: Yes — The Conscious Revolution! And it feels good to be making the soundtrack to your own life, and sharing it with friends. We make all our own decisions, and our own mistakes, too. But that's all part of the game. We aren't ambitious people, but if we do have a vision, it would be to share the mantras and sacred music with the world.

In addition to "The Essence," they have released the following albums:

Deva Premal – *Love is Space*
Deva Premal – *Embrace*
Miten with Deva Premal – *Songs for the Inner Lover*
Deva Premal and Miten – *Satsang*
Deva Premal and Miten – *More than Music (a compilation)*
Deva Premal – *Dakshina*
Miten and Premal – *Strength of a Rose*
Deva Premal – *Sings the Moola Mantra*
Miten with Deva Premal – *Soul in Wonder*

and more to come . . .

For more information contact:
www.DevaPremalMiten.com

$\mathcal{H}$AVI DAS

Ilan Chester, known as Havi Das, enjoys commercial fame in Latin America and has developed quite a name on the kirtan circuit as well. Known for a mix of pop, rock, and Latin styles, his distinct voice and keyboard expertise has won him numerous accolades, so much so that he is currently dubbed, "The Billy Joel of Latin America." With literally dozens of CDs consistently moving up the South American pop charts, his kirtan work is overshadowed by his secular success. Nonetheless, kirtan is his first love.

Born in Israel, he came to Venezuela as a child and quickly felt at home in Latin America. In 1991 and 1992, Billboard *listed his songs, "Sabe A Calidad" and "Ojos Verdes," in its 22nd and 15th "Hot Latin" spots, respectively. After a series of memorable albums, including "Song Books of Venezuelan Love, Vols. 1 & 2," he attracted international attention with the platinum-selling, "Navideno Heart" in 2002. Still, the kirtan maestro is clear that singing for God is where his heart really lies.*

Accordingly, in 1998, "Bhakti" was conceived as an outlet for his spiritual aspirations. Having made a name for himself in the Latin-Pop world, he was now ready to release a devotional CD with songs that were dear to his heart, all composed by stalwarts in the Medieval kirtan tradition. His method is direct: He considers it unnecessary to embellish shabda brahman, or spiritual sound, with elaborate instrumentation and intricate melodies. Thus, on the "Bhakti" CD, he intentionally kept things simple, allowing the original composers' feelings and intent to shine through, without being clouded by unnecessary musical distractions. It's basically just him and a keyboard.

✳ ✳ ✳

Born in Israel, Latin American pop star, and in love with Krishna kirtan—who are you anyway? [laughter]

My birth name is Ilan Czenstochouski, and my body made its appearance, this time around, in Israel. It was the 30th of July, 1952. I was born in a Zionist Jewish household, and we moved to Caracas in Venezuela in 1954. There, I grew up in a Jewish neighborhood and went to a Jewish school. Our Jewish identity was significant at the time, especially because of World War II.

Were your parents victims of the Holocaust?

Not directly, but they were very much affected by it, anyway. You know, they lost most of their family members to the Holocaust, and so my upbringing and the education, the sensibility at the house, was fully influenced by the reality of those times.

And where does music come in?

From the beginning of my childhood I had an affinity for music. In my house we used to hear Jewish songs, Hebrew and Yiddish songs, along with French, Italian, and American tunes. By the time I was four or five, I was playing those songs by ear on the house piano. My mother kept me busy while she did her household chores by playing records, mainly classical music, and I had to guess who the composer was at the end of every record. This was a really good thing. It trained my ear to appreciate the subtleties and the emotions of sound, of music in general.

When did your sense of spirituality develop?

Since I was very small I had natural inclinations toward God. While sitting at the piano I would sing to Him and I tried to relate to Him personally, you know, in a very internal, natural way. Sometimes I was extreme: While sitting in the family car I would give the privilege of the window to Him. [laughter] I would do that sometimes. In Passover festivities, while all the members of my family closed their eyes and opened the door to receive the prophet Elias and drink the wine, I couldn't avoid peeking to try to see him.

Sounds like you were an especially spiritual-minded child.

Spending years with my grandparents in Israel will do that. You see, they were *very* religious — Orthodox Jews. From them, I could understand what spiritual or religious commitment really was. When I inquired about life and God, I naturally directed my questions to them. They seemed to know the subject — why ask someone who doesn't know?

I admired their faith. While I stayed in their house, I was inspired to follow certain rules and to recite certain prayers, mostly to please them. Although many questions were unanswered, I respected their dedication and the inclusion of God in their lives. It seemed real. And it gave their lives a certain value and purpose that others seemed to lack.

One day, in Caracas, in a religious ceremony at the synagogue, I was sitting near my father. Now, he didn't really have any spiritual inclination, not really, but because he was a leader in the community he had to sit there. So, while sitting next to him, I started to talk to God: "Dear God, I know You exist, I don't know *how* You exist, but I know that You do. I know You are everywhere, I don't know *how* You are everywhere, but I feel Your presence. And I know You are listening to me. So please hear this: I want to know You, I really want to know You and to understand You. So, please, You make the arrangement for that to happen. That's all I ask." The sincere prayer of a little boy. And I went on with my life.

So you were blessed early on with faith. When and how did your interest turn Eastern?

Okay, I lived life and took part in most of the youthful frivolities of my day. That should be clear. Then, when I was nineteen years old, in Israel, I stayed in a friend's room at Tel Aviv University. This would be 1971. We were sitting around and playing some music, with guitars and stuff, and a visitor came by, asking for a place to stay for the night. He happened to be an Argentinian student who had just arrived from India. He looked peaceful and, I swear, he had a mystical hue around him. [laughter] Personally, I thought he seemed a bit pretentious, at least initially, with his eccentric and otherworldly behavior.

Anyway, we started to talk, and we talked for many hours. We ended up on the roof at 3 AM, just talking and talking. The subject matter was Truth in all its forms—what it means, and who can really tell what is true and what isn't. We discussed its relative aspects, its opposite, that is, illusion and untruth, and it just went on and on. The sequence of our conversation was fascinating and it ended with me asking, "Okay, so what *is* reality? What is truth?" He just answered, "I know that my hands are like water and I can't really grasp anything. But one day the seed of love is going to be sown in my heart and a huge tree will grow in love of God." I didn't get it, but it sounded nice. We left it at that, and we went to sleep. Out of curiosity, before we went to sleep, I asked my new friend if he had done any yoga. He looked straight in my eyes, with great enthusiasm, and said "Yes, I practice Bhakti-yoga. But please don't ask me anything else."

Next day, I woke up to find out that my new friend had left. And I couldn't help but recall the prior night's experience over and over again. It awakened something in me, touched me in a deep way. Anyway, that day, I decided to go and visit my grandmother and, waiting for a bus, I happened upon a magazine. One of the headlines read, "The Hare Krishnas in Israel." And I started reading: "Krishna is God, we are spirit souls, and we've lost our relationship with Him. Becoming reestablished in that relationship with love is the path called Bhakti-yoga." My eyes scanned those words again: Bhakti-yoga! That was the phrase he had used the night before.

A rush of life ran into my heart. I changed my plans for the day. With new life, I took a taxi to the address that was written in the magazine, which was the place where these Hare Krishnas had their ashram. I remember that from the taxi to the house — which was about 200 meters — I ran with a smile on my face, not understanding why I was so extremely happy. The feeling was as if I was going to reunite with my lost love.

When I arrived, I tried to contain myself, but I just couldn't, not really. I was smiling ear to ear. I knocked on the door and was quite surprised that the gentleman answering the door had a shaved head, looking like a monk. He said, "Hare Krishna. Please come in." I sat on the floor — it was the only place to sit — and he brought some fruits, some *prasadam*. I then started to look at the paintings on the wall, which were fascinating. He started to explain what he had learned about God and life, particularly as expressed through these paintings. Although the presentation was quite alien to me, I maintained an open-minded attitude and I took some books back to my house.

Today, I'm still surprised by the fact that on my way back to my house, everything I read in those little books made perfect sense to me. Not only that, but it was as if the Absolute Truth, the common denominator, the ultimate source, was, in some tiny way, revealing Himself to me.

Two days later, I visited again, and this time it was too much. It was just overwhelming. Dinesh and Krishna Devi, the ISKCON devotees living in Israel at the time, were chanting Hare Krishna with some guests. The vibration created immense impressions in my heart, and I felt this intense happiness. It was beyond me. This was my first encounter with transcendental sound. On my third visit, I put some headphones on and I heard His Divine Grace A. C. Bhaktivedanta Swami Prabhupada chanting the *maha-mantra*. Well, after thirty seconds, I had to take the headphones off. It was *that* powerful. Somehow, it was playing with my emotions, stirring up strong feelings about life and reality, about God and my relationship with Him.

So this touched you in a deep way . . . How would you say this affected you in terms of what you would eventually do with music?

Well, basically my style and technique as a musician today, whenever I do kirtans or *bhajans*, is very much influenced by Srila Prabhupada, and also by His Grace Hridayananda Das Goswami, who has, for many years, been my mentor in spiritual life. I was also initiated, in 1973, by Srila Prabhupada, and that changed my life in so many ways . . .

Other influences?

I was also influenced by the music of the 60s, the Beatles, Ravi Shankar, and that kind of material. I've also been influenced by some elements of Indian classical music, and I began to combine these elements with my natural appreciation for medieval music. Those are the musical influences expressed in my *bhajans* or devotional music. There are many other elements but these are ones that relate to my spiritual music.

You are known as a rather popular *kirtaniya* in the yoga scene in Latin America—I think it would be useful to hear about your approach to kirtan.

Kirtan is a unique form of musical expression, and I like to perform it in its most raw, original form, as presented by Srila Prabhupada. I mean, I like to use voice, *mridanga, kartals* and *harmonium*. That's it. I can also use more sophisticated instruments and production techniques, and so on. But this is what I prefer—the simpler, more grassroots kind of kirtan. In singing, too, I think kirtan is best expressed by simple, direct melodies. You can, of course, do it with complicated changes and intricate vocal patterns, and that can work, too. But, in my opinion, simple is best. Less is more.

Yes, something special seems to come through when chanting simple, direct kirtan melodies. The ego is left aside and one just enters into the sound, without getting distracted by needless complication. The transcendental sound comes through.

Yes. When the kirtan is simple, slow and sweet and the body moves from one side to the other, in a simple dance formation—then it is possible to enter into a very particular trancelike state. Here, each person in the kirtan can feel their individual connection with the mantra and with the object of adoration. That's the perfection of kirtan. Even from an aesthetic point of view, to see a number of people moving and swaying to the same rhythm, with a semblance of almost staged choreography—it just feels good. It shows good taste, too. This type of kirtan could last for many hours, continuously, and can fill the heart with many beautiful feelings. At that moment, the person involved in kirtan feels very fortunate to just be there, to be immersed in the sound.

Can you talk a bit more about the power of sound and how that comes through in kirtan?

The mystery of sound is clear from the Bible: "In the beginning was the word . . ." Wow. Think about that. Everything comes from sound! Think about our vocal chords, and how sound is carried by the ether, and how the ear picks up the vibrations—it's all quite miraculous. In a fundamental sense, sound is a basic element for communicating ideas and emotions, which, really, is just about everything. It has an effect on the way we understand things, and on the way we feel. Now, according to the Vedas, this has to do with the material modes of nature, from ignorance, to passion, to goodness—the barking of a dog, the music on the radio, and the chirping of birds, for example. These are different types of sounds, creating different effects in our perception of the world.

But Sri Krishna, who is described in Vedic texts as the Supreme Lord, states in the *Bhagavad Gita*, "Besides this inferior nature, O mighty-armed Arjuna, there is a superior energy of Mine." This is spiritual. And, curiously enough, this superior energy is accessed and eventually understood by sound. By transcendental sound. I'm talking about a category of sound that belongs to a sphere beyond the conventional form of sound, beyond the usual sounds that we can experience in this world.

Can you elaborate?

In the relative world, an object and its name are different, in as much as the word "water" cannot quench our thirst, for example. Because the word is relative, it doesn't have the same power as the object it represents. In the spiritual world, the exact opposite is true—spiritual vibrations and the objects they represent are exactly the same. That is the nature of Absolute substance. So God and His name are one.

In the art of kirtan, that Absolute dimension becomes an experienced reality. This is due to the benevolent presence of God in His names. So, when chanting, we may not be aware of all these profound truths, but the fact remains the same, and, ultimately, kirtan is the sublime weapon that will not only destroy our misunderstandings about our identity, purify our heart, and develop our dormant love for God, but if we strive in that direction we could end up living in that transcendental realm where every word is a song and every step is a dance.

In the process of self-realization, this sound vibration, this kirtan, is an essential part, and it differs in every way from the utilitarian sounds of the material world. Most sounds bind us to the world of illusion, but kirtan is fundamentally purifying, taking us out of the selfish material mood of this world and situating us firmly in the spiritual realm, in the land of harmony, surrender, and love.

Nicely worded. Let's talk about your professional career in music for a bit and how that led to the recording of your devotional CD.

I've been a professional musician under the artistic name of Ilan Chester for over thirty years, having produced eighteen musical records and composing over 100 songs. These works have been distributed in South America and Spain over the last two decades, with a considerable amount of success. I've been very fortunate in my solo career, which came, of course, after being in numerous bands and working hard with all kinds of musicians. It has all been quite rewarding.

But, I have to say, my CD, "Bhakti: Devotional Songs from India," is more important than all the rest. It is a production inspired by

Srila Prabhupada's melodies and by songs and poems written in the Vaishnava line of spiritual masters. I feel that these songs and poems, in Sanskrit and Bengali, are a window to the spiritual world. And as such, in my particular preference, I try to sing them with the least possible embellishment — with minimal use of instruments.

I notice, too, that in the beautiful, full-color booklet that accompanies the CD, you have all lyrics in English and Spanish, to accommodate your fans and the audience you've cultivated over the years.

Yes, that was very important to me.

I also noticed that you mostly do traditional Vaishnava songs, just your voice and minimal musical accompaniment, as you say, and that kirtan as such—the call-and-response form of chanting—only appears on a couple of tracks.

Yes, I wanted my audience to hear the beautiful songs of the Vaish–navas, and I wanted to present those songs in a way I knew my audience would appreciate. But kirtan is there, too, and I selectively, consciously, chose which ones would appear in kirtan format.

Mainly, it's on Narottam's "Nama-sankirtan."

Ah, you're listening. Very good. In my tours, especially, I have managed to chant "Hare Krishna" in front of thousands — and they often reciprocate with me in this chanting, going back and forth. It's glorious! In moments like that, you can feel the power of the name. So many people, just letting go and chanting. It's quite beautiful. I actually look forward to future performances, with a much more polished way of engaging kirtan methods, maybe with classical instruments and drums from different parts of the world, and perhaps a choir, like the Mormon Tabernacle Choir, something like that. I don't know if I'll do it, but it definitely should be done.

But there's something in the Sanskrit—the mantras as they've been given to us by the sages . . .

Oh, I'm not recommending that we take away the Sanskrit. No. I'm suggesting different kinds of instrumentation, but, no, the Sanskrit must remain. These are the deliberate sounds of the sages, something coming from God directly, and they carry a certain potency of their own.

Sanskrit mantras are compositions of extraordinary strength, phonetically and in terms of auditory value. For example, in the *Bhagavad Gita*, Krishna says that He accepts a simple offering of a leaf, a flower, or some water, if it is offered with a loving attitude. Now, in its original Sanskrit, this verse is a good example of the auditory strength of mantras: *patram pushpam phalam toyam*. You hear the way that sounds? There's a beauty there that gets lost in translation. The meaning's there, and it's true and beautiful. But the sound of the chant, in Sanskrit, carries something extra.

So the scriptures talk about this at length, reminding us of the importance of chanting these mantras and the way these mantras affect the consciousness.

The *Srimad Bhagavatam* tells us, "To hear about Krishna from the Vedic literature, or to hear from Him directly, is itself righteous activity." This hearing and chanting help us on so many levels. These Sanskrit verses, when chanted properly, can lead to extraordinary sonic experiences. That's the power of kirtan.

For more information contact:
www.ilanchester.com

**AGANI**

*Ragani's name is now synonymous
with kirtan. Focusing her work in her
native Milwaukee, which is quickly
becoming the kirtan capital of the U.S., she has led group chanting throughout the world, including India, Malaysia, Singapore, and Curacao.*

*When still a child, Ragani met her teacher, Sri Swami Rama, founder
of the Himalayan Institute of Yoga Science and Philosophy and former
Shankaracharya of India. He personally trained her in the Himalayan Tradition of yoga sciences, meditation, and Eastern music, including kirtan.
She further studied classical Indian vocals under Laxmi Narayan Tiwari,
also a disciple of Swami Rama.*

*Now counted among the "100 Milwaukeeans You Need to Know"
(OnMilwaukee.com), Ragani has been featured on FOX and NBC affili-
ates and in numerous regional, national and international publications
for her work with kirtan and yoga. In addition, she is the featured model
for the award-winning book,* Yoga: Mastering the Basics, *and its two
accompanying videos.*

*Her CDs center on her hypnotic vocals, but they are also rich with
diversified world music instrumentation and the sacred mantras of India.
Her songs "[bring] to mind a winning collaboration between Enya and
the sadly departed George Harrison," writes Nick Dedina of* Conscious
Choice Magazine. *Her recent release, "Ancient Spirit (Kirtan Café, Vol.
II)," was voted the "Top Pick" album with most major music distribu-*

tors, was awarded "Runner Up" in the Best Production category of the International Music Aid Awards, and was named "Best of the Year" (2006) by Backroads Music.

✳ ✳ ✳

Okay, let's begin with some background.

Well, this might be a little awkward—to just talk about myself. I hope that it's useful in some way.

Yes, I think that readers would benefit from hearing about the person behind the kirtan. If they can relate to you, your background, your family, your interests—it's likely they'll better understand what attracted you to the world of sacred mantras.

You're right, I'm sure. So here goes: My legal name is J. Ragani Buegel, though I have dropped the first initial and the last name, since they are no longer names with which I identify. For the astrologers out there, I was born on November 24, 1966.

I see. And where did you spend your early life?

I grew up in the Midwest USA, and I have one younger sister and a nephew. Many of my friends in my early school days were sports friends, since I was really into playing sports, especially soccer. I never really cared for classroom learning, though I did well in school.

Where did you attend school?

I went to a private grade school and graduated valedictorian; a public high school—graduated salutatorian; and I attended Earlham College, from which I graduated with the Kathryn Weber Scholar-Athlete Award and Phi Beta Kappa. My guru, Swami Rama, encouraged me to go to graduate school, so I also hold a doctorate in clinical health psychology and a degree in acupuncture. And after all the schooling was completed, my guru asked me to return to music more seriously. But I'll get back to this later.

Anything significant about your upbringing?

Yes. My parents raised me with a great deal of yoga and alternative health sensibilities in our home, things like homeopathy and a keen sense of nutrition. My mom, especially, emphasized this kind of thing since I was around age five. We became vegetarians—again, my mom leading the way—in the mid 1970s, when people really knew very little about that kind of diet/lifestyle. (I remember when my grandmother used to "sneak" ham into our sandwiches because she was afraid that we wouldn't grow up strong!) My mother was studying homeopathy in Chicago and we used to go see the homeopathic physicians there for any of our ailments. So we had a lot of alternative medicine and yoga stuff around our home.

Any interesting anecdotes from your early days, as a child?

Let's see . . . a few childhood memories and tidbits: One school memory I have is of first grade, when I was learning to write—the teachers kept correcting me about my placement of letters, because I would hang the letters from the top of the lines rather than sit them on the bottom of the lines. That took some undoing—it just didn't make sense to me that the letters should sit on the bottom! Was I being creative or just stubborn? I don't know. [both laugh]

Oh, here's another funny thing about my childhood: As a very small girl, when I was first learning to speak, I used to use the word *baba* to refer to anything big and lovely and wonderful—like a really big cookie!—and it wasn't until later that we came to realize just where that must have come from.*

Interesting that you mention really big cookies as an example: The word *baba* can also refer to any small cake leavened with yeast. That's the way it's defined in the dictionary . . .

[laughter] I didn't know that!

---

*Editor's note: The word "baba" means father or uncle in many Indian languages; it is also used more generally to refer to an Indian holy man.

Any more childhood memories?

I remember taking piano lessons in grade school for some six or eight years, but never really learning to sight-read—I'd play by ear and try to figure songs out the slow way. When I met my first Indian music teacher in 1991 and he showed me the "sa-re-ga-ma" system of Indian music, my heart rejoiced! Oh, the world opened up for me—now *this* was music I could understand! I wonder how many children out there are also looking for something familiar from their past, for something they don't even know how to ask for. How frustrating at times to be a child! In some ways, you can't speak your heart.

Since early childhood I was interested in mystical and spiritual traditions. I recall many memories from two and three years of age and onward, and I especially remember the summer days when I was four years old, standing out in front of our home, wondering why I was feeling a sense of connection to everyone and everything—it was something I couldn't really describe.

I recall very early images from my childhood, though I was aware that others did not seem to look at things the same way I did. One thing I remember thinking about a lot was where I came from, what other lives I may have lived. I don't remember my parents speaking to me about other lives, and these thoughts were more private for me until I became a little older. In fact, I don't recall a time in my life when I was not thinking about these kinds of things. We'd go on road trips and I'd look out the window hoping with anticipation that I might see something that was familiar to me, but, of course, I did not. It was disappointing and I often wondered where I was, and how far away I was from where I'd been in previous lives. Does that make sense? Anyway, that's what my mind was doing when I was younger . . .

And now that you've gotten older?

And as I've gotten older, in many ways I feel I've become a lot less serious. In so many of my childhood photos my beautiful little sister is laughing and joyful—and she was such an angel!—and then there was me, usually frowning and serious. My mom used to say, "It was like you didn't want to be here." Some of those photos make me laugh now, but I also remember what it felt like to be there in that space. I was very contemplative and pensive. I didn't feel like I looked like my face, if you know what I mean—I'd look in the mirror and there I was, looking all different again! How strange!

Although I had a number of friends to play with, none of them ever knew my thoughts about life. I never expressed any of this to them. I couldn't—I *felt* all these things but my little kid's brain and vocabulary could never express them, not even to myself, not fully. I remember sharing some of these thoughts with adults, like baby-sitters and people like that, people who passed through our home. Sometimes they caught on, and they expressed similar ideas. Now, *that* really excited me. I loved the idea that there were others who also thought about past lives and synchronicity and things like that. When I got older, of course, I read about these things with some regularity.

Do you remember reading any spiritual books early on?

I remember the first time I read Paramahamsa Yogananda's *Autobiography of a Yogi*. This was when I was around fourteen years old, and I couldn't put the book down. I felt I'd finally found someone that I could identify with. It was a very powerful experience for me.

Where did your spiritual quest initially take you?

Okay. Well, let me begin by saying that I met my guru, Swami Rama, when I was eight years old, when my parents were attending one of his lectures in a Chicago bookstore, and I met him before his lecture. I remember sitting in the back seat of our car on the way home to South Bend late that night and feeling that I was on my way somewhere in life—I knew that everything was now being taken care of.

And as you got older you saw the Swami more frequently?

Actually, I didn't see Swamiji again until I was in my early teens and he was at his ashram (the Himalayan Institute) in Honesdale, PA. During those teenage years I began my regular daily meditation practices, and it was during this time that I experienced the wave of unstruck sound from the heart, as it passes through the body. Those were very powerful experiences and I often wondered what to do with them. It seemed there must be something more to them than just the immediate experience of bliss, and these vibrations would often fill me even as I moved about during the day. Because of those experiences, I felt that we could dissolve into the sound, that every thing has a sound, a vibration, and that we're all interconnected because of it.

Any other pivotal experiences at this time?

When I was in my early teens, my mother took me to Swami Rama's ashram for one of their International Yoga Congresses. It was here that I met him, once again, and Swami Satchidananda, too, for the first time, among other great teachers, and I was very inspired by my experiences with them. Satchidananda started his lecture by having everyone get ready to meditate, and then we just heard this low rumble sound that got louder and louder until we realized he was laughing! What joy! It was so heartening. So I left the Congress wondering whom I might study with, who I might take as my guru — Swami Rama or Swami Satchidananda.

So what was the deciding factor?

I came home and later that year I had a very powerful experience. I was asleep in bed one night, but I was no longer sleeping, nor was I awake. I felt someone come into my room, and I thought it was Swami Satchidananda. He touched my left knee — where I'd had some physical ailment — and sheer bliss poured into my entire being. I mean, bright light everywhere! I reached out to touch him so that he would know I'd received what he'd given me, and when I touched him I realized it wasn't Satchidananda. I half-opened my eyes and saw a man I'd never seen before. This mysterious person addressed me directly, "No I am not Satchidananda, I am his son."

And then he was gone. I fell into a light dreaming sleep and then quickly awakened to write down the experience.

The next year when my parents went to the Congress, I wasn't able to go. I begged them to go to Satchidananda and to tell him that they were my parents, as I felt he would have something to tell me, especially after that powerful experience I'd had. (I'd also written to him about it.) They missed him twice and on the last day of the Congress they called to say he'd already left the Himalayan Institute and they didn't get a chance to meet him. I was absolutely crushed! I sobbed and prayed in my room for nearly two hours—I was just so upset. And I still didn't know who my teacher should be. It was very upsetting. So there I was in my room and the phone rang, and it was my mother. They had just arrived at the airport and called to say, "You won't believe what just happened. . . . We arrived at the airport and there was Swami Satchidananda sitting in a chair. He said his flight had just been cancelled because of a storm that had broken out in the East." They told him they were my parents, and he gave them a card for me with a note on it. He told them to tell me that I should study with Swami Rama. And that was that.

So this is when you became more directly involved in spiritual life . . .

That was age fifteen. I decided that I didn't want to go back to soccer camp anymore and my mother suggested going to Swami Rama's ashram in Honesdale, PA. The idea seemed inspired. And that next year I made enough money to get myself to Honesdale in the summer for their Self-Transformation Program. I wrote the President of the Himalayan Institute and asked permission to come (because I was a few years under their age requirement), and he approved.

I went for a month and, I must say, that summer marked the beginning of my life. I felt as though I'd picked up where I left off long ago, ages ago. On the hour-plus drive to the ashram from the airport, we saw fifteen rainbows! It would rain and stop and rain and stop—what an amazing beginning for me at that age. It was a visual affirmation of a new phase in my life.

And then you received a lot of association with the Swami. Did you keep records of that?

Oh, definitely. My friend Mick said that many people took Swamiji's words to be like sacred mantras, and people would write them down. So from that first night, after the experience of those rainbows, I began keeping a journal of everything I experienced there, of everything Swamiji ever said to me. And I now have a pile of journals filled with everything that happened during those years.

How many years?

I spent eleven consecutive summers at his ashram, and later — when he stopped coming to the U.S. — I spent more time with him in India at his Rishikesh ashram and the charitable hospital, in Dehra Dun, northern India.

During these years, Swamiji took me under his wing, and I feel really fortunate about that. He taught me yoga and music, basically — and there was something strangely familiar about it, like it was a carry-over from a previous life. I mean, I definitely felt that to be true. I know it's almost cliché, but I *really* felt it.

I have many memories of my time with Swamiji, listening to music and singing with him on a regular basis. He really worked hard to guide me, and I remember very clearly the day he told me that it was my *dharma*, my life path, to sing, that I had been born to sing. It's funny, because I don't think of myself as a singer, not really. But something about this kirtan music is so hauntingly familiar to me — it's a part of me. And now, I *have to* sing, because it's through this music that I feel connected to my guru.

It was during this time that I became Swamiji's assistant and worked with him for over eight years. Kamal was his main assistant and my days with Swamiji and Kamal were clearly the golden years of my life. People often ask if it seems like a dream to remember all of that, but in reality, this now seems much more like a dream. My time with Swamiji didn't feel like a dream — it felt more like I was truly awake.

I've often said that the amazing thing about being with Swamiji and witnessing the reality of his yogic world was not that these incredible things happened in his life, but that when we were with him, we felt those things happening in our lives too.

How did this impact on your personal life?

Well, I did marry, you know. My husband, Dale, and I were married in 1996, a month before the passing of my guru. In 2001, during our time at the Maha Kumbha Mela, we spent time with an incredible Swami named Tapasvi Baba. He was so full of compassion, love and wisdom, and we traveled through India with him and his entourage of swamis. Our time with this Baba brought such joy to my heart—he reminded me a great deal of my guru, of my relationship with my guru. That was a very special time.

Can you tell me a little more about Swami Rama?

Sure. Though it has been written that he was born in 1925, he did tell me that this was not his true birth date. The birth date he shared with me would have made him nearly 300 years old! He dropped his body, as the *yogis* say, in 1996. He was born in the Himalayas and raised by one of the greatest spiritual masters of the Himalayan region, Bengali Baba. Throughout his youth, he journeyed from monasteries to caves, studying with a host of adepts from different traditions. At the age of twenty-four, he became a Shankaracharya, which is the highest spiritual post in the Advaita-Vedanta tradition of India. He later renounced this honor and vanished into the Himalayas to intensify his spiritual practices.

In 1969, Swamiji came to the United States and founded the Himalayan International Institute to create a bridge between East and West, between spirituality and science, and between ancient wisdom and modern technology. He lectured and authored dozens of books on yoga, spirituality, meditation, and holistic health. In 1993, he returned to India and completed his lifelong dream of establishing a hospital to serve the people at the foothills of the Himalayan mountains.

Now what about you and your connection to kirtan? Do you remember the first time you heard it?

Well, when I was about twelve years old, my mother began to bring *yogis* into our hometown to teach yoga—this was in South Bend, Indiana. She also took me to my first yoga classes while I was still in grade school. Anyway, that's where I first discovered chanting and mantras—our yoga instructor was from the Siddha Yoga tradition, a disciple of Swami Muktananda, and we used to chant Om Namah Shivaya very slowly, as a group, at the end of the yoga classes.

After hearing the chanting at the yoga class, I heard my first call-and-response kirtan at the same yoga instructor's house, where I was baby-sitting her four-year-old daughter. It was here that I really fell in love with kirtan for the first time. I couldn't keep myself away from the tiny room where a small group of people were chanting—they were there every week while I was there baby-sitting. I just loved it.

I remember when this woman would drive me home after babysitting—I would ask her to sing the songs for me again so that I could remember them. I remember one of them was "Le Le Vitale," and it had such a sweet melody—we'd sing it all the way home in the car. And back then we really didn't have kirtan cassettes—CDs certainly didn't exist yet. It was only verbally passed on from night to night, person to person. I remember when the Sri Rama Publishing Foundation in Santa Cruz, California, began to produce what have now become classics in the kirtan world. Their kirtan cassettes were the only ones available and I bought them—all of them—as they were released. For many years of my life, through high school and college, those were the only tapes I ever listened to.

So, from high school on—that time was devoted to spiritual practice, yes? Especially kirtan.

You could say that, yes. From the time I was in high school and for eleven consecutive years to follow, I used to spend my summers with my guru, Swami Rama, at his ashram. It was here that

I began to lead kirtan groups on weekends, especially, but also during the weekdays, too. I started singing with Swamiji for all his kirtans, and we'd often have special kirtan events in the summer for the international congresses, where hundreds of people attended. And in 1991, when Swamiji took me with him to India, Malaysia, Singapore and Thailand, we did lots of kirtan.

Tell me about yourself as a kirtan singer, and about your influences . . .

I don't really consider myself a singer, though I do lead kirtan. For me, it's different — it's not so much about the singing as it is about the sacred practice of sound, of connection to the divine. My biggest influence regarding kirtan was my guru. He used to sit me down and he gave me my first Indian music lessons. It's when the light really started to go on for me. He would sing something and have me sing it back. And then he'd write the "sa-re-ga-ma" stuff on paper and make me practice. Then one summer he brought Masterji, Laxmi Narayan Tiwari, a music teacher from India, to give me music lessons, and music lessons we did! Days and weeks of them. I flew to Curaçao with Masterji and studied classical Indian vocals. At the height of my training, I recall long practice sessions of up to six hours a day, plus lots of voice lessons — what an incredible experience that was! And Swamiji would call us in the morning and ask how it was all going. We sent Swamiji tapes of my practices and he'd call to give me feedback. Those days were really special.

You were obviously very devoted to developing your music.

When I was in India in '91-'92, I would sit in a room adjacent to Swamiji's room and practice my vocals. You know, they say you can't make a *yogi* do anything, but I tried: I used to practice music outside his door because I knew if he heard it he would come out. [laughter] And then we would get to spend more time with him. I recorded many of those practice sessions, because Swamiji would come in and start singing with us, and that was really special. It was just Swamiji, an occasional *tabla* guy, and me. Swamiji would often tell me I wasn't doing it right, that I needed to slide my voice more, or that I needed to sing *alap* to the rhythm more, or to do this or that. A fiery master he was! And I felt so honored that he looked after me so much in so many ways. The treasure of my life!

Can you tell me the kinds of kirtan you learned—about its theology and practice?

The kirtan that was taught to me is not associated with any one religion; it comes from the yoga of sound. All of the words, all of the sounds in these kirtans are for that purpose of leading us inwards, of taking us to the source, of reconnecting us to the divine. It's interesting that in the West this kirtan is becoming something quite different than what it is in India. I used to resist this idea, and I used to try to make the kirtan here what it was in India. But now I feel it's becoming something different, something really incredible, something new, right here in the West, and I feel as though I'm watching this amazing thing happening. It's not about religion, as such; it's about sound, and it's about getting out of the mind and into the heart.

All the many sages who came from India must have known what they were doing to bring this kirtan to the West, where no one really understands the words and can only feel the sounds and the effects. In many ways, it's special what's happening here—and it's unique to the West. Kirtan in India has certain connotations for many people—they associate it with temples, with religiosity, and so on. Just like attending church in America. But take it out of India and you have the seed of kirtan without all the connotations, without the baggage. In many ways, it is sort of innocent and the experience has a certain purity about it.

So you're not really about the theological background. You're more about the emotion, the heart, the inner side of the kirtan . . .

Right. So, to this day, when I lead kirtan, I feel the most important thing is the feeling. When our group leads kirtan here in Milwaukee, every night is very different. But the important thing is the feeling, and on some nights, even if the band is not sounding so stellar, if the feeling is there, everyone in the room knows it. They feel it. The feeling in the heart is the most important, and in the end I'm convinced that nothing else really matters. So that is my main focus—that sacred feeling of the heart. Many years ago, in Swamiji's little room at the ashram, he used to listen with us to Vaiyasaki Das and comment that it was very good kirtan, and that good kirtan is difficult to lead. All we can do is clear the space and hold the feeling in our hearts.

And technique? Can you talk about your methods?

I'm not even sure I have a technique, except to select songs with beautiful chord progressions and easy-peasy lyrics. If the lyrics aren't easy-peasy, then people get stuck on the words and aren't able to let go. Just plain simple stuff. I also like to have a full band, because I believe this is useful in presenting kirtan to western participants. I grew up with the kirtan being very simple—just a harmonium many times, sometimes *a cappella*, and a few times with a *tabla*, flute and *tanpura*. I am immensely enjoying the chants with guitar and bass and a heavier drum (like an African *djembe*)—there is something really delicious about kirtan with a full band. And I believe, here, in the West, it's what can draw people in. I know some people come to our kirtan just because they like the music—we polled several hundred of them last year—and I feel if they can taste it once, they'll be back. I also encourage our musicians and backup singers to interact with each other and that's a really big part of the enjoyment for me—to see band members laughing with each other and playing with each other musically during the kirtan.

How do you get participants to get into the sound—to let go, and to open themselves up to the kirtan experience? That's what I mean by technique.

We've often described kirtan as the "back door to meditation." When you chant, it can take you out of your mind, out of your thinking process, and this allows things to become quiet. It's one thing to sing alone, to chant mantras alone in your room. And it's quite another thing to chant with a large group of people, to experience the energy multiplying, increasing all around you. It creates a kind of wave that smooths and soothes things, and it can neutralize even the negative stuff people carry in with them. So I'll explain my philosophy of how this happens; I think that's what you're really asking.

We start the kirtan on a slow rhythm, in part because we want to synchronize all of the energies coming into the room. And because it's repetitive it begins to create a groove in the mind and in the body. It's like getting water to swirl in the same direction—the rhythm starts to bring all of these energies together. When you get everyone's energy on the same wave, it starts to get stronger. It becomes bigger than any one of us individually. The repetition of the ancient mantras of Sanskrit, which is based upon the science of sound, creates a higher vibration. And when you create a groove, a pattern in the mind and body, especially with something that has sound to it, you create entrainment in the mind and body. With entrainment, things begin to function harmoniously. It's like re-setting the mind, re-setting the body. When everything is in phase, then you can feel a certain oneness and connection to everything.

When people see our CD jacket, they often ask me why the songs are so long and repetitive. I tell them kirtan is like jogging for the mind. And you wouldn't go for a five-minute jog, would you? So kirtan is like that. It's not really a musical genre—it is a sacred experience, a sacred practice. And we want to immerse ourselves in it so that we can create these rhythms and grooves in the mind, so that we can benefit from them. When we repeat these Sanskrit words about aspects of divinity, we naturally reflect upon our own divinity—about our relation to the Divine. "All thinking is a habit of the mind," my guru used to say. So if we can train our minds to the purifying grooves of mantras, then we can begin to untie the knots of bondage, the bondage that keeps us from remembering who we really are. The mind needs to have these patterns and this sway of rhythm in order to transcend itself. That is the power of the kirtan and the repetition of mantras.

And do you find it has lasting effect for people? Do they walk out of the kirtan as changed persons?

I would like to hope so! It depends how much they put into it, and what their state of spiritual development is like, how many holes are in their pot, so to speak. Swamiji used to tell us that we have too many holes in our pot, and that's why we don't retain what's poured into us. Kirtan pours the energy in, but the rest is up to us. Kirtan is a multi-fold path—on one side, there is the music and the expression and singing of the participants, and then there is the deeper aspect of the vibration. And in that space between the sounds, when you stop, you'll feel something. And that something is you. It's not anything someone is doing to you. It is that energy that is always within you. And this is when great things can start to unfold. People will comment that they have mystical experiences or profound feelings of peacefulness and grace, or a deep sense of love and connection. These are all things that can happen when you focus on the heart, because the heart is the center of the *anahata nada* ("the unstruck sound"), and when you activate that energy it activates the energy of the heart. It *is* the energy of the heart. And because the energy of the heart is expansive, it can carry us beyond our little sense of self to the larger Self. And that, needless to say, is a profound experience.

Nicely put. Let's talk a little about how your involvement in the world of kirtan led to producing CDs.

Hmm. Alright, but let me back up a little here. Nearly four years after getting married—we were married in 1996—and moving to Milwaukee, I felt I was somehow drying up, starving for a kirtan or a yoga scene. So I called several friends and arranged to begin kirtan events at their various yoga centers. After a few months of kirtan with only three or four people and sometimes no one showing up, I told them that I was having visions of kirtan with 100 or more people. I could feel it in my bones, but it wasn't what was happening before my eyes. So I cancelled all the rest of our kirtan at those locations. I often talk to Swamiji in my heart, since he is no longer physically present, and the day I cancelled the kirtan

I recall saying to him that he would need to run the show, so to speak. I wanted his divine intervention, if you know what I mean. I needed help. I wasn't having any luck, and I was feeling quite frustrated, since many years ago Swamiji had told me that this is what I would be doing with my life. And it wasn't happening. So I told him that, if it was going to happen at all, he'd have to be in charge of it — *completely.*

So about two weeks after that whole "conversation with my guru," a funny thing happened: a woman named Theresa Catlin, who now lives in L.A., called and introduced herself, saying that she heard from someone that I did kirtan. She wanted to know if I might consider doing it at the church where she held her yoga classes. I went and looked at this beautiful little room, where she wanted us to have kirtan, and it was all history from that day on. My husband said that if I wanted to do it, I should do it right — whether for five people or for 500 — and get a good sound system. So we went and got our first microphones and sound equipment just in time for our first night of kirtan in Milwaukee. This first kirtan event was in September 2001, and it has continued on the first Friday of every month since then. A year-and-a-half later, when I saw people cramming into the room, sitting on the piano, in the halls, and on their friends just to get a seat, I knew we had to move. In May 2003 we moved to our second location, and by February 2007, we were again overflowing and moved to our third and present location. We now get some 300-400 people in regular attendance, and it just keeps growing.

Little did I know that this event would push me to learn about so many new things: sound equipment and engineering, CD production, recording equipment, band development, marketing, promotion, and media/press stuff. And this, of course, leads me to answering your question. I am so grateful to our friend, the previous CEO of Narada, who arranged for me to meet his top producers and staff, because they gave me two solid hours of advice on recording my first CD. It was a lot of great advice, and it was also quite overwhelming. I remember walking out of that meeting thinking that if that's what it took to produce a CD, I would never be able to do it! I later also met with David Vartanian, a sound and ProTools engineer referred by Narada, who gave me the best advice yet: "Do it yourself with ProTools—you'll be much happier if you produce it yourself. And then *listen* to what you record. *Listen* to it." Great advice. Basically, I wanted to be sure that I had really good tracks when I went into the editing and mixing process.

So my husband went out to get ProTools and a computer for me, and it sat in our living room for several months. Frankly, it scared me to think I was going to have to dive into computer techno stuff. So I did something I don't often do: I procrastinated. Several months went by and finally my husband sat down, opened the box, installed the software and tried it out himself. When I came home that night, he had made a little song and played it for me. That's what inspired me, and I got interested in doing it at that time. Years ago, Swamiji had said that the man I would marry would inspire me, and he was right. My husband is a profound inspiration in my life, a real testimony to the power of a heartfelt and spiritual connection. And it was because of him that I got the courage to dive into the software and computer aspects of recording music.

So you really got into the whole technical part of production.

I had to. And in order to produce the first CD, especially, I had many steep learning curves to go through, with ProTools, which is music recording software; Photoshop, which is software for photos; In-Design—software for brochure layout; and stuff like that. And a year later I had to learn Dreamweaver to do my own website layout and design. I had had very little computer experience and software experience when I started this recording process. I knew how to read my email and surf the Internet, and that was about it. I really struggled with all that learning, with having so many new things in my life, in my mind, and so I said lots of prayers that year. LOTS of them!

So, these days, the recording process is such a blessing. I'm still learning new things, but the steep uphill curves have vanished, and I'm able to thoroughly enjoy the process with the musicians, with the chants, and with my long days of editing at home. It's like magic to watch it all unfold. It's a sacred process for me, and so many blessings fill our lives these days. I feel like I'm living a wonderful dream, and I'm so thankful for the guidance my guru offers to me.

I'd like to know specifics about your CDs and how you came to record them.

Since returning from India with Swamiji in 1992, I felt I was returning to the U.S. for three reasons: to complete my doctorate, to be with Swamiji, and to complete kirtan CDs. He had told me that this music was my future. In 2002 when I entered a retreat to begin the first CD recording process, my prayer was for the right timing. I knew once the first CD was created, the others would follow and it would then become my life. I definitely received indicators from the universe that the time was right, and so I just went for it. And we did our first CD production.

Shortly after releasing the first CD, in 2003, I was fortunate to have the documentary film producer, David Lee Hendrickson, attend one of our kirtan events. He was moved by the whole thing and asked about the possibility of doing a kirtan documentary movie. So that's another project.

In January of 2005, the International Kirtan Foundation was established in Chicago/ Milwaukee, which is working to bridge the world of kirtan in the West with that in the East, through various projects. We will soon launch its website: www.KirtanConnection. com, and this site will enable the smaller kirtan events — which perhaps can't post their events online, for example — to achieve greater publicity and visibility. It will facilitate the formation of kirtan groups across the West and throughout the rest of the world. It will also provide a forum of communication for *kirtan-wallahs* and kirtan participants, for beginning musicians and seasoned veterans, for CD production tips, live event tips, etc. Gee, I bet it could be a great outlet for this book as well.

We've recorded our second album for the Kirtan Café series, and we plan to complete a total of four kirtan CDs. My purpose in this life is to focus on the heart, to create sacred music. We want to make our CDs memorable, classics, in the field of kirtan, something that would last for years to come, for the next generations, something with richness and layers and all the things that we feel during the kirtan experience. We have also trademarked the phrase, "Turn the World to Love®," for our kirtan because we felt this to be our underlying mission.

I didn't get into kirtan wanting to be a rock star—I found kirtan before I really knew what a rock star was. So you won't likely see me putting out albums that are in English, either. What we do aim to provide are rock solid, beautiful, and rich kirtan albums with no filler songs. The chants we record and do live are what I've dreamed of for over twenty years—having the beautiful traditional chants combined with ancient world instrumentation and modern instrumentation, something that holds the sacredness of the past with the relevance of the present. People will know that when they purchase a CD from the Kirtan Café series, all the chants, all the tracks, will be meaningful and full of life. Because feeling and emotion is so central to the kirtan experience, all of the chants that make it onto the CD must be full of love, full of energy. When people hear a kirtan CD they should feel transformed, transported to a sacred space. They should feel the love that is in the tradition of the masters. That is the blessing of good kirtan.

For more information contact:
www.raganiworld.com

**ASA**

Recording artists Hans Christian and Kimberly Waters decided to make beautiful music together. The result is RASA. Their music is based on Indian love songs from the Vaishnava tradition, sung in Sanskrit and Bengali and arranged with both Western and Indian instruments. Though they rarely use kirtan as such on their CDs, their music attempts to evoke the same spiritual feelings as kirtan, largely by drawing on devotional lyrics and music that harkens to the mode of goodness.

Donovan has referred to their CDs as, "Top quality devotional music." And Jai Uttal has said that they record, "Beautiful devotional music that combines ancient Eastern mystical prayers with lush Western orchestration and ambience. This music really touches my heart."

Their first three CDs, "Devotion," "Union," and "In Concert" have been acclaimed throughout the world, including Amazon.com's choice of being the "Best New Age CDs of the year 2000 and 2001." Amazon also voted them, "Number 1 choice of music for Yoga (for 'Devotion')," and New Age Voice's "Vocal CD of the year (for 'Union')."

And then, in September 2003, came their fourth CD, "Shelter." The work is a monumental offering of meditative prayers to Krishna – in an inimitable style that has now become the trademark of singer Kim Waters and multi-instrumentalist Hans Christian. Overall, the CD is *not unlike their prior three, though the duo has now come of age, perfecting their art with high production quality and with a finesse that comes with years. Using sophisticated programming, cello, electric bass, Indian sarangi, sitara, and Swedish nyckelharpa, among other instruments, Hans underlines Kim's angelic voice in a unique and artful way.*

The next CD (2006) was "Temple of Love," which brings the music to greater meditative heights, with an even more contemplative and reflective quality that is especially suitable for gentle forms of yoga practice. And most recently there is "Saffron Blue," released in 2007, where Hans and Kim have clearly hit their stride. Along with the polished sound of New Age Music's most accomplished duo, there are especially gifted guest artists here as well — Waters sings duets with Vaiyasaki Das, Russill Paul, and Bairavesh Das, making this CD their most delicious and broad-based attempt thus far. "Saffron Blue" has set a new standard for 21st-century devotional music, with its sophisticated production, passionate performances, and energetic deliverance.

✳ ✳ ✳

Okay, let's begin with some background. Hans, can we begin with you? Where are you from and what stands out about your youth?

HC: I was born in Germany to Anne and Guenter Reumschuessel, and I grew up in several small villages in Northern Germany. Eventually, we moved to Hannover, Germany. My father was a minister in the Lutheran church, and my mother was employed as a social worker most of her adult life. Both my parents were socially active, and from early on I was enlisted to help the needy and sick in our community. I also have two older sisters who grew up to be an architect and a filmmaker.

And music?

HC: I started to study the cello at age nine and often played in my father's church — my first temple experience — or for holidays and special occasions in our community. Music grabbed my interest from the earliest years, perhaps as far back as age five, when an accident landed me in a children's hospital, and where I had my first "transcendental experience" — facilitated by a severe concussion — when I listened to one particular music piece over and over again and experienced a floating sensation while being totally absorbed in that piece. This was my first "kirtan," in a sense, since it changed my consciousness through the power of sound vibration.

In 1982 I moved to Los Angeles to study music at Musicians Institute in Hollywood and got involved in the L.A. music scene. I was restless and ambitious and quickly hooked up with local bands, eventually playing with well-known artists on TV and live. But my conscience, I think, kept me searching beyond glamor and fame — I needed to go deeper within myself. So I started to compose my own music, through improvisations on the cello, and found myself on a deep spiritual journey. My music first expressed anger, then a deep longing, and eventually a search for the spirit.

I eventually decided to leave L.A. and devote myself more to my own music in San Francisco. I also opened a recording studio and started to produce other artist's projects. I just wanted to be around music all the time. My explorations guided me towards Indian instruments, and I discovered a deep curiosity for the Indian music tradition; soon I incorporated *tablas* and sitar-like instruments into my compositions. One day, I found a *sarangi*, and an even deeper musical calling was answered — something that definitely reached for the spiritual. This happened around 1997, and in 1998 I met Kim, after having noticed her singing on a recording. Kim lived in Washington D.C. at the time, but we met at a party in the summer of 1998 in Marin County, California.

Okay, Kim. How about your early life and how you came to the spiritual quest?

KW: I grew up in Washington D.C. in an unusual, artistic, slightly bohemian family. My father worked for the government but at heart was a painter and sculptor. I have one sister who is an actress and an artist, and my mother is also a very creative and wonderful person. Although we didn't have a lot of money, I was fortunate to have a relatively gentle childhood full of fantasy, fairy tales, art, and music.

Everything changed during adolescence in the '60s. The angst and self-searching of teenage years, the questioning of one's faith and religious upbringing—in my case, Catholic—the rebellion against authority, and the realization of the illusory nature of the world. Certainly, much of the music of our generation tells that story. So from beatnik to hippie to spiritual seeker—the story goes on. I married at age seventeen, and, together with my husband, Chris Murray, we began our spiritual journey. One that my family had difficulty relating to but ultimately, I think, accepted. Music was always a very important part of all that, but I had no idea that some day I would record and perform devotional music from India.

How did you move East? That always fascinates me.

KW: The first time I heard the sounds of Indian instruments, I was immediately captivated, and I loved it when the Beatles and Donovan began to use these sounds in their music, too. It was an exciting time and this led to many wonderful discoveries, such as the music of Ravi Shankar and others. We were fortunate to meet a few spiritual teachers along the way, such as Swami Satchidananda and Yogi Bhajan, and we also met some special souls, like Allen Ginsberg and Timothy Leary; but, really, I was especially inspired and fascinated by the spiritual and musical journey of George Harrison.

In fact, my then husband and I decided to visit the Krishna temple in London as a result of George's association with Srila Prabhupada and the devotees. I remember the first time we entered the temple room—the altar and deities were dazzling, unlike anything I had ever seen before. Prabhupada was giving a lecture and it was like walking into a whole different world. It was a little hard to understand him at first, with his heavy Indian accent, but his majestic presence was quite incredible, and we were extremely moved by the experience. When it was over, his personal servant at that time, Nanda Kumar, asked us if we could give him a ride across town—not Prabhupada, only Nanda Kumar. We reluctantly agreed, not knowing exactly where we were going. As it turned out, he was going in advance of Prabhupada to prepare for a Vedic celebration in an Indian family's home. He invited us to participate and we ended up having a wonderful, extremely spicy, Indian feast with Srila Prabhupada and several others.

At that time, we asked Prabhupada to autograph our copy of his *Bhagavad-gita As It Is*, which he did, and it was after that loving incident that we were inspired to select some verses, illustrate them, and offer them as a published book dedicated to him. We were even able to show him the work in progress and he approved and blessed our efforts. Eventually, it was published by Harper & Row in 1975, and then it was reprinted by Mandala Media in 1998.

The initial publishing of that book was a turning point in our lives, and our desire to please Prabhupada kept us going for many years. Although we never felt qualified to ask for initiation, we remained friends of the devotees and had a number of very special experiences with Prabhupada.

One of them, I'm sure, was when he looked through your artwork and blessed it. Could you tell me more about the circumstances behind that?

KW: Sure. I worked for about five years doing the illustrations for *Illuminations from the Bhagavad-Gita*. Early in the project, we wanted to show a few of the pieces to Prabhupada, just to be sure we were doing something that he would approve of, especially since we were not initiated disciples. So in New Vrindavan, the ashram in West Virginia, I think it was in 1974, after a morning walk, we stood in a pathway where Prabhupada was approaching. I was pretty nervous holding a stack of paintings on large illustration boards and trying to discreetly adjust the *sari* that I was not accustomed to wearing. Surrounded by his senior disciples, Prabhupada silently looked for a few moments and said, "You are introducing a new art form to this country. You will receive great rewards for this." Chris explained we would try to have a big publisher in New York do the book, and Prabhupada said quite emphatically, "Do it!" and walked on.

Cool story. Do you remember the first time you heard kirtan? Was it in that association—when you were with Prabhupada and the devotees.

KW: I attended a Sunday feast program in Washington D.C at the Newport Place Hare Krishna temple, in 1969, I believe. My former husband Chris Murray followed the sound of *kartals* [hand cymbals] on the street, which led him to the temple. Damodar, Madhusudana, and Kanchabala—all disciples of Srila Prabhupada—invited us for the feast the following Sunday.

The first thing I remember noticing in the incense-filled room was a picture of Srila Prabhupada. He was wearing a crooked pink flyers cap that seemed to be causing one of his ears to fold over slightly. He looked so unusual and yet beautiful in a strange way. We were familiar with some terms and names like "guru" from having looked into Transcendental Meditation, inspired by the Beatles (especially George). It's hard to remember the exact sequence of events, but the Radha Krishna Temple album had a profound effect on us, and little did I know that many years later I would be involved in recording some of those songs.

So, certainly Yamuna Devi, the main singer on that album, who I later became friends with, has been a great inspiration to me. I was blessed to have a special period of time with her and her close friend, Dina Tarine, where we shared many sweet and intimate kirtans with their lovely deities, "Radha-Banabihariji." I was also deeply affected by the singing of Vishnujana Swami and was lucky to experience quite a few extraordinary kirtans with him and Tamal Krishna Goswami. They allowed us to do some special service for Radha Damodar, their deities, and there was one particularly memorable afternoon in a park where the kirtan went on for several hours. It is difficult to describe how ecstatic that was. More recently, I've been inspired by Vaiyasaki and Agni Dev. But I must say that the most amazing and powerful kirtans in my life were the ones in the presence of Srila Prabhupada. Either led by him or by others, they were truly extraordinary experiences—largely because of his powerful presence. There are quite a few Indian singers today that I enjoy and appreciate tremendously, too, such as Lakshmi Shankar, Ashwini Bhide, Jagit Singh, and Russill Paul.

Hans, maybe you could talk about your spiritual quest as well, and how it led you to Kim and RASA.

HC: My initial spiritual quest started in my parents' house, where I was very conflicted about spiritual matters. My initial impression was that people were not authentic in their actions, that they behaved differently in church on Sundays than during the rest of the week, and that troubled me. From early on, I felt spiritual curiosity, but also an aversion to organized religion. In hindsight, it was a blessing to have grown up in church because it instilled in me a living concept of God; at the same time it didn't offer many answers. So I felt a deep split about spiritual matters and kept on trying things out — various chanting, meditation, and mind control approaches. Again, in hindsight, these experiences served a certain short-lived purpose, but I kept moving on rapidly.

My spiritual hunger was also expressed through my music, which initially came out in several solo CDs, titled "Hypnotized," "Phantoms," and "Surrender." While working on those recordings I connected with what I like to call "archetypal forces" within myself — images of fire, blood, and yes, more positive images, too, like grace, love, and surrender. The continuing thread throughout my journey has been the power of sound, and to that end I have explored and developed skills of producing and recording sound — from cello and *sarangi* to Tibetan sound bowls, custom made tubular bells, and many other exotic instruments, too. All of these loose ends connected when Kim and I started RASA, which has become a perfect vehicle to express myself and to offer my music to the world. And as a sideline, in the process of developing RASA, I have also gathered a lot of experience that I now apply in my work as a producer for other artists.

Do you remember the first time you heard kirtan?

HC: Well, growing up in a church environment, people would often sing together in praise of God, but in a Christian setting. Still, that's kirtan, right? My first deep involvement with Indian kirtan came when I played in Krishna Das' band around 1997-98.

It was a good experience, and I learned about the power of kirtan from a performer's perspective. Soon after, I was asked to produce the first of a series of CDs with kirtan singer, Agni Dev; this gave me my first in-depth musical contact with the Vaishnava tradition. Another significant project was a recording of "Hanuman Chalisa" with Jai Uttal, Jay Lakshman, and others from the Neem Karoli Baba lineage. Plus, there were numerous other spiritual projects coming through my recording studio in the late 1990s.

RASA's music is based on *bhajans*, and we never really offer a call-and-response engagement with our audiences, because neither one of us is a "kirtan leader," at least not in the usual sense. Our gifts lie elsewhere. We hope that our music transports people to a "sweet location," and since the songs we perform are too difficult to learn for the general public, we just present them in a concert setting. But if people respond by singing back in their own hearts, that's a form of kirtan, too.

The musical form now known in the States as "kirtan" has tight musical parameters. The musician in me would be somewhat limited trying to fit into those parameters, and so I don't. Instead, we prefer to create a musical journey that is based on these *bhajans* that Kim knows so well, with the hope that it is an infectious spiritual experience for our listeners. Other important parts of our expression are our CDs, which we labor over for many months. Our recordings are our labor of love, our offerings to the world as spiritual musicians.

Could you talk a bit more about your interaction with Krishna Das and Jai Uttal?

HC: I met KD in the mid 1990s when I lived in Marin County. He came through town and was looking for back-up musicians for a concert. The band that was formed included myself on cello, bass, and *sarangi*; Wynne Paris on guitar, and Girish Gambhira on *tablas*. I toured and recorded with KD for maybe a year and played on two of his CDs. He was kind enough to sing on "Devotion," our first RASA release — on the song, "Jaya Radha Madhava" — but I haven't seen him lately.

As for Jai Uttal, we were just living in the same town. We knew of each other but never played together until we recorded the "Hanuman Chalisa" project, and we eventually did play a concert or two together. I also had a brief musical encounter with Bhagavan Das, another noteworthy personality on the kirtan scene. We recorded several hours worth of music, him singing and playing *ektar*, and myself on the cello. I don't know what came of it.

Another name worth mentioning is my friend Dave Stringer, whom I met in L.A. around 1985. I worked with him on his beautiful music, first as a cellist/bassist, and later also as a producer/ engineer. Most recently, I co-produced and engineered his 2007 release "Divas and Devas." Dave went to India around 1990 to a Siddha Yoga ashram and shifted into being a kirtan singer, but we actually shared the love of *tablas* and other Indian instruments before he went. In addition, I had a rich selection of "New Age" singers come through my studio, people who mixed it all together —Shiva, Gaia, Krishna, Dolphins, pet birds as spirit guides, etc. I got pretty fed up with it after a while. I wanted more clarity, cohesion. That's what I do with Kim . . .

Kim, why is kirtan important to you?

KW: I discovered that to sit in silent meditation for any real length of time is not an easy thing for me to do. My mind seems to wander and I become restless. It's easier and more enjoyable to pray or to chant in the form of singing. The drone of a *harmonium* or *tamboura* greatly assists in carrying me into the deeper moods of the songs or mantras, what to speak of all the beautiful instruments that Hans incorporates into our music.

I've always enjoyed chanting with the devotees in the various ashrams I've visited over the years, and for lack of a better way of putting it, had some very high experiences participating in that. But I don't really consider myself a kirtan singer. I prefer to be a singer of devotional songs or *bhajans* rather than a leader of kirtan. It was also wonderful to discover that my love of painting and illustrating could also be a form of prayer or an offering—it was my personal kirtan, in a sense. So the singing of these songs, which I understand to be expansions of mantras, combined with, for example, illustrating *Illuminations from the Bhagavad-Gita*, the book I mentioned earlier as an offering to Prabhupada, was a perfect combination for me in my own spiritual quest.

And Hans—please share some of your realizations about kirtan.

HC: The power of kirtan is directly linked to intention. When we offer our kirtan—or *bhajans*, as we do with RASA—from a deep, devotional heart, then it becomes valid, gains momentum, and inspires the listener. Kirtan is a form of prayer, and the particular surge of interest in Indian-style kirtan may be linked with a deep need to pray, but not along the old and sometimes off-putting lines that we might have grown up with. I'm talking about an innate need—something we're born with.

On the other hand, once we find the nectar in prayer, of calling out to our source, it doesn't really matter in what context the prayer occurs, as long as sincerity is behind it. So, our heart has to shift into a receptive mode, and our mind has to allow it—then we will benefit from kirtan and prayer, or whatever we choose to call it. I believe that all human beings are on the same path, but not necessarily in the same place. You can also say that we are all heading in the same direction, towards the light. Deep down, that's what we all want. Some of us are going through darkness of the spirit while others have the wind on their backs, pushing them in the right direction. But we're all on this epic journey of spirit. Kirtan—real kirtan—just accelerates the process.

For more information contact:
www.rasa-music.com or www.kimwatersart.net

YOFIYAH

Susan Deikman, also called Yofiyah, is the founder of Hebrew or Kabbalistic Kirtan — an ecstatic mystical practice based on the chanting of God's names and sacred Hebrew texts. She is also the creator of "Vocal Discovery," an original method for personal transformation and community building, using the power of sound. Along similar lines, she began the Tone Deaf Choir, which helps self-defined non-singers overcome their perceived limitations.

A leader in the international "Music for People" organization, Yofiyah uses her skills as a voice teacher, artist, and improvisational musician to create a safe, welcoming, and spiritually challenging environment for finding and freeing one's "authentic voice," often locked inside one's own heart. Her initial CD is called "Kiss the Beloved," where she fully engages her unique blend of Indic kirtan and Hebrew chants. This CD was remixed and re-released by Sounds True, Inc., as "Kabbalah Kirtan."

Here, she uses the sefirot — the ten characteristics or energies of God as delineated in the Kabbalah — to show how God is to be found in all people and all things. Rabbi Zalman M. Schachter-Shalomi has this to say about Yofiyah's music: "A marvelous gateway to the spirit, creating holy community through the call and response mastery of a true energizer of the soul. Yofiyah brings yofi (beauty) to Yah (God)."

* * *

Let's begin with some background. You were born . . .

Of course I was! [laughter] May 18, 1962.

Okay. Jewish family?

Yes, a Jewish family. We started out on the East Coast and moved to the West Coast via Colorado.

Where on the East Coast?

Well, I was born in Massachusetts, in Stockbridge, in the Berkshires. Then we moved to Colorado for three years and then to Mill Valley, California. I came back to the East Coast much later.

Was it a religious family?

No.

Oh, you needed time to think about that.

[laughter] We celebrated Passover every year, but we also had a Christmas tree. Go figure. I knew that Santa loved me. [laughter] I mean, I really *did* know that Santa loved me. But there was no God. So I was taught that there was no God, but that there *was* a Santa Claus.

How funny.

I could never figure that one out. Later, my mother clarified by saying that she didn't want me to think there was a man in the sky judging me.

Okay, that softens it a bit.

But that's not what she said at the time. Her idea was clear: There *is* no God. At least that's how I remember it. She would probably disagree with that now. I used to try to enlighten the other children about there being no God, and they didn't like what I had to say. Nor did their parents.

That position is a bit strange, isn't it? I mean, people who disbelieve in God sometimes claim to *know* for sure that God doesn't exist. And

yet they balk when religionists claim to know that God *does* exist. They don't like the certainty exhibited by theists, and yet they often exhibit that same certainty in reverse. I just find that interesting.

It is. It really is.

Okay, so you were raised in a sort of nonreligious Jewish home.

Nonreligious, but my parents were interested in Eastern mysticism.

What form of Eastern mysticism?

Well, it shifted around a bit. First there was the Guru Maharaji phase, and then many other guru types followed.

Can you remember some of them?

Well, there was quite a bit of interest in Trungpa for awhile.

Chogyam Trungpa, the famous Buddhist master.

Yeah, they were also into Suzuki Roshi, who brought Zen Buddhism to California.

Right.

During that time we went to a Tassajara Retreat Center in Santa Cruz, where I spent a month with my folks and a bunch of monks. They all studied and meditated, and I sat in on the talks and learned to meditate, too—but I also ran around and played in the waterfall and the hot springs and stuff like that. My babysitters were women with bald heads. I thought that was pretty cool.

Almost like Hasidic women.

I know. But it was different.

Buddhist nuns were babysitting you.

Zen priests. Then my parents became involved with Sufi study groups. With Idries Shah, who became their teacher. But he was in Europe. They met him once. But he had several study groups over here, and he led the way. That became their spiritual practice.

I see. So they were interested in Eastern mysticism and they found an assortment of teachers. But it seemed that none of the teachers were traditional Hindu teachers. Guru Maharaji certainly wasn't.

No, there was no Hindu anything. In fact, they frowned on ecstatic practices in general. They were not interested in Sufi singing or Sufi dancing, even though they were involved with the Sufis. So it's kind of ironic that I ended up doing an ecstatic practice, you know, that is basically "Hindu" in origin—and singing "God, God, God," all the time. Because they weren't into God at all.

Interesting.

The whole thing is a bit funny.

So how did your evolution into Judaism and kirtan come about?

Okay, so I grew up with, "There's no God—there's Absolute Truth." My father is a psychiatrist. He was part of the Human Potential Movement and all that kind of stuff. I was a real Northern California baby. I moved to New York City, which was an amazing experience for me, to see Jews who were out of the closet, because in California you couldn't tell.

I was really Jewishly identified because my parents were very Jewishly identified, even though they were into all kinds of things, from Eastern thought, to atheism, to humanism. So that's the background. Yet everyone around me told me I was Jewish. They'd say, "You're Jewish, aren't you?" And because of the ancestry, I guess, I'd say, "Uh, yeah." But I didn't have any sense of what it really meant. It felt like a burden. We weren't connected to the Jewish world at all. Then, when I got to New York City, I was surrounded by it. It was incredible, but I didn't know where I fit in. I tried walking in and out of synagogues and it just freaked me out—everyone sitting, facing the same direction, reciting the same words. Well, I was biased against religion to begin with.

Were you going to synagogues that separated women and men?

I walked into all different kinds. I went to reform temples. I thought they were very nice, because they were more inviting—they invited me to have sweets afterwards, too. I went to conservative synagogues. Everything. Finally, a cousin of mine, who is Lubavitch, suggested that I join a Jewish choir. Before that, I had no idea there was such a thing as a Jewish choir. I thought choirs were reserved for churches.

That's what I thought.

So I joined the Jewish choir and loved the music. I started to connect through the music and then . . .

What kind of music was it?

I would say primarily Eastern European Jewish music.

Okay.

Yeah, Western European also. Jewish music. Traditional, I'd say traditional Jewish music. It was a lot of Shabbat and holiday music, so I started learning prayers.

Let's back up a second. When you got to New York, you were going to different Jewish synagogues. But that doesn't mean you were necessarily interested in Jewish spirituality, right?

I was really just interested in connecting with the Jewish community.

Because people kept asking you about your Jewish background?

Yeah, and because, in New York, for the first time, Jews were visible to me and I wanted to know what that meant, what it meant to be Jewish.

I find that interesting, because a lot of Jewish people in New York—myself included—aren't that concerned about our ethnic identity.

But most of those people were at least raised with some background of Hebrew school, and they were Bar and Bat Mitzvahed. They were turned off and they don't want anything to do with it. They had that experience. And then they consciously rejected it.

I see. So you kind of knew you had this Jewish thing in your background but you were never exposed to it. So you were curious.

Right, except for Passover and my grandparents. I experienced a lot of covert anti-Semitism in California. So the whole Jewish thing just felt like a liability, until I got to New York. Maybe this was one of the triggers: I had this friend and I was talking to him one day. He just happened to be Jewish, and all of a sudden, from the way he was talking I realized he was proud to be Jewish. I said, "You're *proud* to be Jewish?" And he looked at me, stunned, and said, "You're *not?*" And that really hit home. I needed to find out what it all meant.

Okay, so you came to New York and explored various approaches to Judaism.

Yeah. And it worked. I connect through the music, and there's a synagogue on the upper West Side called the B'nai Jeshurun . . . Well, the two rabbis and the cantor there were from Argentina. They were conservative, but the whole service was sung, and they used a lot of Mizrahi and Sephardic melodies, which I love. The music just spoke to my soul. So I would go there, regularly, but if I looked at the translations of the text—it was in Hebrew—I would freak out.

Why?

Because the language was incredibly patriarchal and hierarchical, and it was using metaphors and imagery I just couldn't relate to. I worked hard to try to translate it into something that made sense to me: "Okay, when they say God, they're really talking about that energizing life force that separates me from the dead. When they talk about master of the universe, they're talking about the beautifying principle that somehow puts things into form and matter . . ."

So you still had an aversion to the God idea?

Well, yeah, I was struggling with it. I didn't know how to relate to God. And to prayer! I didn't know how to relate to prayer, because who were you talking to?

Right.

I certainly didn't think there was a giant being in the sky with ears that could hear. Meanwhile, just on the side, I had been a singer. As a teenager I had been in a punk rock band, and then I wanted to be an opera singer. After that, I was discouraged by my experience in conservatory, especially at the BU School of Music, and felt really horrible about my voice, and I didn't sing for ten years. Then I joined this choir. There was already some repair going on internally. Judaism and music—these things were growing in me, more and more.

I connected with David Darling and Music for People, and in an attempt to try to figure out what to do with my life, someone had suggested I go there. And I had an experience there with improvisation and letting go, singing over a drum. Voice and drum. I had this great experience—it's quite a unique humanistic approach to music and improvisation.

Darling. He was the cellist for the Paul Winter Consort.

Right. Once upon a time. But he teaches at Omega Institute, and he functions in that world.

Back then, when I first discovered him and Music for People, I had an experience while I was there. The whole thing was very beautiful and profound and magical, but one experience in particular—I did a one-on-one session with a man named Eric Edberg. He played a drone on his cello and he had me sing along. I just closed my eyes, and he said, "Try and sing inside the drone." So I did. Then he said, "When you feel like it, you can try going up a little or down a little and see what happens." He also said, "While you're at it, you might want to try moving your hands around a little; see if you can feel the music with your hands." So I did this, and I had the experience of getting maybe 80% of the way there with my singing, where I was really letting go and in the moment. When I finished, I felt like I was more concretely in the world than I had ever been before. It was a profound experience. And then they said, "Do you want to join our training program?" and I said, "Well, I never imagined myself teaching music, so, no." But then I thought, "Well, at the same time, I've never been able to figure out what to do with my life, so maybe I'll use what feels most alive in me and let that be my guide." And I did. And I'll just keep going as long as it feels like there's still something here, and that was the most alive thing that I ever experienced. Then I ended up doing their four-year training program.

And this is going on while you're developing interest in Judaism.

Right, the music thing is a parallel track that's happening along with the Judaism, which started a little bit earlier. The other thing that was happening was I had found a voice teacher. I had accidentally found her because I'd been having chronic lower back pain and my folks had been begging me to go see a Feldenkrais practitioner. I did — I did this, I did that, but nothing was helping. I got a better chair in the office — I worked a corporate job, too. Finally, my parents sent me a check and a name and said, "Please go see this woman. She'll help you." So I went to see her — her name was Marcy Lindheimer — and I had a session with her. She handed me her card, and at the bottom of the card it said, "Feldenkrais practitioner/ voice teacher."

Ah, a voice teacher—so she was sent to you, in a sense.

And when I looked at that card, I said, "Do you think you could teach me?" Because I was somewhat damaged from my experience in a conservatory. I had a teacher tell me hideous things like, "I really admire people like you who do this even though you'll never have a career in music."

What a thing to say!

Words like that to a nineteen year old are pretty devastating.

Sure.

It's devastating at any age.

But tell me a little about this Feldenkrais principle.

Moshe Feldenkrais started a particular awareness through movement technique that became very popular. He originated two interrelated, somatically based educational methods. The first method involves awareness through movement, which is a verbally directed, body movement technique. The second method is called "Functional Integration" — and this one is nonverbal. It's a manual contact technique designed for people desiring or requiring more individualized attention.

So she taught these techniques and I knew they would be useful to me, given where I was coming from. There was also someone named Carl Stough, who was also known as "Dr. Breath." He worked on breathing coordination. She kind of combined all of these things and had a very interesting approach. I started having experiences with her that were really far out, just stunning. She would say, do this, do that, do the other thing, and I would do what she said, and all of a sudden I'd have this experience of stepping into another world. I mean, there was like a crystalline, narrow, vertical chamber, where everything was resonating. Not vibrating, but just like buzzing. And filled with light. Ecstatic experiences through voice lessons.

This was going on . . .

During my voice lessons with her. Right. She'd say, try this, try that, and all of a sudden some kind of internal alignment would happen. Amazing stuff. What freaked me out was that it had nothing to do with my mind or my intention: I was just very focused on what I was doing, on developing my voice, with deep meditation. But then unexpected things would happen. She'd say, "Imagine that your breath is curving up like a parrot's beak." I mean, it would be something, you know, that you wouldn't necessarily think would lead you there, but that's where it was leading you. It was the most delightful feeling, and my voice would freely move, making sounds that were so resonant . . .

It was really something special — I'd have these white light experiences that I can only relate to things I've read in yoga texts. But I read them much later.

So you had some kind of yogic experience taking singing lessons. Okay. And you were developing your Jewish identity as well, on a separate plane. Where does kirtan come in?

Well, I decided to leave New York, because I couldn't be a musician and a teacher there.

Because of all the competition?

Couldn't afford it, and it's the land of more. It's like, no matter how much you have, more is better. It's the one place I've lived where that's really true. You can have more freedom, more time, more space, more money, and it's never enough. Elsewhere I go on vacation and I need less. I couldn't afford to live there and do the music thing. Also, I had had this very clear vision of my life as a river.

What does that mean?

I had this image that my life was a river and I wasn't even swimming upstream. I was standing on the bank, and it was passing me by. So I left and I moved to Philadelphia, because in the meantime I had met a woman named Rabbi Shefa Gold at B'nai Jeshurun. She was doing Jewish chanting. We did some chanting together: a short phrase with intention over and over and over and then we sat in silence. It was like mantra meditation. I went, "Ah! Finally something I know how to do!" It really felt sooo natural. I couldn't get all the prayers and all the words into my heart, but chanting, you know, some small intentional repetition, like, "My cup overflows," and then sitting in silence and just basking in it. That I could relate to.

I found that the chanting just opened up such a profoundly deep space for meditation. I loved it. So I followed her up to a place called Elat Chayyim—it's a retreat center, a Jewish retreat center in the Catskills. I started going there, and I learned about Jewish Renewal. It was founded by Rabbi Zalman Schachter-Shalomi. Do you know who that is?

Sure. Reb Zalman, founder of Jewish Renewal as a formal movement.

I was really challenged about the whole God/prayer thing. And it took a while. It was like a desensitization process, where every time someone would say "God," I'd cringe, and then I'd cringe less, making baby steps toward recovery. I worked really hard to try to find my way in, to understand what was happening with prayer and what my aversion was really all about. I eventually came to grips with it; I saw where it was coming from, and I worked toward internal healing.

In the meantime, I moved to Philadelphia because there was a Jewish Renewal community there and it was a day trip from New York. It was greener and cheaper than New York City, and it was an integrated neighborhood. I sort of liked that. At Elat Chayyim, I was clear about what I wanted, and so I said, "This is where I want to be. This is what it looks like." Almost unanimously, everyone said, "Mt. Airy," which is a neighborhood in Philadelphia. So I moved to Mt. Airy, where the social circles are pretty small and they all overlap.

What did you do while in Philly?

I was doing improv dancing with Group Motion and improv music with my Music for People friends. I was also doing Jewish Renewal stuff, and there, I found, the yoga community also overlaps. So, because I was a singer, I was invited to do some kirtan at a yoga studio. I went and I thought, "Well, this is neat, but the only person having any fun is the leader, because they get to improvise. Everyone else just has to follow." That bothered me; it sort of went against my philosophy and my teaching methods.

Okay.

I was teaching that everyone has access to music and can tap into that spontaneous flow, which is within them. What I'm talking about is improvised music. I was focusing on people who were concerned about their voice, who thought they were tone deaf or who were very shy. I could relate to them. I had compassion for them because of my earlier experience — back when I quit singing. No one was teaching this population about the beautiful music within them and of their ability to express themselves through song, and I had some ideas about how to do that. That's what I was doing.

But I was running into a recurring problem: In order for someone to really have an internal shift concerning their voice and music, they needed to have a successful musical experience. That's how you gain confidence. For individuals who had little experience going there, it was very hard to get them motivated or to go further. That's when everything started to flow together. It all came together because I was feeling dissatisfaction with the status quo. I felt unfulfilled with distinctly Jewish experiences, with worship services and *davening* [praying] and what have you. Even in the Renewal world, they weren't working for me. They weren't changing my inner state of being; they weren't opening my heart or stilling my mind: they just weren't working.

In my teaching, I was looking for another way to help people move beyond their limited experiences of voice and music. I worked for a full month or more in Omega. I was there taping workshops of all kinds, because I wanted to become a better facilitator. I was observing what different facilitators did for people — where they succeeded and where they failed. So I learned a lot — these are all experts in their own way, and I got quite a bit out of it.

Now, there was a lot of chanting going on there, and it just kind of hit me. It was so obvious when it came together. It's like, "Oh, Hebrew kirtan — Jewish kirtan." Because the kirtan experience worked. People were able to successfully enter into the music through kirtan, to move beyond inhibitions and insecurities. Kirtan does that for people, and it certainly did that for me. It offers the connectedness, the oneness, the open-heartedness, and the silence afterwards. It gave me all those things that I wanted in my spiritual life, and I saw others getting the same thing out of it. It just seemed obvious to do it in a Jewish way, which would help Jewish people who weren't comfortable with their singing. They could benefit from my experience and just follow me there.

So you educated yourself in the kirtan experience.

I started studying kirtan as best as I could. I went to a Sikh temple, and I chanted with them. There's a Krishna temple in the area, and I chanted with them. I listened to everybody's CDs — Americans, Indians, whomever. I got it down, the technique, the style.

But surely you realized that there's more to kirtan than that.

Yeah, and I really didn't want to treat it like a musical technology. I knew there was more to it than just the music. It wasn't just call and response. It was also the intention, the approach, and the text. I knew it was also in the text. I knew about mantras and the power of specific vibrational sounds, the Sanskrit, and also the content. The choices that were made about what to chant were also important. It's very hard to find Hebrew text that resonates in the same way. That's been the most challenging part of the whole project, because I realized that I wanted texts that would bring in the dimensions and depth that you find in the Sanskrit. Like Radha and Krishna, the female and male manifestations of God. I wanted to bring out those feminine aspects for Jewish people, hopefully connecting the masculine and the feminine, bringing in the Goddess, the Mother. Where's the Mother in Judaism?

Besides at home, taking care of the kids?

Exactly. [laughter] Where are those ideas, those metaphors? I started discovering that there are hundreds of names for God in Judaism. Supposedly, the entire *Torah*, when taken together, is a name for God. There's a mystical teaching that talks about that.

But in Judaism you have restrictions about God's name.

There are a lot of restrictions about how to use the text, too, and so I had to make choices about which names I could actually use, because you're not supposed to repeat certain names. So the practice itself of repeating the names sort of contradicted some of the beliefs found in most forms of Judaism.

I've had many interesting conversations about it, and after some time I decided I needed to follow my heart, engaging the kirtan model in the text. I wasn't going to worry about the very orthodox aspects of Judaism, because they're not going to listen to me anyway. There's a tradition — it's called *Kol Isha* — that says a woman's voice is too seductive to be heard by men; so women are not supposed to sing in front of them.

Well, most forms of Judaism don't have a problem with this, but for a long time . . . it was only recently that women started being ordained. Keeping women from singing was one of the ways the rabbis kept them back. By keeping women out of prayer, leading positions in prayer, that was *Kol Isha*. So, not just singing, but leading prayer. This restrictiveness is actually an embarrassment in Judaism, in my opinion, and in many people's opinion.

But even men are not supposed to repeat certain names of God. Is that correct?

Yep. But the same people that hold the *Kol Isha* would have a problem with the repetition of the names.

I've read that the name of God was used by early Jewish mystics to get special powers, like *yogis* used to get mystic powers from chanting mantras. And so the sages, in their wisdom, cut them off from chanting the names, until they qualified themselves by following certain rules and regulations. The ancient rabbis, as I understood it, came to a similar conclusion: They cut people off from chanting the primary name of God, allowing only substitute names, so people couldn't get the powers and thus abuse them.

Well, there's the Tetragrammaton, the original name, and rabbis would work with the letters a lot. They say it's unpronounceable, so . . .

The original name was lost over time.

Well, only the pronunciation was lost . . .

Oh, I didn't know that. That's a whole subject . . .

There were other names, too. And then there's the issue that you're not supposed to use the name out of a prayer context, but you can repeat it out of prayer context because it only has power in prayer. Now, I would argue that this *is* prayer, of sorts, but you're not saying the *complete* prayer? In the end, there's a lot of debate around how I'm using the text. For most of the people I encounter, though, they're just happy to sit down and chant. Really, it's just amazing. Overall, the reaction has been wonderful and fulfilling.

So they're having a spiritual experience and they can connect it to their Jewishness.

Yeah, and that's been very meaningful for people. There are a number of different populations that the group reaches. Many Jewish people are totally alienated from Judaism: They don't want to have anything to do with a synagogue. But still they're spiritual seekers. I'll encounter them in yoga studios where I lead the chanting. When they see where I'm coming from, with Judaism and kirtan, they light up.

I bet.

They *really* light up. I can always see who they are. They have this ecstatic look the whole time, and they come up to me afterwards and just have to express how they feel. They just can't contain themselves. They'll say, "Oh, I've been waiting for this for so long."

These are seekers of Jewish origin, spiritual seekers who aren't connected in any way to the Jewish world. These people are so happy to find a spiritual practice they can relate to. These are folks in the Jewish world who have been sneaking off to yoga centers to chant and to do other things, engage other approaches, because their spiritual life is not being fed. They're not responding to what's happening in the synagogue, even though they like being connected, both to spirituality in general and to their Jewishness.

But it goes beyond Jewishness, doesn't it?

Well, my work is not just for Jewish people. You're right. I really try to find chants and texts that have universal meaning. It doesn't have to be just for Jewish people. I have this friend who frequents yoga centers because she likes kirtan. I said to her, "You've never come to one of my kirtans — are you going to come?" She said, "Well, I'm not Jewish," I said, "Well, you chant in Hindi and Sanskrit and you're not Hindu."

Right, exactly. I was going to say, kirtans are not only for Hindus, so . . .

So, come on! Anyone can join in, regardless of the language.

That's a good point. Your material is marketed well, too. When I came upon it on the web—"Kabbalistic Kirtan"—it just seemed like a good marketing tool. It's attractive and would certainly appeal to modern Jewish people who are somewhat interested in yoga or the kirtan phenomenon. But you don't draw on the Kabbalah much, do you?

I do, actually. The way in which it's Kabbalistic: Some of the text is from the *Zohar*, so that's a Kabbalistic source. Overall, I use the word "Kabbalah" to communicate that we're talking about Jewish mysticism, not mainstream Jewish practice.

I see.

It's not synagogue practice. It's very important to me for people to know that this *is* Jewish spirituality, even if a bit unorthodox.

That's clear, I think.

The Kabbalah is for the mystics. The way it's Kabbalistic, too, is that I'm bringing in the feminine together with the masculine—I'm bringing the feminine back in. In the liturgical writings, in the mainstream, you don't find it. In the mystical writings, the Goddess is everywhere.

I think the Kabbalistic word is "Shekhinah"—the feminine divine.

That's only one name. There's more than one. There's Shekinah, which is the indwelling presence of God, the manifest presence of God.

In the feminine form.

Yes. Well, not in the feminine form, but it is the feminine aspect of God that is manifest in the world.

Oh. Like Radha in the Vaishnava tradition, or Lakshmi. But if it's specifically in this world, then it might be more like Durga or Kali—the Goddess of the material spheres.

I like that: The Goddess of the material spheres. And then you have many other names, too. There's also Elohim . . .

That's feminine?

Yes.

I didn't know that. I thought Elohim was a plural name for God . . .

It is. It's plural, right.

So it's male and female?

Yes. I have a chant, using this text: *Elohim hi ema d'ila-ah*, which means, "Elohim is the Mother of the Above." This is from the *Zohar*. The way I understand it is this: Elohim is God as She appears in the beginning, in *Genesis*, the creation story. It makes sense. Elohim . . . gives birth to the world. Who gives birth? Who creates life? It's a mother. That's why a plural word is used — the mother and father create life. That's God, the creator. I mean, there are a lot of different ideas about why it's in the plural. But the mystics emphasize the mother aspect. So that's definitely Kabbalistic: Having a relationship with God as the beloved.

Sounds Sufi. I always identify that word "beloved" with Sufi doctrine.

Yeah, sounds Sufi. But that's Kabbalistic, too. I also use some of *Shir HaShirim*, which is the "Song of Songs." And in that text it's about love, and longing for the beloved and the union with the beloved.

Right. Some Christian theologians say it was actually a mundane love song, mysteriously included in the Bible, while there are Jewish scholars who call it metaphor. But I think it's about the love of the divine couple.

Oh, well, both of them, the lover and the beloved, are described very erotically. It's a very erotic text, in a sense — it's tantric.

Like the *Gita Govinda* in the Vaishnava tradition. It's very esoteric, and one can easily misunderstand it, thinking it merely mundane. One should qualify oneself to read it through spiritual practice.

The "Song of Songs" is the only tantric text we have. When they were looking to canonize it — they weren't going to include it in the Bible, you know — Rabbi Akiva said, "All of the texts are holy, but *Shir HaShirim* is the holiest of holies." It's the holiest of holy books. He considered it the central text, giving it extreme importance. And if you read it, it's overtly erotic. It describes, "Your breasts are like this, my love, and, hidden in the cleft of the rock, show yourself to me!"

Yes. This is very much like *Gita Govinda* and other esoteric texts on the love of Radha and Krishna.

Hmm.

Those texts have been criticized for being overly erotic, but at the same time they must be understood as conveying *spiritual* eroticism.

That's right. The mystics in the Jewish tradition, at least with the "Song of Songs," believe that it also refers to the relationship of the soul to God.

The soul and God. Yes.

You have the soul as the woman, in the feminine, which is so much like the Hindu imagery, right?

Absolutely.

Right. So I used that text. There's another text, another prayer, from the *Zohar*—it's called the "K'gavna," where we hear about the masculine and feminine divine. I use that, too. And it says, just to paraphrase the Aramaic, "He will not descend upon His throne until She enters into the One, and He will join Her there and One will become One."

"One" is the operative word here, no?

Yeah. I know what you mean. [laughter]

So let's talk about the recording of your CD. Is there a story behind that?

Ah, the story of my CD. Well, I wrote all the music myself, because I didn't want to adapt existing ideas. Music carries meaning, and the traditional kirtan melodies themselves have content—so I didn't want to take the same melodies and just change the words. That would lack a certain authenticity. It would lack integrity, and it wouldn't honor the kirtan tradition in India. So I thought if it's really going to be Jewish kirtan, I didn't want to borrow from existing melodies. I really wanted to come up with something unique, drawing on Indian sounds but also on Middle Eastern and Arabic type sounds, too.

I didn't want this to sound like a basement recording. I really needed it to sound as good as possible because I wanted it to move out past the Jewish Renewal community and to a larger world. So it needed to have that quality.

Right.

I put in my own money, and I recorded the CD. I invested in an *oud* player, *tablas, harmonium* — the works. So I had instruments from different worlds coming together to create a unique sound.

Fantastic.

There's already a history of Arabic and Indian music coming together anyway, in Northern India. It just has this beautiful natural fit. Anyway, I made the CD and people have just been going nuts over it.

And it's selling well?

It's doing well. I had three different record labels interested in picking it up and distributing it, and I went with Sounds True, Inc. They had it remixed and released it as "Kabbalah Kirtan." I'm now working on a new CD that should be coming out in the spring.

I wish you the best of luck.

Thanks. So we're going to try to move it out into a larger world and it'd be really a kick to give the larger world this new fusion music — fusion both in terms of musical orientation and in terms of the Jewish/ kirtan interaction.

One last thing. You have an exotic name. Where did that come from?

Yofiyah. The name was given to me by Reb Zalman. Well, he gave me the name "Yaffe-fiya," which means "the beautiful mouth of God." But then he said, "That might not be quite right." I thought, "It's too many syllables." So, when talking to my rabbi friend, Gershon Winkler, I said, "Gershon, isn't there a name that means the same thing but is only three syllables? Can't we say Ya-fi-yah?" He said, "Well, Yofiyah. *Yofi* means 'beauty,' like in 'beautiful manifestation of God' and *fi* ('mouth') is hidden in there, too, and *Yah* is there as well—which is a name of God. So it still means, 'beautiful mouth of God.'" That's it: Yofiyah. It's a big name to fill, but that's the idea behind these names anyway. With Hebrew names, you can only aspire to fulfill their implications. They're so grandiose! Hopefully, when I'm leading kirtan, I'm fulfilling the name.

For more information contact:
www.kabbalahkirtan.com

$\mathcal{A}$GNI DEV

"Agni Dev's voice doesn't simply imitate traditional bhajan *and kirtan – it is the real thing!"* So says musicologist, author, and award-winning recording artist, Patrick Bernard.

Renowned for his melodious Gaudiya Vaishnava kirtan, Agni Dev sings traditional songs with crossover accompaniment, using both Eastern and Western instruments. In addition to his soul-stirring vocals, he is a master of the mridanga *(the double-headed Indian drum) and the* harmonium.

As a disciple of His Divine Grace A. C. Bhaktivedanta Swami Prabhupada, his study of Vedic philosophy led to the discovery of Bengali devotional music and, in 1972, he began performing kirtan on New York City streets. He later toured with the South Asian Cultural Exhibition, displaying the art of kirtan at university campuses across the United States. He continues to perform at various venues today.

After releasing critically acclaimed cassettes in the 1970s and 1980s, such as "Live in New Dvaraka," "Bhakti Rasa," "Tribute to Prabhupada," and "Treasure of the Holy Name," Agni Dev's work was temporarily sidetracked with managing a vegetarian restaurant in Southern California and ashram leadership. In 2001, however, Mandala Media revived his transcendental voice with "Smaranam: A Garland of Kirtan," a unique CD package that included a small book about sacred sound.

With the success of this project, Mandala soon released the similar "Kirtan: Chanting the Names (Traditional Chants)," with text and music by Agni Dev, Hans Christian of Rasa, and Swami B. B. Bodhayan. The CD-Book format was again reproduced in 2007 with "The Yoga of Sound: Kirtans from the Sacred Forest," including text by Swami B. V. Tripurari and Agni Dev's inimitable kirtan.

✳ ✳ ✳

Let's start by getting some info on your background—your early years, your family, what your influences were—that kind of thing.

Well, my legal name is Alvin Marsden, if that helps. [laughter] I was born on April 9, 1949 in Trinidad and Tobago, in the West Indies. It's one country with two Islands. If you understand that part of the world, you'll know a bit about where I'm coming from. Otherwise . . .

I was raised as a Catholic and went to Catholic schools all the way to high school. Growing up in Trinidad, life was easy, simple, and colorful, especially because of Carnival celebration, which is sort of all pervasive in that region.

I migrated to America two days before my twenty-first birthday and shortly thereafter encountered a small group of Hare Krishna devotees performing kirtan. This was on the streets of Manhattan, in New York.

Tell me a bit more about your home, in Trinidad and Tobago.

Hmm. It's what one would call a melting pot, in a sense. You see, numerous people colonized the country at different times. It kept changing ownership, you might say. We were occupied by the Spanish, the Portuguese, the French, the English, and so on. There's a history of slavery there, too, with a mixture of African, Indian, European, Middle Eastern, and Chinese people all establishing themselves there in one form or another. All these groups managed to leave their mark on the national culture, and so there's a high percentage of mixed-race people.

All of this impacts the regional culture. Now, the last people occupying that area, or exerting control, were the British. As you know, during the time of the British Empire, when the British were powerful, they also occupied India, Africa, and so on. So, as a result, one third of the Trinidadian population is Indian, East Indian. Anyway, there's a real mix of cultures there, all with an island flavor—we have a celebration named Carnival, as I mentioned. You may have heard of Carnival from Brazil or Rio de Janeiro, and places like that.

Sure.

Trinidad Carnival is unique. You've got competitions, costumes, bands, parades. It's amazing—it's the event of the year, every year. People can't wait for it! And it's all they talk about once it's over. It's all quite unique to the area. Here's where you find the origins of calypso, soca music, limbo, and steelbands. Steelbands or steelpan—that's just about my favorite musical instrument.

Really?

It's an amazing thing. It's made from simple oil drums, but it's actually a sophisticated instrument. It's cut in various ways, with the flat top edging into different sections. Those tops are hammered and tempered to give a wide range of musical notes—that is, when it's properly hit. There are these short sticks specially prepared for this purpose, with a rubber knob on the end. You can really play any type of music with the steelpan.

So, anyway, during Carnival time, we're all dancing in the street. The whole island becomes consumed. Orchestras of these steelpan drums, that I was just mentioning, and so many other instruments and styles of music, too. People are out there selling their wares, thousands dancing to the music—and it's all in the streets, festive and colorful.

What time of year does it take place?

It happens just before the Lent season begins. End of March, April.

You know, according to Christian reckoning. Trinidad is heavily Catholic. You should know that. There are actually many Christian denominations there.

Your parents were both Catholic?

Oh yeah. But by the time I came to America in 1970, I was beginning to ask questions. "Who am I? Why am I here? Is there a God?" My Catholic upbringing sparked this in me, too. But I never looked at it that deeply. Being in America changed all that . . .

What brought you to America?

Well, my mother. She was already living in America—she had come soon after my father died—and I wanted to be with her. So when she left . . .

Did you have siblings?

I've got one brother and two sisters.

Did they all come to America?

Well, my eldest sister went to England. She still lives there—settled down, got married, and had a family. But the other two came to America, as I did. They're still here, too. My brother lives in New York; he's a musician. And my sister lives in Portland, Oregon. My mother lives near her, too, in Eugene.

Your brother is a working musician?

Oh, yeah. My family was really musical. As a child, I remember all of my mother's brothers—and there were quite a number of them—getting together during Christmas and playing music. We all joined in.

So you're from quite a musical family.

That's right. I liked a lot of different kinds of music, too, and I was exposed to even more after coming to America. But I must say that the exotic kirtan—those sounds coming from those Hare Krishnas, which, as I said, I heard soon after arriving in this country—wow! It completely revolutionized my consciousness and my whole way of hearing music. Well, really, it changed my whole way of seeing the world.

And, honestly, I didn't know anything about them. I didn't think they were religious or spiritual or anything. No preconceptions, really. You have to understand where I was coming from—the multicultural nature of the islands. And then I saw so many strange things in New York, too, in the 1970s. So I just thought they were another exciting group of musicians.

I didn't know what they were singing about, either. But the fact that they were dancing in the streets with happy faces—that really said a lot to me. They were alive, vibrant, and enthusiastic in their singing and dancing. So I could relate to that.

Hmm. That brought you back to the Carnival?

Exactly. And, you know, one thing led to another—I was so attracted to them that I quickly visited their temple at Henry Street in Brooklyn, and that's when I found out what they were all about. And I loved it! It was easy to develop relationships with these people, too—we were kindred spirits, in a sense. Even so, I started working in New York and developing my own life. So it took a little more than a year before I decided to quit my job and join them full time.

What kind of job did you hold at the time?

I worked for a textile firm, a big textile firm in Manhattan. You know, it wasn't my life's dream . . .

[laughter] Sure, it paid the bills. But what about the music? You said you were introduced to different kinds of music when you came to New York.

Yes, I really had quite an appetite—I'd always be going to one concert or another. Jazz, blues, rock. Everything. You know, because it was New York, and everybody came to New York.

I saw everybody—Led Zeppelin, Chicago, Blood Sweat and Tears, Stevie Wonder; I'd go to the Apollo, Carnegie Hall, Fillmore

East, Madison Square Garden, The Academy of Music. There were so many venues.

And, of course, I formed a band. I was a guitarist and a songwriter. I was pretty good, too, or so I was told. But I was lazy about it. I hated rehearsal. You see, I like spontaneity. And that's what I responded to in kirtan. There's nothing as spontaneous as a good kirtan. When you're really engaged in ecstatic chant, anything is possible! And you know it.

But in the regular, secular world, to play music professionally, you have to practice—and if you want to be good, you've got to practice a lot. Of course, when you play before an audience, you want to make sure it has a spontaneous feel to it. But that actually takes a lot of rehearsal.

Right. Well, to be a good *kirtaniya* takes practice as well.

That's true. But it's also a heart thing, and if you're into it, you're into it. No one can take that away from you. But it *is* an art, you're correct, and you can develop it—both your own expertise at singing, externally, and also your internalization of it. This is really what kirtan is all about. You have to learn how to go deep within. Kirtan helps with that. The more you do it, the more you get good at it.

But you know, it's strange, because I came of age in Trinidad, as I mentioned. And there were so many Indians, Hindus, there—actually, both Hindus and Muslims—and I was friendly with many of them. I remember hearing stray things, you know, like Krishna's name, or something about Indian culture, so there was this distant memory, of sorts, when I met the devotees in Manhattan.

Now, my Indian friends in Trinidad, their Indic culture was pretty much dormant, or maybe they just kept it to themselves—and they certainly never tried to proselytize or anything like that. So even though we lived next door to them, we never knew much about what they believed in. Still, when I met the devotees, I sensed something familiar, something struck a chord. Maybe I'm making too much of this. Maybe the familiarity had to do with a past life. I can't say . . .

You didn't have India in your blood?

No. No, my father was Chinese.

Oh. You didn't say that. That's interesting. And your mother?

My mother is, again, Spanish, black, French, Irish — that Trinidadian mixture. Years later, my mother married an Indian man. After my father died. And so my two younger siblings — their father is Indian. And my older sister and I — our father is Chinese. But this kind of thing is not uncommon in Trinidad.

Okay, interesting though this is, it *is* a bit of a tangent. Let's get back to your kirtan involvement.

Right. So I would regularly go to hear the kirtan in the streets and that got me interested in Krishna devotion. I would sometimes join in with the chanting; sometimes not. So I started visiting the temple in Brooklyn. And I eventually joined the ashram, living amongst the devotees. All I really wanted was kirtan, though. I just couldn't get enough of it. Still, I knew I had to conquer inner demons if I really wanted to taste kirtan on a deeper level.

Inner demons in what sense?

Well, I had this sense of identity — I thought of myself in terms of the body and mind, and I found it difficult to transcend those conceptions, even though, intellectually, I knew that I was spirit, beyond body and mind. I still couldn't get myself to function at that level. I couldn't let go of my prior conception of the self.

So, even though I was living in an ashram — with people at various levels of spiritual attainment, and most of them far more advanced than me — I still had a difficult time going out in the streets. I loved chanting. Don't get me wrong. But I didn't want to be seen doing it in front of other people. I had a phobia about it — I didn't think it was the kind of thing that "Alvin Marsden" should be doing. To put it bluntly, I was self-conscious, in the most materialistic sense of the term.

I see. That's understandable, though. You didn't want to be seen as a

monk, with shaved head and robes, chanting religious mantras and such.

Right. It was basically a weird kind of vanity, too. You see, I had a big head of hair, like Jimi Hendrix or Sly Stone. People knew me like that. I was a musician, a "cool guy." Then, all of a sudden, I reveal a new side, with a new identity. It freaked me out, probably more than it would have freaked out those who knew me.

It was primarily in my own mind, of course. And even though I was, in a sense, proud of the new me—and I identified with the new me more than I ever did with Alvin Marsden—there was this blind spot, or this "block," that really stifled me. Something just made me timid as a new devotee. So I didn't want to go out. I didn't mind staying at the temple, but I didn't want to be visible to the outside world, to go on a chanting party, singing in the streets. Even though I loved doing it. And this is what I told the temple leaders.

I said, "I'll do anything you want; I really love all of this; I like everything about it; but there's one little thing that I'd rather not do." And what was their response? "We have just the service for you: We want you to go out in the street and . . ." [laughter]

Well, there was a certain wisdom there. It was a shock to the ego. And in spiritual life, that can really help . . .

You're absolutely right, but I didn't know it then. Anyway, what could I do? I was committed to this process of spiritual elevation. And I respected the temple authorities. So off I went. I would go out every day with, maybe, six to a dozen devotees, the whole day.

Morning to evening.

We'd go out right after breakfast, like 9 AM, or thereabouts. And then we'd return to the temple at 6 or 7 PM. This became my life for quite a while, and I came to love it.

Now, there were great kirtan leaders in those days, singers with emotion, experience—having been to Bengal or otherwise steeped in the tradition. Jai Sachinandana was one of them. Man, that guy could sing. Or Janardan. Bharadvaj. There were so many. So I listened, and I learned.

And how did you become a kirtan leader?

That started with Janardan. It just happened one day, while we were out there on the street. He was leading the kirtan party and had to go to the bathroom or something. As he walked away, he just said, "You chant, you lead." And that was it.

It became a regular thing, pretty much every day. And the more I did it, you know, the more I got stronger and better.

Right. More confident . . .

Yes, more confident. And learning the *mridanga* helped a lot — taking that drum out with me every day added to the kirtan. I was taught to play by a German devotee named Vasudeva. He gave me a few early lessons, and I just kept playing.

It's interesting how this evolved. It started when I was coming to the temple, before I actually joined. Vasudeva approached me and said there was a *mridanga* for sale. Some other devotee was selling it. Now, Vasudeva could really play but he had no money to buy it. And he told me that if I bought it for him, he would give me free lessons. He'd teach me how to play. He really just wanted to have it around — he said it was good for his soul. I remember that.

So, I thought, well, great! I can help him get this *mridanga* and I can learn how to play at the same time, even before moving in to the temple. So when I actually moved in as a novice . . .

You already knew how to play.

I already knew, exactly. When I moved in, I was already playing like a pro.

Very interesting. Krishna was preparing you . . .

Yeah, I was being groomed, even though I was unaware of it.

Who were the *kirtaniyas* influencing you at the time?

Well, Jai Sachinandana and Bharadvaj, for sure. Dravida — he was great, too. He would bring his flute and he would just play — those kirtans were . . . celestial.

I know. I attended some of those, in the early '70s.

And then after the Sunday feast, and after the lecture and *prasa-dam*, Jai Sachinandana would lead a kirtan, and that was another flavor altogether.

Right.

And then there was Vishnu Gada; there was someone named Vishnu Das, too. He was an artist, a painter. He would also lead. There were quite a few, actually. They were all good—all very different, but all good in their own way.

And I remember the turning point, when it all moved up a notch. They went to India, to Bengal, the home of ecstatic kirtan. One year—I think it was the first big Mayapur festival, so maybe it was early-to-mid-1970s—the kirtan leaders came back with something special. They went to Mayapur, where Mahaprabhu engaged in loving kirtan 500 years earlier, and they brought back the real thing; they brought back a sort of authenticity. You could sense a certain *shakti*, an energy, that was just transcendental. I didn't go that year, but Jai Sachinandana went, and when he came back he brought with him this indescribably sweet Bengali flavor.

And so I began to follow his lead. That's when New York temple became famous for its kirtans. You were there. So you remember, I'm sure.

It was special, no doubt. It had a lasting effect—it was transformative. I would say that even this book, my desire to do it, originates from those early New York kirtans. But let's talk more about the philosophy of kirtan and what kirtan means to you.

You know, Prabhupada said that kirtan was the safest position in the material world. And I often meditate on the truth of that statement. When you're in kirtan, you lose your sense of false identity. You've reached the perfection of yoga. The trick, of course, is to make it last, to keep it with you in your day-to-day life. That isn't easy. But at least while you're there, if you give it all you've got, it's as if you become protected by a fortress of spiritual energy—

nothing can touch you. You're protected from anger, pride, fool-ishness, sloth, materialism. To the degree that you let the kirtan enter your heart, to that same degree you're actually in touch with God, and He won't let you go, that is, until you let Him go.

So kirtan is my protection. And I take solace in that, in the under-standing that even someone in my fallen condition can actually attain what great *yogis* attain, but only through kirtan. Because it's easy. That's why it's safe. With just a little sincere endeavor, I can reach high spiritual goals, by the grace of guru and Krishna, by the grace of the holy name.

Right. And you were doing this in New York, on the streets! Everyone who came in contact with you benefited from your kirtan, too. Kirtan is not just for those who chant, but also for those who hear the chanting.

Absolutely. That's one of the special features of this process. Other spiritual practices are mainly good for the people who undergo the effort. The results are reserved for practitioners. But God really showers His mercy in regard to the chanting: The chanters and, as you say, those who hear the chanting—even the animals, insects and trees that are nearby—everyone gets the mercy. Everyone within earshot—they all benefit from the chanting process. And the truth is, there's no place like New York City for Hari-nam, or for taking the holy name out into the streets.

That's true.

It *is* true. When I moved to L.A. in 1976, I thought there were no good places for going out on Hari-nam. I was spoiled by New York. [laughter] Because L.A. doesn't have the same amount of people, at least not out in the streets. And they are certainly not as visible or as in your face as in New York. Manhattan never sleeps, as they say. You know, in New York, we used to sometimes stay out—well, on Friday, Saturday nights—we would be out in the streets until midnight, and people would just join in with us until all hours!

And remember, we were out from early in the morning. In all

kinds of weather. You know what New York winters are like. But it was foreign to me, coming from the islands. That's what I mean about kirtan being the safest place — it gives you a special spiritual potency. You can overcome anything when you're in the midst of kirtan.

That's right, you went out in the dead of winter. Amazing.

Yeah. In fact, one winter I went out in freezing weather, causing me to have a near-death experience.

Really?

That's right. I blacked out; I went totally unconscious. It was so cold, but I just went on chanting, leading, and really loving it. But every time I hit the *mridanga*, my hands — I mean, it was so painful. Because it was five below, and that was the coldest I had ever experienced. And so, after about twenty-five minutes, I couldn't take it anymore.

Now, I am aware of the distinction between body and self, and spiritual philosophy is all well and good. But I was just plain suffering! So I told Janardan, "I really need to go somewhere . . . I think I'm going to be sick. I'm dizzy. Maybe I should go into the subway and . . ."

I was really at my limit here. So I turned and stumbled toward the subway, the entrance of which was just around the corner. When I turned the corner, I was out of sight — the other devotees couldn't see me. And that's when it happened: I just blacked out and fell on the sidewalk.

Oh, God.

And the next thing I remember, I heard voices from people on the street. "Hey, look! Something happened to one of them! It's one of the Krishnas.

And so I'm lying there, face down. Next thing I know, Janardan and the other devotees came to help me: "Get up, get up." And at that point, I wasn't feeling anything. Totally out of it. There was no pain. I was just sort of exhausted and dreamy. So I told them,

"Leave me alone; I'm taking some rest." But, really, I was oblivious to where I was, lying face down on the cold concrete.

You were numb.

I was beyond numb. [laughter] Afterwards, they told me it was hypothermia. That's the medical term for it. They say that's how people die out in the snow. They get to that stage where they're not feeling anything and then they just go to sleep.

Right, right.

I was like that, and Janardan realized that I was in bad shape. I didn't realize it, but he did. I was just feeling really tired and strange. So Janardan lifted me up, right off the street. Threw me over his shoulder. Because I couldn't even walk. It's like I had taken some heavy drugs. I'm sure that that's what the people on the street must have thought: "There's a Hare Krishna on drugs!" [laughter]

Anyway, Janardan was carrying me toward a nearby restaurant, to lay me down in a warmer place. But as he started walking I became extremely nauseous and I vomited all over the sidewalk.

Oh, man!

Yeah. And so, he just took me into this Italian restaurant; it was on 34th Street, across from Macy's. Basically, it was a pizza place.

So you had all these Italian guys, you know, with mixed feelings. Some were concerned; others wanted to get me out of there as quickly as possible. But overall they were compassionate, seeing my condition. I mean, I was frozen, and they had to thaw me out.

Don't tell me they put you in the pizza oven to warm you up.

[laughter] The main guy was nice, though. For most people, the chanting on the streets was an enjoyable spectacle. The cops would sometimes come and chase us, telling us to move. But it was all in good fun. They didn't really care, and many of them would join in and chant with us. And then, if we were chased away, we'd just go one block and start up again. The cops would see us, but they didn't care. We were out of their jurisdiction. And immediately we had 500 new people surrounding us, joining in with the singing and dancing. We were like free entertainment in New York City.

But what happened when they brought you into the pizza place?

So they carried me in there. And the guy took me in a booth and he brought some hot towels. The towels were in boiling water. And they started putting them on my hands and on my head and on my feet.

What a scene.

Well, they had to thaw me out, right? It was amazing, though, because when they brought me in there I wasn't feeling anything. And after they put the towels on me, I started feeling again—I went back to feeling pain. That was a good thing, because I was getting sensation back in my limbs. Otherwise, it could have been really dangerous. It could lead to amputation or serious medical conditions, even death. So it was difficult; the pain was intense. Like needles in all parts of my body—it was just really horrible.

And then, after a while, it subsided. I was back to normal, and Janardan immediately asked, "So, you want to go back out and chant again?" I think he asked half in jest. But I answered in no uncertain terms: "No! I want to go back to the temple. This weather is too much for me."

And after that, every day, I would always ask at the temple's front desk: "What's the temperature out there?" I wasn't going out if the weather didn't permit it. As much as I loved street chanting—I wasn't taking any chances. Once bitten, twice shy.

That's especially true if you're frostbitten! [laughter] That might be the most amazing kirtan story I've ever heard, but let's go off on a tangent for a moment: Tell me about your influences. Basically, you do Bengali kirtan. So was there an India connection?

First time in India was 1977, in Mayapur, West Bengal. Yes, this was an important period in my life, and a big influence on my kirtan style. Soon after my arrival in India, I heard this otherworldly sound. It was the sweetest of kirtans; it was coming from a nearby temple.

So I followed the sound, and there were three Bengalis sitting down chanting for the Deities. Nobody else was there, just the three of them, in an empty temple room. Three Prabhupada disciples, older Indian gentleman: Mayamanush, Sarvajna and Murari Hari. I'll never forget them. Simple: voice, *mridanga*, and *kartals*, but it sounded so full, so complete.

And they were just there, with no other thought or occupation. This is what they did, and they were so good at it.

Amala harinam amiya vilasa: **"Chanting the Lord's name is my pastime . . ."**

Right. This was their life. And I didn't want to disturb them, but I wanted to study them, too. So I was very discreet, but I recorded them — right then and there. I kept my tape recorder in a bag, a cloth bag, and I sat down, without distracting them. I gently turned on the recorder . . . And so, I listened to those tapes intensely. I brought them back with me and I would listen to them constantly, even while going to sleep at night . . .

Naturally, traces of it would come out in my kirtan, or melodies that would be partially reproduced . . .

And then you achieved some renown as a *kirtaniya*. **You started recording, first with cassette tapes, I guess, and then CDs, right?**

Yeah. I moved to Los Angeles in 1976, just before that first trip to India. Many devotees went to California, because the Bhaktivedanta Book Trust, the art department — they relocated to LA. And so a lot of devotees followed.

I remember *Back to Godhead* magazine, at that time, did a feature story on the Los Angeles community. And I was still struggling with New York weather, too. So I thought, "It's sunny and warm out there — maybe that's the place for me." When I arrived, people seemed to know me. I was famous for my kirtans. I didn't realize it until I got there.

Rameshvar and Jayatirtha, the two ISKCON leaders in Southern

California at the time, were real happy about my arrival. I remember one morning, they introduced me to the larger body of devotees, and they said: "Now L.A. is complete — we have a real *kirtaniya*." So I was known as a kirtan leader, and they were glad I was there.

Now, you were already initiated by this time, correct?

Oh, yes. I was initiated back in New York. But, gradually, L.A. became my home, though, in some ways, I really missed New York. There's no street life in Southern California, not like in New York. But still, I would take the Hari-nam party out every day, even if it wasn't the same. It had a sweetness of its own, though. Really. Still, I was scouting for areas where there were lots of people. I was hoping to find a place that might capture that New York vibe. Hollywood Boulevard, and places like that. As I say, we had great kirtans. But New York will always be special.

Did you have any outstanding experiences in L.A.?

Oh, don't misunderstand me — L.A. was amazing in its own way. It just wasn't New York. I'll tell you one amazing story, when we met and recorded with Stevie Wonder.

Stevie . . .

That's right. We went out on Hari-nam one day, and we were there from morning until evening, just chanting on the street. Then, when we returned to the ashram, in the evening, the temple president told us, "Don't put down your instruments. Don't get comfortable. You're going out again." We were exhausted, so we weren't really listening to him. We certainly weren't going to go out again. But then he told us the story: While we were chanting on the street, Stevie Wonder passed by in his car. He was being driven to his music studio, and he heard the devotees chanting, and he just loved it. So he called the temple and asked if we would come down to play on one of his songs.

You must have been ecstatic.

To put it mildly. We regrouped and called in a few experienced *kirtaniyas*—we got Jai Sachinandana to come along, Duryodhana Guru, Bharadvaj, Rukmini, and some others, along with the original group that had initially gone out on the street. When we arrived, Stevie was there with his secretary—just the two of them. He greeted us graciously and told us how great our kirtan sounded. He also said that he admired the devotees as people who had really given their lives over to God. He then played some of the songs from his forthcoming album for us—this was "Songs in the Key of Life," which was released as a double-LP set.

After that, he explained the tune he wanted us to play on. It's called "Pastime Paradise." It's a song about the temporary nature of material enjoyment. It expresses, in a poetic way, how people live for the past, or they live for the future—but they don't appreciate the present. It's about the need to see what's real, what's now. Not what once was or what is yet to come.

Kind of like "Be Here Now."

Right. Exactly. So he had us do our kirtan thing toward the end of the song, and as we were leaving, I noticed a gospel choir coming into the studio. As it turns out, he used both, I guess to show the universal nature, the non-sectarianism, of true religion. Sort of like Harrison did in "My Sweet Lord."

What year was this?

It was soon after I arrived in 1976, and the album came out later that year. It eventually won Grammy Awards for Best Pop Vocal and Album of the Year. We're given credit on the album's liner notes—me and Bharadvaj and the others. It was a great experience, and we could see that Stevie Wonder was a warm, sensitive, and, really, a very spiritual human being.

And soon after this, someone started recording you in L.A.? How did your own recording career start?

Yes, It was Jayatirtha, in L.A. They had a subdivision of the Bhaktivedanta Book Trust. It was called Golden Avatar.

They had set up a music studio there. That's where they used to produce Prabhupada's tapes, both music and recorded lectures. So, Krishna Kanti wanted to make a record of my kirtan singing. He was the technician there; he knew a lot about recording, and the music industry, and what have you. Jayatirtha had the initial vision; he arranged the whole thing. They began by recording me at the Sunday Feast. This was always a well-attended, enthusiastic kirtan. Tons of people, devotees and non-devotees, just letting go — it always became a raucous, bring-down-the-house kirtan. Really lively.

I remember: "Live In New Dvaraka."

Right. That's what they called it. That was my first recording. It was spontaneous, at the Sunday Feast, and it became an instant hit because it was live and ecstatic.

That tape went around the world. I was getting letters from people in countries as diverse as Germany and Japan, India and Australia. Then we decided to produce something in the studio. But that didn't really get off the ground; we only managed to complete one song. Something happened and we got sidetracked. But I kept chanting, leading kirtans in Hollywood and at the temple, and then Prabhupada came to L.A. Now, this was special, because I had the opportunity to go and greet him at the airport, bringing my entire kirtan party with me.

You must have been excited.

It was always a thrill to greet Prabhupada at the airport, and I had experienced this several times back in New York. But in those days, Jai Sachinandana was always the one to lead the kirtan. He was more experienced and so everyone naturally wanted him to lead.

But this time *I* got to lead the kirtan. Now, I didn't want that to go to my head. I wanted to lead purely, or at least without thinking of myself as anything more than an instrument, as someone playing a role. I was just one of the many devotees in that kirtan. Okay, I happened to be leading, but, really, it's just service. It would be nothing without everyone else. What's a one-man kirtan?

Furthermore, I wanted to be conscious that I was doing this for *his* pleasure — for Prabhupada's glorification. I was singing for guru and Krishna, and that's it. This was not meant to feed my ego, but rather *to free me from ego,* or at least false ego, to free me from the idea that I am the center of the universe. I am simply a servant. I was trying to focus on that.

Hmm. I like the distinction you're making here between "ego" and "false ego." The word *ego* means "identity." The Vaishnava doesn't want to lose his individuality, his identity. Rather, he wants to become established in his *real* identity, as an eternal servant of Krishna.

I was consciously thinking like that. So before Prabhupada emerged from the door, I was trying to consider what he would like, what would be pleasing to him. If I could please Krishna's pure devotee, that would also be pleasing to Krishna — and that's my duty, my service: to please Krishna. And just then, almost out of nowhere, a melody appeared in my mind . . .

A melody?

A melody we used to sing in New York. One devotee had told me that this was one of Bhaktisiddhanta Sarasvati's favorite melodies. Now, Bhaktisiddhanta was Prabhupada's guru. So I reasoned that Prabhupada would love to hear a melody that was dear to his own spiritual master. Logical, right?

Sure.

So this was going on in my mind, and as Prabhupada came through the door, I began the kirtan. I began by singing invocation prayers to the spiritual master, which was simple enough. But then I started chanting "Hare Krishna" in that melody, the one his guru liked, and after I got through the first verse, the first mantra of that melody — Prabhupada stopped walking, because I was behind him, and he wanted to turn and see who was leading.

So Prabhupada stopped and turned around, and he looked at me through the throngs of devotees that were jumping and singing and glorifying Krishna's name. Now, I was nervous. Was he going to be pleased, or was he going to look at me with displeasure? His eyes met mine and a big smile came across his face, and then he shook his head in that distinctly Indian way, showing approval. He gestured, "Come on, let's go." And I was in bliss.

I took that as encouragement from Prabhupada, that he was pleased with the way I was chanting. The ego swelled, but I immediately caught myself. Kirtan is really about pleasing the Lord and His pure devotee. And as I reminded myself of that, I felt an even greater bliss. Self-centered pleasures can't compete with selfless devotion. So I strive for the latter.

That's an important realization. Maybe you can talk about that, about the importance of selflessness in chanting—not for fame, adoration, and distinction.

Not for fame. Right. If you chant for any length of time, with any regularity and sincerity, you'll know. I could sense it from the beginning. Because I knew that this was not ordinary, that it was sacred. I knew some humility was required. Because, after all, who are we? This is God and His name, and they're nondifferent. It's a very sacred thing. So it's an honor to chant, and we should remember that. It should be humbling.

Lord Chaitanya, as you know, made this same point. It's the shortest verse in the *Shikshashtakam*, his eight prayers of glorification, but in some ways it's the deepest. His words are potent: *trinad api sunichena, taror api sahishnuna*: "One should be more humble than a blade of grass and more tolerant than a tree." He says that if one adopts *this* mood, one can chant constantly. One becomes blessed, in a sense, by one's own humility.

Right. That's an extremely important verse. Central for kirtan. In fact, Krishnadas Kaviraj Goswami singled that out and said: "String these words around your neck and wear it." It's that important.

And if you really enact that, if you consciously try to bring humility into your life, you feel purification set in. Be humble and chant, constantly. Then your bad habits start to fall away. Like dust, they just fall away in the act of kirtan.

For more information contact:
Govinda's Restaurant, 1899 Mendocino Avenue,
Santa Rosa, CA. 95404; Tel. 1-707-544-2491

Photo by Ganapathy Das

DAVID NEWMAN

David Newman, who is also known as Durga Das, is a triple threat: kirtan chant artist, singer songwriter, and a practicing yogi. His chanting evokes the ancient yogic tradition of sound as a tool for healing, and he contemporizes his methods with folksy song and modern musical know-how.

His approach is both celebratory and transformational, maintaining the essence of ancient Eastern traditions while bringing them up to date. He frequently shares this unique form of kirtan in workshops and seminars worldwide, as well as by regularly performing in yoga studios.

His fervent desire to spread the magic of kirtan is counterbalanced by his passion for yoga. Along these lines, he is also the creator of "Inner Fire Yoga," a yogic technique that emphasizes spiritual discovery, mantra meditation, controlling the breath, physical movement, and the application of yogic principles in daily life.

In 1992, he founded "Yoga On Main" in Philadelphia and since then has taught aspiring yoga teachers and seekers who want to learn the mystical arts. He has made it a point to teach his particular brand of yoga to diverse audiences as well, including the elderly, cancer patients, and children. But his first love is kirtan, and his unique sound is captured on his CDs: "Soul Freedom," "Lotus Feet: A Kirtan Revolution," "Leap of Grace: The Hanuman Chalisa," and his latest CD/DVD set, "Into the Bliss."

David Newman was born . . .

I was born in Philadelphia on December 31, 1963, and I grew up in the suburbs of Philadelphia.

Was it a musical family, a religious family . . .

I grew up in a Jewish family. My parents were definitely conscious of the fact that they were Jewish and celebrated the holy days, but it wasn't a particularly religious family. My parents were big listeners of music, and my uncle, my mother's brother, who I was very close with growing up, was — and is now — an attorney. But he was a guitar and banjo player, too, and a songwriter and a bluegrass musician. He bought me my first guitar when I was thirteen, at my Bar Mitzvah. He also played rock and roll for me for the first time.

Who were some of your favorites when you started to get into music?

Oh, I began with the real founders of rock and roll, like Chuck Berry, Jerry Lee Lewis, Bo Diddley, Little Richard, Elvis Presley. From there I started listening to the music of the 60s, like the Doors, who I really liked, or the Rolling Stones, and then I got into a lot of the more progressive English music, like Yes and Genesis and King Crimson; these were some of my early influences. I've always had an eclectic ear. Later, I went on to study music as an undergraduate and got into jazz and classical music as well.

What about the virtuoso guitarists like Hendrix and Jeff Beck? Were you into that kind of stuff?

Very much so, yeah. Jeff Beck, Jimi Hendrix, Santana. I was always a big fan of . . . not so much a virtuoso, but I liked Steve Howe from Yes, Steve Hackett from Genesis, Robert Fripp from King Crimson — these were all inspirations to me, among others.

Robert Fripp is a particularly gifted player, underestimated I think.

I like his early stuff, and then when King Crimson got back together, when he teamed up with Adrian Belew.

That was special music. Unlike the more popular rock music of that

time, there was some sense of spirituality about that kind of music, a sort of otherworldliness. Was that what led you to kirtan?

Well, my original introduction to meditation was probably when I was around twelve or so, or thirteen. My parents got me and my brother initiated into Transcendental Meditation as taught by Maharishi Mahesh Yogi. That was my first experience. There was some chanting I heard as part of that. Then . . .

What do you mean they "got you initiated" into it? Was it something they just wanted their kids to do?

It was sort of in vogue back in the 70s, when it was very popular. They decided to do it themselves and they thought it would be a nice thing for the family to do together. So my parents and both my brother and I were initiated into TM. We were all given a mantra.

A secret mantra, right?

A secret mantra. To this day, I haven't told anybody my TM mantra.

You know, there's a great story about Ramanuja, the spiritual master from Medieval India. He was given a secret mantra, *om namo narayanaya*. His teacher told him: "Ramanuja! Keep this mantra a secret. This is a very powerful mantra. Those who repeat it will attain salvation. Give it only to a worthy disciple." But Ramanuja's heart was large. He was extremely compassionate. So he wanted to share the mantra with everyone—he wanted the eternal bliss of Lord Narayana, the deity of this mantra, to engulf everyone's life. So what did he do? He immediately called all neighboring seekers, irrespective of caste and creed, to assemble before the temple. He stood on top of the tower above the front gate of the temple, and he shouted out the sacred mantra for all to hear.

His guru became furious. So Ramanuja said: "O my beloved Guru! Please prescribe a suitable punishment for my wrong action. I will gladly suffer the tortures of hell myself," he said, "just so long as others can get salvation by hearing the mantra." He thought that even if he didn't personally get the fruits of the mantra—that would be okay, as long as others could benefit from it. Needless to say, his guru was ultimately pleased with him.

That's a beautiful story.

Anyway, I'm sorry for going off in another direction. You were saying . . .

I was just giving you a little chronology about my life, sort of an introduction to my spiritual journey, because I think it's all part of the mix. I went to Bowdoin College in Maine, where I was a music major and where I was introduced to all kinds of music, including some world music that had chant elements and "repetitive mantra style" elements to it — which I later used in kirtan. I graduated in '86. Then, after that, I ended up in the music business for a few years, and then I went to law school for three years.

Where?

Cardozo Law School in New York City.

You said you were in the music business . . .

In between law school and college — I was an aspiring singer/songwriter. After graduating college I moved to Los Angeles, because some people in the industry had interest in my songwriting and my performance abilities. But that really didn't pan out and I ended up working in other capacities, still in the music business, for two years. I worked as a creative manager for several music publishing companies, the most well known of which was Island Music. I worked for Chris Blackwell, the owner of Island Music, and then sort of became disenchanted with the industry side. I decided to go to law school, and — backtracking a little bit — I took my first yoga class when I was in Los Angeles at that time. We're talking about 1987 and 1988, and I really enjoyed it. I started practicing yoga, regularly visiting the Shivananda Yoga ashram. They had also introduced some chanting into the mix; so again I was exposed to it.

Was the early experience with TM a real part of your life?

To some degree it was a part of my life, but not consistently. I remember as a young child, though, I just realized that through meditation I could leave the world as I knew it. That came from TM. Even as a young person of thirteen or fourteen years of age, I could recognize the existence of stress and how it affects people. Maybe

I didn't call it that, but I definitely recognized its existence and found that through meditation I was able to enter into a space that bypassed all kinds of stressful feeling. You know, whether it came from my homework, school, inadequacy problems, insecurity, even girls — TM kind of stayed with me, as a way to cope. Even if it wasn't TM specifically, at least the essence of meditation stayed with me, in terms of mantra repetition and meditation. But during law school, I met a yoga teacher in New York City who was visiting from Hawaii, a guy named Gary Kraftsow who represented the yogic lineage of Desikachar and Krishnamacharya.

So he brought you to a more traditional yogic path?

Well, we shared a lot in common. He was Jewish, he was from Philadelphia, and he had gone to a small Ivy League school. When I met him it was sort of an eye-opener, because suddenly I realized that I had an alternative. You have to understand my background: My father was a cosmetic surgeon and my mother was a Supreme Court justice in Pennsylvania. As a child, I grew up somewhat in a box, feeling that there's a certain way you're supposed to live — "first you do this, and then you do that . . ."

I was Premed in college, but I didn't have the energy to go to medical school and go that route; so I chose law school, because in my family, you're off the hook once you've gone to graduate school. So I was sort of doing my family *dharma* in a way. Now, when I went to law school, I met Gary and studied with him and visited with him in Hawaii, and sort of an inner light went off because of that, "Wow, this is another option in my life." I mean, here was this person, who I had a resonance with, who was giving retreats, traveling, teaching yoga. Right? So I thought, "This is what I want to do with my life." I met him a year-and-a-half into law school and immediately knew that this was what I wanted to do, and I immersed myself in studies with him, both when he traveled to give retreats and in Hawaii, and as part of that particular lineage. I started studying Vedic chanting.

I was going to say: That lineage is sort of Ashtanga-yoga mixed with

Ramanuja Vaishnavism, no?

Ashtanga-yoga in the Patanjali sense, but not in the Pattabhi Jois sense.

But isn't there an element of the Ramanuja Sampradaya?

Very much so. That's their lineage. They trace their lineage back to Ramanuja. Ashtanga in the sense of the eightfold path, but they definitely do not practice the *ashtanga* sequence. It's very different. It's much more of a therapeutic thing based on the needs of the individual rather than a formalized *ashtanga* practice.

Like Ayurveda, it's adapted to the needs of the individual.

Ayurveda was part of that system, studying the *Yoga-sutras*, doing the Vedic chanting, yoga therapy, adapting the poses and modifying and creating sequences to meet the needs of individuals. So it was through that particular system that I started doing Vedic chanting, which immediately seemed familiar to me. I've never been a particularly language-oriented person, but when I started studying and practicing Vedic chanting, the Sanskrit came very natural to me.

When you say Vedic chanting, do you mean actually from the four Vedas and the Upanishads?

Yeah, transliterated though. They would use a system where it was transliterated into English with different symbols, vertical lines, horizontal lines, to tell you which pitch and how long. I wasn't actually reading the Sanskrit, but the transliteration was very particular and the melodies were very particular to that lineage or tradition.

Do you remember any specifics?

There were many chants, at that point, that I was chanting regularly such as *saha na vavatu, gayatri mantra*, and many others. I was studying with one of Desikachar's senior students named Sonia Nelson, who was very focused and gifted in teaching Vedic chanting.

Okay. Where do you go from there?

What happened was, while living in New York, a friend of mine took me up to the Siddha-yoga ashram, Gurumayi's place. Interestingly, part of the program that night was this: they did kirtan by chanting one mantra for about forty-five minutes. So that was where I initially experienced more of a kirtan orientation towards chanting.

Do you remember what they were chanting?

Kali Durga Namo Namah. I was sort of intrigued and I definitely felt it, in a deep way. It was all very new to me.

Were you thinking of taking initiation in that tradition, Siddha-yoga?

I certainly thought about it.

What happened?

Well, I graduated, took the bar exam, and opened up a yoga school about two weeks later in Philadelphia, which is called "Yoga on Main," which still exists. It's been there for about fifteen years.

So that had staying power.

We have a very strong spiritual community here around it.

You're still a part of that?

Yes, I am. I'm not a very active part of it, but I participate in the teacher training, when I'm in town. I give kirtans every few months there. So I opened "Yoga on Main" and at that point my lineage was squarely focused on Desikachar Krishnamacharya. I was doing Vedic chanting, and the continuation of kirtan entered into my life through two channels at that point, which was in the early '90s, maybe '93 or '94. One was this: We brought in Kali Ray and Mercury Max, yoga teachers, to do a workshop, because somebody had seen them and they gave a kirtan as part of their workshop on a Saturday night. I was very touched by the kirtan. It was deeply moving. Also, at that time, I was into this Brooklyn Jewish guru named Rudi, whose work I had sort of serendipitously found at a bookstore; he lived in the 1960s. He was a devotee of Bhagavan Nityananda and of Baba Muktananda. Rudi died, in 1973, but one of his successors named Swami Chetanananda had an ashram in Portland, Oregon, that I attended for some time. Whenever he would give a program, it would always start out with kirtan as well.

So as a result of the Kali Ray influence and the chanting at Chetanananda's ashram, I bought a couple of CDs. I had been a guitar player since I was thirteen, and so I started listening to the chants and learning some of them. Also, being a songwriter, I started creating my own melodies to some of the mantras. Somebody had given me a harmonium in Oregon and I started playing with that a bit, and then started to, you know, do a little bit of kirtan. The dilemma was that the lineage of Desikachar and Krishnamacharya was very Vedic, and while I wouldn't say they were against me singing kirtan and engaging in other forms of *bhakti* practices, it wasn't really their thing. I didn't get a real sense of approval.

Conservative.

They were more conservative. Eventually it led me to leave that yoga lineage, because I felt constrained in a lot of ways. In terms of my Hatha-yoga studies, I started doing some of the techniques of Erich Schiffmann and John Friend and others. I just really started to find my own voice and my own sense of *asana*, if you will, and as I was continuing to be a Hatha-yoga teacher, giving teacher trainings, finding my own voice, my interest in kirtan and *bhakti* was growing, too. At that point, I was introduced to a CD by Jai Uttal and thought, "Wow, this is not only kirtan, but this is musical. This is fusion. This is a real musical experience."

His stuff is great.

I was inspired by what he was doing, and then I became aware of Krishna Das. Now, when Krishna Das put out his first CD, which was "One Track Heart," we actually had him come to "Yoga on Main," and in the same way that I was touched by Hatha-yoga back when I met Gary Kraftsow, Krishna Das carried something in the kirtan that made one of those other lights go off.

Or on.

On, right. [laughter] I felt a resonance with him, and something touched a deep chord. We had come from the same background, the same religious affiliation, and there was just something familiar about him. After spending some time with him, I started to feel even more drawn to singing kirtan, giving kirtan, writing kirtan chants, and things of that nature. I really thought that Krishna Das was going to be a significant teacher for me.

Was he?

Well, what happened was this: A few months later I received a packet from a woman who was managing Bhagavan Das at the time. We invited him to visit "Yoga on Main," and at first his presentation seemed strange, at least to me. Oddly, though, he and I had a very strong *karma* together, if you know what I mean. He ended up getting very close with the Philadelphia community, spending a lot of time in Philadelphia, and I started doing some traveling with him, singing with him, though I never formally studied with him. Just singing with him sort of opened me up to certain frequencies.

You're talking about Bhagavan Das.

Bhagavan Das. The thing about Krishna Das and Bhagavan Das — they are sort of like brothers. They've had their struggles. I don't think it was a conscious choice, where I said, "I'm going to study and travel with Bhagavan Das and not Krishna Das" — it was nothing like that. Although Krishna Das had touched me deeply, my connection with Bhagavan Das just seemed more predominant and more intimate. We just had this connection, and so I started following in his footsteps — I got an *ektar* and I learned his songs and his chants and we developed a friendship, traveling together and doing our thing.

He's an interesting person . . .

Well, the thing is, he *is* an interesting person and I've always been very inspired by him. And, in a way, he was one of the early pioneers to bring kirtan to the West, so . . .

Yes. Bhaktivedanta Swami's "Happening" album was already in circulation in 1967, and there were others. The only prior non-Indian kirtan was Yamuna's, and Harrison's "My Sweet Lord," and maybe the Broadway production of "Hair," which included "Hare Krishna" . . .

He was certainly one of the first. So his presence in your book is important.

His initial CD came out in 1972. Hmm. Well, interviewing Jai and Krishna Das and yourself, and other followers of Neem Karoli Baba, I kind of feel like I have him here in spirit.

You know, he left for India on December 31, 1963, and he left from Philadelphia, where I was born on the same day. We just have a weird sort of connection there, with things like that. What I also wanted to just share with you was this: In addition to my connection with Krishna Das and Bhagavan Das, Neem Karoli Baba came to me also, but in a mystical way. I mean, in a lot of ways, Krishna Das brought a vibration to me and his stories from India led me closer to Neem Karoli Baba, and I would say that Bhagavan Das sort of drove the nail home. But Neem Karoli Baba himself came to me in what I would call a sort of telepathic vision, back in 1998, and he has been with me ever since.

Have you had visions like that before or was this something really unique?

This was the first. You see, I had sort of strived to be with certain gurus because, ever since I was young, I was always intrigued by the guru-disciple relationship. I guess I was looking for the perfect relationship, but every relationship I looked into was unfulfilling for me. In 1998, I got divorced and went out on my own. At that time, my sister-in-law came to my house and asked me what I wanted for a housewarming gift. I immediately pointed to books of saints that I had in my cabinet: Nityananda, Ramakrishna, Neem Karoli Baba, Amma, Ramana Maharshi—the lives and experiences of such *sadhus* were always very interesting to me.

Anyway, my sister-in-law gravitated to *Miracle of Love*, opened to a picture of Neem Karoli Baba, and was dumbfounded by the picture.

She was just inspired. She said, "I'm going to paint you a painting of this picture." So she went back to her place, and she took some months to do it, and I thought it was going to be this small painting. I had no idea what to expect. But when she invited me to her house to present it to me, I couldn't believe what I saw. It was an oil painting that was as big as a garage door. It was huge. When I looked at it, it just appeared as if nectar was dripping off the painting. It was surreal.

Is that the famous picture of him lying down with the blanket . . .

No, it's sort of a close up of his face. I'll send you a postcard with the image. It's really gotten around among the Neem Karoli Baba people.

And what about the vision?

Well, when I took the original painting home and put it on my wall, I closed my eyes and went into a very deep meditation, just sitting in front of this huge piece of art. And, while I was in meditation, he came to me and said, "I manifested this painting for you because I want to be this big in your life."

Interesting. And it felt real, I'm sure.

It *was* real. That's how real it felt. Let's put it this way: When it happened, it was the beginning of my spiritual life. Not the beginning, but it was a whole new chapter, because, prior to that, there wasn't a feeling of direction, not spiritually. It was as if his form reflected back to me my own spiritual nature and the realization of what really following a guru means: it basically means following your own true nature, and, in that way, finding out who you really are. The realization is based on love. Through falling in love with his form, with him, and with everything that he stood for, I fell in love with my own spiritual essence, with my own spirituality. And it has been a trip ever since. About two weeks later is when Bhagavan Das rolled into town. In that way—just continuous experiences come into my sphere to remind me that He, Neem Karoli Baba, is with me, and these experiences are so concrete.

So you told Bhagavan Das about that initial experience, no doubt. What was his reaction?

He was very supportive of it, and one of the things that endeared him to me was the realization that the guru was not just a person who takes and leaves a body at will—the guru is ever-present and omniscient. He very much honored and supported my vision, respecting my unique relationship with Neem Karoli Baba.

Where did you get the name Durga Das?

Bhagavan Das gave me the name.

Was it a friendly gesture or was it a type of initiation, or what?

It was, I would say, a type of initiation and a friendly gesture as well.

What exactly did he base it on?

Well, he also initiated me into the chanting of mantras. It's such a casual sort of brother-to-brother relationship. I experience him as a spiritual brother and a spiritual friend. Neem Karoli Baba is my guru, and I consider Bhagavan Das an elder who has been great support along the path.

Okay, and how did you get more and more into kirtan, to the point of putting out CDs?

I started getting more and more into kirtan, I would say, with an *ektar*, in the mood and style of Bhagavan Das. People started to hear me do it, and eventually they said, "You should put a kirtan band together." So I did, in Philadelphia, and "The Electric Kirtan" was born. I hadn't picked up a guitar in at least five or six years, and I was playing *ektar* more than anything else, but we eventually put an eight-piece band together.

"The Electric Kirtan"?

Yeah, that's what we called ourselves. It was pretty cool. It was a really interesting band. I started putting my *ektar* through a wah-wah pedal, you know, and getting that sort of sound. We would usually rehearse in the evenings. Anyway, one night I went to see Richie Havens at a local venue and I came home and picked up my guitar. All of a sudden there was all this creative inspiration that hadn't been there for years. My mind was flooded with these devotional songs that were singer/songwriter songs, maybe in the vein of someone like a George Harrison or a Van Morrison, in that genre. I started writing songs like that, and they would just come. They were just flowing. So as "The Electric Kirtan" was still going on, I went out and I got a new guitar. I began incorporating my guitar-playing into my music. In due course, "The Electric Kirtan" was not only a kirtan ensemble but an avenue through which I could explore my songwriting. It was so wonderful because it had come full circle, and now my songs were inspired by my guru and by my spiritual path. They were, at their heart, devotional songs . . .

In English.

In English, yeah, and they came from more of the singer/songwriter folksy kind of energy. I weaved them with my message in a way that the listener wasn't beaten over the head with the spiritual element. Even some of my songs mix personal love and the universal love, but it was sort of a genre that just started to develop within me. Then I met this gentleman named Kit Thomas.

Kit Thomas?

Yes. He would often come back to Philadelphia to care for his ailing mother. But he had done a lot of production of spiritual music in Los Angeles, where he had lived for a long time. He had produced Sting's "Rain Forest" documentary and had also directed a lot of music videos. When in Philadelphia, he sort of kept his identity secret from me, because he wanted to have a different kind of life while he was here.

But we ended up with a very lovely connection. I convinced him to pick up the bass, which he hadn't played in a while, and I got him to join "The Electric Kirtan." As a result of that, he started to help me develop my songwriting, and then—I guess it was during the summer of 2002—I was taking a month off, and I said, "Hey Kit, I'm thinking about recording some of these songs." That's when he told me that he was actually a record producer and that his production partner, Ben Dowling, lived in L.A. So eventually I met his partner. That summer, I spent the entire month making my first CD, which was this mix of singer/songwriter songs with kirtan tagged onto the end of the songs. That CD was called "Soul Freedom," which was released, I think, at the end of 2003. It was devotional in nature and included kirtan, too.

A fusion, hybrid kind of thing. That's cool.

That record did its thing and I toured, and I was still balancing my many worlds. Then I started to make "Lotus Feet." It was in the summer, after I was introduced through a mutual friend to Frank Wolf, a record producer and mixing engineer in New York City. He had done remixes for Santana and Dido and Pink and Jennifer Lopez. He had done a lot of stuff with Elton John and Barbara Streisand. I mean, really, the list goes on and on. He had a side interest in chanting and spirituality, which I found out when we were introduced. It became apparent that we were meant to make this record together.

He was like your Rick Rubin, huh?

Yeah, kind of like my Rick Rubin, exactly. I spent nine months in New York City making "Lotus Feet" with him in his home studio, and that was really an effort for me. You see, "Soul Freedom"—although I really love that record—it just wasn't the kind of product I could show up at a yoga center with and say, "Hey, I'm a kirtan singer," because it was more a singer/songwriter record. It's a funny distinction in markets because although many people responded to "Soul Freedom"—I mean, for an independent record it sold well—it's not necessarily the kind of CD you put on in a yoga class and do yoga to.

So my second attempt, "Lotus Feet," was an effort to move in that direction, to make a well-produced, sonically up-to-date guru-oriented record that people in the yoga market would go, "Yeah, this is great. I like doing yoga to this."

So you consciously set out to make a record that would appeal to the yoga community.

Right, but what happened in the making of it is interesting: I became less of a kirtan singer, in the style of Bhagavan Das with the *ektar*, singing traditional songs. Instead, I started to develop my own voice in that particular genre. This was partially due to the fact that people in my life, including Kit Thomas, whom I mentioned, said, "You know, what distinguishes you is your musicality, your chord structure, your melodies—and that's really what I see you moving into." And, to boot, I had a dream where the great saint Nityananda* came to me in a loincloth holding a Martin acoustic guitar in his hands.

Oh, you should definitely have someone paint that and put it on a CD.

Yeah, that would be a great visual. So, anyway, everything was leading me in a particular direction. The universe had something to say, and I couldn't help but listen. You know, Bhagavan Das has his market, and those are people who really like that sort of traditional kind of sound; and even Krishna Das has his market, because he took it and made it a little sweeter and a little more palatable for Westerners; and now I was guided, too, from within and from without, to incorporate these Folk-type songs, which has been very well-received.

Sharon Gannon from Jivamukti is one of my biggest supporters and she just thinks it's the greatest service to mix the two genres and idioms. "Soul Freedom" was mostly songs with a little bit of chanting, and "Lotus Feet" is mostly chanting with a little bit of song. And then there's "Into the Bliss: A Kirtan Experience."

This is a CD and DVD double disc set that captures the devotion, mystical beauty, and musical spontaneity of live kirtan—it's really special. A good number of musician friends helped out on this one: Mira, Philippo Franchini and Morgan Doctor—and also an enchanted vocal choir. The DVD was filmed and recorded in an intimate and elegant setting in Topanga Canyon, California. It really is an experience watching it—it's like being there.

---

* This refers to the 20th-century saint, Nityananda Baba, and not to Nityananda Prabhu, Sri Chaitanya's associate in Medieval Bengal.

So, things really shifted for you with the second CD. I mean, you were into kirtan early on, but that second CD really gave you the crucial push . . .

Yes. With "Lotus Feet," that's when everything shifted. When that record was released there was such a great response. I started to receive many invitations to chant at various venues, especially yoga centers. I also started to feel more impetus to contact more yoga centers, because I had this product that I could send to them, knowing that a majority of them would say, "Hey, this is cool, you gotta come here and sing." So with the release of "Lotus Feet," my life really shifted from yoga center owner/ yoga teacher to kirtan singer and traveling musician. Also, around that time I became more intimate with a dear friend who I had known for a long time. Her name is Mira, and I had met her initially many years ago through our community in Philadelphia and had developed a stronger friendship with her during the years that she traveled with Bhagavan Das.

We became partners right around the time I began my extensive touring. Mira is an integral part of my life, music, and devotion, as well as a wonderful singer-percussionist. So, together with Mira, and the many wonderful musicians who join us along the way, my time is spent singing kirtan, giving workshops on devotional yoga, offering concerts, and making music. This is a great blessing!

And let's not forget your tribute to Hanumanji, which I think is among your most beautiful work.

Oh, thank you. Yes, that's a special disk. It's called "Leap of Grace" — it's the "Hanuman Chalisa."

You recite it eleven times on the CD. That's significant . . .

Right. That's an auspicious number, and it's said that Hanuman bestows his blessings on sacred occasions if you chant it eleven times. So that's what we did. I like to think of "Leap of Grace" as a modern-day CD prayer wheel — manifesting its message as it spins in your player.

You know, it's interesting that there are so many different styles of

kirtan coming out. I mean, from you to Krishna Das to Jai Uttal—it's really great, all these different nuances of style.

Different and one at the same time. Deep down, I'm of the same ilk as KD and Jai. I'm rooted in *bhakti* and devotion and into the practice of *guru-kripa*—the mercy of the guru—and so on. Although my presentation is contemporary, it's very much rooted in my inner guidance, in what comes through me. When I sit at home, I often just sit with my *harmonium* or with my *ektar* and just sing traditionally. But I've been guided differently for outward presentation—I feel deeply that the modern West needs a different approach. So that's what I do. In any given kirtan performance, I might flip from "Shiva Shambho" to "Don't let me down"—a Beatles song. That's just how I'm guided.

And then the Beatles song takes on new meaning. Actually, people, often subconsciously, have a fundamental yearning for God. And when they compose songs, they're really calling out to the divine. Superficially, it might be a call to one's girlfriend or to something else. But deep down, underneath it all, we're looking for God.

Absolutely. I have this one chant that I wrote; it's very similar to the Beatles song—"Don't let me down." So when I'm singing "Shiva, Shiva" and then I sing, "Don't let me down," it takes on more of a devotional quality.

Sure. It's funny, growing up I've always listened to rock music, or blues, and, in the song, a guy loses his girlfriend and starts to feel vacant, discouraged in life. But somehow I always read it in a spiritual way, like a person moving away from God and lamenting about that.

Yeah, a sort of feeling that they've lost their connection to the divine source.

Exactly.

That's exactly what I try to do—but I do it consciously. Most of the music we're talking about does it inadvertently. But I do it directly, with intent. In other words, I write songs that help people go beyond the face value of the lyrics. The songs are written in such a way that people can easily look at them from a different perspective, and I'm always infusing devotion to God into it, too, which makes it still easier. That's always my intention when I sing. Devotion to my guru, devotion to the divine Mother, devotion to God.

Let's conclude with what kirtan means to you.

Sure. When I'm singing, when I go out to sing a kirtan, my *bhava*, my mood, is that I'm always singing for my guru, to please the divine. For me, I feel that the mantras in and of themselves—whether it's the Hare Krishna mantra, Sita-Rama mantra, Om Namo Shivaya mantra—have a certain potency. It's like spiritual medicine. If you take a prescribed medicine, it will have a certain effect. If you have faith and belief in the medicine, it will have a stronger effect, or there's more of a chance that you'll allow it to work.

So I feel that the people relate to mantras differently. For me, I relate to the relationship between *bhakti* and Nada-yoga, that spiritual life is nurtured by music, which speaks to the divine in each of us. When the divine Mother shows up in the form of music, that's Her form. She incarnates in the vibrational current of the sound, and She should be respected—She should be listened to. So when I'm singing, I'm opening myself up to Her as a vehicle to then communicate Her presence, Her love, Her energy, Her vibration, to the people that I'm singing for. If they receive it in a musical way, where they just feel their hearts open up, that's great. If they're tuned into the mantra, to the significance and to the essence of the mantra, that's great, too. It's a feeling. Some connect with that *bhakti* energy more than others. But it's all good.

For more information contact:
www.davidnewmanmusic.com or www.myspace.com/davidnewmandurgadas

$\mathcal{S}$RI PRAHLAD

Sri Prahlad was born into kirtan. His father was a devotee of Krishna, a member of the International Soci-

ety for Krishna Consciousness (ISKCON), and set him on his life's path when he was only a child. Having received training in gurukula board-ing schools around the world, Sri Prahlad received his most valuable experiences in Vrindavan and Mayapur, both of which are considered the most sacred of Indian holy places. There, he studied Vaishnava cul-ture and took part in daily kirtans, honing his skills and developing his talents.

Often returning home to Australia to visit family, he was one day informed about the plight of the Soviet Hare Krishnas, who, in the mid-1980s were imprisoned and sometimes killed by an oppressive government. Sri Prahlad conspired with other devotees to right this wrong, organizing protests and writing letters to the powers that be.

In 1986, when he was only twelve years of age, he and "The Krishna Kids" — young musically inclined ISKCON devotees from Australia — recorded an album on the international EMI label, including a plea to Gorbachev to free the Soviet Krishnas, which was soon also released as a single.

In due course, his efforts proved successful, and he appeared frequently on television and radio shows — promoting the album but also sharing his concern for the devotees in Russia. Eventually, the devotees were liberated from their prison cells. But Sri Prahlad went on. He continued singing for peace by working hard to spread kirtan around the world. He formed several bands — from rock to reggae — and kept the holy name in the center, recording several albums as the years passed. Becoming well known on the kirtan circuit for his accordion/ harmonium techniques and his unique style of singing, he gradually teamed up with dedicated kirtaniya Indradyumna Maharaj and, together, they sponsor and perform at festivals throughout the world, particularly the huge Woodstock-like kirtan festivals held annually in Poland.

✹ ✹ ✹

Okay, let's begin with some vital statistics: Your name, date of birth, place of birth, and so on.

Ace Volkmann Simpson, born March 16, 1974 in Wellington, New Zealand.

It's really something that, like Karnamrita Dasi, you grew up hearing kirtan!

Yes, my father, Kunjabihari Prabhu, then known as Michael Simpson, was associating with devotees and practicing Bhakti-yoga when I was a child. He even lived in the ISKCON temple in Adelaide, Australia, for some time. While there, he received a phone call from my mother in New Zealand, informing him that she was pregnant with his child. He left the temple and flew back to be with her, to assume responsibility as husband and father. While he was away from devotee association, he gradually gave up his Krishna-conscious practices, but then took them up again when I was three or four years old.

Is that when you were first introduced to Krishna consciousness?

My first memories of meeting a Hare Krishna devotee: I must have been three or four years old. I was walking down the street with my father and we saw a devotee distributing books. He appeared effulgent, like he was from another world. I can still remember his face in my mind. We purchased a copy of the *Srimad Bhagavatam* from him, a single volume. I obviously couldn't read, but I loved that book, because I knew it was something spiritual. It just had a special look and a special feel to it—I could tell it was connected with God.

But you actually joined the movement much later, no?

Well, my uncle came to visit. He was doing yoga and chanting *japa* while standing on his head. [laughter] I was attracted to his unique ways, his eccentric personality, and his Krishna consciousness, although I didn't know what that was, not at that time. When he was leaving to go back to the devotee community, 500 kilometres away, in Auckland, I remember crying because I wanted to go with him, to leave the family and join the Krishna temple. Of course, my family didn't allow me to do that. I was only a kid.

So you were attracted to chanting and to Krishna devotion from a really young age . . .

Yes. I mean, I can remember when I was maybe four years old: I was playing with some friends and we were singing "Hare Krishna, Hare Krishna, Krishna Krishna, Hare Hare/ Hare Rama, Hare Rama, Rama Rama, Hare Hare"—we were just singing as we played. One of the kids then said, "That's not a song; it's a chant." I said, "No, it *is* a song, and I even have the record in my house." But he insisted, "No, it's a chant." So we went to my father to settle the dispute: "Is 'Hare Krishna' a chant or a song?" My father told us that "Hare Krishna is both a song *and* a chant." I was excited about this—you know how kids are—and I would approach people, informing them, "You know, 'Hare Krishna' is a song and it's a chant, too. You can sing it or you can just chant it."

Tell me more about your first impressions of Krishna devotion.

One day in May, 1979, my father told me, "Tomorrow we're going for an airplane trip—we're going to join the Hare Krishnas in Auckland." I was excited and, of course, a bit weirded out at the same time. I had some reservations about joining the Hare Krishna movement, even though I was only a kid, following my father. I had just started school, maybe kindergarten, and I had the impression that devotees were like Buddhist monks, from Japan, or something like that. I saw this picture of a *sannyasi*, with a *danda*, the staff of renunciation, and so I thought that Hare Krishna life was about stick-fighting and really austere monastic life. Anyway, these were my kid-like concerns, and my father was fun-loving and attentive. He allayed my fears. As long as I was with him, I was okay.

So, as he said, we left the next day. The temple was situated on a farm near to the town of Kumeu, on the outskirts of Auckland City. Our plane landed at the Auckland airport and we took a bus to Kumeu. As evening approached, we started walking through the rain, and my father was trying to hitch us a ride to the temple. A man driving a Volkswagen van picked us up and dropped us at the entrance of the farm. There was a front entrance around the other side from where we walked in, but somehow we walked through the kitchen door. A *pujari* cook was there. It was Kalashambar Prabhu. My father said: "We've come to stay."

So that was it, huh? Your father wanted to stay and you were part of it—kind of like a package deal.

That's right. But, don't get me wrong—I fully trusted my father, and we had a great time there. It was quite an educational experience, and, as a kid, what could be more exciting? Singing, dancing, playing, musical instruments, community. It was a rich, colorful life.

Did you receive a Sanskrit name at that time. "Sri Prahlad"?

That's an interesting story. Everyone there had an intriguing spiritual name, and I wanted to have one too. Guests would come to the temple and they would often ask me: "What's your name?" I was too embarrassed to tell them my civil name, "Ace Simpson." I mean, I was a devotee, so it seemed like I should have had a more exotic name. I kind of sensed that, even though I was quite young at the time. So I made up a name for myself. The problem was that I didn't know enough Sanskrit to find a really good name. Basically, I knew four words: "Hare Krishna" and "Hare Rama."

That's three words.

Oh, you're right. [laughter] Anyway, I thought, "Hare Krishna" is too common; so I called myself "Hare Rama." Whenever a guest or a visiting devotee asked my name, I would tell them: "Just call me 'Hare Rama.'" Eventually, the temple president gave me the name "Prahlad," after the five-year-old devotee-saint described in the *puranas*. Later, when I was initiated by Hridayananda Maharaj in 1990, I was given the name Sri Prahlad.

The benefit of being a child in Krishna consciousness is that you learn quickly — the mind soaks things up when you're that young. So it was easy for me to learn scriptural texts, cultural traditions, Sanskrit and Bengali, cooking, playing instruments, and what have you. It all came to me quite naturally.

So this was in conjunction with your schooling?

Oh, of course. Shortly after joining the Krishna community in Auckland, I was enrolled in their co-ed boarding school. It was situated on a beautiful thousand-acre community in Murwillumbah, Australia. For those of us at the school, of course, mantra meditation, in terms of *japa*, kirtan, and *sankirtan*, were a regular part of our daily lives. I would often lead the kirtan at the community temple. Oh, I just loved to sing. It was a good life, and the program "60 Minutes" did a very positive feature on the school, with a short segment of me chanting Hare Krishna, standing in the Tweed River with water up to my neck.

It does sound like a good life, actually. Did you visit India at all?

Hmm. In 1983, when I was nine, I went to the Hare Krishna boarding school in the holy town of Vrindavan. That's where I received deeper training in the wisdom of the *Bhagavad-gita*, and in Vaishnava culture more generally. It was my desire to be transferred there, actually. I had heard a lot about the Vrindavan *gurukula*, about the high quality of the kids there. I had heard that they were really learned and qualified in so many ways — serious practitioners. That was what I really wanted. So I asked my father and my teachers if I could go to Vrindavan *gurukula*. And they eventually fulfilled that ambition of mine.

Was it all practice and no play? Did you go out and have fun? Did you go on vacation?

There was so much fun—swimming, playing music, dramatic performance—you name it! When it came time for school holidays, my father wasn't always able to fly me back home, to Australia—we didn't always have the money. So I went with the boys to Bombay, where the devotees would organize programs for us *gurukulis* each night. And it was really a lot of fun!! We would attend big festivals, sing kirtan into the wee hours of the morning, and one of us would even give a lecture—and the hosts would prepare such big feasts, and sometimes we would help with that too. We would also swim quite a bit and wrestle on the beach. We were all very happy.

Did you ever give one of those lectures?

Yeah. In fact, I remember the first time. One evening, during the program, Giriraj Maharaj asked me to speak. He was our very wise and greatly respected teacher, so I decided to do as he asked, even though I didn't really feel qualified to address such a large audience. Anyway, I got up, folded my hands in traditional *anjali* style, and I gave my talk. Basically, I spoke about the power of the holy name. People appreciated it. Everyone seemed so happy—they clapped and even cheered. The next day, Giriraj Maharaj asked me to talk again, and I couldn't think of anything else to say. So I gave the same speech. Then the day after that, Giriraj Maharaj asked me to speak and I again spoke about the power of the name. Finally, Maharaj asked me to infuse some variety in my presentation. So one evening I told the story of Valmiki—that he started out as a killer and a hunter, a murderer. But Narada Muni came and told him to change his ways. Narada told him to chant the name of Rama, but Valmiki said, "No, I can't. That's for pious people. And I like to kill." So Narada said, "Can you chant the name of death—Mara?" And Valmiki responded, "Yes, that I can chant." From that day on, Valmiki chanted: "Mara, Mara, Mara, Mara . . ."

And this is "Rama" in reverse—it's inverted. So by chanting the holy name of Rama, the sinful Valmiki had a transformation of heart and became a great saint. Everyone liked that talk, too. So it became my standard talk. And I gradually realized that every talk I ever gave was always focused on the holy name. I instinctively knew that this was the essence of our Gaudiya Vaishnava philosophy, even though I couldn't have been more than ten at the time.

Aside from these lectures and holiday tours, you stayed in Vrindavan for your formative years?

Well, in March 1984, some of the students—including me—were taken to Mayapur for the annual celebration of Sri Chaitanya's appearance. Mayapur, in West Bengal, is famous as the birthplace of Sri Chaitanya Mahaprabhu, who popularized chanting the holy name on the authority of Vedic teachings. And I felt blessed to be there. In Mayapur I saw *gurukula* boys performing ancient-looking fire sacrifices and chanting Vedic mantras during a deity procession. That really intrigued me. I thought: "I want to join this Mayapur *gurukula*." I mean, I really liked where I was, in Vrindavan, but this would be an interesting change—these kids were really doing something special.

So, no, to answer your question—I started out in Vrindavan, but after only one year in Krishna's holyland, I moved to the Bhaktivedanta Gurukula Village, the school in Mayapur, West Bengal. It was based on traditional *gurukula* techniques from ancient times, and I really responded to that. The environment here was unique in that all of the buildings were made from traditional materials—bamboo walls, earth floors, and thatched roofs. In this simple setting, the students would bathe in pure water, hand pumped from a well, or regularly swim in the Ganges River during the summer. It was like living in Sri Chaitanya's time. Simple and sweet.

Living in the area once graced by Sri Chaitanya would certainly prime you for a life of kirtan.

Yes. Soon after I arrived, I was trained in the ancient tradition of chanting Vedic mantras, like Purusha-sukta, Narayana-sukta, and

Sri-sukta, as well as the *Isha, Taittareya* and *Narayana Upanishads*. There was also great emphasis given to training the students in performing kirtan. In fact, I was having such a good time, that I was sad when, in 1986, at the age of twelve, I had to return to Australia to renew my Indian visa. And what's worse, my father decided to hold me back from Mayapur for some time, because my English was like Indian English. He decided to keep me in Australia to catch up on my English studies. I mean, I understood that it was for my own good, but I just loved being in Mayapur. Anyway, I entered the Australian *gurukula* again, knowing that after some time I'd go back to Mayapur.

I know you were involved in helping the devotees in Russia—there was horrible religious persecution there, and you helped to alleviate that situation. You became well known for your kirtan soon after that. Maybe you could talk about that whole history.

Yes. In 1986, news came out about what was happening to the ISKCON devotees in Russia, the Soviet Hare Krishnas. They were put in jails, psycho-prisons, and labor camps—all part of the Soviet Union's policy to repress religious activity. Devotees around the world were shocked by the events in Russia, especially hearing about Premavati. She was pregnant and she was put in prison because of her religious beliefs. When her child was born, she was only allowed to see the baby for one hour each day. Can you imagine? Then, at one point, she was told that her child had died, even though the baby's health was fine just one day earlier. Obviously, it was killed or mistreated to the point where death was inevitable. Maybe because we were also children in ISKCON, these horror stories hit us hard, harder than most—we were just totally shocked with the very idea of it. It seemed unbelievable that just because we were chanting Hare Krishna or just because we had the *Bhagavad-gita* in our homes, we could go to jail or be put into labor camps.

So how did you get involved in all of this?

I used to talk quite a bit to Gaura Gopal Prabhu, the public relations manager from the farm community, New Govardhan, which is where the Australian *gurukula* was located. One day, he had an idea — we would write a letter to Gorbachev in my name. You see, he was inspired by my interest in the topic, and by my genuine concern. I would talk about it constantly, asking obvious questions — "How could people be so irreligious? How could they persecute people just for believing in God?" I was really confused or shocked by the whole thing, but the idea to write a letter to Gorbachev was his. I helped to write it, but actually he was more the brains behind it. It was a great idea — you have an incensed child write to a political leader about the madness of religious persecution. It grabs the heart strings.

Then he took that letter to the media, saying, "This small boy has written this letter and he is going to send it to Gorbachev." So the press did an interview with me. I told them more about the situation. Then my picture appeared on the front page of a local newspaper: "Local boy writes to Gorbachev." After this initial success, Gaura Gopal had the idea that I could go to other newspapers and do the same thing, which is exactly what we did. Here's how we did it: We would drive the car and park in front of some newspaper building. I would go to the front desk and ask, "Can I please speak to the person in charge?" I would just get right to the point: "I have a very important message about the persecution of Hare Krishnas and the violation of human rights in the Soviet Union." They would immediately respond, across the board: "Okay. We'll send someone down right away." So the journalists would come down and I would show them my letter, tell them what was happening. It was a big story, and they were all into it. I mean, like, countless newspapers. They would take photos and the story was always published. We would drive from one newspaper to the next with the same strategy. Then we started going to radio stations. Gaura Gopal would drive, park the car, and stay there. I would go inside and say: "Can I speak to the chief of staff? I have a very important message." Same formula. They would always take me in and record an interview about the Russian situation — sometimes I would immediately go on air, live.

And this led to your famous recording on EMI Records . . .

Well, that came in due course. I used to lead lots of kirtans and played *mridanga* as well. Gaura Gopal even arranged for me to lead the first Hari-nam party in Surfers Paradise, a famous resort city in Australia. Devotees were not allowed to chant there, but he organized it and received official permission. We went with the other *gurukula* kids and I led the Hari-nam — we did kirtan in the whole area. It was really something special. So Gaura Gopal was aware of my singing abilities. The next step was a natural progression from that. We would use my singing for our current cause — to stop the violation of human rights in Russia, at least as it pertained to us, to the Hare Krishnas. Naturally, then, Gaura Gopal decided that we should record a song. He had an idea to turn my letter to Gorbachev into a hit record. A radio talk show comes and goes, but if a song about the same subject would be played throughout the day, many times, then people might get the message.

Again, he wrote some words for the record, and I added some ideas too. It was a collaborative effort. Our friend Havir was a good musician, and he agreed to help me write a song and record it at another friend's studio. And after the song had been recorded, the newspaper came to the studio to hear the music, and to meet the artists. After the newspapers came in, a popular television program called, "Good Morning, Australia!" aired the story. They did a special on the song and also aired interviews where we spoke about the campaign to free the Soviet Hare Krishnas.

I remember that. It was big news. The song was called, "Mr. Gorbachev, Please Let Our Friends Go." But how did it get to EMI? That must be a story in itself.

Oh, yes. Well, EMI Records. That was something. One of their chief executives in Sydney saw the "Good Morning Australia" program and called up the television station. He wanted to release the song as a single and distribute it on the EMI label. So we signed a contract with them, and they wanted another song for the flip side of the single. So we recorded the song, "Message for Tomorrow," for the flip side. Again, it was about the plight of the Soviet Hare

Krishnas. EMI really liked these two songs and they gave us a contract to do an entire album with ten tracks in total. We spent six
months recording it. In the end, it was called, "Through the Eyes
of a Child." What an experience! During the week, we were in
school, and on weekends, Saturday and Sunday, we would spend
the whole day at Springbrook Recording Studio. Throughout the
week, Havir Hari Prabhu would compose the music—he would
sometimes visit the school on weekdays to teach us the songs, and
on the weekends we would record them. It was a busy time. During
the week, there were always interviews for newspapers, radio, and
television. TV stations would come in and film, and radios would
call us and we would give interviews over the phone. In that year,
1986—which was also the 500th anniversary celebration of the
appearance of Sri Chaitanya—we had so much publicity in the
media. It became quite intense for a twelve year old to always be
in demand like that, not to have any free time. Weekends were for
recording, through the week there was school, but, like I said, even
school routine was always broken for different interviews and different promotional engagements.

So things started to change for the devotees in Russia?

Right. Well, we had some effect. In addition to the record, we pro-
tested outside the Soviet consulate in Sydney. On the same day,
devotees worldwide held protests in front of Soviet embassies,
high commissions, and consulates in their respective areas.

Things started to break down around us, and this affected our
campaign. The larger ISKCON world was having problems, as institutions tend to have, and this got out into the media. Frankly, it was
a difficult time. ISKCON was going through some real changes.
There were many great devotees—and still are—but now it became
obvious that not everyone was necessarily as holy as they seemed.
And this affected our work. You see, near the end of our promotional
tour in January 1987, the EMI executives saw the negative news arti-
cles about ISKCON, so they became reluctant to promote the Krishna
Kids, as our band was called. They had invested a huge amount of
money up until that point, but they didn't want to take it further.

That's understandable. So you went back to India?

For a time, yes. After spending eight months in Mayapur, there was a terrible flood and the school was disrupted. At that time, my father decided to bring me back to Australia. About a month after my return, at the end of 1987, I noticed an article in a national newspaper saying that Australian Prime Minister, Mr. Bob Hawk, would be visiting Moscow for a meeting with Gorbachev — to discuss the persecution of Soviet Jews. I immediately thought to write Hawk and request him to also represent our appeal for the freedom of the Soviet Hare Krishnas.

I thought they were already liberated by this point.

Not yet. I'm going to tell you how it happened. Just as I was thinking about writing to Hawk, I received news that Gaura Gopal had contacted the Prime Minister's secretary in my name, and that Mr. Hawk had agreed to deliver a letter to Gorbachev for me. The letter included a list of all of the Soviet Hare Krishna devotees who were imprisoned. Well, Mr. Hawk delivered the letter in his first meeting with Gorbachev and, the next day, in their second meeting, the letter was returned with a check next to each name, indicating their release.

Incredible. In the end, it was that easy.

It came after all our hard work, but, yes, the right people can do amazing things, just by their say-so. The Australian media picked up on the story of Mr. Bob Hawk's involvement in freeing the Soviet Hare Krishnas. The story appeared on the front page of all major newspapers in Australia, and in some other parts of the world, too.

Was the release of these people actually confirmed?

Oh, definitely. Gaura Gopal immediately called Sweden to speak with Kirtiraj Prabhu, who was the leader of the international campaign to free the Soviet devotees. By cooperating with Amnesty International, coordinating demonstrations in front of Soviet embassies around the world, informing the media of developments and keeping in touch with the Soviet devotees, Kirtiraj Prabhu had for years led this effort. With a choked voice, Kirtiraj informed Gaura that the devotees had suddenly been released. Now all of his efforts had come to fruition.

The devotees in that part of the world, especially, must have been relieved. Actually, they must have been thrilled.

Everyone was so grateful — Krishna wins out in the end! That was the end of a chapter, and it was a happy ending.

So after that, what avenues did you pursue in life, especially in regard to kirtan and the release of CDs?

In 1990, I left school — at the time I was at a *gurukula* in New Zealand — and started traveling with my spiritual mentor and dearest friend, Indradyumna Maharaj. I had been praying to Krishna to give me direction on how I should lead my life — I wanted to move forward in a sincere, spiritual way. ISKCON, for all the good it did, in so many ways, was falling on hard times, and I needed some spiritual guidance from someone I could trust. I wanted to make a significant contribution to the world by helping people in various ways, but mainly by helping them to lead more spiritually fulfilling lives.

Anyway, I left school, got a job, and collected enough money to purchase a plane ticket to circle the globe. My idea was to take off a year, seeing the world and learning how to lecture, how to play the *harmonium*, and how to lead kirtan. At the time, Indradyumna Maharaj visited Australia for the first time, and he offered me the opportunity to travel with him. I realized, in this, that Krishna was answering my prayer. Together, we visited Russia, where I finally had a chance to meet some of the devotees who had been persecuted under the Soviet regime. We visited Poland, too, where local devotees organized a number of public festivals for Maharaj's visit. The public's favorable response to the chanting so overwhelmed Indradyumna Maharaj that he cancelled the remainder of his European tour so the devotees could organize more festivals for him in Poland. We traveled all over the country with a group of fifteen devotees performing Hari-nam Sankirtan and holding public festivals.

But you're downplaying these festivals. I understand they were eventually compared to Woodstock—like kirtan-infused versions of massive rock celebrations.

Well, let's go step by step. The next year, Polish devotees planned summer festivals in advance and rented a forty-seater bus to accommodate participants, mostly students who were free to travel and chant during summer vacations. From these humble beginnings, in 1990, the tour has continued to grow in leaps and bounds every year. Today, the "Polish Festival of India Group" has a professional stage program and tons of festival equipment. Each year the group travels with over two hundred volunteers and organizes over sixty indoor and outdoor events in different parts of the country. On average, the events anually attract over 1.5 million participants. The festivals include dramatic performance, huge kirtans and *bhajans, prasadam* distribution—hundreds of thousands of plates of spiritualized vegetarian food, sanctified by having been offered to Krishna. It's just amazing.

So this all led to further involvement in kirtan for you, didn't it? How did your particular style develop?

In 1991 I learned to play the *harmonium*, and in 1993, noticing how similar the accordion was to the *harmonium*, I started playing accordion to accompany our street Sankirtan. It was a nice addition, which quickly caught on. Now I see devotees all over the world adding the accordion to their kirtan. It's practical, because you can walk and dance while playing. Later, in the year 2000, I made a two-hour, live recording of these accordion kirtans at a friend's studio in Moscow. We released this recording as two CDs, called, "Harer Nama—No Other Way," parts 1 and 2.

And you took your kirtan band to various festivals, too?

Yes. In 1993 our festival group was invited to participate at the prestigious Sopot Music Festival, an annual event held in Poland's northern region. The organizers asked if our group had a rock band, and our festival team told them we did (when, in actuality, we did not). For the following week, the musicians from our group practiced with several other musicians—people more inclined to rock music. We composed music for an electric mantra concert that would entertain over five thousand people. Well, the concert was a smashing success. Many people asked for recordings then and there, and a live recording of the concert was eventually released. We decided to keep playing together, calling our group, "The Celibate Lovers." For three years we played at all of the Festival of India events and many other shows too.

In 1997, The Celibate Lovers finally dissolved, and some of the musicians—including me—regrouped as a reggae band, and we called ourselves, "Village of Peace." We chose reggae music because we found that the passionate nature of rock sometimes made the audience too wild. With reggae, the music is both heavy on the bottom, with strong bass and drum rhythms, but sweet on the top. We found that this combination satisfied the wide variety of people who attended the festivals. The youthful people were pleased with the strong grooves at the bottom end, and the older people and even the young children could enjoy the sweetness aspect of it. We also considered that the principal of reggae, which uses simple musical arrangements and chord combinations, along with strong and steady and almost monotonous grooves, was more closely related to kirtan, where devotees often chant the same mantra and melody for hours in a trance-like state.

Also, reggae has traditionally been message music—it's often listened to by people who are questioning and looking for answers.

That's true. We were conscious of that. The songs we sang were both English and Hare Krsna *maha-mantra* compositions. The English tunes, of course, carried positive messages, ranging from upbeat, mode of goodness ideas, to directly spiritual messages. In the four years I was with this band, we recorded two albums, "Where We Come From," which has included a number of mantra tracks, and

"Pastimes," also including mantra tracks. Though I left the band in 2001, "Village of Peace" continues to play concerts to this day.

This summer (2007) I had an interesting experience in Poland. Our festival group was singing street kirtan in the Baltic town of Kolobjeg when we decided to take a short break in a park. As we were resting, we heard a familiar voice singing Hare Krishna over a strong beat being played loudly at a nearby game parlor. As it turned out, some Polish DJ had remixed one of my "Village of Peace" Hare Krishna mantra tracks, which was one of the most popular tracks played in Polish discos and radio over the past year. It is also a popular ring tone—on phones. The DJ who created the remix also produced a video that appears on some TV stations. It's kind of weird but also quite a bit of fun. You can see it on U-tube by searching for the Alchemist Project.

Let's conclude with a little philosophy. Can you tell me what kirtan means, both to you and in general?

Many spiritual traditions of the world teach that the name of God is holy and that it is, in fact, nondifferent from God Himself. The spiritual tradition of India is no different. In India, devotees perform "Hari-nam." In the Sanskrit language, *hari* refers to God and *nama* means name. The holy names are chanted as mantras. Mantras are spiritual sound vibrations consisting of names of God that are chanted over and over as a meditation. *Mantra* is a Sanskrit word consisting of two syllables: *man* ("mind") and *tra* ("to free"). And so mantra meditation frees the mind of negative emotions, such as fear, anxiety, hatred, envy and greed, and awakens awareness of our spiritual nature—allowing spiritual love within the heart to truly blossom. It reconnects the chanter with the supreme soul, God, and in this sense, it's the perfection of yoga—since yoga is ultimately about "re-linking" with the Supreme. Material conditioning and negative emotions affect our health, relationships, physical endeavors—it affects everything. When the mind is purified, we experience deep inner satisfaction and peace. By internally maintaining a condition of meditation, one's simplest labors become an offering of love to God, a meditation in and of themselves. By learning the art of chanting, one learns how to accomplish this.

In India, mantras are composed of the names of various deities, like Surya, the Lord of the sun; Chandra, the Lord of the moon; Durga, the personified material nature. Most often, chanters glorify these names for the fulfillment of various material desires. Other names are chanted for the attainment of release from material suffering—or for liberation from the cycle of repeated birth and death. Such mantras include the syllables AUM, Brahman (all pervasive spirit), and Ishvara (supreme controller).

Vaishnava tradition teaches that God has an unlimited number of names—like Krishna, Rama, Vishnu, and so on, which all indicate the same supreme Lord in His various forms. Now, these names can also be chanted for the fulfillment of material desires or for liberation. But these goals really miss the point. These things are actually insignificant side benefits of the real benediction that the holy name can bestow—that is, pure love for God, *prema*. This is the real fruit of chanting.

Therefore, Sri Chaitanya Mahaprabhu, the most recent incarnation of God, who appeared in West Bengal 500 years ago, gave emphasis to the chanting of the *maha-mantra* in a pure state of mind. He explained that the *maha-mantra*, in its purest form, is the inner prayer of the soul crying out for its source—for loving union with God. It's a prayer that basically means, "Oh, all attractive Lord, Oh, reservoir of all happiness, please let me love You; let me serve You."

Is there something you would advise people to keep in mind while they chant?

Although the name of the Lord is absolute, He manifests according to the purity of the chanter. When you chant for name, fame, money, or other forms of sense gratification, and not out of love, then the name will not fully manifest on your lips, or in your heart. So I would advise to focus on purity of purpose. I pray to the Lord to play me as His instrument and I ask Him to lead the chanting, even if it externally appears that I am leading it. Leaving your ego aside and chanting in a humble state of mind is when you can experience real miracles in kirtan. When kirtan's going on, everyone in the room becomes a channel for the transmission and reception of spiritual energy. And you can tangibly feel your heart jumping with spiritual ecstasy. When you're singing prayerfully and in the mood of a humble servant—you're singing with heart.

Sometimes pride is compared to a great mountain, which squashes one's endeavors in spiritual life. But the great Vaishnava saint, Raghunath Das Goswami, reminds us that Krishna is the lifter of Govardhan Hill, so lifting our prideful mountain is no great thing for Him. If only we'd really want Him to do it.

For more information contact:

www.narottam.com/category/personalities/sri-prahlad/

EAN JOHNSON

*Sean Johnson is a kirtan powerhouse
who brings together New Orleans
soul and the spiritual chanting of
ancient India. He has been featured in* Yoga Journal, L.A. Yoga Magazine, Yoga Chicago Magazine, Fit Yoga Magazine, Yoga Life Magazine, Aura Magazine, The Philadelphia Inquirer, The New Orleans Times-Picayune, *and more . . .*

*"Kirtan has been called the gospel music of India," the New Orleans
kirtaniya tells us. "It's got that flavor to it. It's devotional music from the
heart."*

*But he's quick to add that its heart is not limited to India, and to
prove this, he draws from multiple cultures and religions: Irish, Indian,
Catholic, Buddhist, and Muslim, among others. He does his best to present kirtan in an ecumenical, non-sectarian way.*

Dan Cowan reviews Sean's latest CD "Calling the Spirits" in Music Design In Review: *"Sean Johnson & the Wild Lotus Band are a New
Orleans-based collective that offer a unique twist on classic kirtan chant.
Acoustic guitar, bluesy rhythms, lots of clap-style percussion . . . the
band takes the essence of the bayou and merges it with Indian spiritual
music for a sound that bubbles with soul and unbridled passion. Johnson provides lead vocals on the album, and his voice has a low, smooth
quality that melds well with the earthy, acoustic-based backdrops. Their*

take on the perennial 'Om Namah Shivaya' is fresh and original, with a light jazz sound and joyous singing that captivates. The same could be said for another favorite, 'Govinda Gopala,' which makes great use of Kristen Jensen's violin to provide an upbeat yet tender melody. Johnson and his band perform regularly at yoga studios around the country and have frequently put on benefit concerts to help rebuilding efforts in their New Orleans home."

As his one-time teacher, Russill Paul (author of The Yoga of Sound) *writes, "Sean brings home the devotion in his voice: this is* bhakti *in full measure. He is also living proof of the power of the Hatha-yogi who also understands the power of sound. This, I believe, is the future of yoga, especially in the West, where a unique yogic culture is being developed, authentic in its spirit and meaningful in the form of its expression."*

✳ ✳ ✳

Let's get your basic background info out of the way.

Sure. I was born on January 24, 1971 in New Orleans, Louisiana.

I guess we should start with your spiritual roots and evolve into your musical roots—and that should bring us to kirtan.

Well, my spiritual and musical roots were both sunned and watered long before I was born. I come from an ancestry of (mostly former) Catholic nuns, monks, priests, and deacons that goes at least a few generations back. On my mother's side of the family several uncles were Trappist monks at Gethsemani when Thomas Merton was there. A great grand uncle of mine was the first Catholic priest to be ordained in Houston, Texas.

That same great grand uncle was a former football star at Notre Dame under coach Knute Rockne, and he later flew planes and served as a missionary in India for over thirty years. How interesting it is that four generations later, I would be sharing Sanskrit mantras with fellow Westerners!

That *is* interesting. Any other religious luminaries in your ancestry?

Another uncle was a Jesuit for twelve years, and an aunt a Poor Clare nun for fifteen years. In fact, my mother was a Poor Clare nun before she left the convent and met my father, who was in a Jesuit seminary for two years studying to become a priest. On the paternal side of my family, my grandfather was a deacon for many years, and I have an uncle who was also in the same Jesuit seminary as my father.

Wow. So there's been a lot of religion in your family.

A lot, yeah. Not all of it has been good. There was a lot of dogma, guilt, and that kind of stuff. At times I've felt like a part of my destiny involved healing my family's past, renegotiating our family karma by creating opportunities for positive, inspiring spiritual growth — the kind that transcends dogma, proselytizing, and guilt.

That's a lot to digest. What about your musical history?

My paternal grandfather was a Vaudeville banjo player, and my maternal grandmother was once offered a music scholarship to Juilliard, which she turned down because she wanted to become a nun. And my brother Matt, who often plays in our kirtan band, is considered one of the most talented jazz guitarists in New Orleans. So there's a bit of music in the family.

But religion seems to have had an overriding presence in your life and family.

In a sense, yeah. That's right. But, in another sense, no, not really. My two younger brothers and I were raised with no religion at all. My parents, bitter about their years of what they called brainwashing by the Catholic Church, protected us from having a similar experience. Being raised with no religious traditions actually left me more open-minded to experiencing what religion was really all about. In other words, while I wasn't affiliated with a particular church, I was deeply interested in the universal threads that tie the planet's spiritual traditions together; at least this interested me later in life.

I feel incredibly blessed to have parents who always encouraged us to follow our hearts and always supported our interests.
I was an imaginative child and fascinated by otherworldly creatures like fairies, leprechauns, and ghosts. I loved mythology. I
spent a lot of time alone, completely content, playing outside or
in the sanctuary of my room. As a child, I loved to sing, by myself,
in musical theatre, and in The New Orleans Symphony Children's
Chorus. I also played piano. One of my favorite pastimes was making tapes and singing songs. I was fascinated with the power
of the microphone, and I did lots of experiments with sound. In
fifth grade I composed an experimental piece of protest music on
an electric organ called "Yet War Goes On." This focused heavily
on the black keys of the organ. I really tried to express my sadness and confusion about the history of human bloodshed — it just
never seems to end. That's the kind of kid I was.

Ah, the sensitive, creative type. Tell me about school and growing up.

I attended New Orleans public schools from kindergarten through
high school. We lived in a modest home and my parents cleaned
houses for a living. That's how we spent our summers — cleaning
houses, which gave me a great work ethic and a lot of humility.

When I was in junior high, rap music and break dancing had
just hit the mainstream. I was in awe of the joyful dancing, singing, and rhyming of my African-American classmates. I learned to
"beatbox" and would compete with other kids at parties, creating
three and four sounds simultaneously with my mouth. Through
these kids' inspiring company, I was introduced to the unique
rhythms of New Orleans street culture, which resonates with me
to this day. In high school I played basketball, ran track, edited the
school newspaper, partied a lot, and, oh yeah, I was intrigued by
the altered states created by drugs and alcohol.

[laughter] And in New Orleans! That must have been intense.

Oh, yeah! There are many reasons to love New Orleans. It has a
culture all its own. If you look at the elements that really define a

distinct culture, you'll find them all here: our own music, cuisine, holidays, accent, architecture, a unique history, rituals.

I never thought about it quite that way. New Orleans is exceptionally colorful, isn't it?

Much of the United States, with its acres of strip malls and homogeneous culture, feels sterile compared to New Orleans. I mean, maybe I'm just biased, but New Orleans has real contrast, paradox, nuance. The dark and the light are at play here, making it a fascinating and romantic place to live. Isn't it true? New Orleans is lush, humid, sexy, heavy, laid-back, decadent, traditional. Hey, man—we have it all. [laughter] As you can see, New Orleans is in my blood. It's an energy that has a big influence on my interpretation and expression of kirtan.

That's interesting. Most *kirtaniyas* are influenced by a certain region in India, where their particular style of kirtan might have originated. But your kirtan is heavily influenced by your own background, your surroundings, growing up.

There's a running joke among New Orleans yoga teachers that because of our geographic position at the mouth of the Mississippi River, which is like the spine of the U.S., New Orleans is the first and second *chakra* of America. This is just one energetic map—and I don't want to oversimplify—but the lower *chakras* buzz with our soulful energy and the upper *chakras* hum with our spirit energy. And if we can embrace both those energies, there is the potential for wholeness, for integration.

Love it! [laughter]

In New Orleans you can embrace your own soul: the rich, dark, mysterious, primal, creative, part of yourself that doesn't always make sense. You can feel both parts of the self—the body and the essential being within—coming together. At a time when our country's culture is becoming more and more homogenized, and everything is beginning to look and sound and feel the same—I invite people to come experience what New Orleans has to offer. Usually, people make a pilgrimage to a mountaintop to attain great spiritual heights. That's the usual image, right? I say this: Come make a sacred journey to the deep south, to the swamps and bayous in and around New Orleans. Here you'll experience the depth of your soul, and the soul of this nation.

Overstating it a bit, no?

[laughter] Well, there's something to be said for looking into our own roots, digging down to see where our ancestors come from, where *we* come from. But, of course, we all have a deeper spiritual side, too, one that has nothing to do with bodies and minds, one that transcends the material world altogether.

Let's talk more about that spiritual side. How did that open up for you?

My heart cracked open and a part of me woke up to the world in the summer of 1991, when I was nineteen years old. I fell in love for the first time. The gift of that love burned through so many illusions. I had been a high-achieving student in high school. In my first two years in college, at Boston University, I was studying Broadcast Communications. I had worked and begun moving up the ladder at a television station in New Orleans and secured prestigious internships at TV and radio stations in Boston. I wanted a fancy house, a nice car, a respected job—all the usual material trophies. Then IT happened. She and I met—it was a great love that blossomed like a fantastic lotus out of the thick mud inside me, and I was filled with a brightness I had never felt before. We spent three blissful months together and then I left for school in Boston and she was home in New Orleans. Even though we were apart, the love roared inside me, and I asked myself the question—"What do I do with this love? She's not here. I could sit around and feel sorry for myself, or is there a way to channel this powerful energy into my present life. Could I express my love for her through everyday life?"

So your love for this girl opened you up to spirituality? Usually, it's the demise of such a relationship that opens a person up . . .

Well, let me flesh this out for you a bit. In that relationship, I was possessed by a newfound creative energy that put me in a very special space, emotionally, psychologically. For one thing, it made everything seem alive. For the first time, I experienced life as a work of art. I downplayed the mandatory core requirements at B.U. and began to take classes based purely on my passion for the topic. I studied art, music, mythology, dreams. I think my newfound relationship gave me a taste for the spontaneous, a love for the endless possibilities of creativity.

I took a job at a daycare center, expressing my love toward the innocence and open-mindedness of the children. I wanted to be with kids, who love to play, laugh, and dance. They don't know the same restrictions that we do; they're not held back by the same reservations. They were my teachers.

Does your girlfriend enter the picture again?

Well, one day while driving through the New England countryside, an idea hit me like lightning. I decided that I wanted to drop out of school and just travel around the country with her, particularly exploring the West Coast for the first time. I discussed it with her, and she was into it. So we saved up money for a year, bought a little camper and went on a three-month adventure. I really enjoyed the spiritual landscape of the West Coast — the edge of the continent, and edge of Western consciousness. A year after our trip, our relationship ended in a tragic betrayal and I asked myself again — "What do I do with this love? She's not here, and won't be here. Does this tremendous love power just exist in relationship to her, or is it inside me and her presence just sparked it into consciousness? Can I fall in love with life itself?" So she made me realize just how much love was actually inside of me — her personality, in a sense, was only incidental. There was something larger here than just a male/ female exchange. Later, I would recognize the relationship between these questions and the more universal qualities of longing, separation, union — the cosmic love affair expressed in Bhakti-yoga. I poured my grief and longing into a unique education that would change my life forever . . .

Ah, okay, so your first love was a catalyst for something else. Where does it go from here?

Well, while traveling, we had discovered a little liberal arts college in Olympia, Washington, called The Evergreen State College, and, later, I picked up my studies there. It was at Evergreen, from about 1994 to 1997, that so many seeds were planted for my spiritual life and current work, even with kirtan.

Okay, can you give me some background on Evergreen?

It's a boldly alternative college, founded by a small group of liberal professors in the late '60s. The school prides itself on interdisciplinary education, written evaluations instead of grades, and independent study programs. Rather than taking four to five unrelated classes, at Evergreen, students participate in one program that lasts anywhere between two and three quarters, team-taught by a group of professors coming from different fields of expertise. One could essentially map out one's own education at Evergreen. We called all the professors by their first names. My transcript is as thick as a book with details of all I learned while I was there, rather than a GPA.

In my first year at Evergreen, I took a program called "The Irish Experience," exploring deeply my Irish heritage, culture, and spirituality. I was taught "old-style" Irish songs by an ethnomusicologist named Sean Williams, who would become a close friend. She was a student and daughter figure to the legendary Irish *sean-nós* singer, Joe Heaney. On his deathbed he asked her to pass his songs on. She fulfilled his wish by giving some of his songs to me and to several other fortunate students. *Sean-nós* singing is a highly personal solo vocal art form categorized by intricately ornamented melodies that have been passed on from generation to generation of traditional Irish singers.

So this gave you some singing background and some familiarity with your Irish roots. Did you use these singing techniques later?

Well, the summer after I initially learned this stuff, I went to Ireland for the first time and sang in pubs all over the country. After a couple of pints of Guinness, I would close my eyes and begin to sing, entering what seemed to be a dark tunnel. When I'd enter that state, I felt possessed by the spirit of my ancestors, and I sang like I never had before. It was a highly spiritual experience. After a given song, I'd come out of the tunnel and be greeted by mad applause from the people in the pub. We would then all sit around and talk, and they'd usually be real curious about what county in Ireland I was from. When I told them that I was from America, they were invariably shocked. Anyway, I found this singing to be the ultimate way to commune with my ancestry. The ornamentation and technique of the Irish singing would later prepare me for studying the basics of Indian vocal music, one of the most sophisticated vocal arts in the world.

Were there any personal spiritual teachers? Did you meet anyone along the way, especially back when you were in college?

Yes. At Evergreen I met my first spiritual mentor, a renaissance woman named Doranne Crable. Doranne was a Hatha-yoga teacher and long-time student of Mahayana and Vipassana meditation. She was a passionate dancer who had lived with gypsies in Spain, studying Flamenco. She also studied with the revolutionary dancers in Japan who created Butoh dance. Doranne eventually became a great guide and friend.

She introduced me to yoga, too. In her classes, I entered into a deep relationship with my body, learning to explore movement as meditation, and many forms of creativity. In this way, I became much more open to a deep exploration of the inner life. I began practicing Vipassana meditation after a ten-day silent retreat at a local center.

At that time, I created an independent project with a small group of peers, called, "Art, Mysticism, Movement, and Fear," which explored the relationship between creative expression and spirituality. The last program I took with Doranne was entitled, "PATH: Practices Acknowledging The Heart." In hindsight, I see now that it was basically an introduction to what I now know as Bhakti-yoga. Doranne invited many guest artists to come and work with our class who would have a profound impact on my musical and spiritual path. Flamenco artists visited and I was awakened to the passionate power of the *canté*, flamenco singing that has its roots in India.

It's mainly connected to Punjabi singing . . .

Right. Oh, how I wanted to sing like that! I yearned to sing with that unbridled freedom and feeling. Then around that time, a "sound healer" and instrument maker named Catherine Favré came to work with us. She taught one exercise, in particular, that really moved me: We learned to tone vowel sounds over each other's bodies. When I first discovered this, I remember writing in my journal: "I want to be a sound healer."

So you were learning about spirituality and sound, in relation to singing. Were there any other teachers who inspired you back then?

A prominent Sufi master and *shaikh* in the Mevlevi Order visited at that time, too. His name was Kabir Helminski, and I experienced my first *dhikr* with him.

The repetition of the names of Allah. So we're moving toward kirtan.

Yes, and I immediately fell in love with this form of sacred chant. I was struck by the trance-like state that comes out of it. I was also introduced to Rumi's poetry at that time, which has been one of my constant companions ever since.

Sounds like you were having a meaningful experience at Evergreen— the spiritual and educational journey of a lifetime.

I was really enjoying it, so much so that I kept petitioning the college to take more credits. I didn't want to graduate. Finally, they said I needed to move on. So I did. I began searching for graduate programs where I could continue the holistic education that had been sparked at Evergreen. And I did find something. I discovered a graduate program in Oakland, California, called The University of Creation Spirituality, which became the West Coast campus of The Naropa Institute while I was a student there.

Oh, Creation Spirituality—that was Matthew Fox's concept. He's a Christian theologian with whom I'm somewhat familiar. He empha-sized *via positiva*, looking to the good of creation, as opposed to *via negativa*, the philosophy that the world is a negative place. You went to his University?

Yeah, and, you know, Fox was silenced by Cardinal Ratzinger— who's now the Pope. And he was eventually dismissed from the Dominican order. His vision of the Catholic Church was in line with the mystical philosophies of medieval visionaries, like Hildegard of Bingen, Thomas Aquinas, Meister Eckhart and Nicholas of Cusa— he dared to question the Church's belief in original sin; he experi-mented with reinventing the mass by integrating rituals from other spiritual traditions, using multimedia, and inviting people to dance to ecstatic techno music; he integrated findings from astro and quantum physics to tell contemporary creation stories that would inspire awe, wonder, and gratitude.

Special soul, a visionary.

Right. Of his books, one of my favorites is called *Original Blessing*. On the faculty were spiritual teachers and artists from many dif-ferent traditions who shared a common purpose: to celebrate the blessings of creation and creativity. Each classroom was named after a different mystic: The Rumi Room, The Aquinas Room, The Eckhart Room. It was a very creative place to stretch and grow at that time. That's where I met Russill Paul, who was a teacher in the program there. He's an extremely talented musician, *yogi*, and teacher from South India who had lived as a monk at the Hindu-Christian ashram founded by Father Bede Griffiths.

I'm familiar with Paul's work. I read his book, *The Yoga of Sound*, which, in some ways, inspired my vision for this book about kirtan. I've also always been intrigued by Griffiths, particularly his commentary on the *Bhagavad Gita*.

Griffiths was devoted to the dialogue between Hinduism and Christianity. He was a father figure to Russill.

Do you remember the first time you heard Russill sing?

Yes, it was during the first week of graduate school, and I was blown away. At the time, I was a great admirer of the Pakistani Qawwali singer Nusrat Fateh Ali Khan, as well as other singers who have such power and beauty in their voices. But this was the first time I heard such a voice from the East live—in person. That afternoon I was introduced to Russill briefly. Our conversation was short and casual. So I was a bit surprised when a bold stream of words flowed, almost involuntarily, out of my mouth: "I want to be a devotional singer," I told him. I think this was the first time I had consciously verbalized this intention.

So he took you under his wing?

That week, Russill facilitated art-as-meditation sessions in the afternoons, particularly during that initial orientation period. He taught us several Vedic mantras, too. The final day, we had a ritual in a room at school called, "The Sacred Cave." Russill invited everyone to sing and create music freely, integrating the mantras we'd learned that week. He played keyboards, *unitar* (a hybrid sitar), the *tanpura*, and the harmonica, while a percussionist wove rhythms into our chanting.

At a certain point I had an incredible experience of letting go, surrendering to the ecstasy of song. I just let everything in—it felt like rather than me singing, I was being sung. My voice traveled to places I didn't know it could go, sliding and quivering in what I can only describe as vocal acrobatics. Suddenly, I realized that everyone doing that exercise was following my lead. Russill was concentrating on playing the *unitar* and had stopped singing. For a few moments, I became very self-conscious, until I released myself again to the power of the mantra. Actually, I savored the sensation for as long as I could. This was honestly one of the most amazing experiences I had ever had. I really wanted more. After class, I was excited when several students thanked me and told me that my voice and my ability to let go had inspired them and helped them release into a deeply ecstatic state of being.

Was your experience with Russill Paul just this short-lived exchange, enacted during a few classes at orientation?

Oh, no. For the next two years, 1997 to '99, I engaged in an intensive apprenticeship under Russill, studying mantra, Shabda-yoga, Karnatic (South Indian) vocal music, Kundalini-yoga, and Bhakti-yoga. With Russill as my adviser, I titled my masters project at Naropa, "Initiation Into Devotional Singing And Teaching Sound And Music As Spiritual Practice."

So is this where you started with kirtan?

Yes. At Naropa, several days a week, I led morning kirtan sessions in "The Sacred Cave" for my classmates. Elements of the project included lots of personal yoga and music practice, research and study; group learning with Russill; private devotional singing lessons and assistant teaching with him; local performances with Russill and on my own; and eventually leading kirtans and teaching workshops independently. In recent years, Russill has released a series of CDs. But you know this, since you've read *The Yoga Of Sound.*

Since this was going on in the 1990s, were you exposed to any of the popular *kirtaniyas* at the time?

While I was at Naropa, I was turned onto a recording of Jai Uttal's music. The depth of devotion and passion in his voice resonated deeply with me. I also admired the way he integrated Eastern and Western music in a unique way—it felt sincere, unforced. Jai has been a great guide and friend since 1999. Last year he visited New Orleans for the first time and blessed our studio with a rockin' kirtan! That night, guided by Jai and Daniel, it felt like we were sending healing vibrations across the entire New Orleans landscape. I have attended a couple of Jai and Daniel Paul's ten-day kirtan camps. Though I had already been guiding kirtan for years before the camp, I received so much inspiration from the community Jai created. I have a great admiration for his humility, honesty, sense of humor, and his family, and I love singing with him. I feel very grateful to Russill and Jai for their support along the path.

I guess this leads us to Wild Lotus Yoga. How did that come about? And what impact has your studio had on New Orleans?

In 1999, after graduate school and seven years of spiritual adventures and learning, I received an invitation to return home and to teach yoga in New Orleans. I was glad to come full circle and share what I had learned with people in my hometown. For the first few years, I taught yoga and led kirtan at universities, fitness centers, and local and regional yoga studios. As a result of all that, in 2002 I decided to open "Wild Lotus Yoga."

The studio began modestly with a staff of three friends teaching seven classes a week. Today, Wild Lotus is the largest and one of the most respected yoga schools in the gulf south. We offer forty-three classes per week and serve an average of 500 students a week, too. Over 7,000 students have taken classes at Wild Lotus over the last five years. It was the first yoga studio in New Orleans to reopen after Katrina and has served as a peaceful refuge in a time of stress and uncertainty — forces that have been very present in the post-Katrina era.

So Wild Lotus is only five years old, but it has accomplished a great deal in that time.

Right, and we've been blessed to be voted "Best Place To Take A Yoga Class In New Orleans" five years in a row in our local *Gambit Weekly*'s annual readers' poll — since the beginning. Every Monday night when we're not touring, we offer kirtan at Wild Lotus. I also integrate kirtan into many of the Hatha-yoga classes that I teach, and have been invited to share kirtan at health fairs in a local hospital, cancer survivors' retreats, churches, universities, and retreat centers. I feel so blessed by the presence of kirtan in my life.

Do you have any kirtan singers who you would call your favorites, or who influence you in your own kirtan?

The kirtan singers that move me most have an ability to move my heart, to transmit love through the sincerity and through the authenticity in their voices. It doesn't feel like they're trying to sound like someone else, or trying to force the music to sound too traditional, on one side, or too poppy, on the other. They are singing from their center. That type of chanting fills me with joy—it makes me cry. I really have a very strong, emotional, and kinesthetic reaction to their voices.

Russill was most influential in the early years, and Jai, I would say, in the later years. What I admire about their singing is their ability to utilize their voices as a mantric instrument that can be subtle and soft and beautiful and also incredibly powerful and dynamic, when the kirtan calls for it. I have to tell you, though, it has been a joy to meet and experience the music of other contemporary kirtan singers, such as KD, Wah!, Girish, Saul David Raye, Dave Stringer, Bhagavan Das, Shyam Das, Govindas, David Newman, Joey Lugassy, Kamaniya, Diana Rogers, Lily Diamond, Steve Ross, and others. There are so many, with more and more people joining the ranks every day.

Finally, I'm interested in your philosophy of kirtan. Would you compare kirtan to prayer and to other forms of invoking God's name? What would you say to that?

So many of my teachers were cultural bridge builders, passionately integrating East and West, and I've picked up on that myself. My vision as a kirtan singer living happily in the deep South, has been to bring the practice to many people who have never experienced it before; and to find a voice for kirtan that springs out of the musical and cultural influences that move my heart and soul. I have always felt most passionate about a non-sectarian approach to kirtan—I like to present this art as a spiritual practice that celebrates the universal. Everything I've ever seen, heard, smelled, tasted, and touched impacts on my approach to kirtan. These golden mantras have been marinating in the street rhythms of my New Orleans childhood; the haunting songs I sang in Ireland; the Indian vocal practices that I continue on a daily basis; the middle-eastern rhythms that other teachers and friends have brought to the mix; the urban jazz sensibilities so vital to the ambience of New Orleans; the mystic poetry of Rumi and Kabir; the rhythmic and melodic flow of a Vinyasa-yoga practice; and of course my own life joys and struggles and those of our home and community. I also want to acknowledge and honor the gifts brought by my musical family — The Wild Lotus Band — My brother Matt Johnson, and my dear friends, Gwendolyn Colman and Alvin Young.

Let's not forget the beauty and the disappointment of your relationship with your first love.

That was a big part of it. All such relationships offer us a hint of the love that exists between the soul and God. For me, the experience with her — it was the blessing of falling in love for the first time, then losing the woman who awakened that love, and then seeking to channel that love into a relationship with the divine. Kirtan is a form of lovemaking, isn't it? It's a form of becoming intimate with our source, with the supreme divinity. It's an act of kindling the connection with the sacred presence within us, through the sincerity of singing. Just as we stretch our bodies with yoga *asanas*, kirtan stretches our hearts and cultivates emotional flexibility. In kirtan, we celebrate our longing and our thirst for God — in numerous ways. We can sing our love, sing our doubt, sing our anger, sing our fear, sing our passion, sing our compassion — all these raw emotions can be offered up to the divine. Whatever we're feeling at the time.

Kirtan is a form of purification. The mantras sensitize us, polish away the clutter in our heads and melt the numbness in our hearts — so we feel clear, awake, and brilliantly alive. The singing melts our inhibitions. The frozen places inside us defrost and we start to move more freely, which enables us to play, almost like children.

Kirtan is a a form of meditation. Our wandering minds have the opportunity to return again and again to the touchstone of the repeated mantra, an invitation to truly exist in the present. The mantras themselves are like medicine, freeing us of our spiritual ailments and tuning the head to the heart. Kirtan is also the ultimate *pranayama* — the repetition of the mantras regulates our breath pattern, stoking the *prana*.

When you get down to it, kirtan is fundamentally therapeutic. So many people have lost touch with the power of their voice and their creative expression and kirtan is a direct path to freeing the authentic voice within. Many folks who have attended kirtans over the years have offered gratitude for the opportunity to sing without being judged, and they really appreciate the cathartic and liberating power that comes with that experience.

In this sense, kirtan creates community. Singing together, we feel a fundamental bonding with each other, and we feel in sync with the divine vibration. Thus, kirtan is the most sublime form of *satsang*, gathering with fellow seekers of truth to sing, to reach within by the power of our own voices and hearts.

Such a beautiful thing. It's seems we have a duty to share this with others.

Since I started leading kirtan in 1997, I have spent most of my energy introducing people to it as a sacred art. When I haven't been on tour, I've offered kirtan in New Orleans every Monday night since 1999. My focus in introducing the practice is to appeal to universal qualities of human experience.

Contemporary chanters are intuiting what our ancestors took for granted—that the fabric of the world itself is comprised of sonic vibration. We can find references to the power of sound and speech in the creation stories of so many cultural and spiritual traditions. The Hindus say "Nada Brahma" or "Shabda Brahma"— the world is sound! Contemporary science, in its own language, tells a similar story. Today's physicists say that subatomic particles in all matter—even in the hardest, densest material—are in fact vibrating. If we look at that in the deepest possible way, we see that both the poetic narratives of our ancestors and the empirical data identified by modern science are telling us that the world is sound. People who chant are participating in the song of life. And when you dedicate yourself to this practice, you become consciously aware of that.

For newcomers, I usually just explain that the practice of kirtan awakens specific aspects of our divine nature, depending on the deity we attract by our chanting. Through kirtan, we coax these energies from within our soul of souls, and we invite them into our presence.

Can you give some practical examples?

Well, I tell them that chanting the name of Ganapati, for instance, will remove obstacles in life, because Ganapati is the remover of all obstacles; Vishnu is the spirit of peace and preservation—so chanting his name helps one in that way; Krishna brings out the spirit of love, abiding in all things and in whom all things abide; Hanuman represents the embodiment of unswerving service and absolute spiritual devotion; Durga—great mother; Shiva—the divine spirit of transformation . . .

Oh, I see. So you don't necessarily introduce them as personal deities but rather as ways of accessing specific qualities.

At a certain level, I find this really works for people. Sometimes the idea of a personal deity comes with too much baggage, especially for people with a Judaeo-Christian background. So I keep it simple and thus less intimidating.

And what kind of musicians do you work with? Who might accompany you during one of your usual kirtan performances?

Many *kirtan-wallahs* travel with a single percussionist or even travel alone and work with local musicians who sit in with them. Over the years, I have played with a variety of musicians and it's just so much fun to jam. But it has been even more rewarding over the past two years to work with the same musicians in a trio or quartet format—percussionist Gwendolyn Colman, my brother Matt Johnson on guitar and tenor sax, and Alvin Young on fretless bass. We've cultivated a certain chemistry, a musical intimacy, and skill that just keeps getting deeper and juicier.

Because of our familiarity with each other, we're able to fine-tune the dynamics of each chant in a way that would be difficult to do with folks you aren't used to playing with. We've been experimenting with ways of integrating the improvisational spontaneity of kirtan with loose arrangements that enable us to navigate the chanters through subtler and subtler variations of sacred ambiance.

You're talking about facilitating a certain *bhava*, or emotion ...

The *bhava*! Exactly. These arrangements sometimes include instrumental solos whose purpose is to serve the mantra, and to feed the *bhava*, rather than distract from it. It takes a great deal of sensitivity on the part of the musician to pull this off. This is a yoga practice in and of itself.

Let's hear more about your work with your kirtan band and then about the CDs you've produced.

We are currently working with traditional mantras, chanted with mostly original melodies. The melodies are never forced. I feel like they come "through" as gifts from the Divine Presence. We explore the new melodies through a process of improvisation, leaving lots of room for our spirits to speak. Oftentimes a kirtan melody grows through the practice of trying it out live with a group. The spirit moves the music in unexpected ways. It develops a life of its own. I'll tell you: I'm a worshipper of that mystery!

We've been touring more and more over the last few years, developing a following particularly on the East and West Coasts. Some highlights have been kirtans at Laughing Lotus in New York City, the Kripalu Center in Massachusetts, The Midwest Yoga Conference, The Las Vegas Vinyasa Yoga Conference, The Ojai Yoga Crib, The Global Mala Project in Los Angeles, and dozens of yoga studios and churches nationwide. Next year we've lined up several yoga conferences, including The German Yoga Conference, which will be the anchor for a European tour.

And the CDs?

I recorded my first CD in 2002. It's titled "In The Moment," and I did it with multi-instrumentalist Hans Gruenig. The album is a studio-enhanced collection of live chants in which I wanted to capture the improvisational spirit of making music as a form of meditation. We recorded original songs and some live kirtan on the album.

For the second CD, titled, "World Peace Chants," I was invited by a group affiliated with The Parliament of The World's Religions to create a soundtrack for a labyrinth walk at their 2004 international meeting held in Barcelona, Spain. The intention of the recording is to heal the conflict between religions by celebrating the harmony between all spiritual traditions through music. The album consists of original songs with lush instrumentation, featuring chants that honor the Buddhist, Hindu, Jewish, Christian, Muslim, Sikh, Yoruba, Vodun, and Native American spiritual traditions, and the sacredness of all spiritual paths. The songs are a prayer for spiritual awakening and world peace—for people of all religions to walk together in beauty. People from many different spiritual traditions, in their ceremonial robes, walked side by side on the labyrinth in Barcelona listening to these cycles of meditative peace chants.

My latest album with my band—The Wild Lotus Band—is entitled, "Calling The Spirits," and I feel this one really represents where ten years of kirtan have taken the music to date. It has been picked up for distribution and is being sold nationwide, and it's receiving really positive reviews.

All of the songs on "Calling The Spirits" were composed post-Katrina and capture the soul and spirit of our life in New Orleans. Chanting these mantras with people has been a nourishing and therapeutic experience, and a big part of our service to the renaissance of New Orleans.

New Age/ Yoga albums often have a strong spiritual vibe—lots of synthesizers, chimes, bells, beautiful sounds that stimulate the upper *chakras*. I love these albums. But, sometimes it feels like there's something missing . . . the soul, the roots. Bhakti-yoga is about devoting all the parts of ourselves to the Divine. With "Calling the Spirits," we're trying to merge the sublime spirit of yoga with the rich soul of New Orleans. Cultivating this balance is what I love so much about living in New Orleans and having a yoga studio here.

Musically, the album was created with a lot of improvisation, which is the heart of New Orleans music. Many of the melodies are unscripted, raw, alive. Also, except for the amplified bass, "Calling The Spirits" is exclusively acoustic—there are no synthesizers—which creates a rootsy, earthy feel. There's a real presence of wood on the album, which is really brought forth by Gwendolyn's hand-drumming. Most of the live music in New Orleans is acoustically based. Many of the songs are percussion driven. The bass line and rhythm of the song "Calling The Spirits" and the rap-like delivery of a portion of the "Durga Chaleesa" on "Om Shakti" are a tribute to New Orleans rap, which Matt and I both grew up with going to New Orleans public schools. There are some jazz harmonies on the album, too, particularly "Jai Ma," which is influenced by Bossa Nova. The sax lines on "Om Nama Shivaya" remind me of brass bands playing on the streets of New Orleans.

Future plans?

I'll be establishing a 200-hour yoga teacher training in the coming year that will be focused on integrating Hatha- and Bhakti-yoga, one of the few training programs in the region. The goal is to re-seed New Orleans with yoga teachers who can help serve the renaissance of New Orleans. Many yoga teachers left after Katrina, but this might draw them back in.

I've been involved with a powerful group of people who are seeking to establish a downtown healing center that will bring yoga, meditation, healthy food, healing arts, and educational opportunities to the area's mixed income neighborhoods, including the 9th Ward, so heavily hit by Katrina. The plan is to open up "Wild Lotus Yoga-Downtown" inside this state-of-the-art operation, which will provide a holistic, safe, sustainable center that heals the individual and community by offering services and programs that promote physical, nutritional, emotional, intellectual, and spiritual well-being for the fulfillment and empowerment of all. Wild Lotus will offer several community classes there at discounted rates and host visiting expert teachers, artists, and musicians from around the country. Kirtan, of course, will be a big part of the center as well as the energizing focus of all that I do. We will continue to tour the globe and record new material, sharing the love power of kirtan with an ever-expanding circle of people! Jai Ma!

For more information contact:
www.seanjohnsonkirtan.com
www.wildlotusyoga.com

AI UTTAL

Jai Uttal is a pioneer in the world music community, using kirtan as a bridge to harmonize diverse cultures. His eclectic East-meets-West approach, with his virtuoso singing and musical dynamism, has put him at the forefront of the world fusion movement.

Born in New York City by way of West Bengal, India, Jai Uttal came of age with music. When he was only seven he began playing piano and learned banjo, guitar, harmonica, and some other instruments as his years moved forward. Discovering American roots music, and then jazz, rock, and blues, his musical and spiritual life gained direction when he was a teenager — it was then that he first heard Indian music, which "touched my heart like sounds of my home," he said. "Then I got all the Indian albums I could, jamming along on guitar with Ali Akbar Khan records."

By 1969, at the age of eighteen, he emerged on the West Coast, studying sarod and taking voice lessons with the legendary Ali Akbar Khan. Almost two years later, he found himself in India, for here, he knew, he would grow closer to the music and culture he so loved. During this first stay on the subcontinent, he met his guru, Neem Karoli Baba, which was transformative in every way, solidifying his love affair with the land of Krishna — and with the "soul support system" of kirtan and Bhakti-yoga.

His second trip to India, two years later, deepened his experience, as he lived in a simple house in the Bengali city of Bolpur, becoming friendly with the street musicians – the Bauls of Bengal. He gradually started play-ing and traveling with them, gaining experience and "chops," as they say in the music industry.

After some time he returned to America and, in 1990, released his debut CD with Triloka Records, "Footprints," a monumental contribution to the East-West fusion genre and the New Age Movement, including guest appear-ances by jazz artist Don Cherry and Indian vocalist Lakshmi Shankar.

With his newly formed band, the Pagan Love Orchestra, Jai Uttal continued to develop his sound – a concatenation of Western rock and jazz influences along with Indian-inflected moods, mantras, and exotic instruments from the East. He soon released "Monkey," which enjoyed Top Ten status on the World Music charts.

His next release, 1994's "Beggars and Saints," was a tribute to the Bauls of Bengal, an attempt to thank them for his formative time in Bolpur. Here his music shows signs of maturation, the dawning of the signature style for which he would soon become well known. Three years later brought the world "Shiva Station," which was mixed by renowned producer Bill Laswell. This was a breakthrough CD, winning worldwide acclaim and a new audience of yoga practitioners and kirtan enthusiasts.

Next came the self-released album, "Nectar – Live Kirtan and Pagan Remixes," followed by another remix EP, "Guru Brahma/ Malkouns," which was mixed by Asian Underground artist, Talvin Singh.

Meanwhile, Jai Uttal found himself leading kirtan workshops and con-certs throughout the world. His unique chanting brought him to Israel, Fiji, Brazil, Germany, Switzerland, India, and elsewhere.

In February of 2002, Jai Uttal recorded what was to become his seminal release: "Mondo Rama," on Narada Records. An ambitious work combin-ing Brazilian sounds, Hebrew prayers, Appalachian hillbilly music, blues, a 1960s rock sensibility, and – what he was now known for – Indian music and sacred chanting, Jai Uttal had finally arrived, not only on the yoga kir-tan scene but as an internationally acclaimed recording artist.

The CD was nominated at the 45th Annual Grammy Awards as "Best New Age Album" of 2002. Several years later he released "Kirtan! The Art and Practice of Ecstatic Chant," as well as several other CDs specifi-cally aimed at a yoga audience. And he continues to produce and play for the benefit of all.

✳ ✳ ✳

Okay. You weren't born with the name Jai Uttal, right? I mean, you're a Westerner.

You want my full American name?

Yes, your legal name.

Douglas Zion Uttal.

Zion?

Yeah.

That's pretty cool.

[laughter] And "Uttal" — it's pronounced "you-tall," rather than "oo-tall." It's Lithuanian, not Sanskrit. And I was born in Brooklyn.

As was I.

[laughter] At the Women's Hospital in Brooklyn. Where were you born?

Brooklyn Jewish Hospital.

I was born on June 12, 1951.

Okay. And were you born into a religious family, or no?

No. You mean because my middle name is Zion?

Not necessarily. I'm just curious . . .

My mother was very Jewish, both politically and socially. My father was Jewish, too, from the left, though. No, it wasn't a religious family, even if I did have religious or spiritual thoughts from early on.

Again like me.

But my mom, especially, was really connected to the whole political thing — that was their thing. They never prayed or lit candles or anything like that.

Was she an intellectual?

They were both intellectuals. Sort of. They fashioned themselves to be. [laughter]

I know what you mean.

No, they were. My mother was an artist, a painter. She was a writer, too. But mostly she was a somewhat troubled person.

Hmm.

God bless her. My dad was in the music business.

Yes? In what capacity?

He was an executive for various record companies over the years. He'd find groups, put out records. . . . He was quite successful in the 70s.

Any significant record companies that I might have heard of?

Bell Records? Private Stock Records?

Bell Records. My brother collects doo-wop stuff from the 50s—that was one of the labels . . .

Right. My dad put out Al Green's first album; he got Blondie for the company. He had tons and tons of big hit records. We lived in an environment of hot music. And my dad would bring home every week the top 20 singles from the major radio station. So that was cool.

You're talking about the late '50s, early '60s?

Well, let's see. I was born in 1951, and we moved to New York when I was six. We moved to Manhattan, rather, when I was six. So, yeah, late '50s early '60s. But all through the '60s, until I left, around 1969, I guess. It was the first half of the '60s.

That was great music.

Yeah, great music. He worked a lot on R&B, and then he got heavily into disco, too. That was after I had already left. He was just working with whatever was popular.

Right. So did you take to music personally? I mean, more than just by listening to it? Were you a musician early on?

Yes. I started playing the piano when I was around six, I think. No, we were in New York, so maybe seven or eight. My parents started me on piano lessons. They started me on piano lessons because I was playing the piano. They had a piano in the house. I was just loving it—picking out little songs, and just doing what I could. So we started piano lessons when I was pretty young. I did that for several years, until I was a young teenager, and then I didn't want to do it anymore. I stopped, and then I started playing the harmonica for a little while, which led to one of my great, great loves: the banjo.

With the harmonica, were you playing blues harp, or different stuff?

I was into old-time music, Appalachian music. I don't know—I was just playing harmonica. I don't know what I was playing. [laughter] But when I got into the banjo, I got *very* into Appalachian music. I took lessons from some great banjo players and good people. One of them was Julius Lester. Have you heard of him?

Julius Lester. That name sounds familiar, but I don't know. Civil Rights Movement, children's books . . .

Yeah. He became a writer. He's a black man, and he eventually became a scholar of Jewish studies.

Oh, right.

Funny how he converted to Judaism. Probably because he played at my Bar Mitzvah, and . . . No, I don't think so. That was a joke.

[laughter]

But he did play at my Bar Mitzvah.

He did?

Yes. Banjo was my first real passion. And he played a mean banjo.

So as the '60s were evolving, did you get into the hippie scene?

Yeah. That's when I kind of switched from banjo to electric guitar.

Who were some of the people who inspired that? Was it the usual Clapton, Beck, Page thing?

Well, no. It was Jimi Hendrix. Although I liked Clapton, and one of the greatest concerts I saw was one of the first Cream concerts. But I would have to say it was *totally* Jimi Hendrix. Because he resonated with his inner pain. Because *I* resonated with his inner pain. He awakened the inner scream that was within me, a scream that needed to be screamed.

He really did. He had a whole vibe that went so far beyond the guitar.

Exactly. It was an expression of that place inside—the part of us that's in agony, the part that needs to be released, to cry, to call out to someone. Ultimately, to cry and call to God. And I heard that in his playing. I saw that in his playing more than in anybody else. He had mastered that expression. You know, I should say, too, that I am still, to this day, a total Beatles maniac.

Oh, yeah? Yeah, yeah? [laughter]

[laughter] But I still could have kept on loving the Beatles and kept playing the banjo. So it was Jimi that made me switch to the guitar. But, meanwhile, I was listening to Indian music, too.

Back then?

Yes, back then. I continued to listen to old-timey music. Do you know what I mean by old-timey music?

Old-timey? The Big Band stuff?

No. It's the pre-country, pre-bluegrass music of the Appalachian Mountains. They call it old-timey music, but I don't know exactly why. That's what I still do with the banjo. I was always listening to that kind of stuff, and also a lot of Indian music, like Ali Akbar Khan and Ravi Shankar. You couldn't get much variety in those days. I was also listening to Indian folk music, like the Bauls of Bengal. I really liked Jimi Hendrix, the Mothers of Invention, the Beatles, and that kind of stuff. And Bob Dylan, always. And John Coltrane.

You were into jazz, too? Like Coltrane?

Yeah, some jazz. Coltrane and others; mostly Coltrane. There was some classical stuff as well. You know, I was a music fanatic. I tried playing some Eastern *ragas* on the guitar a little bit, too. I would read the album covers and find the scales. So that was going on.

What about when the Mahavishnu Orchestra came about? That must have knocked you for a loop.

Well, yeah, of course. But I wasn't really into jazz-fusion at all. At that point I was getting into Reggae sounds.

I think that was the early 1970s, so maybe you were already on a different path.

I started studying with Ali Akbar Khan in 1969.

Oh! Tell me about that. That sounds intriguing. Or are we jumping ahead?

Okay. I was a hippie. I was proud to be a hippie, although I was only about eighteen. So around '66 or so I was still in New York, and I started hearing the Hare Krishna chant. Amazing. I was transfixed by them and I just loved it. The sound entered my heart, I mean, on a very deep level.

So you saw and heard the Hare Krishnas in the mid to late '60s.

Yes. I kind of followed them around New York — and this happened on a number of occasions. Whenever I saw them, I just followed; I couldn't control it — I *had to* follow that sound. The chanting really spoke to me. I felt that it awakened memories in me, something that's been covered forever. I just loved it.

Did you meet any of them? Speak to any of them?

No, I didn't. For some reason, I wasn't drawn to the people as such, to join them or anything. I joined them on the streets, singing, but that's about it. I was just into the sound of the chanting. I loved it. I was into meditation and stuff like that. I got into Zen Buddhism, some early teenage version of it, and the whole psychedelic thing, too. But the Hare Krishna lifestyle—that was too serious for me.

So what did you do after that? We're leading up to your study with Ali Akbar Khan.

Yeah. So then I went to college, Reed College in Portland, Oregon. The eve of registration, you know, the night before our first classes, Ali Akbar Khan came and performed there.

So you went to that show.

I went to that concert and I was just turned inside out by it. For one thing, I had taken Mescaline.

That'll help.

That'll help. [laughter] But you know how, in life, there are certain memories that never go away? Certain events and certain things happen to you in life, or even certain dreams—most of it fades with time, but some things just become a part of you and they don't go away . . .

Forever stays with you. Yeah.

That night was one of them. What happened was that when the music stopped, when Ali Akbar stopped playing, the music continued in my ears, in my mind, in my heart. I was hearing the *raga* continuing on and on, and I was hearing the *tabla* beats in everyone's footsteps. People would come up to me and ask, "What's up? Why are you still sitting here? Didn't you like the concert?" And I would say, "Quiet, please; it's still going on!" That must have seemed pretty out there, I guess.

It's obviously a *samskara*, an impression, from a previous life.

It was. There was this feeling that Indian music—when executed properly—was the most direct expression of the soul, a tangible emanation of the life force, in musical form. That's what I felt at that moment.

So, I stayed in college for three months, and then I dropped out and came down to California to study with Ali Akbar Khan. I thought I was going to study guitar, because he teaches classical music with all instruments, and I was already playing guitar. But as soon as I came to the school and heard the students practicing *sarod*, I packed away my guitar. I somehow scraped together the money to buy a cheap *sarod*, and then I got into that.

That's a lifetime of study . . .

By the way, I still study with him.

Oh, I didn't know that.

Many, many, many years later. I'm pretty close to him, and I'm close with his family. He insisted that everyone who studied music with him had to study vocal music. They would have to study singing. Now, I did not consider myself a singer by any stretch of the imagination, and I had no ambitions as a singer . . .

That's funny, because I think out of most of the *kirtaniyas* in the West, your singing is probably the most *pukka*, the most professional sounding.

Thank you. I appreciate that. Well, this was 1969, and I was a pretty unhappy little guy . . .

What do you think was causing your sadness?

No, no, no. Not just sadness. It was a deep, deep dissatisfaction with life. I guess it could be traced to something from my childhood. Definitely. I don't know how far we want to get into that.

Well, let's just get an idea about why you were so disturbed. You know, it's not uncommon for a teenager to question life, wondering what it's all about, and that can cause deep disturbance.

Right, but this went deeper than that. My family was essentially dysfunctional, with a lot of emotional abuse. Let's just say it was an unusually unhappy family environment. I had extremely low self-esteem. But music was the one thing that brought me out of that. It gave me renewed spirit; it rejuvenated me in so many ways.

And so when I started singing—which, again, I only did because of the insistence of my teacher, Ali Akbar—that singing tripped something. It just vibrated something in my heart that was longing to be vibrated. It reached me in a place that instruments just couldn't reach, although instruments always made me feel safe. They made me feel comfortable, enabled me to set aside the pain. But singing somehow opened up the gates of my heart and gave me a sense of freedom and divine presence and happiness. But I was desperately inhibited at first, because I was so convinced that my voice was horrible.

That sounds like Jimi Hendrix. He also had that insecurity.

That's true. The only time I could sing was when I was locked up in my room and no one else was in the house. I don't think I would have ever sung if it hadn't been for those classes with Ali Akbar Khan. But you can't really hide yourself when you're singing. Well, you can, but it's harder to hide when you're singing. When you sing, you're so vulnerable. So, at first, it was very, very difficult for me to sing. Psychologically. But, you see, that difficulty was counterbalanced by the realization that singing was the one thing that gave me almost total joy. It made me feel whole.

How paradoxical.

It was extremely paradoxical. And it was an odd kind of joy, because music put me in touch with the sadness as well. I guess you could say it was more relief than anything else.

Cathartic. It was cathartic for you.

Cathartic. It was cathartic for me every time I opened my mouth.

[laughter]

But it was a real struggle. So, anyway, I was studying with Ali Akbar for several years at that point and really, really getting into it. I was mostly playing *sarod*. The singing was still very backseat, but bubbling, you know, because it was the strongest thing; it went deep.

Right. Did that lead to more involvement with India? Did you want to go? By that point you hadn't yet traveled to India, right?

I very much wanted to go to India. This came about when I got into a particular yoga society, a group led by an Indian guru, who I think should remain nameless. So there I started doing more kirtan. They taught a very complete yoga thing, and we did *asanas*, meditation, and *pranayama*, as well as kirtan and . . .

Where was this?

We had a little ashram in Berkeley, and remember we were all still very young. But I was singing kirtans and leading kirtans and playing kirtans in the ashram. Mostly doing it with a guitar. I knew a few simple, devotional songs. I was very much a *bhakta*, a *yogi*-type kid. My idol was Sri Ramakrishna. I was really, really into that. Just crying and longing and singing and . . .

If Ramakrishna was your idol, how come you were involved with that particular yoga group and not with the Ramakrishna Mission?

Well, that's a really good question. It's got two answers. For one thing, that yoga group sent a bunch of very lovely, charismatic gurus to America, to initiate people. And the guy we connected with was really very nice—he drew us to him in a very substantial way. I still know him a little bit, all these years later. But there was also this thing that the guru gave us the guarantee of enlightenment. [both laugh] It was a written guarantee, that if we did such and such, you know, followed some observances, and meditated and did a particular practice for twenty minutes a day, we were guaranteed enlightenment in this life. That was very, very appealing at the time.

Sure. That's a good deal . . . if you can buy it.

[laughter] So, being a good, American boy, who understood a deal when he saw one . . .

And probably because you were suffering, you had some sense of *mukti*, or liberation, of being free from your pain. That was what you wanted in pursuing enlightenment, no?

Absolutely. What was my idea of enlightenment, anyway? What could I get out of this? Basically, I think "enlightenment" — at least for me, at that time — was more about becoming a different person, someone I could love a little more. It wasn't so much about *mukti*; it was more about becoming somebody else. It certainly wasn't about coming to the core of who I really was. There was so much self-loathing that I just wanted to be somebody else. So I decided I wanted to be a *yogi*, someone with great confidence, and great inner strength, and connection to God. That's where I was back then . . .

It was more about escaping, I think.

Right. Okay. That's one way of putting it. I wanted to run away from who I was and become somebody else. So, I had a deal, I had a contract. Things were looking up, you know? So I went to Ali Akbar Khan and I said, "Oh sir, I have decided to go to India to see this guru." You see, we were told that in India, we could go to this ceremony that occurred once a year and the guru would put his hands in a certain *mudra*, a certain position, and that this would fling us into *samadhi*, some perfected state, or something. Thousands of people. And I was fully buying into this — I so needed it at the time. So I went to Ali Akbar Khan and said, "I have to go to India." I was feeling I needed to go to India to meet this guru. And Ali Akbar Khan said, "Don't go. Don't go. I'll let you study with me for free."

Wow!

But I went. [both laugh] You know, for a nineteen-year-old kid, this is a big adventure.

That's about when I first went to India, too. I was about nineteen or so.

We were brave. [both laugh]

Well, it was a whole different time. It really was.

So I sold my electric guitar and just pulled it together and went—
me and a couple of friends. When we got to the airport, in India,
we were greeted by a friend from California who had left for India
about three or four weeks earlier. He also went to become a monk
with this guru. We said to him, "Wow, how did you know we were
coming?" and he said, "Well, I've been waiting for you for twelve
hours—yesterday I had a dream that you were coming, but in my
dream it didn't say *when* you were coming."

How Strange.

Very weird, I know. But it gets worse. He said, "The reason I am here
is to tell you that the guru is in jail for mass murder."

You're kidding!

He said, "I needed to tell you this before you went on to Patna, to
find him." That's where he was, in Patna.

That's in Bihar, on the southern bank of the Ganges, right?

Right. So he said, "Come to Old Delhi and I'll tell you all about it.
There's a bunch of monks who are waiting there, and they'll tell
you the full story." So we went to this hotel in Old Delhi and it was
pretty amazing. The culture shock was crazy. The thing is, I was so
happy—not because he was in jail for murder but because I felt so
immediately at home when I arrived in India. I remember walking
off the plane and smelling India. It was a revelation . . .

Yes! I had the same experience when I first entered Vrindavan.

Well, in Vrindavan it's even more intense, for sure. Anyway, when
I arrived in Delhi, I felt like my entire life, up until that point, I had
been in exile, and that I was finally home. This was just in the airport in Delhi, which is no great place. But it was instantaneous. It
was mostly the smell of all those fires, those little cooking fires. But
it was so much more.

I know what you mean.

When we went to Old Delhi we stayed with all these young monks who appeared in the hotel in orange robes, and somewhere in the hotel they changed into Calvin Klein jeans and then left. The hotel was under surveillance because this yoga group was involved in leftist politics in India. They were doing great things, too, with orphanages and schools, and stuff like that. So I think politically it was pretty cool.

But, anyway, all these monks, these young guys in their late-teens, early twenties, thought that they were getting away with their lives, after being involved with this questionable yoga group. We were like, "So, what happened? What's this about a murder?" We had heard that the guru would touch people on the head and they would instantly go into Nirvakalpa Samadhi, just by the power of his touch, or by the power of his look. These were the things we were told. We were totally indoctrinated with that stuff.

The short version is that the bubble was quickly broken. So, suddenly — after hearing about all the hanky-panky and downright illegal and immoral activity — the illusion shattered. My identification with this guru collapsed and I felt like I was walking on air. Rather than being highly disillusioned and disappointed, I found myself walking around in India — totally free. It was an amazing feeling. The stuff that we heard was pretty astonishing. He would hit the monks on the head and they would pretend to go into *samadhi*, because if they didn't he would beat them. He was mistreating so many people. We heard so many awful things. I didn't find out the whole story about the numerous murders until many years later. No need to go into that here.

Okay, so you were floating around Delhi without a real agenda. This was 1971?

1971. Yes. I guess I was involved with that yoga group for about two years. I was very into it in America. They sent a bunch of us young disciples out to different parts of America to teach yoga to other people. I lived in Bakersfield for a while. I went there as a yoga missionary on their behalf. I had only forty dollars or so in my pocket, a guitar, and a *sarod,* and I hitchhiked to Bakersfield. I sat down on the lawn of the college campus and started playing *sarod* and chanting. People gathered around me and I talked about yoga. Gradually we got a house there and, you know, the *yogis* came and initiated people.

When you say, "I talked about yoga," are you talking about *ashtanga-yoga,* like the exercises, and things like that?

They called it *ashtanga-yoga* in those days, but it was not *ashtanga-yoga* like what people do now. It was *ashtanga-yoga,* the eight-limbed path of yoga. *Asana, pranayama,* etc.

But that's what you were basically teaching people?

Yeah. I was nineteen years old and I was teaching *asanas.* That's pretty funny, in retrospect. What could I really teach? But mostly, I was gathering people with the music. That was always my focus. I would wail on the *sarod* and sing some kirtan.

And what kirtan would you sing?

We did many different kirtans in those days — and I learned them through my yoga connections. Shiva kirtans, Krishna kirtans. Yeah, we definitely sang Hare Krishna tunes, and Rama, Sita-Rama. We sang lots of different tunes. I really enjoyed them, though it was all quite basic.

Okay, so you were in Delhi without a guru and without an agenda. What happened next?

Now, I had known Ram Dass back in the States.

You're referring to Richard Alpert, the LSD researcher and writer . . .

Right. I won't say that we were close friends or anything like that, but we hung out a bit. He came over to our house one time, for kirtan, and we had an amazing time. And then we met up in India.

I was at this bookstore, and the bookseller said, "Hey, did you know Ram Dass was in town?" And I said, "No, I didn't. Where is he?" So the shopkeeper told me what hotel Ram Dass was staying in. He said that Ram Dass was giving classes. I thought that was kind of cool. For me, it was kind of like following the breadcrumbs in the forest. So I went over there and they said he had gone to see his guru in Vrindavan, which was a couple of hours away. So my friends and I thought we'd go and see Ram Dass in Vrindavan. Because what else were we going to do?

So we went there, but there was no desire to see the guru. I had had it with gurus, naturally, given my previous experience. But I was excited about being in India. Particularly in 1971 — it was really magical. It's still very magical, but back then it was much less decayed and polluted and toxic. Even in Delhi, the air was relatively clean. We went to Vrindavan and the *tonga* driver, the driver who took us from Mathura to Vrindavan, delivered us right to the ashram of Maharaji — Neem Karoli Baba. We didn't want to get out of the *tonga*. We said, "No, no, we're not going to another ashram . . ."

Had you heard of Neem Karoli Baba?

Yes. I had read *Be Here Now*. But I didn't know much about him And I certainly wasn't looking for a guru at that point. So the driver took us to one *dharmashala*, the guesthouse. I think it was the only guesthouse in Vrindavan at the time that Westerners could come to, where they'd feel comfortable, and, actually, we'd been welcomed there. It was called Jaipuria Bhavan, and we stayed for several weeks. We were there with a bunch of other Americans, including Ram Dass, most of whom were waiting a week to see Maharaji, because Maharaji had told everyone to leave for a week. Which is what he would often do: He'd tell people to go, or he would disappear, and then he'd tell them when to return.

So I hung out with these people for the week, just walking around Vrindavan. As you know, it's such an amazing, magical town, and particularly at that time. I still love it. You know, there were no cars then. It was so different — it seemed so ancient. It was much cleaner, and, of course, as always, mystical. Every night, on the rooftop of the Jaipuria Bhavan, just around sunset, we'd gather around this huge altar — the altar had lots of different things, pictures of sages and gods and goddesses, and in the middle some pictures of Maharaji, too. We would sing prayers, songs, and light some lights every night. So it created a really nice atmosphere—it was a beautiful ceremony and I really enjoyed watching it, and taking part in it.

But, you know, I was more *watching* it; I wasn't really doing it. And so the end of the week came and everybody was all excited to see Maharaji. I was just like, "Okay, I'm along for the ride." Somehow, I woke up that morning and I was the first one at the temple. I don't have any idea why, because in my mind I was still very, very disinterested in gurus, or looking for another guru. I was interested in God and spirituality, don't get me wrong, and I just loved the energy that was around me. But I wasn't ready to give focus to one person. I just didn't believe in it.

Okay. Still, I got to the temple and I was the first one there. To this day, I really have no idea why that is. I mean, I can make up ideas about it, but, in any case, there I was and I was waiting in the middle of the courtyard, where Maharaji was expected to appear.

In those days, it was just a big, dirt courtyard in between the buildings. Now it's quite different. In the middle of the courtyard, there was a table with a blanket on it. They said that that's where Maharaji was going to meet with everybody, but he was still in his room. So I was sitting there, waiting. I was sitting in the morning sun, listening to the most beautiful kirtan coming from the loudspeaker of the temple. Vrindavan, of course, is a town of kirtan, as I'm sure you've experienced. Sometimes it seems like every third house is a temple, with chanting going on. Most of the houses, most of the temples, have some small loudspeaker system to amplify the chanting. I just loved walking those streets, listening to the songs, listening to the kirtans.

Right. But what happened? I'm anxious to know if you saw Maharaji at that time.

So I was sitting in Maharaji's temple, the courtyard of the temple, which is a Hanuman temple, and I was relishing the chant of Hare Krishna, Hare Krishna, Krishna Krishna, Hare Hare/ Hare Rama, Hare Rama, Rama Rama, Hare Hare. It was coming out of the loudspeakers and the chanters sounded like celestial beings. I could almost see them reaching up to the heavens, you know? It was such beautiful singing.

Anyway, people started gathering, sitting around, waiting for Maharaji and listening to the chanting. There was a tremendous air of expectation. Everyone was coming in and bringing offerings of food and placing them on a wooden platform. The place felt calm, and people were meditative. And then, suddenly, forcefully, Maharaji burst out of his room. Prior to this, the peace in the courtyard was so deep, so strong. But then Maharaji's doors burst open—you know those hinged wooden doors, the really large ones you see in India? The doors burst open and smashed against the outside of the building, making a loud noise. Out he prances, like a big elephant. There are guys trying to hold him up, but they can't keep up with him. He bounds across the table and starts talking, three or four conversations at once and throwing food around. It was just madness.

He was speaking in English?

No, no. In Hindi. But he spoke to Westerners. His close disciple, Dada Mukherji, was translating. But it was unlike anything I'd ever experienced. Suddenly, I felt like I was in this three-ring circus. In fact, he threw some food and it hit me in the chest. [both laugh]

It's like, "What's going on here?"

Right, right. We were crying because we were laughing so hard. Then he looked to my girlfriend—the girl I was traveling with at the time—and he said, "Who's your guru?" She looked at him and mentioned the name of our previous teacher. That kind of surprised me because by now it was clear that we weren't following him anymore.

Maybe she just didn't know what else to say.

Yeah, maybe she didn't know what else to say. Right. He said, "Oh, that's Ananda Baba, the railroad clerk. You Americans are so easily deceived."

Ahh.

Yeah. He knew the guy in an entirely different light. But so much stuff was happening at once. Right after that exchange with my girlfriend, this Indian man comes up to him and sits down in front of him cross-legged, and Maharaji hits him on the head, on the forehead, and the guy goes into what appears to be some kind of trance. A couple of other Indian men come in and carry the guy off.

And by now, I'm saying to myself, "Oh, man, I guess this is just the guru shtick all over again. Here's another one. Watch out." Maharaji told my friend, who I was traveling with, "Go in there and poke his eyes, and see if he is still breathing." My friend went in there and came out a little while later, saying, "Well, I don't know, I poked his eyes and he didn't blink. I couldn't detect any breath, but I don't know." So, in retrospect, I think it was really funny; he was totally playing with my mind.

But all judgment was suspended. It wasn't like, "This is my guru—I love him and he loves me." Rather, it was like, "Wow, what an amazing, intoxicating scene. I can't go anywhere else. This is so cool." So I just stayed there, listening to the kirtan and sitting in front of Maharaji for hours every day.

He made sure we had great food, and he would engage in many simultaneous conversations with people about their lives, their families, their jobs. Now and then, he'd get very quiet, whispering, "Ram, Ram, Ram, Ram, Ram." Now and then he would say a few words of teaching—but the real teaching was simply his presence. Then he would tell the Westerners to sing kirtan. So, for hours we would just sing different kirtans. Without a leader, really. Different people would say, "Okay, let's sing that song," and so we'd all start singing. And that was kind of the way we'd pass the time. It was singing and eating.

Was the food consecrated—was it *prasada*? Or was it whatever you happened to pick up in the market?

It was definitely *prasada*, offered to the Deities and to the guru. It was food that was cooked in the temple. Cooked and offered, so it was all *prasada*. But big meals, many courses. It wasn't just *dahl* or something. It was all *prasada*.

Well, what more needs to be said? You're getting the purification of the *prasada* and the kirtan.

And the divine love of a Maha-siddha! Every day I would wake up very early and just dash through the streets of Vrindavan to get to the ashram. And then one morning, when I arrived, the doors to the back courtyard were locked. And I was told to go away. They said that Maharaji had left during the night and that they didn't know when he was coming back. They didn't tell anyone where he was going. Remember, at this point, I wasn't feeling that this was my guru. But still, you know, my heart just broke. I suddenly felt like my beloved had departed—this feeling that seemed to come out of nowhere. I didn't even know that I felt that strongly about him.

So even though you weren't thinking in terms of a guru, you had developed some attachment for him.

But I wasn't aware of it. Until that moment. And it was more than some attachment. It was the feeling that the beloved of my heart had left me. It was huge. I didn't know what to do, except to keep coming to the temple every day, hoping he'd return. But instead of going to the back, to be with Maharaji, I would sit in front of the big, beautiful *murti* of Hanuman, and I'd sing. From that moment, singing became fully connected to the deepest longing in my heart—to longing and pain that I hadn't even known I had.

I'd been singing kirtan for years, but at this point—because of Maharaji's sudden disappearance—it became the life support that kept my heart and soul alive. It became the very expression of my innermost feelings. I was singing to desperately connect with my beloved.

That's the heart of kirtan.

I'm not sure what happened, but because of him, when Maharaji wasn't there anymore, everything really changed.

Sort of like "love in separation." This is known as *viraha-bhakti* in the Vaishnava tradition, though there it's directed toward Krishna Himself.

Yeah, well, there's a parallel there. The thing is, I hadn't been aware of love *until* the separation. Because I was so involved in the daily *lila*, in my everyday life, and because I was just nineteen years old. It took Maharaji's sudden disappearance to begin the process of waking me up to my own self, my own feelings, a process that's still continuing today.

Sometimes separation serves to enhance one's love.

Hmm. Right. I don't know. I will say that my relationship with Maharaji has changed thousands of times, and continues to change, because my perception is just my perception, which is limited by my own understanding and by my own intellect. There are some things that the mind can't understand, and exactly who the guru is and what our relationship is to him — that's a couple of those things. I believe that the relationship with one's guru is really so deep — it's so ancient and so beyond the mind. My understanding has evolved and changed over the years, and still, really, I know nothing.

Did you make any lasting friendships at that time, with other disciples of Neem Karoli Baba?

Yeah. Well, we developed a lot of lasting relationships; but not necessarily friendships. We're like a huge dysfunctional family with a lot of love for each other.

There's a bond.

There's a bond, right.

I have the same thing with ISKCON people from when I joined those many years ago. There's a bond even if I don't really know them.

The few people that I actually went to India with, you know, who I traveled with, are surprisingly still some of my closest friends. So that's quite a long friendship. It's amazing to still have people in my life from that time. What was that, almost forty years ago?

Almost forty years. It's amazing that we can talk about forty years ago!

Yes, because some aspects of it seem *so* present. Like time doesn't exist. One thing I know for sure: My life changed at that moment, all those years ago. I was a planet flying through the universe without any center of gravity. Maharaji became my sun! And he gave me the practice of kirtan to nurture the sweet seed of devotion that he planted inside of me. Later on, several months later, I had some experiences, particularly in dreams . . .

Had you already returned to the West?

No, I was still in India. I was once in Allahabad — because we were told that Maharaji was going to arrive there, at a certain place. And I was waiting for him, wallowing in the fact that my girlfriend had just broken up with me because she loved this other guy. I had my first experience of bacterial dysentery at that time, too. So I was pretty sick and depressed, staying in this little apartment, and every day I was going to this private home where Maharaji was expected to appear. I was just sitting around, doing kirtan, and waiting for him to show up.

That night I went to bed and had a dream in which I was waiting for Maharaji at the train station in Allahabad, and it was just me there. Finally, Maharaji stepped off the train onto the platform, opened his blanket and wrapped his arms around me and I wrapped my arms around him. We both wept and wept, continuously, with the sense of, "Finally, we're together again. Finally, I'm home."

Reunited.

At that point I woke up, totally euphoric, and I looked at the clock. It was 1:28, or something like that — you'll see why the exact time was important — and then I went back to sleep. In the morning, I went to that private home again, where everyone was waiting for Maharaji, and there was a very different energy there. Everyone was talking softly and scurrying around very cautiously. I asked someone, "What's up?" and they said, "Maharaji arrived last night. He got off the train at 1:28 in the morning."

There's a divine connection, no doubt.

In fact, I didn't even need that person to tell me, because the dream was so strong. But maybe there was a part of me that needed it confirmed. It was in this dream/*darshan* that Maharaji revealed to me our eternal connection. I knew that he was my guru, although to this day I don't really know what that means . . .

It certainly doesn't hurt when you get some kind of affirmation.

No, it doesn't hurt, because the mind tends to doubt. It's one of the things my mind does quite well.

So, anyway, years and years pass by. And my life went through many ups and downs—many dark places. I wasn't a happy-go-lucky young *yogi*. I went through some very painful relationships, and various addictions . . .

Addictions?

Yeah. Drugs and drinking, trying to get away from myself. And still through it all, I did kirtan. That's what saved me. Whether it was on my own in my own home or with others, I still did *japa*—I still chanted. It was always with me, no matter what. It kept my connection to God and to my guru and to my own soul, sometimes by the barest thread. There were times when I was pretty out there. I don't know why exactly, but I do know that Maharaji was always holding me. And there was some part of me that always felt I didn't deserve his love.

Humility.

No, not humility, but rather a deep sense of unworthiness. I always believed in God; I always believed in spirit. Just the same, part of me believed that God didn't care about me because I was below His radar; I wasn't deserving of His grace. So I created a life—on a subliminal level, unconsciously—where I kind of fought away the light.

I was conflicted; there were two sides of me. Both sides were very alive. One side was devoted to spirituality and kirtan and so on, and the other believed that I belonged to darkness, and I acted in that way, too. But now I'm more thankful than anything else, because the light side is now winning out. I'm actually thankful for all my experiences, because even the darkest of those experiences give me a sense of humanity, and a sense of compassion—a sense of understanding, so I can relate to others.

I was going to say that, too. The dark experiences, in some odd way, could have contributed to your success—well, success might be the wrong word—your accessibility. Your kirtan speaks to people, perhaps partly because they can relate to you. They see you as someone like them, but you have this extra thing, this kirtan, and so you can share that with them.
　　As Sri Chaitanya says, "If you chant the holy name in a humble state of mind—which is the proper way to chant—then you can chant consistently." Your darker experiences seem to have created a sort of humility for you, and people can sense that, and they respond to that.

Well, maybe so, maybe so. I certainly have so much . . . gratitude. I see the power of God's name. I've been to the bottom and back, and kirtan is what helped me get back. I guess that's what I'm saying. Kirtan was with me all along, and that helps me believe in the power of prayer.

Sure, because you see that the holy name brought you to your present state. Now, let's allow the reader to follow you on that journey. You went back to the West, and then what happened? Maybe you could briefly describe that period and how it led to the making of CDs, explaining when and how you achieved your current popularity. What happened after you met your guru?

Well, briefly . . .

I know we're talking about many years . . .

Yeah, 1973 to 1990. So a lot went down in terms of my life and my music. I came back and held down a variety of jobs—one of which was extremely interesting. I was living in the ashram of Swami Muktananda, and the reason I was living there was because they gave me room and board in exchange for kirtan—they wanted me to sing a little bit every day, leading their group in devotional chanting.

This was in the West?

Right, in Oakland, California. So I thought this is a great thing for me. I was living like an ascetic at that point. I was living there, in fact, when Maharaji died. That was a very strange, sobering moment for me because I always thought that I would just go back to him, to spend time with him, but it was always tomorrow, tomorrow, tomorrow. "I've got plenty of time." Right. And suddenly Maharaji died and I realized that I didn't have plenty of time. It was kind of harsh, but, you know . . . life went on. I started getting different jobs; I got married, and I got divorced . . .

Children?

Well, Ezra Gopal is almost three years old now.

Oh! Congratulations!

We'll get to that. But I don't know how to summarize this.

It's difficult, I know. It's because we're trying to cover a lot of space in a short time.

Well, let me say this: After I came home from India, from that first trip, people would invite me to lead kirtan, all over the place. And so I did that, and there was no sense of it being a career of any sort. It was a real challenge for me because I've always been a shy person, particularly, as I was saying before, because of my struggles with feeling at ease with my own voice, which still continues to this day. But when people would ask me to do kirtan, I felt like it was Maharaji asking me to do it. Like it was coming from above.

Still, life went on. I was involved with the Maharaji community. I toured a bunch with Ram Dass, which was really fun. I really loved it and it also gave me a taste of large audiences. Actually, when I was younger, I wasn't interested in becoming a performer or a recording artist. I just wanted to play music, and my vision of myself was really as being this musician *yogi* — musician/ *yogi*/ *sadhu*/ shaman/ healer. That was my desired self-image.

That's kind of what you became.

Strangely, yeah. Although, really, I imagined myself on a hill with a little house and well . . . no, it's pretty much the same. [laughter] I just got a television about a week ago. Someone gave us a TV, so that kind of destroys the asceticism aspect.

Anyway, when I got back from India that first time, I was studying Indian music again. I was studying with Ali Akbar Khan and just singing and playing *sarod*, and just absorbing myself in that kind of stuff. I made enough money to just barely get by, taking odd jobs, doing this and that. Then my first marriage started to dissolve, and I got into playing electric guitar again; I put a band together. It was a sort of sophisticated punk band. It wasn't punk rock in the raw sense, but it was coming out of that same place, with a bit more musical sophistication. I was really expressing a lot of anger . . .

What year was this?

Oh, the 1970s. It was somewhere in the late-'70s. Then we started recording and trying to do some stuff like that, and I got into a reggae band with a Jamaican guy, which was great training for me. We started traveling around together.

I loved some of that reggae stuff on "Shiva Station."

Yeah, I just love reggae, and playing with the Jamaicans was really an education for me. Also at that time, I started using more drugs and drinking, too. I was out in that world. Then I got into a Top 40 band. This was a trip for me because I had to sing. I wasn't the only singer, but I sang, since we covered a lot of different kinds of material requiring several voices. This was scary as hell. But it was also challenging, in a good way, and I worked at it. I sang Al Green songs at the time, too, and some of my other favorite singers—I really worked on learning how to sing that stuff.

Like who? Who are some of your favorite singers?

Well, I have Indian singers that I love, but in the Western world, Al

Green is one of my all-time favorites. Strangely enough, Bob Dylan was one of my favorites, too.

Yeah, I can understand that.

But it's bizarre because he's not a technically good singer. Not really. I love John Lennon's singing. Otis Redding, Stevie Wonder, Marvin Gaye. Those kinds of singers I just adore. Soul singers, you know, real singers.

Now, about that Top 40 band . . .

Top 40 band, traveling around, drinking a lot. But still, I had a beautiful *murti* of Hanuman in my home. I was singing to him every day, and every Saturday I would do a longer *puja*, which a friend of mine from India, an older mentor, of sorts, suggested I do. It was a very funny, strange life for me, to have both extremes going on at the same time, the dark and the light.

Then I had a pretty serious car accident, and I sort of bowed out of the scene for some time. That's when I got into narcotics.

What kind of narcotics?

Codeine, for pain in my back. The doctor that gave me that . . . well, let's just say that he was somewhat irresponsible. So that got me more involved with drugs. Because I couldn't work, I couldn't do anything else — my back was really bad.

But through it all, I always felt connected to my spiritual side. There was some part of me that had to play itself out. I don't know why. I can only have faith that Maharaji was taking me through what I needed to go through. From that point on I got deeper into drugs, of all kinds, deeper into drinking, into that whole world. All the while I was developing my music, the Eastern and Western style music, the confluence of both worlds.

It was in that period when I started making my CDs, which is amazing to me. Because, so many times, people have come up to me and said, "I've listened to your CD and it gave me so much light and strength — there's so much spirituality in it." But for me, the CDs were expressing my anguish.

I can see that. People were able to relate to your kirtan because it spoke to them—everybody has some degree of anguish; everyone's life is touched by pain. At the same time, though, your kirtan offered them hope; it brought them to another place altogether.

All of that was also going into my kirtan. To make a long story short, given the limited amount of time we have to go through my whole life, I should just quickly tell you how amazing my life is now and how full of light and full of grace it is. I've been totally away from drinking and anything like that for quite a while. I am married to the most beautiful, wonderful, amazing, divine Goddess . . .

You were always blessed—it just manifests in different ways at different times. But a good wife is always a special blessing . . .

She's a Brazilian woman that I met in Sao Paulo, Brazil—she's a yoga teacher, a healer. We have the most beautiful child, Ezra Gopal, whom I've already mentioned—he's our little Baby Krishna.

Sweet.

Externally, I'm still doing the same kind of stuff that I've been doing in terms of music, in terms of kirtan. And being with people, in all my workshops, I'm very, very honest about all I've gone through in life. I often tell them about my times of joy and my times of sadness—how kirtan has always been the savior for me, bringing me to a deeper place that reigns beyond all that. Nowadays, along with my practice of kirtan and my chanting of mantra, I always spend some time—even if it's just a couple of minutes each day—in gratitude, in conscious gratitude. You know, I am constantly taking a moment to thank God, to thank my guru, for the gifts in my life, even if I wasn't always able to fully appreciate them. The gifts were always there. The grace was always there. Now by that same grace, I'm able to let it in, in a way that I wasn't able to before. And the kirtan just keeps going deeper and deeper.

So maybe we should jump to that and talk about how it became a part of your professional life, how it evolved in that way.

Before even saying that, let's say, "How did it become the heart and soul of my spiritual life?" Because, again, I didn't plan for that to happen. I didn't know. How could you plan that? Some people plan those things, I guess. But I feel that it was planted in me. I feel that Maharaji gave me the blessing of devotion. He gave it to everyone around him, but he gave it to me, too. Now, devotion can be such an ephemeral state of heart, state of mind, state of consciousness. It can seem to come and go, but along with that he gave me the gift of God's name. He gave God's names as a way to nurture that devotion and to water the plant of *bhakti*, to let it—however slowly—take root.

So, in this way, for you, devotion would not be ephemeral. Rather, through the gift of chanting, you had something tangible, something that would allow you to keep devotion in your life, instead of slipping through your fingers like so many grains of sand.

Exactly! And that's how it implanted itself in my life. So then how did it become a profession? It's funny. From there it goes back to the long development of my own music—my journey into Indian music, Indian classical music and Indian folk music and devotional music, as well as Western music, that I grew up with—and how that started long ago.

It seems that Bengali kirtan, especially, informs your style. I wanted to ask you about that.

Well, that's the Bauls of Bengal. They influenced me tremendously, in my melodic style, the singing style, and also in terms of instrumentation. The little miniature *sarod* that I play, the *dhotara,* is a Baul instrument. A lot of the rhythms that I'm drawn to are from the Bengali region. That's where I got it—that's the planet of kirtan. The Bauls taught me about the world of *bhakti,* where emotions are our fuel, our rocket fuel to get to *bhava,* higher spiritual emotions, which in turn takes us to that spiritual planet of *bhakti.* Kirtan is the catalyst.

I lived in West Bengal, in a house with some amazing people. And that changed my life early on. This takes us back to our earlier discussion, when I first went to India. I lived in Bengal for seven months at that time, and this one beautiful Baul musician would come to our house three times a week. None of us could speak Bengali and he couldn't speak English—it was rather like a comedy. But there was beautiful communication in terms of musical connection.

What was his name?

Baidyanath Das, a remarkable guy. We also met Purna Das Baul, who is rather well known. At the time, we had a little ceremony in which he pronounced my friend and me, "international Bauls." Anyway, while all that was going on, I was also exploring and developing in Western music, as I mentioned, and playing all kinds of things. Finally, around the time of "Footprints," around the late 1980s, I started combining the two worlds. I had experimented a little bit before that, but that was the first real, serious experiment, and it just clicked. It just went from there.

All the musical stuff that I had absorbed became like the foundation, the bedrock, of all my kirtans and other musical compositions. And it still is. Even if I'm just playing *harmonium* and singing—because most of the time nowadays I'm just traveling with a *harmonium*—all my past, all my music, impacts on what I do. Even though the melodies that I make up, and the chords I accompany them with, are usually very, very Indian. Sometimes they're very, very Western, too. I'm a mix, and that's that.

It's interesting to see how you're a merger, in a sense, of everything you have experienced up to this point. From Hendrix, to Dylan, to the Beatles, to seeing those Hare Krishnas on the Lower East Side of Manhattan, to the Bauls of Bengal, to your guru . . .

Well, that's all *in* me.

For sure. And that's what we wanted to uncover in this interview. But you've actually been able to produce music that conveys these influences. Your work enables people hear how you've gone through all these things. It can all be heard in your music.

Right. All the things I love.

I wanted to ask you about "Shiva Station," because that's probably one of my favorite CDs of all time. I just love that CD.

That was done during a time when my band was playing a lot. We were performing constantly, and it was quite a phenomenon because we were doing this music, which is basically devotional music, over very Western rhythmic structures. We were playing nightclubs and bars, and it really felt like we were bringing two worlds together.

Live . . . we were basically a rock band. I wouldn't call it rock music, but we had the energy of a rock band. We were loud and raw around the edges, and really explosive. I tried to capture that on the CD, "Shiva Station." It's hard to capture that live vibe in a recording studio. I still don't feel that I have ever successfully gotten that. But "Shiva Station" came close to it. It really reflected what we were doing live, and there are a lot of jumps from very meditative to explosive and then back to very meditative.

You worked with Bill Laswell there?

He did the mixing on that album. He's very diversified, and a fascinating guy. I kind of thought of him as like a Zen master. After that, I did a gig and his wife sang with me. She's an Ethiopian singer named Gigi—absolutely fantastic. So we did a gig, inviting her to sing on a couple of songs. That was a very cool collaboration.

Your tune "Never Turn Away"—I just love that song. Usually I don't like kirtan CDs that incorporate English lyrics, but that song moves me on a very deep level.

Well, "Shiva Station" isn't essentially a "kirtan" album. It's a devotional album with lots of different moods and flavors. That's the Bauls of Bengal singing on "Never Turn Away." Those are some of the guys that I met in Bengal, singing on that song. It was a sample from a Baul CD, and I went very out of my way to make sure we got permission and that they were aware of it. I saw Purna Das and I specifically told him about it. I love that song, too, especially because of the Baul singing. The English words are so expressive of what I was feeling—what I still feel about life, about devotion, and about what this crazy world really has to offer.

For me, as a Westerner, I sometimes need to express this in my own tongue, in my own language. But, these days, I'm actually much more at ease expressing these feelings through kirtan which, really, is a universal language.

That's the last thing I was going to ask you: What is your philosophy of kirtan? Tell me what you think about kirtan, what it does, how it affects people, and so on.

Okay. Well, I don't really have a philosophy. After all these years, kirtan still amazes me. It's still a huge mystery to me. What does it do? How does it do it? Well, technically, we sing, and the repetition of the mantras and the beauty of the music enter our hearts. In one chant we can go through a rainbow of emotions that in our daily life we're not really feeling, or at least not admitting to ourselves. In life, most of us live a very narrow field of human feelings, because the alternative is not allowed, or it's uncomfortable, you know? But in my life, part of my own healing has been for me to become comfortable with all of the feelings inside of me.

Kirtan is such an amazing form of worship because it can carry and express and hold and nurture everything inside of us. By going through the repetition, of course, the mind just kind of chills out. We go into meditation without even really knowing we've gone into meditation, not even caring that we're going into meditation. Because the mind takes a backseat to the heart.

Mantra literally means "mind release."

That's perfect. That's what happens. Then the heart steps forward and unfolds—it unfolds and opens. And we cross the bridge of God's names to the land of divine *rasa*. Also, with kirtan we're encouraged to sing with abandon. Again, this is something most of us don't ordinarily do, so we can easily have trouble with it. But, step-by-step, we enter into that space. The walls of the heart seem to come down. And behind those walls is God and His infinite divine love.

We get there simply by not blocking ourselves, by not judging ourselves: "I should be feeling this. I should be experiencing that." Just hear the sound of the mantra and repeat it without preconceived notions or getting in your own way. Feel whatever you're feeling and let happen whatever happens. The great mystery here is that God is in His name. There's no difference between the name and He—or She—who is named. So we take that name and sing it over and over again, and by doing that, God's presence is felt deeply in our hearts and souls. God is always manifesting within us anyway, but we don't perceive it.

The sound of His name awakens us to that.

On some level, it takes us into that place and pulls us away from the illusion that God is somewhere else . . . I don't know. I see it with so many people when they actually open up to kirtan. Everybody comes with different motives, with different intentions, different reservations. Including me. One day my inner world is different than another day. It's always changing. And yet, we sing kirtan for a while and the externals, the hardness . . . melts away. To some extent. For some, just a little; for others, a lot.

I think it depends on our spiritual evolution, on where we're coming from.

Maybe it does. But I really don't know anything about spiritual evolution. I do feel that there's an element of grace, though. We perform our spiritual practices and we purify ourselves and maybe we become better people, hopefully, more compassionate, and all that stuff. But grace, to me, is something entirely different. Grace comes from the absolute love of God. Love coming from the universe, from the angels, from the guru, and in our love for them. It has nothing to do with our spiritual practice—with what we do or don't do. Grace isn't a work exchange or a business contract. It has nothing to do with our efforts.

Right. It's God's gift.

So somebody could come to a kirtan and have been wired in a world of absolute ego and still something in there will touch them.

Not always, again, and you never quite know why it will happen sometimes and other times it just remains far, far away.

Well, you're right, it's grace. It's mercy. Really: It's the kindness of God, His causeless mercy.

Causeless mercy. That's a beautiful and true phrase. That's what you get from the yoga of sound, too. It attracts that mercy. So sometimes it comes of its own accord, and sometimes it's drawn to you by kirtan and other practices. I would say that grace is natural and fine, and it will definitely come in its own time. No question. And kirtan is like a magnet, inviting and begging grace to enter our hearts and our lives. Kirtan is a most precious thing, something to be cherished and practiced with total gratitude, and those who learn how to enter into it will feel God's grace and presence as the closest of the close, the dearest of the dear—our true beloved.

For more information contact:
www.jaiuttal.com

VAIYASAKI DAS

Born in London, Vaiyasaki came of age in Winnipeg, Canada, and after many years in the music business —
and a personal search for the divine — he is now one of the premier singers on the kirtan circuit. Starting out as a rock and blues guitarist with a penchant for singing, his taste for Indian culture came early on.

By 1970, he found himself back in London and enamored by Krishna devotion. Soon, in 1973, he was committed to the path, and, just two years later, he received formal initiation from His Divine Grace A. C. Bhaktivedanta Swami Prabhupada, the founder and spiritual preceptor of the International Society for Krishna Consciousness (ISKCON).

On Prabhupada's request, he journeyed to India, both for personal purification and to proclaim the renaissance of Chaitanya Mahaprabhu's bhakti movement in the modern era. He traveled the entire subcontinent, and Southeast Asia, distributing his spiritual master's books.

By 1978, he arrived in Bangladesh, where he fully imbibed the culture through his pores, becoming fluent in Bengali and learning the ways of the local people. On a boat trip down the Meghna River, he chanced upon a local kirtan band on their way to a festival. Deciding to follow these happy minstrels and their soulful kirtan music, he would also attend that same festival, changing his life forever. It was there that he discovered the ancient Bengali art of Raga-kirtan, which touched his soul in

the deepest possible way. Never before had he heard such depthful sing-
ing, and he resolved to use his own considerable vocal talents to spread
this technique around the world.

His first tape was released in 1982, with numerous CDs following that,
all of which are now considered seminal in the yoga/kirtan/world music
universe. Vaiyasaki is a much sought-after performer, conducting work-
shops and leading yoga festivals and retreats worldwide.

✳ ✳ ✳

So, to begin, I like to ask people about their background: legal name,
date of birth, and so on.

Are you also issuing visas? [laughter] My birth name is Per Sinclair.
I was born in London, England, April 25, 1943. We immigrated to
Canada when I was almost six, and I grew up in Canada.

Some more background would be useful—musical inclinations, the
type of work you did, and so on.

My mother sent me for violin and music theory lessons when I was
seven years old, and I sang in my school choir. I was something
of a classical violinist, but at thirteen I switched to guitar, mainly
influenced by blues, rock, and soul music. After that, I went to college but found it boring. I ended up working for IBM in 1967.

What did you do for IBM?

I was with the Scientific Services Division in Toronto. As a representative of IBM, I would help my clients run their programs on big
mainframe computers. Two of my clients were from India. One of
them, Bhanu Sud, would tell mystical stories about India, attracting my curiosity. These stories touched me in a meaningful way.

The second person was Mr. Sengupta. He was a Bengali Vaishnava
and talked about otherworldly things, in general, and Krishna, specifically. The talks really peaked my interest. He wore a pearl ring
and he said the pearl would counteract bad influences—it would
bring out positive astrological benefits. That was intriguing.

When he saw that I was interested in his culture and tradition, he invited me to his home for dinner one Friday evening, and so I went there with my girlfriend at that time, Linda. It was very interesting because . . .

What year was this?

Summer of 1968.

So, exotic Indian things appealed to a lot of hippies at the time . . .

Well, I was working at IBM, remember, so I wasn't a hippie.

And music . . .

Well, I was into music my whole life, really, since I was a kid. Anyway, I went to Mr. Sengupta's home that evening, and when I arrived, his wife was in the kitchen. She came out briefly and he introduced us. We sat and chatted in the living room about things from India while his wife finished preparing food in the kitchen. Linda had just come back from a trip to California, and in San Francisco she saw these people playing musical instruments, wearing robes, shaved heads, with ponytails in the back — and she was mentioning it, casually. At this point, Mr. Sengupta said, "Oh! Those are Vaishnavas!"

The word "Vaishnava" caught my attention; I don't know why. I had never heard it before, but the word stuck in my mind. During the conversation, his wife came in with a tray of food, walked past us, and put it on the mantle and began ringing a bell. I didn't know what was going on then, but now I understand that she was doing an offering — saying prayers and turning the food into *prasadam*. That's all I remember because I wasn't aware of those kinds of things at the time, but it was the first time I had *prasadam*. Mr. Sengupta saw that I was interested because of my questions. It was enjoyable for him, too, because someone from IBM wanted to know about his culture and tradition. People respond to that. When you show interest in someone's tradition, you show interest in them.

At one point, he said, "We have a temple where the Indian community meets every Sunday. Would you like to come?" So I responded: "Sure, what time?" So that Sunday morning, in the summer of 1968, I had my first Hindu temple experience.

Do you remember where it was, or anything specific about it?

The building was in downtown Toronto, an old building where they have lofts. I climbed the stairs to the third floor and entered a long room with a little stage at one end. There were pews in there, too. I sat down toward the back because the service was already in full swing. The place was packed with Indian people and on the stage some musicians were playing *tabla, harmonium, kartals,* and singing. I listened carefully to the sounds, closing my eyes and trying to get into it, because that's how I listened to music at home.

As I focused more and more, I made out the words of the *maha-mantra*: Hare Krishna, Hare Krishna, Krishna Krishna, Hare Hare/Hare Rama, Hare Rama, Rama Rama, Hare Hare.

These were not ISKCON people . . .

No, I had never heard of ISKCON. These were Indians. Mr. Sen-gupta was from Bengal. "Sengupta" is a Bengali name. It was very interesting because I was moved by the chanting. I mean, *really* moved. Tears were coming to my eyes. Somehow, I was emotionally involved. It was more than just enjoying it, and I didn't know why. I remember thinking to myself, "Why is this affecting me like this?"

Something was awakened . . .

Because I had been listening to music my whole life. So that was my first experience hearing the *maha-mantra* and associating with Indians and enjoying their food, and so on.

At the same time, I was reading a small paperback edition of the *Bhagavad Gita* and becoming more and more bored with IBM. I was starting to ask those perennial questions: "What is the meaning of life? Where do we come from? What's it really all about?"

And so life moved on, attempting to bring you answers. Where did you go from there?

In the fall of 1968 I left a promising career at IBM and enrolled at Simon Fraser University, in Vancouver, to study anthropology. I had been to college before, but I decided to try again to answer some of my questions—to study the origins of mankind. So I looked into these things through anthropology but at the same time I was reading yoga books by Ramakrishna, Vivekananda, Yogananda, *Autobiography of a Yogi*, like that. But again, the second time around—I got bored with university education. It was just not taking me where I wanted to go.

You saw that you had to go inward, that you had to look into things in a more spiritual way.

Well, right, I began getting deeper into yoga. In Vancouver I came across the Krishna devotees chanting in the street and I thought, "Oh, these are the Vaishnavas. These are the people that Linda saw in San Francisco." I took their magazine but I was thinking — "They're doing their thing, and I'm doing my thing." I really didn't get into it because I didn't understand Bhakti-yoga at that time. I kept seeing them, but I just let it go.

Around this time I also wanted to further my career in music, because I had a band, a power trio called "Genesis," and all of us could sing . . .

Was it before the popular band by the same name?

Long before, yeah. Anyway, to carry on: I began to think about where to go to further my career. Either Los Angeles or London. Those were the places for moving forward with music, professionally. So I chose London, because I knew people there, and because I was born there. One day, I remember walking down Oxford street and I heard that distinct cymbal sound, "ching, ching, ching/ ching, ching, ching," and I thought: "Wow, they're here, too." So I came across the Krishna devotees again. I liked it, but again I let it pass. Around this time, I joined a band called "Quintessence."

Where you playing keyboards?

No, guitar.

Oh, right. . . . Because you're such a good *harmonium* player now, I thought . . .

Guitarist, always the guitars. So, at the first rehearsal, something interesting happened. The lead singer's name was Phil Jones, but he had this other name, Shiva. That's what people called him. He was from Australia, and he was there with his girlfriend: She was a Krishna devotee, an initiated disciple of His Divine Grace A. C. Bhaktivedanta Swami Prabhupada.

What was her name?

Jill. When she found out I was vegetarian, she decided I was ready to hear what she had to say.

As a side issue, how is it that you became a vegetarian—is there a story there?

How I became vegetarian. Well, in Simon Fraser University, I was into yoga, experimenting with consciousness and things like that. At the time, I was a broke college student, trying to scrape together money just to get by. I remember I was alone for Thanksgiving 1968. My Thanksgiving dinner was a box of Ritz crackers. But soon after Thanksgiving, my group of friends went camping in the mountains, and we visited some people who were strict vegetarians. I remember the food didn't impress me much, but what did impress me was that they were trying to live a cruelty-free diet. That was between Thanksgiving and Christmas in 1968. So, New Year's Day, 1969, I made a resolution that I was going to become a vegetarian.

And you've been one ever since.

Yeah.

So, okay, back to Quintessence.

Jill became my friend and she began inviting me back to her place and talking a lot about Indian philosophy, Bhakti-yoga, and so on. I was kind of impressed, because I had done a lot of reading and I thought I was pretty well-versed on Eastern philosophy. But she was off the charts! She was far better informed than I was. And as I argued with her—because we disagreed on some points—she defeated me many times, in a gentle and good-hearted way. When

I complimented her on her deep understanding, she always said that it was her guru's knowledge, not hers. So we became really good friends and I became interested to meet her guru. And, naturally, she wanted me to visit the Krishna temple and introduce me to other devotees.

Let's hear about your first visit to a Krishna temple.

My first time was at the London Radha-Krishna temple, at 7 Bury Place, one evening. They were doing *tulasi-puja*, dancing around Krishna's favorite plant. Seemed strange, but I was open. And all of a sudden, Peter Sellers came in . . .

Really?

There was a devotee who brought Peter Sellers to the temple, and he honored the traditions of the temple: he folded his palms in traditional *pranams* and went down on his knees to offer obeisance before the deities. He obviously knew the culture. I thought it was interesting that he was there — it seemed cool, and celebrities were into it, which made it even more cool. And then I took *prasadam*, which I didn't particularly like. I was on a macrobiotic diet at the time, just eating dates and drinking goat's milk. The *prasadam* just seemed too rich . . .

I would put a date in my mouth and then drink some goat's milk and chew them together so I would get sweet goat's milk. That was my diet at the time. I was living very simply and playing music and trying to make it in the music business. So the *prasadam* didn't attract me so much. The kirtan didn't attract me that much either, not at that time. The ashram singing didn't move me — I preferred the way the Indians chanted in Toronto. Plus, I was a musician — I was into really cool music and accomplished musicianship; so the simple temple chanting didn't attract me on that score, either. What attracted me, believe it or not, was that the devotees were always paying obeisance to one another, bowing down and showing respect and love to each other. And I was thinking: this is real humility. Because I had read that the real path to spiritual advancement is humility. And I could understand that. I had visited many other yoga groups by that time, and none showed this kind of humility. So that said something to me.

You visited various spiritual groups? Like who?

No need to mention names, but I visited all the popular groups at the time and it was only in the Krishna group that I saw this "bowing down" phenomenon. So, I thought, "Okay, this is a real sign of humility." I liked it.

Can you remember any specific experiences with the other spiritual groups?

I remember that Jill wanted to hear a famous *yogi* speak, so we went to hear him, because he was the guru. After he spoke, he asked for questions. She raised her hand and said, "Can you talk about death?" He was taken aback by that—he didn't know how to answer her and made a comment about the glory of life, something like that. After we left, she said she wasn't impressed—a true spiritualist knows about life *and* death, because death is a part of life. Ideally, life is a preparation for that final journey. That's what the *Gita* says. So, in this way, I was getting insights into the spiritual path, what to look for, what to focus on, etc.

Did you meet Prabhupada around this same time?

Yes, I met him in 1973, at the London Ratha Yatra Festival. At that time, George Harrison had donated a manor estate outside London, in the country, so we went there to help fix it up, because Srila Prabhupada was coming.

Had you gotten into chanting?

No, not yet. I was just hearing. I mean, the devotees were chanting, but it didn't mean that much to me, not during that period.

That's interesting.

Then the day of Ratha Yatra came, and during that parade, was the first time I saw Prabhupada. After that, I'd go to the temple to hear Prabhupada speak, give classes, *darshans*, everything.

Okay. So you saw Prabhupada, started chanting Hare Krishna, and you became serious about the path of *bhakti*.

Hmm. Prabhupada touched my heart and gave me the inspiration to commit to spiritual life. His chanting was so profound, full of spiritual emotions. His voice was ancient. The sound vibrations entered deep into my consciousness. I left London a year later in 1974, because my music career wasn't taking off as I had hoped it would. I went back to Canada and joined a band in Toronto. At that time, I would visit the Toronto Krishna temple where I met two devotees who had both been in bands before, so they knew how to talk to musicians about Krishna Consciousness. As soon as I arrived in Toronto, I found a band and we were gigging in clubs until 2 AM, most nights, and then, after the gig, I would pack up and drive to the temple. I'd get there about 3 AM, and the temple *pujari* — a really sweet guy — would be up, and he'd let me in. It was almost time for their morning service, which was way before sunrise, as in all Hare Krishna temples. I'd go in the temple room while he got everything ready for the pre-dawn *arati*, the morning service, and I'd chant *japa* on beads. So I'd be there for the morning program . . .

When did you sleep?

Let me tell you. After the *arati* service I would go up to the *brahmachari* ashram and crash. So I would sleep when most devotees were chanting *japa*, and during the scripture classes, too. I'd come back down for breakfast.

During the day, sometimes, they would go out for street chanting, and their kirtans were very good. They were structured, because those two devotees, Uttama-shloka and Vishvakarma, were musicians. I remember we were downtown doing this really incredible kirtan and I was thinking, "This is *real* music, street music, music for the people." So, here's where I developed a taste for chanting. Gradually, I left my band behind, put on robes, and . . .

Became a monk.

I was in Toronto for six months and then went to Los Angeles, because Prabhupada was coming to L.A. At the San Francisco Ratha Yatra Festival in 1975, I was initiated. That's where I got the name, "Vaiyasaki Das." I had met Prabhupada at the London Ratha Yatra Festival in '73. And then, at the San Francisco Ratha Yatra Festival, in July '75, I got initiated.

And you went from being Per Sinclair to Vaiyasaki Das. Prabhupada gave you that name.

Yes. "Vaiyasaki" is another name for Shukadev Goswami, a very important saint in ancient India. Shukadev is known to have attained perfection through kirtan, as depicted in the *Bhagavata Purana.* For me, I think it was a foretelling of sorts.

Hmm. Srila Prabhupada had a way of knowing those things, though, didn't he. Okay. When did it hit you that you could lead kirtan, that you could be a *kirtaniya*.

Well, in L.A. I didn't lead kirtan because they had so many great kirtan leaders there. Since there were great kirtans already, I didn't even consider leading back then.

Not even occasionally?

No. Nor did I do it in Toronto. Vishvakarma and Uttama-shloka did most of the leading in Toronto. But I was right at the front playing *kartals* and . . .

. . . And you soon became a kirtan leader?

Not until I went to India, which happened in autumn 1975. I was in Vrindavan for a few months, went to Bombay, and I ended up in Calcutta, spending some of my time in nearby Mayapur. Now I was in Bengal, the heartland of Chaitanya Mahaprabhu, original home of kirtan, and things started to change.

This is what happened. In 1977, some Bengali kirtan groups came to Mayapur and one particular group was tremendous. I just loved them. They were fantastic musicians, singers, everything. I was really attracted to that and wanted to do kirtan like that myself.

You knew how to play the *harmonium* at this point?

I didn't play *harmonium* at this point, no; that came in 1978 when I went to Bangladesh.

How did you come to go to Bangladesh?

Because I was traveling throughout Southeast Asia in 1977 with the Bhaktivedanta Book Trust (BBT) Library Party. We went to all the different countries distributing Prabhupada's books at every single library you can imagine. First we did all of India, and then we went to Thailand, Malaysia, Singapore, Indonesia, Bali, Hong Kong, and Philippines. We finished the Philippines in February 1978, and that was the time of the huge ISKCON Mayapur Festival; so we wanted to go back to Bengal for the 1978 festival. But on the way back, I said to my colleague, Satya Narayana, who was distributing books with me, "Why don't we go to Bangladesh? They probably have a few universities and colleges there."

Did you know Bengali at this point?

A little, yeah. I had been studying Sanskrit. And I knew Bengali because, when I was living in Mayapur, I had read that Prabhupada's guru predicted: "One day people from Western countries will come to Mayapur and they will learn Bengali, simply to relish the nectar of the *Chaitanya-charitamrita*." So when I read that, I decided I wanted to be part of that prediction. I gave up studying Sanskrit and started studying Bengali, so that I could be part of the prophecy. Anyway, on we went to Bangladesh. We ended up staying at the Gaudiya Math in Dhaka, the capital of Bangladesh.

Of course, we didn't just stay in Dhaka—we visited many places in Bangladesh, and after traveling to a few places we separated and went in different directions to different colleges somewhere else. Chandpur is a big place for boats. People travel by boat because there are so many rivers in Bangladesh. These are large motor launches, too, like buses, except on water. So we split up, and as soon as I got on my boat, I noticed at the end of the boat, a group of musicians with their Bengali instruments. There were seven or eight musicians. They looked really cool, with their instruments. So I thought, "It's a band. Real musicians. Great!"

Indian guys?

Yeah, of course. Bengalis. I was in Bangladesh. So I kind of wandered over and started chatting with them in Bengali. I told them I was also a musician. I asked, "What are you doing? Where are you going?" They told me that they were going to a festival—to do a gig. I was kind of excited.

I was hanging out with them and just really enjoying it, when all of a sudden the boat pulled up and docked. They said: "Haribol," and they got off. I watched them walking across a field, as the boat, with me on it, was about to pull out. And that's when I made a life-changing decision. As the boat started to take off, at the last second, I jumped off and ran after them! I just wanted to experience their music.

That brings to mind Malcolm Gladwell's recent book, *Blink*. It's the idea of thinking without thinking. In the blink of an eye, you make a decision, and your destiny unfolds as a result.

Right. That's true. Anyway, the town was called Mohanpur, and they were attending a festival there in honor of the passing of the host's father. So when I arrived, and the host saw me, a Westerner, he thought it was an auspicious omen of some sort, because he quickly discovered that I had adopted Bengali culture and tradition.

So you were accepted as part of the gang, so to speak, part of the group. And the festival host accepted you, too.

They were really impressed. You know, they took me to their temple and they saw that I knew the culture, and that I behaved like a Vaishnava. They fed me *prasadam*, and I was speaking a little Bengali, so they were intrigued, and thought it was auspicious. They were curious how I came to all of this, so I told them about what was happening in the West—how Srila Prabhupada came there and brought kirtan and Vedic culture, how young people were getting into Krishna, by Prabhupada's grace. So they gave me a room near

the band at the festival. They were called Gauranga Sampradaya —
that was the name of the band . . .

What kind of music was it?

Kirtan. *Raga-kirtan.*

Okay, it was kirtan. Because when you initially mentioned a band, with instruments, I pictured these Bengalis playing rock music.

No, no. They were playing *mridanga, harmonium,* flute, violin, *kartals.* They were a kirtan group.

Did you record their music?

You bet. I had a tape recorder, and I asked if I could record their kirtan. So they chanted four different *ragas* and I was totally knocked out by their singing, the devotion, the music. And after they finished, they called it a night. But I couldn't sleep — I was listening with my headphones all night. Fantastic kirtans like I had never heard before. Raga-kirtan.

It was completely different than what we usually think of as kirtan, and it was unlike any other kirtan I had experienced before. These Raga-kirtans were long and drawn out — very emotional — going through different phases, carefully delineated but fully spontaneous at the same time. No one in the West had ever heard kirtan music like this.

So tell me more about that festival.

Well, the next morning, the festival started, and there were six kirtan groups. So I made friends with another group, and I recorded them also. They were called Nityananda Sampradaya. So, that was pretty interesting. The two bands I met, one was called Gauranga Sampradaya and the other was called Nityananda Sampradaya — named after the two central deities of Gaudiya Vaishnavism, which is what I was into. I'm not sure about the other four groups — I just made friends with these two. I spent a good deal of time taping both groups, just feeling excited to have come into contact with people who were expert at chanting kirtan. I asked them about their next gigs, and they gave me their itinerary. I just wanted to go with them.

But first I would meet up with Satya Narayana back at the Gaudiya Math temple in Dhaka, and told him what had happened. I said that their next gig was in this town Sylhet, and that we should go there.

Did you keep up your program of distributing Prabhupada's books at the time?

Well, that was the plan. There was a college there, in Sylhet, so we could hear the band and do our service as well, distributing books. In every town, we did this. It worked well in Sylhet. We always went to a temple or an ashram, and they always welcomed us, because we were into their culture. We always asked to hear kirtan, and in Sylhet they brought out these four young boys, about eight or nine years old and they sang for us. It was fantastic — beautiful young voices, gorgeous melodies. And then we did the college, distributing books, and went to the festival, where I saw the Gauranga Sampradaya again and other bands . . .

So where does it go from there? You're developing a taste for kirtan but not quite leading kirtans yourself . . .

Subsequently, I went back to Mayapur, for the Mayapur Festival, and I was asked to go to Bangladesh again to start a Krishna center, an ashram.

Because you had some experience in that part of the world.

Right. So I accepted that service and left the Library party. That was a big decision. Once I made up my mind to do it, though, I actually started a center in Bangladesh. But even while doing that, I was always looking for kirtan groups at local festivals, and I was always hanging out with these kirtan musicians. Through that association, I started to learn the Bangladesh style of chanting and singing.

Okay, so that's how it evolved.

Yes. And I remember that as we met people, they would come to our ashram and they would play with us. I remember one guy, a *mridanga* player, said, "You are sounding just like a Bengali now." They sang so high—I could never sing those high notes. I was always learning to sing higher and higher, because they told me the higher you go the more *bhava* you experience. You can get more *amrita*, nectar, *ananda*, bliss, in the higher notes. So that's how I got into it. I traveled around the country and met all these groups while establishing the ISKCON ashram in Bangladesh.

And you were becoming more fluent in Bengali.

Yeah, and I was recording these great *kirtaniyas*, in these bands, and I would listen to those recordings over and over again. And that's really how I learned that style of kirtan—by listening to those recordings that I made. And I made many, many such recordings. Pure nectar!

Do you still have any of those recordings?

I still do, and I still listen to them. That was 1978, '79, and '80—I was recording there for three years.

In Bangladesh.

Yeah, and in '79 I brought some Bangladeshi devotees with me to the Mayapur Festival and we were chanting together. It wasn't quite Bangladeshi style, but it was different than the usual ISKCON style, too. And everybody really was attracted to our kirtans. So this became like a new phase in ISKCON kirtans . . .

Were you leading at all?

Oh, yeah. At this point, I was the kirtan leader, singing up front all the time. So then, in 1980, we went back to the Mayapur Festival and this time we had super *mridanga* players, we had learned how to play the *kartals* properly, and to chant and play Bangladeshi style—we were hot, and everyone knew it. Word had already spread in '79, so by the time we got to the Mayapur Festival in 1980, everybody knew about us. Everywhere we went, whenever we were chanting, there were like ten or twelve walkman recorders, and people would be recording it. They would say, "Come here and chant." We would go to this place and that place and everybody was recording us. Then we went back to Bangladesh after the festival. A year after that, I left Bangladesh and came to Europe. Wherever I went people said, "Oh! We love your tapes." Everybody knew me. Everybody knew my sound. I said, "I don't have any tapes!" But tapes were circulating, nonetheless.

People were making tapes of you and sending them back to the West?

Yes, so many tapes — made unprofessionally — were sent all around the world. After the festivals, devotees went home to their respective countries and made copies, and copies of copies, and shared them with their friends. This was the case in Europe, Australia, India, Africa, America . . . I didn't know anything about it. So, finally, I said to someone: Can I hear one of these tapes? And he let me hear it — that's when I realized they were recorded in Mayapur, at the festivals.

I'm sure you were encouraged that people liked your stuff.

That's right. But I thought, "God, this sounds horrible, and it's full of mistakes." You know, no quality control or anything. It was disturbing. And they were thinking: "How wonderful." So then when I came to America in 1982 I decided: "If people are going to listen to me, then at least I want it to be good quality, with quality control." All the tapes that people were listening to — I just didn't like them.

The idea of making more professional tapes occurred to me on the way to America, in Toronto. So I started recording there. And as I continued traveling in the summer of '82, making my way to L.A., I again recorded there. After a while, I took the best of what I recorded in Toronto and L.A. and I put out a cassette called, "Vrindavan Chandra." And it sold like hot cakes.

You mean mainly in ISKCON.

At the time, yes, but that constituted a huge amount of sales around the world—ISKCON is international, with many devotees and friends of the movement who are into kirtan. And then, a year later, I went into a studio with some Indian musicians in Los Angeles and recorded another album, "Transcendence." That was an incredible hit, even more so than the prior cassette. Everywhere I went, people would come up to me congratulating me and asking me to lead kirtan in their ashrams and temples, and at major festivals, too. So that's the reason I started to put my kirtan on recordings—because people were listening to all these bootlegs and I thought the quality was just horrible. I mean, the singing was not properly executed, either. I didn't like it. I just wanted some quality control, so that's why I started putting out tapes.

Interesting. But let's backtrack for a second. I'd like our readers to have some background on Bangladesh. For example, why do you think Bangladeshi kirtan is so special?

Well, it is for me; maybe not for someone else.

It has *bhava*, emotion. It has drama. It also has style—a certain gravitas and yet, simultaneously, a sort of free-form spontaneity as well. And it has years of tradition. Maybe you can talk a little bit about the background, about the history of Bangladesh, which can lead into a discussion of Bengali kirtan . . .

Well, in 1947, the British partitioned India based on religion. Bengal and Punjab got sliced in half. Bengal became East Pakistan (which later became Bangladesh) and West Bengal. Bangladesh is a predominantly Muslim country, with about 85% Muslim people and 15% Hindu, Buddhist, and Christian. The minority groups are naturally marginalized. The only way the Hindus could maintain their culture—the prior, natural culture of the area—was to propagate their own tradition through kirtan, dramas, festivals, and so on.

Previously, Bangladesh was East Bengal, part of undivided Bengal. The British divided Punjab in the west and Bengal in the east. That's how they divided India. Muslims were in East Bengal and also in West Punjab. That's how Pakistan came into being. There was

West Pakistan on one side of India, and East Pakistan on the other side. This new country, Pakistan, was separated in the middle by India. It was insane.

In 1971, there was a war of liberation in which East Pakistan separated from West Pakistan. West Pakistan was trying to impose its language, Urdu, on East Pakistan, whose indigenous language was Bengali. Of course, the Bengalis wouldn't accept this foreign language foisted upon them. Why should they? So the Bengalis in the east fought a war of independence and the nation of Bangladesh came into being. But it was still a Muslim country.

So Muslims were on both sides.

Right. In contrast to West Bengal, in India, Bangladeshi Hindus were into the teachings of Sri Chaitanya Mahaprabhu, because this is their tradition. In West Bengal, the Hindus were more into Ramakrishna, and not into kirtan. So, in Bangladesh, kirtan took root more and more, and they developed their own styles in which the local people became expert.

Because they were an oppressed minority, they clung to the teachings and kirtan culture of Sri Chaitanya Mahaprabhu — who brought kirtan as we know it to this planet, and who prophesied that the kirtan movement would spread worldwide. It was Prabhupada's mission to fulfill that prophesy, and indeed he was the initial force that got the whole kirtan movement going.

And I think I should mention at this point that Prabhupada is really the person who brought kirtan to the West. I mean, before he came to America, in 1965, there were maybe one or two people doing kirtan in the Western world, but on a small scale. Now kirtan has become prominent, and, if you look at it, it's in no small measure due to Prabhupada, who introduced it all over Europe and America in the '60s.

Right, that's certainly true. But let's return to the subject of Bangladesh and the development of kirtan as we know it today.

The Bangladeshi kirtan style is based on *ragas*, with long, wonderfully drawn-out kirtans evoking the different *bhavas* associated with the pastimes of Radha and Krishna, the female and male dimensions of God. These kirtans go through different delineated moods in their kirtan performance, bringing out the various *bhavas*, like separation, union, and all the moods in between.

Okay, let's talk about the distinct nature of Bangladeshi kirtan.

Well that's where you see it, because kirtan is based on mood, on *rasa*, on *bhava*—inner feeling. And this was developed in Bengal. It's not just singing, there's *bhava*, there's sentiment that you're trying to evoke, and that sentiment matures into spiritual love, love for God—for Krishna.

Now, each *raga* is carefully crafted to bring out a particular emotion, and that emotion is connected to, or in harmony with, Radha and Krishna's pastimes, known as the *ashta-kaliya-lila* of Radha and Krishna. So, in Bangladesh, they do kirtan according to the *ragas* and the *ashta-kaliya-lila* pastimes of Radha and Krishna with all the moods and emotions in the kirtan that correspond to eight different facets of the day in the spiritual world.

At midnight, for example, they sing midnight *ragas*, evoking that particular mood, to better appreciate the mysteries of what Radha and Krishna experience at that time. And, in the morning, they do morning *ragas*, evoking that mood, and so on.

Hmm. And the origins of these *ragas* can be found in . . .

. . . the scriptures and the writings of the self-realized souls. For example, the Six Goswamis of Vrindavan, Bhaktivinode Thakur, and from Sri Chaitanya Mahaprabhu, whom Vaishnavas accept as the combined incarnation of Radha and Krishna. Then the *kirtaniyas* express it with their own realizations.

Another component of these kirtans is "union and separation"—kirtans that help evoke those feelings and that bring the chanter to the point of understanding these complex moods in the pastimes of the divine couple.

Oh, absolutely. This is what it's all about. Each kirtan evokes the coming together of Radha and Krishna and the separation of Radha and Krishna. They usually start off with the anticipation of reunion, coming together. Rejoicing.

Triumphant.

Real grandiose and luxuriant chanting, very wonderful, you know. And this leads to full-fledged union. And the mood of the chanting, the *raga*, reflects these emotions. But when the divine couple part, both Radha and Krishna experience a tremendous sense of separation, with tears coming to their eyes. They're crying and experiencing intense longing.

Totally forlorn. But these are fully *spiritual* emotions, of which their material counterpart—as experienced by finite beings—is just a limited reflection. The transcendental feelings of Radha and Krishna are the genesis, the origin— it's where it all comes from.

Right. These kirtans, properly experienced, can lead you right into an appreciation of Krishna's world – a world of intense emotion and feeling.

And so you were talking about the divine couple's intense longing . . .

This is the *bhava* of love in separation. During the kirtan, the chanting reflects these moods in so many different ways. And when Radha and Krishna come back together, back into union, the kirtan again becomes very joyful . . .

This is all reflected in the music.

All reflected in the music. But it always ends with very joyful, happy moods, because Radha and Krishna are reunited, together again. I saw so many really good kirtan bands do this in Bangladesh. Band after band would reenact the same cycle of emotions and moods – but with countless variations on the *raga*, because it was a different time of day, or a different nuance of mood.

Most people stay and listen for a full twenty-four hours, because then you can hear all of the *ragas*, and all the moods of the *ashta-kaliya-lila* that correspond to each part of the day. I would go to twenty-four hour kirtan festivals, called *akhanda-nam-kirtan*. Some–

times they have twenty-four hour *akhanda-kirtan*, sometimes forty-eight hours, or seventy-two hours, or a whole week, of non-stop kirtan.

Fascinating.

Practically every village in Bangladesh has one of these festivals, known as *utshabs*. So I got in on the circuit. I'd find out where the kirtans were and go to all these different *utshabs*, and I met all the different groups. Over time, I found the best singers, the most famous groups, the best *mridanga* players, and I'd go there and tape them and hang out with them.

This is before you started singing . . .

No, I was singing; this was in Bangladesh, so I was already sing-ing. And they liked me, because I was so interested in what they were doing—they were happy to show me technique and to give me tips on kirtan. They could see that I was into it and that I was singing, too. They thought I was cool because I was a Westerner and I was into their music.

Are there any *kirtaniyas* from that time that you remember? I know you associated with Purna Das Baul in Bengal, correct?

Yeah, I played with Purna Das, and he invited me to his home for lunch, too. I hung out with all those guys. I particularly remem-ber, in Bangladesh, three guys who were amazing kirtan singers. Absolutely amazing. Monoranjan Sheel, Ajit Chakravarty, and Govinda Lal Mazumdar. They sang as well as opera singers, but even better, because it was kirtan.

Really.

These guys were unbelievable singers. I mean, their kirtan was obviously inspired from the spiritual platform, something they've developed over lifetimes—it had a transcendent, spiritual quality to it. But also it was just plain good, even materially speaking. They all had their own styles, different voices, but the emotion they put into the kirtans and how they built up the kirtans and hit the high notes—it made me cry, like when I first heard Prabhupada or when I first heard the Indians in Toronto. I was absolutely breathless hearing these guys sing. Words cannot describe . . .

I see you're getting choked up just remembering them.

[laughter] Yeah. And I also watched *mridanga* players and the other musicians very closely. I watched how they played . . . I observed it all. I just hung out with these guys for three years and absorbed the whole thing. So, even though I can't play *mridanga*—I don't have a knack for it—I know exactly how it should be played, and when it should go from this rhythm to that rhythm, and so on. It's sort of like driving a manual shift car—first gear, second gear, third gear, fourth gear, overdrive—I know what *mridangas* should be doing, how they should do it, when they should do it, in such a way that the kirtan gradually builds and gets where it needs to go. I try to impart this to drummers I play with; But they haven't heard the beats I'm trying to communicate to them, so it doesn't happen.

Forget the drum: you play a mean *harmonium*.

[laughter] In Bangladesh they all play *harmonium*, so I learned their style of playing it, the Bengali way, which works for me. I learned a lot there—I learned how to sing; I learned different exercises they do; the techniques they use for developing voice and style, everything. I learned all that from those musicians.

And now you're quite successful on the kirtan circuit.

Well, now I have a following, and I'm invited to different countries to chant and people like it; so that's great. I've also learned different styles, too, so I can accommodate different tastes. For example, when I'm with Gujarati people, I sing the Gujarati style; when I'm with Bengalis, I sing Bengali style. If people just know Hindi, then I do the Hindi songs, not just Sanskrit. And for Westerners I adopt a simple approach, some *bhajan*, some kirtan, with melodies they can relate to. So I've learned the different styles, and each style is wonderful in its own way.

I've played with Gujarati musicians who are fantastic and just as impressive as the Bangladeshi players. But the difference is, in the Gujarati style, for example, it's mostly about the union of Radha and Krishna—the joyful experience of Radha and Krishna being together in a state of bliss. There are no expressed feelings of separation and longing for God. That you only find in Bengal. And the separation makes the union sweeter—that's the thing. This is the realization of the Bengalis. Separation makes the heart grow fonder; it solidifies the *bhakti*.

In my own experience, too, singing about these feelings of longing and separation for Krishna—it's more fulfilling and satisfying to me, as a person, because it evokes more powerful feelings in my heart. And it's common sense that it would be that way, because we are in fact separate from Krishna, aren't we? We're here in this material world and we want to go back to Him. So that's why the mood of separation is so poignant, so real for me, personally. But some people can only relate to the joyful experience of union— they respond to the *shanti*, the peace. And that's fine. They haven't come in contact with the more intense emotions of separation. They haven't been trained to understand the deeper meanings of mantra meditation, of Bhakti-yoga, of the deeper significance of divine sound vibrations. But it all comes in due course, simply by the kirtan itself.

And can you talk about the different kinds of chanting, specifically the different forms of kirtan?

There are many different types of kirtan. Here in the West we just think of kirtan as call-and-response chanting, focusing on a particular name of the divine, but there are different kinds of kirtans. First, there are three main styles of Bengali kirtan, based on the personalities of Rama, Krishna, and Sri Chaitanya.

Right. Let's get into that a little bit.

There's Krishna-lila-kirtan, there's Rama-lila-kirtan, and there's Gaura-lila-kirtan. So that's chanting the elaborate pastimes of Radha-Krishna, or the pastimes of Sita-Rama, or the pastimes of Sri Chaitanya. This style is called Lila-kirtan, where devotees sing songs

that evoke the pastimes of these manifestations of God—the actual *lilas* performed, both in the spiritual world and when these
manifestations of the divine descend to earth to bless the conditioned souls.

Then there's Pala-kirtan. This is also of three types: Again, we're
talking about Rama-lila, Gaura-lila, or Krishna-lila. Pala-kirtan is
when you tell the whole story of one particular *lila* by singing and
by speaking. All the Pala-kirtans—like any kirtans—are based on
scriptures and on songs written by the Vaishnava poets throughout the ages. So, in Pala-kirtan, one evokes a particular pastime
by singing, speaking, and by acting it out. The speaking is like a
bridge for the narrative, and then one goes on to the next song to
continue the pastime.

There's some narrative, some story, as opposed to just chanting names.

Yeah, narrative, but also acting out. They dress up, and they act
it out also—very beautifully done. And that's how they lead into
the next song, the next part of the pastime. For example, you know
Damodara-lila?

**When Mother Yashoda is upset with Krishna. She attempts to tie Him
up with rope . . .**

Yes, she tries to bind Sri Krishna with a rope because He's been a
naughty boy. But she can't, no matter how many ropes she ties
together—it's always too short. Not enough rope. Finally, Krishna
agrees to be bound by her love, and that's called *bhakta-vatsala*. So
the *kirtaniyas* will sing and speak about all the different actions
that give rise to that pastime, acting it out. So, that's one kind of
Pala-kirtan.

Then, there is the Pala-kirtan about Rama-lila, where they sing
and speak about the pastimes of Sita and Rama. And they act it
out. They build up emotions, moving from one story to another:
The demon is coming, and the arrow is on the bow, and it's aimed
at Rama! And then they break into a song, written by a famous
poet, but then Rama is ready to retaliate. On and on.

It's done like this in Bangladesh?

Yes. And they perform it. They go into the many villages and they perform. And the most amazing kind of kirtan is called the Ashta-kaliya-kirtan, which is a twenty-four hour nonstop kirtan by one group recounting the entire day and night of Radha-Krishna's pastimes.

We spoke about this already.

No, that was *akhanda-nam-kirtan*, which is related but different. This is not Nam-kirtan, but rather Lila-kirtan — pastimes. In the West we are pretty much familiar with Nam-kirtan, or Mantra-kirtan. Ashta-kaliya-kirtan is different. The kirtan begins before dawn, when Radha and Krishna have just woken up in their *kunja*, or forest bower, and have to return home, before their families discover they're missing. And the singer sings all the pastimes of when Radha comes home, and when Krishna comes home, meeting with their parents, and then all the pastimes through the day when they go to the forest with the cowherd boys and Radha and Krishna meet again.

This goes on all the way into the evening, when they come together for their tryst and then again all night — to just before daybreak, when they wake up and have to go home. Kirtan groups that do this usually have one singer who sings twenty-four hours nonstop, expressing every single *lila* and its corresponding emotion — *lilas* that occur between Radha and Krishna.

One singer throughout the day, without sleeping or eating?

Yeah. That's yoga! The band sits there, and he sings. Sometimes the music will go on for a bit, and he'll take a breather, or someone else may sing, another singer in the band may sing a little bit. But one singer is standing up, prominent, while the rest are sitting, the musicians. But the main singer is acting it out and singing with such feeling. In this way, Krishna's day is broken up into eight parts of three hours each, each three-hour segment is called a *prahor*. So, *ashta-prahor* — eight segments — this is the Ashta-kaliya-kirtan. And people in Bangaldesh come from all over and listen for the entire twenty-four hours and enjoy the entire day of Radha and Krishna's pastimes.

The various melodies and tunes and stories must be endless.

Oh, I'm glad you mentioned melody. There are different melodies because everything is sung by *raga*, according to the time of the day. This relates to Gaura-lila too. Because when they sing the Nam-kirtan at midnight, they sing the *sannyasa* melody, which means they're singing the Hare Krishna *maha-mantra* using the melody from the corresponding Lila-kirtan—when Lord Chaitanya takes *sannyasa* and He's leaving Vishnu Priya. It corresponds to Krishna leaving Radharani, which is a heavy mood of separation. And everybody in the audience—at least every cultured listener—starts feeling intense emotions, or even weeping, because when they hear that melody they know that Krishna is leaving Radharani, or that Lord Chaitanya is going to take *sannyasa* while his wife, Vishnu Priya, is sleeping.

Then, in the morning, Vishnu Priya will sing like this, "Where is my Gaura? Where has He gone?" Just by hearing the *maha-mantra* in that melody, the audience knows what's coming, because they're familiar with the melodies, the moods, the sentiments, and how they all interrelate. This is advanced *shravanam*, hearing—for those experienced in kirtan.

This brings to mind "Gaura Chandrika," which is, as you know, the overlapping of Chaitanya Mahaprabhu's pastimes and Krishna's pastimes. This is essential in this kind of kirtan, no?

Gaura Chandrika. This is another important thing—that is, in Lila-kirtan—because before you can sing Krishna-lila you have to first sing and glorify the parallel pastime performed by Chaitanya Mahaprabhu. Every Lila-kirtan begins like this: First you ask for the mercy of the guru, then for the mercy of Mahaprabhu, and only then can you be empowered to sing the Gaura Chandrika—the *lila* of Sri Chaitanya that corresponds with the Krishna *lila* that will be performed right after it. Sri Vasudev Ghosh, a famous Gaudiya

Vaishnava poet, wrote many Gaura Chandrikas, which were put to music. So that's important: For every pastime in Krishna-lila, there is an exact, corresponding pastime in Gaura-lila.

Because Gaura and Krishna are actually one. So there is an ontological connection.

Exactly. If it is to be done properly, the *kirtaniya* must sing the Gaura-lila song first before beginning to sing the Krishna-lila. This is the culture. If one sings Krishna-lila directly, bypassing Lord Chaitanya, omitting the Gaura Chandrika, that's considered a huge offense, at least in Bangladesh. They can't even imagine such a thing. Just like they would never imagine singing an evening *raga* in the morning. It's just not done. Prabhupada taught us the same principle — we sing the Pancha Tattva mantra of Sri Chaitanya before starting a kirtan.

Okay. And now a little about the basic philosophy of kirtan . . .

Well, there's certainly quite a bit of philosophy in what we've been discussing . . .

Yes, but now let's turn to the holy name more directly.

Wherever you find the holy name, you'll find the eternal abode of Krishna — *jekhane krishna nam, shekhane vrindavan*. So the underlying philosophy of kirtan is that Krishna and His name are non-different. Because of that, depending on the purity of the chanting, and the sincerity of the chanting, and the feeling of devotion in the chanting, to that extent Krishna becomes revealed through His divine name. Or, due to a lack of these moods, Krishna remains hidden. That's why it's a process of purification, a process of God realization. It's gradual. The more you develop the qualities of a devotee — humility, selflessness, love, compassion — then that's how much you can taste the essence of the name, the nectar of the name; then that's how much more you're in touch with the deity of name, Nam-Prabhu, the secret dwelling of God in the name.

Why do you think the Bengalis, their particular approach to kirtan,

resonated so strongly in your heart? I mean, you're describing a general principle of God and His name, that they're non-different—why the Bengali approach?

Well, in Bangladesh, I found them to be like blues and gospel singers, and so I was able to relate to them, because that's what I was into. The blacks in America were singing blues and gospel because they were oppressed . . .

Hmm, right.

It came out in their music, that they were oppressed by white people. Similarly, in Bangladesh, these Vaishnavas were oppressed by the Muslims. That's one level of it. They were pining for days when they would no longer be oppressed. I mean, there was the whole transcendental reason for their pining, and they were singing of the love of Radha and Krishna, which is totally spiritual. But, just on a mundane level, I could relate because of this blues phenomenon. And it came out in their music. So it is very similar to blues. In fact, this one *raga*, known as *malkauns*—it's basically a blues *raga*. But they would use it for singing the Hare Krishna *maha-mantra*.

Yeah. That's right—it's a pentatonic *raga*, right?

[laughter] So, that was Krishna's arrangement, I guess, that I grew up on blues music—it facilitated, in a way, my attraction to kirtan. I mean, coming from the blues background, listening to black blues and gospel singers, and now listening to Bangladeshi singers . . . it all sort of gelled. I could experience the similarity—singing from the heart. That mood impacts on the music, and so the connected scales and the *ragas* are quite similar.

But kirtan is, obviously, more pure—it has the Vedic component. It's involved with self-realization, with developing love for Krishna. That's why I ultimately went for Bengali kirtan instead of ordinary blues music. But the emotions, at least from an external point of view, are expressing similar feelings, only blues is not directly for communion with God.

Srila Prabhupada once explained it like this: One should chant the holy name of Krishna in the same way that a child cries out in separation from his mother, "Krishna, Krishna." In this way, if one cries out with that kind of intensity and purity — one can get out of the entanglement of the material energy and return home, back to Godhead, in full blissful consciousness. So that was the mood.

Can you tell me more about the *maha-mantra* specifically? This is the most important of all mantras used in kirtan, no?

It really is. Alright, let's look at the three words that make up the mantra: Hare, Krishna, and Rama. "Hare" is that divine feminine energy of the Lord. That energy is spiritual energy, or divine love energy — it's called *hladini-shakti* in Sanskrit. It's the energy of the heart, the energy of love. More, it is God in feminine form. And this is embodied in Sri Radha, Krishna's eternal consort. So "Hare" refers to Her and everything She represents.

Next, "Krishna." The sound vibration Krishna designates the Supreme Lord Himself, and it means, "the all-attractive one." He has the potency to attract the mind, to attract the heart, to attract the senses, to attract every conscious living entity. Every quality that a person may be attracted to, Krishna has that quality in complete fullness and perfection. So, in that sense, God's most complete name is "Krishna."

And then "Rama" is the reservoir of pleasure — that's what it means. And that's what you experience when you connect to the all-attractive Krishna, through the emotion and potency of the spiritual energy, Hare. So that's the *maha-mantra*. I compare it to an electric current. When you flick on the switch, the electricity connects to the bulb, and the light goes on. Similarly, when we connect to the Supreme through the vibration of "Hare," and we flick on the switch of pure devotion, then we become enlightened, and we experience that reservoir of pleasure, known as Rama.

So those three words — Hare, Krishna, and Rama, which make up the *maha-mantra* — give the underlying philosophy of the mantra.

And yet there are many deeper understandings of the mantra as well . . .

Oh, it's endless. Some *acharyas* describe it like this: They begin with "Hare Krishna, Hare Krishna," the first four words of the mantra. This, they say, refers to Radha and Krishna together, in union — they are celebrating their love together. It's called *milan* or *sambhoga bhava*. The joy of being together. Then, "Krishna Krishna," the next two words of the *maha-mantra* — this signifies their separation. And Radharani is calling, "'Krishna Krishna' — where is my Krishna; oh, please tell me, where is my Krishna?!" In the next two words, Krishna calls out, too: "'Hare Hare,' where is My Radharani?" So they're both experiencing intense separation at this point in the mantra.

I see. So just in the first half of the mantra, one already finds the two emotions of union and longing.

Yes, and these are spiritual emotions, because it's the *lila*, the pastimes of the Supreme, of Radha and Krishna, God in female and male forms. We can relate to this because similar emotions occur in the world of matter, too, but we only get a hint of it in the material world. It's only a dim reflection of the original phenomenon, which exists in Krishna.

And the second half of the mantra?

Here the emotions increase and intensify. Krishna is called Radha-Raman because He is the darling of Radha. "Hare Rama, Hare Rama" means Krishna is experiencing the ecstasy of His darling Radharani — so the divine lovers, Radha and Krishna are together again, experiencing the reservoir of pleasure simply by being in each other's company. Radharani and Radha-Raman, which is Radha and Krishna, "Hare Rama, Hare Rama."

But then, "Rama Rama" — they're separated once again. She's crying, "Where is that ecstasy I experienced with Krishna? Where is He?" She calls out His name twice: "Rama Rama!" And He is also crying, "'Hare Hare' — where is that ecstasy I experienced with Radharani? Where is My beloved?" So in both halves of the mantra there is union and separation, union and separation. And as one advances spiritually, one can appreciate these emotions more and more.

The depth really does seem limitless.

The mantra is full of spiritual emotions, deep spiritual emotions of divine love, and that's what you're supposed to experience when you chant this *maha-mantra*. The mantra reawakens the original divine love in our hearts. But it takes time and sincerity.

You know, there's a reason why it's called the *maha-mantra*, or "the great mantra." It includes the potency of all others. Just by chanting "Hare Krishna," one can gain the benefits of all other kinds of chanting. This is because it connects you directly to the supremely divine lovers—with God in His most confidential features as Radha and Krishna. Therefore, it's the most potent of all mantras. *Man* means "the mind," and *tra* means "to deliver," so because it is a pure spiritual sound vibration, the mantra delivers the mind from material consciousness to spiritual consciousness. This is what Sri Chaitanya experienced and taught, and that's why he wanted to spread kirtan all over the world.

Is there a specific meditation that works best with chanting?

Just hear the name, focus in on the sound of the mantra and remain open to whatever Krishna sends your way. There's no question of thinking. It's all in the sound of the chant—*cheto darpana marjanam*, the sound vibration enters the heart through focused hearing. In this way, the mantra cleanses the heart of all *anarthas*—of all unwanted things, like lust, anger, greed, envy, and so on—and our hearts become like a clean mirror, reflecting back our eternal spiritual identity in relationship with the Supreme. That's how it works.

Krishna is the supreme lover. He is the bridegroom and we are the bride—you can think about it like that. And the *maha-mantra*, when chanted with focused attention, with the right feeling, emotion, and consciousness, brings bride and groom together in a divine embrace of love. That's what kirtan is all about.

And that mood of kirtan purifies us from all material conceptions, from our false material identity, which we've been developing not just in this one life but for numerous lifetimes. Our conditioning

d up for countless generations, countless forms, and count-
ives. By chanting, we become free from our ego and from
erything mundane, so that we're able to experience our actual
identity as the eternal beloved of the supreme lover, Krishna.

**Is any other type of worship necessary? It seems that everything one
needs is in the recitation of the holy name.**

It is. Other forms of worship exist, *nava-vidhi-bhakti* — the nine limbs
of *bhakti* — and there's certainly no reason to avoid them. But you
should also know that chanting the Hare Krishna mantra is sufficient. Besides, it's also *puja*, or worship. Just like we see worship
in the temple. We see people decorating the Deity of the Lord. But
now — in this Age of Kali — the Deity is the *maha-mantra*, Krishna
Himself in the form of His name. As it is said, *kali kale nama rupe
krishna avatar* — that in this age of Kali, the supreme Lord Krishna
incarnates in the form of His holy name. So, just as Krishna, the
Deity, manifests in brass or wood or marble, as we see in temples,
He also comes in the form of sound vibration.

**But the Deity in the temple is cared for in such a loving way. By that
ensuing, loving service, the devotee develops closeness with the Deity, a personal relationship. The devotee dresses the Deity, offering
food, flowers, and so on—it's one on one.**
  **On the other hand, it seems that the Deity of the holy name is simply
about chanting—the practitioner could easily have trouble developing a close relationship with this aspect of God, because here He's
merely envisioned as a sound vibration, not as a person.**

Yes, that's true, so for those who want to do it through Deity worship, or other methods, that's fine. The *acharyas* give us teachings
and facilities so we can make it happen. But don't underestimate
the personal relationship one can develop with the holy name.
That's there, too. For example, how do we decorate the Deity of
the *maha-mantra*? With beautiful melodies. The melodies are the
different beautiful garments with which we can dress the Deity of
the *maha-mantra*. And the rhythms are the beautiful ornaments:
the necklaces, the bangles, and the earrings. There are really so

many ways to develop a personal relationship with the Deity of Krishna's name.

Beautiful. This is very important.

In *puja*, we offer the flame—that's part of traditional worship, when one serves the Deity in the temple. So, in kirtan, the flame is the fire of our devotion, the fire of our energy while singing. In *puja*, we offer the Deity a flower; so in kirtan that flower is the flower of our life, in devotion to Krishna. As we chant more and more, and become more realized, we're offering the flower of blossoming realization.

In *puja*, too, we offer water, so, in our metaphor, that water is our emotional feelings, the tears that, when we become advanced, we'll naturally shed while chanting the name. That water is the nectar that's coming through the chanting—the nectar that's experienced not just by the chanter but also by Radha and Krishna, who are receiving the kirtan, because it's reciprocal.

So kirtan is a serenade of love—it's a love song! We're serenading the Supreme Lover. That's what Krishna kirtan is.

Let's conclude by giving our readers a run-down of your kirtan history—CDs and performances—thus far.

Well, I recorded my first kirtan album, "Vrindavan Chandra," in the summer of 1982, as I mentioned, as a response to the poor quality bootlegs of my music that were circulating at the time. I also recorded a video giving formal *harmonium* lessons at that time. The following year, I recorded my second album, "Transcendence," which was a blend of kirtan and *bhajan*. Then, in 1985, I did "Chaitanya Chandra," a tribute to Sri Chaitanya Mahaprabhu, who actually began the kirtan movement in the sixteenth century. In 1991, I returned to India to record another, similar album, "Bhakti Ratna Mala," and I did a tour of the U.S., Europe, and India. In 1993 I recorded, "Charana Kamal," which really circulated well, and won some international acclaim at that time. Then I did my first tour of Latin America in 1994—I toured Brazil, Peru, Ecuador, Guyana, Trinidad & Tobago. People were so encouraging, and I was being invited to lead kirtans all over the world.

I then recorded "Way of Love" in 1995. I traveled all over Western and Eastern Europe promoting that CD, which led to the recording of a live album, "Kirtan Rasa," in Slovenia in '96. It became my most popular album up until that time. So then I did another live album, "Hari-Nam-Ananda," in London in 1997. In 1998, I published my first book, *Radha-Damodara Vilasa*, a historical novel describing how kirtan was transplanted from East to West, as seen through the eyes of one of my heroes, Vishnujana Swami, who gave his life in the '70s to spread Krishna kirtan in the Western world.

Then, I did a second tour of Brazil in 2000, where I recorded "The Turning Point" with a group of Brazilian musicians. In 2001, I released the CD, "Best of Vaiyasaki," which was a tribute to George Harrison's devotion to Sri Krishna, when Harrison's health began to fail.

His use of the *maha-mantra* on "My Sweet Lord," in 1969, was one of the first kirtans recorded in the Western world by a Westerner—only Yamuna's recording came before that. So he is hugely important in the history of kirtan, though most people are unaware of this. But go on . . .

Right. I then did "Sri Krishna Divya Nam" in Calcutta, in 2003, taking my kirtan technique in yet another new direction. Actually, last year I recorded another album in Calcutta taking that direction one step further, and I'm constantly traveling, doing festivals and workshops. I also recently founded KSI—Kirtan Satsang International—to preserve and disseminate kirtan music.

And recently, my wife, Kaisori, and I began 2007 with a six-week tour of fourteen cities in Brazil, did three radio programs and an interview for *Yoga Journal Brazil*. Then I toured the USA, Hawaii, Spain, Portugal, the Canary Islands, Andorra, Ireland, Scotland, England, the Philippines, and India.

Whew, you've been busy!

[laughter] In November 2006, I led the kirtan event in Rishikesh, India, on the occasion of the ten-year Maha-Samadhi of Sri Swami Rama, founder of the Himalayan Institute. They contacted me be-

cause Swami Rama used to listen to my kirtans and he appreciated them. In Madrid, I did kirtan at the home of the Indian
Ambassador to Spain. The invited guests were embassy people
from the various international missions to Spain and other important dignitaries.

In Portugal, we held a kirtan event at the University of Lisbon.
Our special guest—the Consul General of India—just loved the
kirtan. So, yeah, as you say, I've been keeping pretty busy.

Any long-term goals?

The goal of my life is to help uplift the consciousness of people,
and of the planet, by purely presenting kirtan without personal
motivation. I pray that my kirtan is pleasing to God and guru—to
Sri Krishna and my divine teacher, Srila Prabhupada.

Now that kirtan has become fashionable, I'd love to see kirtan have its own music category at the Grammy Music Awards,
instead of it being lumped in with World Music.

From your mouth to God's ears!

For more information contact:
www.myspace.com/vaiyasaki or www.kirtan.org

SRI CHAITANYA MAHAPRABHU: THE FATHER OF MODERN KIRTAN

"O merciful Sri Chaitanya, O sea of compassion — may the beautiful flow-ing waters of your spiritual activities find a home on my desert-like tongue. These waters are made even more beautiful, no doubt, with the lotus flow-ers of singing, dancing, and the loud chanting of Krishna's holy name — which is kirtan, the special wealth of unalloyed devotees. These devotees are compared to swans, birds, and honeybees, whose hearts are immeasur-ably gladdened by the ocean of your being."

— KRISHNADAS KAVIRAJ GOSWAMI

In the late fifteenth century, European kings sent their ambitious explorers in search of new routes to treasure-filled India. Many returned home on ships laden with silks, spices, artwork, and magnificent jewels. Valuable though these assets were, the visiting foreigners had in fact bypassed India's real treasure, which was just then being widely distributed by Chaitanya Mahaprabhu. His mis-sion: To make accessible the essence of Krishna-*bhakti*, or the mysti-cal path of yogic devotion, which had for so long remained hidden in esoteric texts and in the minds and hearts of spiritual adepts.

Prior to Sri Chaitanya's time, a reawakening of Krishna-*bhakti* had swept the subcontinent, drawing on centuries-old Sanskrit texts and vernacular poetry composed by Sri Chaitanya's distin-guished predecessors. Now, he and his followers would add spice to an already flavorful Vedic recipe, showing how to put the deep theology of devotion into practice by emphasizing the power of the holy name. And through this method, he enthusiastically gave love for Krishna to all who would have it.

Along the way, he pioneered a momentous social and spiritual movement that continues to spread its profound influence world-wide. At the very least, he transformed India in four ways: philo-sophically, by establishing the logic of a personal Absolute named Krishna and the need for rendering loving service unto Him; socially, by opposing the blindly rigid caste system and setting in place a universal doctrine that is open to everyone; politically, by organizing India's first civil disobedience movement against a repressive secular government; and, most important, spiritu-ally, by teaching and demonstrating that Divine love is the secret meaning behind all Vedic texts; that it is a cooling balm capable of healing the world's woes; and that it is the ultimate nonsectarian teaching at the root of all religion.

Who is Sri Chaitanya?

Bengal, India, 1486. It was a time of change. The political and social climate was dense, creating paradigm shifts not only among intel-lectuals but among common people as well. Even religion, which had always been at the center of Bengali life, was moving toward radical transformation, with practitioners questioning core values and well-established beliefs. In many ways, this was the perfect time for Sri Chaitanya to appear, for his methods of God-realiza-tion, though grounded in traditional scriptures and supported by the philosophical conclusions of his predecessors, were revolution-ary, augmenting age-old practices with new approaches and staid interpretations of scripture with explications of inner meaning.

Sri Chaitanya was born into a world of *yogis*, *pandits*, and saints —a world he would soon dominate, not by political strategies or managerial prowess but rather by wisdom, strength of character, and unremitting love.

As a teenager, he had become a scholar of significant renown, but by his early twenties he had set all academic pursuits aside in favor of love of Krishna. His transformation took place under the tutelage of Ishvara Puri, an accomplished teacher in the well-established Madhva lineage, who initiated him into the chanting of the holy name.

With this blissful name on his lips, he became like a live wire, rousing everyone in his path with the electricity of devotion. Divine love emanated from his very being, like an unstoppable current of spiritual power. The *pandit* (scholarship) gave way to *prema* (love of God). The path of knowledge, *jnana* (dialectics), moved aside, and *bhakti* (devotion) reigned supreme. Though he initially married and led a responsible family life, he eventually set aside worldly concerns, preferring instead the life of an ascetic, an itinerant monk.

His approach to monastic life, however, was revolutionary. Unlike other mendicants of his time, who emphasized serious Vedic study and rigorous meditation techniques, he merely wandered from town to town, singing and dancing. He shared his considerable philosophy only when necessary, focusing instead on the love, joy, and the understanding that comes from Krishna's name. His was a practical form of yoga: "Don't deny the senses," he taught, "but rather use them in Krishna's service. Don't run away from the world, but, instead, run single-pointedly toward the Divine." This was his strong recommendation, to be performed with a sense of exuberance that was unknown to previous forms of yoga and meditation, with their solemn practice of mantras and severe austerities. His was a colorful world of song, dance, art, and dramatic performance. Sri Chaitanya was an aesthetic ascetic.

With his vibrant yet simple teaching of divine love, he spent many years traveling India's countryside, attracting numerous followers and disciples. In the north, he met Sufis and Muslims, and in the south, Buddhists and Advaitins. All would find harmony and respite in his dance of love.

And yet he was not a mere sentimentalist. When the greatest of scholars found themselves in his company, he would not disappoint them. Indeed, leading philosophers of the day sought him out, just to enhance their knowledge of ultimate truth as embodied in the Vedic scriptures. Even the Six Goswamis of Vrindavan—

who were arguably the most accomplished theologians of the time—became his disciples. They systematized his teaching and produced numerous volumes of profound philosophy.

As a result of his personal charisma, learning, and exemplary character, and because of the notable personalities who surrounded him, he became something of a celebrity, with hundreds of thousands adopting his teaching—he would give them the holy name, proclaiming kirtan as the yoga of the modern age. All of India's elite came to see him, to learn his methods and to receive his blessings. His personality was irresistible, his approach to life, contagious.

One might naturally ask: Who was Sri Chaitanya, really? The earliest Gaudiya Vaishnava texts tell us that he was Vishnu, come to earth to inaugurate the *yuga-dharma*, or the process of God-realization for our current epoch in world history: the chanting of the holy name. But this, say those same texts, was only the external reason for his appearance. There was an internal reason as well. On the deepest level, he was Krishna—the source of all *avatars*, the primary manifestation of the Supreme - appearing in a humanlike form. He comes as a human to taste the love His devotees have for him—to taste it from their unique perspective, as humans.

Additionally, he wanted to taste it from the perspective of his most dedicated devotee, Sri Radha, who is none other than Krishna Himself in female form. In Sri Chaitanya, then, God is said to take on the mood and emotional disposition of His female counterpart, Sri Radha, merging lover and beloved in one spiritual body. Thus, according to Gaudiya Vaishnava theology, Chaitanya Mahaprabhu is a combined manifestation of Radha and Krishna —one in which God fully experiences His own love and that of His devotees as well.

For the final twelve years of his manifest pastimes, he settled in Puri, deeply absorbed in meditation. His consciousness immersed in the mystical dimensions of union and separation—the twin emotions of love, central to Krishna devotion—he shared these inner feelings with his most confidential devotees, not only with words but by the symptoms he exhibited in day-to-day life. He would cry and laugh simultaneously, like a madman; run after shadows, hoping they were in fact his beloved; and passionately call out, "Krishna!, Krishna!," like a victim of unrequited love.

His followers observed him carefully, taking scrupulous notes. Documenting his every move, they devised a science of devotion, noting exactly how love of God develops, the symptoms one experiences along the way, and how to gauge proper advancement on the path. This was, after all, part of Sri Chaitanya's reason for being—to experience the emotions of a genuine devotee of the Lord and to show how this experience could be replicated by those who sincerely adopt his process.

By the time of his departure for the spiritual world, in 1533, his love resembled a tsunami, a tornado, the solar ejecta. Shridhar Maharaj, a pure devotee in the line of Sri Chaitanya, said it best—his love was comparable to a golden volcano, with eruptions of ecstasy that flowed like molten lava. This volcanic emission continues to flow, throughout India and, in recent years, the rest of the world.

His Miracles

Aside from sharing the bliss of kirtan, Sri Chaitanya exhibited many miracles, situating him on a par with the greatest of spiritual masters and the most powerful of mystic *yogis*. Though his biographers relate numerous accounts of his miraculous deeds, a few examples should suffice here.

It is said that when he was an infant he would weep continually, more than other children. But when his mother and the neighboring ladies finally cried, *Haribol*—"chant the names of God"—he would invariably stop crying, with his temperament immediately changing to one of glee. For this reason, his childhood home frequently resounded with the chanting of Krishna's names, presaging his future mission.

During his married years, he displayed a number of miracles, too, especially in the house of Shrivas Thakur, which is where he inaugurated the Sankirtan mission. It was here that his nocturnal kirtans transformed his followers into the best of yogis, adepts in the spiritual practice of intonating the holy name. The sheer ecstasy of these kirtans nearly drove all attendees mad, causing them to jump, howl, and shed tears of bliss.

One day, after such an ecstatic kirtan, Mahaprabhu casually asked the devotees what they wanted to eat. When they unanimously expressed their desire for mangoes, even though the fruit was then out of season, he took a mango seed and quickly buried it in Shrivas's courtyard. Immediately, the seed sprouted, miraculously appearing as a full-grown mango tree right before their eyes. It supplied enough ripened fruits to accommodate each of them, and it continued to do so for the rest of their lives.

On another occasion, Mahaprabhu journeyed to Puri through the dense jungles of the Jarakhanda Forest. The uncharted terrain frightened his inexperienced associate, Balabhadra, his sole traveling companion, who had heard about the wild beasts who made it their home. As the two pilgrims journeyed through the wooded area, however, Balabhadra's concerns were eventually set aside: He saw that Mahaprabhu's chanting and dancing soothed the savage beasts appearing in their midst, causing even lions, tigers and elephants to dance with abandon. Hearing Sri Chaitanya chant the names of Krishna, they all howled in their respective tongues, and Balabhadra, who later reported the incident to the other devotees, could hardly believe his eyes.

In due course, Mahaprabhu cured a leper known as Vasudeva, raised Shrivas Thakur's son from the dead, and healed many needy souls in Jesus-like fashion. Most such miracles were not witnessed by the masses, only by his inner circle of associates. Word spread fast, however, and his following grew.

Other miracles were seen by the multitudes. Perhaps the most famous of these occurred in Puri, during the Ratha-yatra festival, with millions watching. At this massive celebration, in which a huge wheeled chariot is pulled by hundreds of enthusiastic devotees, with hundreds of thousands watching, the cart suddenly stopped. It simply would not move. All the assembled devotees tried with their combined strength to push it forward, but their endeavor proved futile. The gigantic elephants of Puri's Raja were brought in, but they too failed to move the cart. Everyone present was baffled by this inexplicable dilemma, not knowing what to do.

Just then, Mahaprabhu arrived and placed his head up against the immovable cart. Applying minimal pressure, the enormous vehicle moved forward, to everyone's amazement. All the visiting pilgrims shouted "Haribol!" in appreciation of Sri Chaitanya's miracle.

At the same festival, because of his insatiable desire to taste the bliss of kirtan, he appeared in seven different chanting parties simultaneously. His numerous associates cried with ecstasy as they watched him manifest in several places at once—a mystical yogic feat that few can actually perform. King Prataparudra, the regional king, was particularly awestruck by this magical happening, and surrendered his heart, then and there, to Sri Chaitanya.

It should be mentioned, too, that Mahaprabhu frequently revealed his divinity to his intimate followers, but with the caveat that they not disclose this truth to anyone, at least until after his manifest pastimes. Such disclosure, he said, would hinder his ability to experience the mood of a devotee. If people knew his divine status, they would openly worship him as God, and this would go against the project of his particular incarnation—to live as a devotee and to experience love for Krishna from a devotee's unique perspective.

Even so, early on Mahaprabhu revealed his divinity in the house of Shrivas Thakur, when all of his associates became aware of his identity with Vishnu. At various times, he showed his Universal Form, including all universes and living beings together in one spot, inconceivably; and he displayed his six-armed form to Lord Nityananda and others—this included the two arms of Krishna, playing His flute, as well as Ramachandra's arms, with bow and arrow. Ultimately, he revealed his Rasaraj-mahabhava Svarup — his form as a combined manifestation of Radha and Krishna —to Sri Ramananda Raya, who was a loving devotee and a well-known governor in the Rajahmundry District of South India. Mahaprabhu's divinity was anything but secret, even in Bengal during his own manifest pastimes.

Miracles alone, of course, do not establish Godhood, nor do they legitimize a given religious path. Indeed, the Hindu religious tradition would eventually be overrun with those claiming to be God, and with nuances of belief that led to many diverse traditions. Anticipating this, Sri Chaitanya's more scholarly associates developed a series of complex theological tests by which such things can be determined. The most important is this: An *avatar* is generally described in scripture — if not explicitly mentioned by name and parentage then by innate personal characteristics. A close look at Vedic and post-Vedic texts confirm Sri Chaitanya's divinity. In but one of many scriptural references, Lord Krishna says in the *Vayu Purana:* "In the Age of Kali, when the Sankirtan movement is inaugurated, I shall descend as the son of Sachidevi."

Conclusion

He inspired hundreds of thousands in his own lifetime, and many millions more after that. His mission engulfed all of India and has gradually burst out, as already mentioned, into the rest of the world. Even religious scholars, who have little or no connection to the Vaishnava tradition, have become aware of his unique contribution and the power of his personal example. Christian theologian John Moffitt — to cite one example — wrote of him in adulatory terms:

> If I were asked to choose one man in Indian religious history who best represents the pure spirit of devotional self-giving, I would choose the Vaishnavite saint Chaitanya, whose full name in religion was Krishna-Chaitanya, or "Krishna Consciousness." Of all the saints in recorded history, East or West, he seems to me the supreme example of a soul carried away on a tide of ecstatic love of God. This extraordinary man, who belongs to the rich period beginning with the end of the fourteenth century, represents the culmination of the devotional schools that grew up around Krishna. . . . Chaitanya delighted intensely in nature. It is said that, like St. Francis of Assisi, he had a miraculous power over wild beasts. His life in the holy town of Puri is the story of a man in a state of almost continuous spiritual intoxication. Illuminating discourses, deep contemplation, moods of loving communion with God, were daily occurrences.[1]

Although widely known as a scholar in his youth, Sri Chaitanya left the world only eight verses, called "Shikshashtaka," which sum up his teaching. At first glance, the verses seem rather simple, but they are not. They express an appreciation for the holy name; an awareness of exactly how the name should be chanted; an element of regret, showing how one should hanker for greater taste in the practice of chanting; the importance of humility in approaching the name; and finally the overwhelming feeling of love in separation, where one is virtually consumed by the desire to unite with God. Here are the eight verses in full:

1. Glory to Sri Krishna Sankirtan, which cleanses the heart of all the dust accumulated for years and extinguishes the fire of conditioned life, of repeated birth and death. This Sankirtan movement is the prime benediction for humanity at large because it spreads the rays of the benediction moon. It is the life of all transcendental knowledge, increasing the ocean of transcendental bliss and enabling one and all to fully taste the nectar for which they are always anxious.

2. O my Lord, Your holy name alone can render all benediction to living beings, and thus You have hundreds and millions of names, like Krishna and Govinda. In these transcendental names You have invested all Your transcendental energies. There are not even hard and fast rules for chanting these names. O my Lord, out of kindness You enable us to easily approach You merely by chanting, but I am so unfortunate that I have no attraction for it.

3. One should chant the holy name of the Lord in a humble state of mind, thinking oneself lower than the straw in the street; one should be more tolerant than a tree, devoid of all sense of false prestige and ready to offer all respect to others. In such a state of mind, one can chant the holy name of the Lord constantly.

4. O almighty Lord, I have no desire to accumulate wealth, nor do I desire beautiful women, nor do I want any number of followers. I only want Your causeless devotional service birth after birth.

5. O son of Maharaja Nanda [Krishna], I am Your eternal servitor, yet somehow or other I have fallen into the ocean of birth and death. Please pick me up from this ocean of death and place me as one of the atoms at Your lotus feet.

6. O my Lord, when will my eyes be decorated with tears of love flowing constantly when I chant Your holy name? When will my voice choke up, and when will the hairs of my body stand on end at the recitation of Your name?

7. O Govinda! Feeling Your separation, I am considering a moment to be like an eternity. Tears are flowing from my eyes like torrents of rain, and I am feeling completely vacant in Your absence.

8. I know no one but Krishna as my Lord, and He shall remain so even if He handles me roughly by His embrace or makes me brokenhearted by not being present before me. He is completely free to do anything and everything, for He is always my worshipful Lord unconditionally.

What more needs to be said?

Endnotes

1. John Moffitt, *Journey to Gorakhpur: An Encounter with Christ Beyond Christianity* (New York: Holt, Rinehart and Winston, 1972), p.129, 135-136.

{ APPENDIX 11 }

WHAT DOES OM REALLY MEAN?

"Just as the gentle rays of the moon open the tender petals of the lotus,
May the power of chanting OM open our hearts."

— TRADITIONAL MANTRA

Walk into any yoga studio and you'll encounter the OM mantra. Though it is easily identifiable as a sound that is distinctly Indian, associated with yoga and meditation, few can explain what it really means.

Its origins are found in the ancient Indic texts known as the Vedic literature, where we find the seminal seed-mantra, *Omkara*. But before exploring such early references to the mantra, it might be worthwhile to know that, in essence, OM is hardly a sectarian sound, nor is it peculiar to Hindu notions of meditative chanting. Indeed, the sacred syllable is evoked by the well-known Judaeo-Christian utterance "amen," which is a variation on OM. Similarly, Muslims say "amin." Many of our English descriptions of God, too, begin with OM—omnipresent, omnipotent, omniscient. The prefix *omni*, then, might be seen as a slightly veiled manifestation of OM.

The Power of Sound

Vedic texts, as well as science, inform us that there's more to hear than meets the ear. In fact, human beings are physically unable to perceive certain portions of the known vibratory spectrum. While extremely sensitive to sound waves of about 1,000 to 4,000 cycles per second (cps), we are all but deaf beyond 20,000 cps. Dogs and cats, on the other hand, can hear up to 60,000 cps, while mice, bats, whales, and dolphins can emit and receive sounds well over 100,000 cps. In other words, there are certain things that we as humans are physically unable to hear.

And yet hearing is special. We all know this. It surpasses the visual sense and all others, as Katharine Le Mée explains in her book *Chant*:

> The sense of hearing . . . connects experientially with the heart, and music and sound touch us most directly. We do not resonate so deeply with the visual as with the auditory. This may be explained by the fact that our visual apparatus has a frequency range of slightly less than one octave, from infrared to ultraviolet, whereas our auditory system has a range of about eight octaves, approximately 60 to 16,000 hertz, or number of vibrations per second. We are sensitive to sound frequency as pitch and to light frequency as color. The frequencies of the visual field are much higher than those of the auditory field (by an order of 1010), and, as is well known, the higher the frequencies, the lesser the penetration of a given material. For instance, a piece of cardboard shields us easily from the light, but it takes a thick wall to block out sound, and the lower the pitch the deeper the penetration. We are very sensitive to sound, not just through the ear but through our whole skin, and all our organs are affected by it.[1]

One wonders, therefore, just how many categories of sound lie beyond our grasp.

According to the ancient Indian traditions articulated in the Upanishads, all speech and thought are derived from that one sound: OM. The ancient *Chandogya Upanishad* (2.23.3) states: "As leaves are held together by a spike, so all speech is held together by OM." According to the Puranas, sound is the origin of ether, or space, the most subtle of natural elements, and it is also the source of hearing. Sound is how we convey the idea of a given object, which exists in space, or ether, and it is also, in a sense, considered a subtle form of that object. Further, sound indicates the presence of a speaker, or an initial source, and thus hints at the existence of the Supreme Speaker, or God.

Indeed, OM is described throughout the Vedas and by the great spiritual masters of India as the seed conception of theism. As a tree or fruit begins with a seed, so does everything begin with OM; the Vedas begin with OM, the Upanishads begin with OM, the *Vedanta-sutra* begins with OM, and the *Srimad Bhagavatam*, the essence of all Vedic texts, begins with OM. Therefore, it can safely be said that the divine journey, or the search for transcendental knowledge, begins with this sound vibration.

Patanjali's *Yoga Sutras* (1.23-1.29), for example, recommend recitation of the OM mantra as a direct path to self-realization. According to the *sutras*, focusing on this transcendental sound, along with developing sensitivity for what it represents, brings both God-realization and the removal of all obstacles on the path. The same idea is found in the *Rig Veda*, earliest of India's sacred texts: "One who chants OM, the sonic form of Brahman, Spirit, quickly approaches ultimate reality."

Om: More Than the Sum of Its Parts

Although OM, as a divine syllable, is recognized in nearly all spiritual traditions originating in the East—from the Buddhists of Tibet to the Vedantists of Benares—few elaborate on its actual meaning. More often than not, OM is thought to be little more than an impersonal utterance—an abstract feature of the Absolute, chanted by *yogis* and swamis in India (or by Westerners adopting an Eastern form of spirituality).

Although the mantra is generally written as "OM," the letters "A - U - M" more accurately convey its inner meaning. According to Vedic seers, these three letters represent the first (A) and last (U) vowels of the Sanskrit alphabet, along with its last consonant (M).

Taken together, they say, these letters form "the perfect word," encompassing "all truths that words can convey."

Along similar lines, yoga texts explain that the letter "A" symbolizes the conscious or waking state. The letter "U" is the dream state, and the letter "M" the dreamless sleep state of mind and spirit. The symbol as a whole, then, stands for all states of conscious awareness. Additionally, these same yoga texts underline the seven levels of consciousness and how chanting AUM addresses each one. Initially, there are four primary levels described in yoga texts, and these, in turn, are complemented by three transitional levels, which give us a total of seven. Serious practitioners of yoga will experience each of these levels while on their inner journey.

The *Deeper* Significance

And yet AUM goes further than that. In the *Bhagavad Gita* (9.17), Krishna Himself identifies with the mantra—"I am nondifferent from the syllable AUM." As such, this sacred syllable is known as the *maha-vakya* ["the great saying"] of the Vedas, and can thus be considered on an equal level with the *maha-mantra* (Hare Krishna, Hare Krishna, Krishna Krishna, Hare Hare/ Hare Rama, Hare Rama, Rama Rama, Hare Hare).

Consequently, AUM should not be thought of as solely impersonal. Rather, it is a preeminent sonic manifestation of the Supreme, identical to the Lord in both essence and character.

It is also said that the syllable, properly vibrated, is the sound of Krishna's flute: Oral traditions associated with the *Brahma-samhita* tell us that when Brahma, the first created being, tried to articulate the sound of Krishna's legendary instrument, he uttered "AUM."

Going Deeper Still

The *Gopal-tapani Upanishad* brings our understanding of the mantra still further—reinforcing its identity as the Supreme Divinity.

> The letter 'A' denotes Balaram [Krishna's immediate expansion], who is the substratum of the entire universe. The letter 'U' denotes Pradyumna, who is the Supersoul of the universe.

The letter 'M' denotes Aniruddha, who is the Supersoul of each individual being in the universe. And the 'dot' above the 'M' denotes Sri Krishna, the fountainhead of all Vishnu incarnations. (2.54-55)

Interestingly, according to the *Srimad Bhagavatam* (12.11.21-22), the Deities mentioned in this verse preside over the four levels of consciousness cited earlier. More, they are said to bring practitioners to the final three levels as well. In this way, the *Bhagavatam* unites the esoteric understanding of the mantra with that of the *yogis*.

While the *Gopal-tapani Upanishad* begins with the explanation of AUM cited above, it gives further nuance to the mantra in its next verse (2.56). Here we learn that Krishna's divine energy, Sri Radha, is part of the AUM continuum as well.

Jiva Goswami, one of India's greatest philosophers, elaborates: "AUM is a combination of the letters, A - U - M. The letter 'A' refers to Krishna. The Letter 'U' refers to Radha, and the letter 'M' refers to the ordinary soul." Here we learn the most evolved understanding of the mantra: AUM is everything.

Endnotes

1. Katharine Le Mee, *Chant* (New York: Bell Tower Publishing, 1994), pp. 28–29.

{ SELECT BIBLIOGRAPHY }

Assorted contributors. *Chant and Be Happy: The Power of Mantra Meditation*. Los Angeles, California: The Bhaktivedanta Book Trust, 1982.

Bake, Arnold A. "Kirtan in Bengal," in *Indian Art and Letters*, n.s. XXI (1947).

Beck, Guy L. *Sonic Theology: Hinduism and Sacred Sound*. Columbia, South Carolina: University of South Carolina Press, 1993.

_____. "An Introduction to the Poetry of Narottam Das," in *Journal of Vaishnava Studies*, Vol. 4, No. 4, Fall 1996. Issue Focus: "Vaishnava Poetry."

_____. "Vaishnava Music in the Braj Region of North India," in *Journal of Vaishnava Studies*, Vol. 4, No. 2, Spring 1996. Issue Focus: "Vaishnava Music."

_____. "The Devotional Music of Srila Prabhupada," in *Journal of Vaishnava Studies*, Vol. 6, No. 2, Spring 1998. Issue Focus: "ISKCON/ Bhaktivedanta Swami."

_____. "Hare Krishna Mahamantra: Gaudiya Vaishnava Practice and the Hindu Tradition of Sacred Sound," in *The Hare Krishna Movement: The Postcharismatic Fate of a Religious Transplant*, eds., Edwin F. Bryant and Maria L. Ekstrand New York: Columbia University Press, 2004.

477

Berendt, Joachim-Ernst. *Nada Brahma: The World is Sound*. Rochester, Vermont: Destiny Books, 1987.

Bernard, Patrick. *Music as Yoga: Discover the Healing Power in Sound*. San Rafael, California: Mandala Publishing, 2004.

Chakrabarty, Ramakanta, "Vaishnava Kirtan in Bengal," in *Journal of Vaishnava Studies*, Vol. 4, No. 2, Spring 1996. Issue Focus: "Vaishnava Music."

Chakravarty, Sudhindra Chandra. *Philosophical Foundations of Bengal Vaishnavism*. Calcutta, India: Academic Publishers, 1969.

Chandidasa, Baru. *Singing the Glory of Lord Krishna*, trans., Klaiman, M. H. The American Academy of Religion, 1984.

Choudhury, Basanti. "Love Sentiment and its Spiritual Implications in Gaudiya Vaisnavism," in *Bengal Vaisnavism, Orientalism, Society, and the Arts*, ed., Joseph T. O'Connell. East Lansing, Michigan: Asian Studies Center, Michigan State University, 1985.

Coward, Harold and Goa, David. *Mantra: Hearing the Divine in India*. Chambersburg, Pennsylvania: Anima Books, 1991.

Dasa, Achyutananda. "The Descent of the Holy Name: A Gaudiya Vaishnava Perspective," in *Journal of Vaishnava Studies*, Vol. 2, No. 2, Spring 1994. Issue Focus: "The Power of the Holy Name."

Dasa, Hayagriva. "Sankirtana in the Bible," in *Back to Godhead*, Number 37 (1970).

_____. "The Potency of Sound," in *Brijbasi Spirit*, Volume 7, Number 2 (May 1981).

_____. *The Hare Krishna Explosion*. Wheeling, West Virginia: Palace Press, 1985.

Das, Krishna. *Flow of Grace: Chanting the Hanuman Chalisa*. Boulder, Colorado: Sounds True, Inc., 2007.

Das, Raghava Chaitanya. *The Divine Name*. Bombay, India: np, 1954.

Dass, Ram. *Miracle of Love: Stories about Neem Karoli Baba* (New York: E. P. Dutton, 1979)

Davis, Richard, "An Interview on Bhakti Poetry," in *Journal of Vaishnava Studies*, Vol. 4, No. 4, Fall 1996. Issue Focus: "Vaishnava Poetry."

Dehejiya, Vidya. *Antal and Her Path of love: Poems of a Woman Saint from South India*. Albany, New York: State University of New York Press, 1990.

Delmonico, Neal. "Chaitanya Vaishnavism and the Holy Names," in *Krishna: A Sourcebook*, ed., Edwin F. Bryant. New York: Oxford University Press, 2007.

Dimock, Edward C., Jr. "The Place of Gauracandrika in Bengali Vaisnava lyrics," in *Journal of the American Oriental Society* LXXVIII (July-September 1958).

Dossey, Larry. *Healing Words*. San Francisco, California: Harper, 1993.

Dwyer, Graham, and Cole, Richard J. *The Hare Krishna Movement: Forty Years of Chant and Change*. London, England: I.B. Tauris, 2007.

Gass, Robert. *Chanting*. New York: Broadway Books, 1999.

Goswami Maharaj, Bhaktisiddhanta Sarasvati. *Sri Chaitanya's Teachings*. Madras, India: Sree Gaudiya Math, 1967, reprint.

_____. *Sri Brahma-samhita*, translation and commentary. Los Angeles, California: The Bhaktivedanta Book Trust, 1985, reprint.

Goswami, Rupa. *Mystic Poetry: Rupa Goswamin's Uddhava-sandesa and Hamsaduta*, trans., Jan Brzezinski. San Francisco, California: Mandala Publishing, 1999.

Goswami, Satsvarupa Dasa. "Planting the Seed," *Srila Prabhupada lilamrta*, Volume 2. Los Angeles, California, Bhaktivedanta Book Trust, 1980.

_____. *Japa Reform Notebook*. Washington D.C.: The Gita Nagari Press, 1982.

Guha, Manindranath, *Nectar of the Holy Name*, trans., Neal Delmonico. Kirksville, Missouri, Blazing Sapphire Press, 2005.

Hall, Manly P. *The Therapeutic Value of Music Including the Philosophy of Music*. Los Angeles, California: The Philosophical Research Society, 1982.

Hawley, John Stratton, and Juergensmeyer, Mark. *Songs of the Saints of India*. New York: Oxford University Press, 1988.

Hawley, John Stratton. *Sur Das: Poet, Singer, Saint*. Seattle, Washington: University of Washington Press, 1984.

Hein, Norvin J. "Chaitanya's Ecstasies and the theology of the Name," in *Hinduism: New Essays in the History of Religions*, ed., Bardwell L. Smith. Leiden, Netherlands: E. J. Brill, 1976.

Hopkins, Steven P. "Singing in Tongues: Poems for Vishnu by Vedantadesika." in *Journal of Vaishnava Studies*, Vol. 4, No. 4, Fall 1996. Issue Focus: "Vaishnava Poetry."

http://kirtans.blogspot.com/

Johnsen, Linda, and Maggie Jacobus. *Kirtan!: Chanting As a Spiritual Path*. St. Paul, Minnesota: Yes International Publishers, 2007.

Khan, Hazrat Inayat. *The Music of Life*. New Lebanon: Omega Publications, 1988.

_____. *The Mysticism of Sound and Music: the Sufi teaching of Hazrat Inayat Khan*. Boston, Massachusetts: Shambhala, 1991, reprint.

Klostermaier, Klaus K. "Reflections on Divine Names in Hindu and Biblical Traditions," in *Journal of Vaishnava Studies*, Vol. 2, No. 2, Spring 1994. Issue Focus: "The Power of the Holy Name."

Lamb, Ramdas. *Rapt in the Name: The Ramnamis, Ramnam, and Untouchable Religion in Central India*. Albany, New York: State University of New York Press, 2002.

Le Mée, Katharine. *Chant: The Origins, Form, Practice, and Healing Power of Gregorian Chant*. New York: Bell Tower, 1994.

Mallison, Francoise. "From Folklore to Devotion: Dhol Songs in Gujarat," in *Living Texts from India*, ed., Richard K. Barz and Monika Theil-Horstmann. Weisbaden: Otto Harrassowitz, 1989.

Manuel, Peter. *Thumri in Historical and Stylistic Perspectives*. New Delhi: Motilal Banarsidass, 1989.

McDermott, Rachel Fell. *Singing to the Goddess*. New York: Oxford University Press, 2000.

Mukherjee, Sudhir. *By His Grace: A Devotee's Story by Sudhir Mukherjee* (Santa Fe, New Mexico: Hanuman Foundation, Indian Reprint, 1996).

Narayanan, Vasudha. "Music and the *Divya Prabhandam* in the Srivaishnava Tradition," in *Journal of Vaishnava Studies*, Vol. 4, No. 2, Spring 1996. Issue Focus: "Vaishnava Music."

Padoux, André. "Mantra," in *The Blackwell Companion to Hinduism*, ed., G. Flood. Oxford, UK: Blackwell Publishing, 2003.

Paul, Russill, *The Yoga of Sound*. Novato, California: New World Library, 2004.

Prabhupada, A. C. Bhaktivedanta Swami. *The Golden Avatar: Teaching of Lord Chaitanya*. Los Angeles, California: Bhaktivedanta Book Trust, 1981, reprint.

_____. *Sri Namamrta*, compilation, ed., Steven J. Gelberg. Los Angeles, California: Bhaktivedanta Book Trust, 1982.

_____. *The Nectar of Devotion: The Complete Science of Bhakti Yoga*. Los Angeles, California: Bhaktivedanta Book Trust, 1982, reprint.

_____. *On Chanting Hare Krishna*. Los Angeles, California: Bhaktivedanta Book Trust, 1999, reprint.

Ramanujan, A. K., trans. *Hymns for the Drowning: Poems for Visnu by Nammalvar*. Princeton, New Jersey: Princeton University Press, 1981.

Rosen, Steven J., ed. *Vaisnavism: Contemporary Scholars Discuss the Gaudiya Tradition*. Delhi, India: Motilal Banarsidass, 1994, reprint.

_____. *The Hidden Glory of India*. Grodinge, Sweden: Bhaktivedanta Book Trust, 2002.

_____. *Essential Hinduism*. Westport, Connecticut: Praeger, 2006.

_____. *Krishna's Song: A New Look at the Bhagavad Gita*. Westport, Connecticut: Praeger, 2007.

Rosenstein, Ludmila. "Svami Haridas and Dhrupad," in *Journal of Vaishnava Studies*, Vol. 4, No. 2, Spring 1996. Issue Focus: "Vaishnava Music."

Schelling, Andrew, trans. *For the Love of the Dark One: Songs of Mirabai*. Prescott, Arizona: Hohm Press, 1998.

Shukla-Bhatt, Neelima. "Nectar of Devotion: Bhakti-rasa in the tradition of Gujurati saint-poet Narasinha Mehta." Ph.D. Thesis, Harvard University, 2003.

Singer, Milton. "The Radha-Krishna Bhajanas of Madras City," in *Krishna: Myths, Rites, and Attitudes*, ed., Milton Singer. Chicago: University of Chicago Press, 1966.

Sivananda, Sri Swami. *Music as Yoga*. Rishikesh, India: Yoga Vedanta Forest University, 1956.

Slawek, Stephen M. "Kirtan: A Study of the Sonic Manifestations of the Divine in the Popular Hindu Culture of Banares." Unpublished Ph.D Thesis, the University of Illinois at Urbana-Champaign, 1986.

_____. "The Definition of Kirtan: An Historical and Geographical

Perspective," in *Journal of Vaishnava Studies*, Vol. 4, No. 2, Spring 1996. Issue Focus: "Vaishnava Music."

Staal, Frits. "Vedic Mantras," in *Understanding Mantras*, ed., Harvey P. Alper. Albany, New York: State University of New York Press, 1989.

Swami, Mahanidhi. *Art of Chanting Hare Krsna: Japa Meditation Techniques*. Vrindavan, India: np, 2002.

Swami, Prajnanananda. *The Historical Development of India Music: A Critical Study*. Calcutta, India: Firma KLM, 1973.

Swami, Sacinandana. *The Nectarean Ocean of the Holy Name*. Schona, Germany: Gayatri Publishers, 1999.

_____. *The Gayatri Book*. Schona, Germany: Vasati Publishers, 2005.

Thakur, Bhaktivinode. *Sri Hari-Nama-Cintamani* (in Bengali). Svarupaganja, Nadiya, West Bengal, India: Gaudiya Mission, 1963, reprint.

Thielemann, Selina. "The Musical Manifestation of Bhakti," in *Journal of Vaishnava Studies*, Vol. 4, No. 2 (Spring 1996).

_____. *Sounds of the Sacred: Religious Music in India*. New Delhi, India: A.P.H. Publishing, 1998.

Tripurari, Swami B. V. *Gopala-tapani Upanisad*, translation and commentary. Philo, California: Audarya, 2004.

_____. *Siksastakam of Sri Caitanya*. San Rafael, California: Mandala Publishing, 2005.

White, Charles S. J. *The Caurasi Pad of Sri Hit Harivams*. The University Press of Hawaii, 1977.

Wulff, Donna M. "On Practicing Religiously: Music as Sacred in India," in Irwin, Joyce, ed., *Sacred Sound: Music in Religious Thought and Practice*. Chico, California: Scholars Press, 1983.

_____. "The Akhar Lines in Performances of Padavali Kirtan,"

STEVEN J. ROSEN (SATYARAJA DASA) is editor-in-chief of the *Journal of Vaishnava Studies*, a bi-annual academic publication exploring Eastern thought. He is also associate editor of *Back to Godhead* magazine and the author of over twenty books on Indian philosophy. His recent titles include *Essential Hinduism* (Praeger, 2006), *Krishna's Song: A New Look at the Bhagavad Gita* (Praeger, 2007), and *Black Lotus: The Spiritual Journey of an Urban Mystic* (Harinam Press, 2007). He is an initiated disciple of His Divine Grace A. C. Bhaktivedanta Swami Prabhupada.

{ FOLK BOOKS }

Folk art is, indeed, the oldest of the aristocracies of thought, and because it refuses what is passing and trivial, the merely clever and pretty, as certainly as the vulgar and insincere, and because it has gathered into itself the simplest and most unforgettable thoughts of the generations, it is the soil where all great art is rooted. Wherever it is spoken by the fireside, or sung by the roadside, or carved upon the lintel, appreciation of the arts that a single mind gives unity and design to, spreads quickly when its hour is come.

—W. B. YEATS